THE EUROPEAN UNION SERIES

D1756084

General Editors: Neill Nugent, William E. Paterson

The European Union series provides an authoritative library on the European Union, ranging from general introductory texts to definitive assessments of key institutions and actors, issues, policies and policy processes, and the role of member states.

Books in the series are written by leading scholars in their fields and reflect the most up-to-date research and debate. Particular attention is paid to accessibility and clear presentation for a wide audience of students, practitioners and interested general readers.

The series editors are **Neill Nugent**, Visiting Professor, College of Europe, Bruges and Honorary Professor, University of Salford, UK, and **William E. Paterson**, Honorary Professor in German and European Studies, University of Aston. Their co-editor until his death in July 1999, **Vincent Wright**, was a Fellow of Nuffield College, Oxford University.

Feedback on the series and book proposals are always welcome and should be sent to Steven Kennedy, Palgrave Macmillan, Houndmills, Basingstoke, Hampshire, RG21 6XS, UK, or by e-mail to **s.kennedy@palgrave.com**

General textbooks

Published

Laurie Buonanno and Neill Nugent **Policies and Policy Processes of the European Union**
Desmond Dinan **Encyclopedia of the European Union** [Rights: Europe only]
Desmond Dinan **Europe Recast: A History of the European Union** [Rights: Europe only]
Desmond Dinan **Ever Closer Union: An Introduction to European Integration (4th edn)** [Rights: Europe only]
Mette Eilstrup Sangiovanni (ed.) **Debates on European Integration: A Reader**
Simon Hix and Bjørn Høyland **The Political System of the European Union (3rd edn)**
Dirk Leuffen, Berthold Rittberger and Frank Schimmelfennig **Differentiated Integration**
Paul Magnette **What is the European Union? Nature and Prospects**
John McCormick **Understanding the European Union: A Concise Introduction (5th edn)**
Brent F. Nelsen and Alexander Stubb **The European Union: Readings on the Theory and Practice of European Integration (3rd edn)** [Rights: Europe only]
Neill Nugent (ed.) **European Union Enlargement**

Neill Nugent **The Government and Politics of the European Union (7th edn)**
John Peterson and Elizabeth Bomberg **Decision-Making in the European Union**
Ben Rosamond **Theories of European Integration**
Sabine Saurugger **Theoretical Approaches to European Integration**
Esther Versluis, Mendeltje van Keulen and Paul Stephenson **Analyzing the European Union Policy Process**
Hubert Zimmermann and Andreas Dür (eds) **Key Controversies in European Integration**

Forthcoming

Magnus Ryner and Alan Cafruny **A Critical Introduction to the European Union**

Also planned

The Political Economy of European Integration

Series Standing Order (outside North America only)
ISBN 978–0–333–71695–3 hardback
ISBN 978–0–333–69352–0 paperback
Full details from www.palgrave.com

The major institutions and actors

Published

Renaud Dehousse **The European Court of Justice**
Justin Greenwood **Interest Representation in the European Union (3rd edn)**
Fiona Hayes-Renshaw and Helen Wallace **The Council of Ministers (2nd edn)**
Simon Hix and Christopher Lord **Political Parties in the European Union**
David Judge and David Earnshaw **The European Parliament (2nd edn)**
Neill Nugent **The European Commission**
Anne Stevens with Handley Stevens **Brussels Bureaucrats? The Administration of the European Union**

Forthcoming

Wolfgang Wessels **The European Council**

The main areas of policy

Published

Michele Chang **Monetary Integration in the European Union**
Michelle Cini and Lee McGowan **Competition Policy in the European Union (2nd edn)**
Wyn Grant **The Common Agricultural Policy**
Martin Holland and Mathew Doidge **Development Policy of the European Union**
Jolyon Howorth **Security and Defence Policy in the European Union**
Johanna Kantola **Gender and the European Union**
Stephan Keukeleire and Tom Delreux **The Foreign Policy of the European Union (2nd edn)**
Brigid Laffan **The Finances of the European Union**
Malcolm Levitt and Christopher Lord **The Political Economy of Monetary Union**
Janne Haaland Matláry **Energy Policy in the European Union**
John McCormick **Environmental Policy in the European Union**
John Peterson and Margaret Sharp **Technology Policy in the European Union**
Handley Stevens **Transport Policy in the European Union**

Forthcoming

Karen Anderson **Social Policy in the European Union**
Michael Baun and Dan Marek **Cohesion Policy in the European Union**
Hans Bruyninckx and Tom Delreux **Environmental Policy and Politics in the European Union**

Sieglinde Gstöhl and Dirk de Bievre **The Trade Policy of the European Union**
Christian Kaunert and Sarah Leonard **Justice and Home Affairs in the European Union**
Paul Stephenson, Esther Versluis and Mendeltje van Keulen **Implementing and Evaluating Policy in the European Union**

Also planned

Political Union
The External Policies of the European Union

The member states and the Union

Published

Carlos Closa and Paul Heywood **Spain and the European Union**
Andrew Geddes **Britain and the European Union**
Alain Guyomarch, Howard Machin and Ella Ritchie **France in the European Union**
Brigid Laffan and Jane O'Mahoney **Ireland and the European Union**

Forthcoming

Simon Bulmer and William E. Paterson **Germany and the European Union**
Thomas Christiansen, Emil Kirchner and Uwe Wissenbach **The European Union and China**
Tuomas Forsberg and Hiski Haukkala **The European Union and Russia**
Brigid Laffan **The European Union and its Member States**

Issues

Published

Derek Beach **The Dynamics of European Integration: Why and When EU Institutions Matter**
Christina Boswell and Andrew Geddes **Migration and Mobility in the European Union**
Thomas Christiansen and Christine Reh **Constitutionalizing the European Union**
Robert Ladrech **Europeanization and National Politics**
Cécile Leconte **Understanding Euroscepticism**
Steven McGuire and Michael Smith **The European Union and the United States**
Wyn Rees **The US–EU Security Relationship: The Tensions between a European and a Global Agenda**

Forthcoming

Graham Avery **Enlarging the European Union**

Theoretical Approaches to European Integration

Sabine Saurugger

First published 2014 by
PALGRAVE MACMILLAN

This is a very substantially revised, recast and extended edition of the work first published in 2009 by Presses de Sciences Po under the title *Théories et approches de l'intégration européenne*.

Palgrave Macmillan in the UK is an imprint of Macmillan Publishers Limited, registered in England, company number 785998, of Houndmills, Basingstoke, Hampshire RG21 6XS.

Palgrave Macmillan in the US is a division of St Martin's Press LLC, 175 Fifth Avenue, New York, NY 10010.

Palgrave Macmillan is the global academic imprint of the above companies and has companies and representatives throughout the world.

Palgrave® and Macmillan® are registered trademarks in the United States, the United Kingdom, Europe and other countries

ISBN: 978-0-230-25142-7 hardback
ISBN: 978-0-230-25143-4 paperback

This book is printed on paper suitable for recycling and made from fully managed and sustained forest sources. Logging, pulping and manufacturing processes are expected to conform to the environmental regulations of the country of origin.

A catalogue record for this book is available from the British Library.

A catalog record for this book is available from the Library of Congress.

Printed and bound in Great Britain by TJ International Ltd, Padstow, Cornwall.

Contents

List of Boxes, Tables and Figures		vi
List of Abbreviations		viii
Acknowledgements		x
Introduction		1

Part I Why Integrate? Theories of Integration

1	Original Debates	16
2	Neofunctionalism	34
3	Intergovernmentalism	54

Part II Mainstreaming European Studies

4	Institutionalist Approaches	79
5	Governance	102
6	Europeanization and Public Policy Transfer	123
7	Constructivism(s)	145
8	Sociological Perspectives on European Integration	162
9	Political Theory	184

Part III The European Union and the World

10	International Relations and European Integration	207
11	Comparing Forms of Regional Integration: Beyond European Studies	226
Conclusion		249
References		256
Index		292

List of Boxes, Tables and Figures

Boxes

2.1   Core neofunctionalist assumptions   37
3.1   What is intergovernmentalism?   55
3.2   Conventional intergovernmentalism   59
3.3   Regional integration: a three-stage process   72
5.1   What is governance?   106
5.2   Horizontal and vertical interdependence in multi-level
       governance   111
6.1   Falkner et al.'s variables explaining non-compliance   132
7.1   Three constructivist core ideas   148
11.1 Warleigh-Lack's five types of regionalization   241

Tables

0.1   Functions of theories and conceptual frameworks   6
0.2   Four dimensions of EU research   7
1.1   Original debates in brief   17
1.2   Perspectives on original debates   32
2.1   Neo-neofunctionalist hypotheses   50
2.2   New perspectives in neofunctionalism   51
3.1   Intergovernmentalism in brief   55
3.2   Perspectives on intergovernmentalism   74
4.1   Neo-institutionalisms in brief   81
4.2   The four neo-institutionalisms   98
5.1   Three origins of governance   103
5.2   Governance perspectives in brief   108
5.3   Marks and Hooghe's Type I and Type II multi-level
       governance   113
5.4   Governance perspectives   120
6.1   Definitions of Europeanization   126
6.2   Jacquot and Woll's typology of usages   134
6.3   Europeanization/policy transfer perspectives   142
7.1   The three logics   147
7.2   European studies constructivism in brief   152
7.3   Constructivist perspectives in European studies   160
8.1   Sociological perspectives in EU studies in brief   169

8.2	Sociological perspectives in EU studies	181
9.1	Ideas on Europe and its integration	187
9.2	Normative theories on the EU as a political community	191
9.3	How can we analyse legitimacy in the EU?	202
10.1	Contemporary international relations in EU studies in brief	215
10.2	Contemporary international relations in EU studies	223
11.1	The establishment of regional organizations	230
11.2	Comparative regionalism in brief	232
11.3	Old and new regionalism (Hettne 2003; Warleigh-Lack 2007)	236
11.4	Factors leading to a degree of rationalization	236
11.5	Comparative regionalism perspectives	246

Figures

5.1	Network continuum	118
6.1	Risse, Green Cowles and Caporaso's sequential causality	127
6.2	Circular Europeanization	128
6.3	Types of transfer (Bulmer et al. 2007)	140

List of Abbreviations

ACP	African, Caribbean, and Pacific Group of States
ASEAN	Association of South-East Asian Nations
BRICS	Brazil, Russia, India, China and South Africa
CAP	Common Agricultural Policy
CARICOM	Caribbean Community
CEEC	Central and Eastern European Countries
CFSP	Common Foreign and Security Policy
COREPER	Committee of Permanent Representatives
CSCE/OSCE	Conference on Security and Cooperation in Europe/Organisation for Security and Cooperation in Europe
CSDP	Common Security and Defence Policy
EC	European Community
ECB	European Central Bank
ECJ	European Court of Justice
ECOFIN	Council of Economic and Finance Ministers
ECOSOC	UN Economic and Social Council
ECOWAS	Economic Community of West African States
ECSC	European Coal and Steel Community
EDC	European Defence Community
EEC	European Economic Community
EMS	European Monetary System
EMU	Economic and Monetary Union
EPC	European Political Community
EU	European Union
EURATOM	European Atomic Energy Community
GATT	General Agreement on Tariffs and Trade
GCC	Cooperation Council for the Arab States of the Gulf
IPE	international political economy
JHA	Justice and Home Affairs
MEP	Member of the European Parliament
Mercosur	Southern Cone Common Market
NAFTA	North American Trade Agreement
NATO	North Atlantic Treaty Organisation
NGO	non-governmental organization
NPM	new public management
OECD	Organisation for Economic Cooperation and Development

OMC	Open Method of Coordination
QMV	Qualified Majority Voting
SAARC	South Asian Association for Regional Cooperation
SADC	Southern African Development Community
SEA	Single European Act
SGP	Stability and Growth Pact
UN	United Nations
UNASUR	Union of South American Nations
WTO	World Trade Organization

Acknowledgements

When Steven Kennedy told me in 2009 that Palgrave would be interested in publishing an extended and revised version of my work *Théories et approches de l'intégration européenne*, I did not know that I was about to engage in what turned out to be a very long and exciting, but almost never-ending story. Writing a book on theories seems at first sight to be an easy enough task. However, the sheer abundance of detailed theoretical works on European integration, every one deepening, enlarging and slightly changing the main hypotheses of previous theories and concepts, has made writing such a book an extremely challenging intellectual adventure.

My gratitude goes first to Steven Kennedy, William E. Paterson and Neill Nugent. Without ever losing patience, they have provided suggestions, support, encouragement and meticulous reading of the various drafts of this book. The anonymous reviewers have challenged the book where necessary and have provided suggestions and extremely constructive critiques. Ben Rosamond's excellent book in Palgrave's European Union Series was a constant inspiration.

I am immensely grateful to Paul Stephenson, who has helped me to produce a book in a language which is not my own. Without him, reading it would have been much more difficult.

I am also grateful to Céline Belot, Clément Fontan, François Foret, Charlotte Halpern, Patrick Le Galès, Christian Lequesne, Frédéric Mérand, Franck Petiteville, Uwe Puetter, Claudio Radaelli, Alex Warleigh-Lack and Nikos Zahariadis who, despite their busy schedules, found time to read and comment on parts of the manuscript. The book would not be what it is without the intellectual companionship and warm friendship of Fabien Terpan, who provided support, enthusiasm and an abundance of constructive criticism and who has read this whole book so often that I am sure he has had enough of it.

The Institut universitaire de France offered me a period of sabbatical leave to enable me to carry out my various theories-projects, and Sciences Po Grenoble gave me the time and funding I needed to complete this book.

A special thank you goes to my students at Sciences Po Grenoble, the Université Libre de Bruxelles and the University of Cologne, who have asked complex and challenging questions, as only students are able to do. My family has seen me less than they should have, and I am immensely grateful for their patience and laughter when things have not always functioned as they should.

Introduction

Theoretical and conceptual accounts of European integration abound. It is rare these days for an academic publication on European integration not to be anchored in a conceptual framework of one kind or another, while claiming to deepen, test, enlarge or reinterpret a theoretical account.

At a time of increased strains and contestation for the European Union (EU), it is more important than ever to understand the range of theoretical perspectives that have helped explain its evolution and present state and provide the resources for addressing new developments and challenges. This book is designed to provide an introduction to and critical assessment of the wide range of theories that currently prevail in the study of European integration. It does so both in terms of an analysis of their substantive contributions to the field but also in terms of their historical context and origins (including what they were developed to explain and the impact of real-world events on their fortunes) and their philosophical underpinnings. While the first theorists specifically focused on explaining European integration, i.e. why states have agreed to abandon all or parts of their national sovereignty and what results this integration process has produced, since then others have sought to apply more 'mainstream' approaches from comparative politics, public policy and beyond to explain the day-to-day politics of European integration.

The book will argue, however, that neither of these two perspectives is sufficient to understand contemporary European integration. This means, more precisely, that the EU cannot be analysed merely as an intergovernmental entity in which member states make central decisions, nor that it is a political system similar to that of a (nation)-state – an interpretation introduced by general comparative politics approaches. This book argues that only a combination of both international relations and comparative politics approaches will allow us to answer crucial empirical contemporary European studies questions both on its internal and broader external – or international – aspects. In other words, this book aims at 'mainstreaming' theoretical accounts of European integration. What do we mean by that?

Mainstreaming European integration theory

Theoretical 'mainstreaming' means drawing out the relationships between key concepts and frameworks in EU studies with broader theorizing in political and social science both today and historically.

1

While this attempt was undertaken as early as in the 1980s (Bulmer 1983), and has became even more systematic since the 1990s (Hix 1994, 1998; Pollack 1996; Caporaso 1999; Gabel, Hix and Schneider 2002), this book aims to give it another twist.

Mainstreaming European integration theory means, to the understanding of these authors, not only looking at the construction of new institutions at a supranational level. European integration is also about the transformation of domestic structures, policies and politics. Thus, instead of developing theories and frameworks solely designed to study European integration, conceptual tools broadly used to study the state should be applied to European integration.

This particular understanding of mainstreaming European studies is reflected in the development of contemporary European integration frameworks such as institutionalisms (Chapter 5), governance (Chapter 6), Europeanization (Chapter 7), sociological approaches (Chapter 8) or political theory (Chapter 9). I refer to this understanding as 'bottom-up mainstreaming' because its origins can be found in the study of the state.

However, this particular movement has a serious flaw: it neglects the international and intergovernmental aspect of the integration process (Hurrell and Menon 1996, 2003). Bargaining among member states inside the EU, negotiations between the EU and other states, bilaterally or multilaterally in international organizations such as the EU, takes place in an intergovernmental arena where contemporary conceptual international relations frameworks provide precious tools for analysis. These interactions are shaped by sovereignty-based considerations such as 'national interests' or 'power'. Theoretical tools developed by 'bottom-up mainstreamers' do not systematically take these sovereignty considerations into account, as they consider the EU as similar to a nation-state. Yet the intergovernmental aspect of European integration remains crucial. This, of course, concerns the external aspect of European integration (all areas of external relations – trade, defence or diplomacy, as well as internal policies that have an external impact, such as Justice and Home Affairs (JHA)). Sovereignty and power, however, also concern the internal aspect of European integration, i.e. the bargaining that takes place among the EU member states (Chapter 10).

Furthermore, the EU is not the *only* regional integration project, neither in time nor in space: NAFTA (the North American Free Trade Association), MERCOSUR (the Southern Cone Common Market) and ASEAN (the Association of Southeast Asian Nations), to mention just three, are other cases with which comparisons might be extremely beneficial. These comparisons would allow for a better understanding, not only of regional integration processes, but also of the consequences of regional integration for states and society more generally (Chapter 11). It is in all these areas that new international relations approaches offer promising avenues for research because, in one way or another, they recognize an actor's role as being influenced by sovereignty and 'national interest' considerations. This research attitude is what this book calls 'top-down mainstreaming'.

This book differs from earlier calls for academic mainstreaming in a number of respects, most importantly by looking to a broader range of disciplines, including both international relations and comparative politics, alongside sociology. Linking the concepts of 'bottom-up' and 'top-down mainstreaming' in this book is not necessarily about developing one single homogenous conceptual or methodological approach to European studies. Here it means insisting on the fact that only the combination of theoretical concepts originating in comparative politics, public policy *and* international relations will allow for any nuanced understanding of the different aspects of European integration.

Introducing the reader to the richness of theoretical accounts in EU studies and guiding them through the complexity of these concepts, however, also requires putting these theoretical approaches into their political and historical context.

Contextualizing theories and concepts

Contextualizing theories and approaches in general is central for our understanding of where the origins of theories lie, and what the underlying scientific and methodological paradigms are. The analysis of processes, institutions or real-world phenomena more generally is always influenced by the particular social context within which the observer evolved (i.e. was trained to analyse and observe) and operates today (some academic institutions are renowned for their particular approach or 'school of thought'). The development of theoretical and conceptual approaches in EU studies is no exception: approaches and frameworks are influenced by the prominent academic but also political paradigm of their time, i.e. by trends. Thus, presenting the historical origins of theoretical approaches to European integration helps us explain the structures of thought generally implicit in these tools for analysis.

Let us take three moments in European integration in order to illustrate the importance of the social, political or academic context in developing theoretical frameworks. First, the theoretical accounts introduced in the 1940s and 1950s were developed to explain the origins of European integration. Three theories competed in explaining European integration in the 1950s, all of them influenced by the traumatic events of the Second World War: neofunctionalism, intergovernmentalism and federalism. As will be shown in Chapter 1, federalism argued in favour of supranational integration, developing ideas on how to best structure regional integration in order to hinder the outbreak of a new armed conflict on the European continent. On the contrary, neofunctionalism

(Chapter 2) and intergovernmentalism (Chapter 3) emerged during a period of change in scientific paradigms: behaviourists introduced scientific methods stemming from hard sciences into social sciences. Influenced by this debate, these approaches developed hypotheses that sought to identify what had pushed sovereign states to abandon their room for manoeuvre and adhere to a new form of international organization. Their ideological standpoints were discarded: neither neofunctionalism nor intergovernmentalism believed that member states accepted to create the European Community (EC) mainly because of their wish to secure peace on the European continent. While neofunctionalists argued that European integration was due to the perceived benefits of this integration: positive results in one integrated policy area would lead to pressure for increased integration in another policy area, intergovernmentalists specifically emphasized the role of state interests driving the integration process forward.

While the latter interpretation remained largely valid for 20 years, the mid-1980s saw the emergence of new frameworks explaining European integration providing the second example of the importance of theories and conceptual frameworks in interpreting 'real-world events'. Contrary to the dominant intergovernmentalist thinking of the time, which emphasized the minimal interest of the major member states in European integration and, as a result, the relative apathy of the EC, the rise of institutionalist accounts brought change to the theoretical mainstream. More precisely, it allowed for an alternative interpretation of this 20-year period, but with hindsight. When adopting an institutionalist viewpoint (Chapter 5), we observe that, under the calm surface, a large number of changes and reforms were afoot. These include the introduction of the European Monetary System (EMS), the first elections to the European Parliament, the implementation of intergovernmental cooperation on foreign policy and integration through European law via the European Court of Justice (ECJ). Thus, far from being dependent on state interests alone, 'institutions mattered'. The existing institutions, as well as those established during the 1960s and 1970s, helped further European integration. Such an observation would have been impossible had the theoretical framework been based purely on a single variable – namely, state interests being for or against increased European integration.

The analysis of the negotiations for the Single European Act (SEA) in 1986, a document that 'relaunched' the European integration process by creating a single European market, is a third example that illustrates how the same events can be read very differently depending on the theoretical lens one chooses to look through. Thus, we may understand the SEA as an instance of purely intergovernmental negotiation between member states, and more precisely Germany, France and the UK (Chapter 3) or, on the contrary, as having been largely influenced by non-state actors and, more precisely, economic interest groups such as the European

Round Table of Industrialists. From this perspective, the preparation of the SEA becomes a phenomenon better explained using the conceptual approach of network governance (Chapter 5), according to which a broad and pluralistic number of actors – both public and private – negotiate in order to define and implement a policy.

What we observe here are cyclical or dialectical patterns of challenges to, and the reinforcing of, existing theoretical perspectives (Paterson 2010). Sets of real-world events, crisis and caesuras provide challenges, but also opportunities to reformulate theories and conceptual frameworks. The academic and sociohistorical context largely structures the emergence and subsequent importance of these theoretical approaches.

European integration studies have also been influenced by conceptual debates going on in other fields of political science and international relations. At the same time, European studies have exerted their own influence, contributing to the emergence of a number of considerable controversies in the social sciences more generally (Wiener and Diez 2004, 2009; see also Bache and George 2006; Rosamond 1995, 2000; Kelstrup and Williams 2000). For instance, governance approaches (Chapter 5), developed at the beginning of the 1990s in EU studies, opened up new possibilities to conceptualize the integration of the state into a supranational entity, by cutting the state into small constituent elements – public and private actors. This also led to normative questions about the democratic character of the EU in general, dealt with by political theory approaches (Chapter 9).

The relevance of theories

In short, this book is based on the basic and perhaps obvious assumption that theories matter. But why do they matter? Is it not enough to study the history or detailed workings of the EU as historians and lawyers do? Albeit important, this approach is not entirely satisfactory. Theories and conceptual frameworks matter precisely because they allow us to understand how a specific hypothesis can influence the interpretation of a given research question. To put it bluntly, if no effort is made to structure our observations, no proper understanding is possible (Marsh and Stoker 1995).

The origin of the notion of theory comes from the Greek verb *theorein*, meaning 'observing, identifying and understanding'. It refers more precisely to the idea of bringing order and meaning to phenomena observed. In a restricted sense, 'theory' is defined as an argument of correlation or determining variables of universal, historical and nomothetic validity which can be tested by a set of refutable hypotheses (Przeworski and Teune, 1982; King, Keohane and Verba 1994). This book, however, deals not only with theories, but also presents key concepts and frameworks. Contrary to theories that attempt to develop an argument about causality, concepts and frameworks offer ideas for interpreting social facts. In the case of concepts and approaches, social phenomena are part of a specific context and must be interpreted rather than explained – i.e. any explanation is first and foremost (merely) an interpretation.

The link between concepts and theories can be understood as a continuum. On this continuum, multiple positions are possible. On the one hand, not all authors presented in this book who advocate an explanatory theoretical approach necessarily defend conceptualizations based on unidirectional links between causes and effects. On the other hand, adepts of the interpretive, conceptual approach do not all reject the use of language based on hypotheses and variables, be they dependent, independent or intervening – in fact, the majority of scholars take a position somewhere in the middle of this continuum.

This book will use the notion of *theories* or *theoretical approaches* when these frameworks allow us to develop a system of hypotheses. The notion of *conceptual framework* is used in a wider sense, referring to what Gerry Stoker called 'frame[s] of references in which reality can be examined ... [by] providing interpretations of relationships between variables' (Stoker 1995: 18).

The theories and conceptual frameworks analysed in this book can be distinguished according to two functions: their explanatory function, on the one hand, and their critical and normative function, on the other.

Although *explanatory theories* differ very broadly in their epistemological underpinnings and, therefore, in the methods used by scholars when employing such theories, these theories do share a common objective: to explain why and how events take place. Their added value lies in systematic research aimed at uncovering the reasons for, and determinants of, the policy processes observed. Critical or normative theories, on the contrary, do not take European integration as a given. They aim to

Table 0.1   *Functions of theories and conceptual frameworks*

Functions	*Theories and conceptual frameworks*
Explanatory	Federalism, transactionalism, neofunctionalism, intergovernmentalism, institutionalism, governance, Europeanization, constructivism, sociology, political theory, international relations, comparative regional integration
Critical and normative	Federalism, functionalism, constructivism (post-positivist variant), normative power Europe (NPE), political theory

Table 0.2   *Four dimensions of EU research*

Dimension	Main question
Ontology	Does the world exist independently from actors' perception?
Epistemology	What are the necessary and sufficient conditions of knowledge?
Sub-disciplines	Should we study different areas of integration with different disciplinary tools?
Scope of theoretical approach	Can we explain the EU's political system in its entirety or only parts of it?

provide avenues allowing for developing alternatives to political and economic processes at the EU level. Political theory, for instance, led to reflections on what the EU should be or become.

However, distinguishing between the explanatory and normative functions of theories and conceptual approaches does not allow us to fully understand all the fundamental differences between the approaches presented in this book. Joseph Jupille's (2006) differentiation between four metatheoretical dimensions seems better suited to explain the architecture and cleavages present in scientific research on European integration (see also Wiener and Diez 2004, 2009).

The first dimension concerns ontology: 'What is the world made of?', 'What is a cause of the social world, and what is an effect?' Ontology deals with the question whether the world exists independently of the perception or experience of actors (and therefore, objectively), or if it only exists via the perception of individuals or the individual (subjectively). Are actors moulded by their environment and where they are situated in it, or are their preferences formed independently from external influences? This debate is best known as 'structure versus agency 'debate. It can be understood as an issue of socialization against autonomy of an individual: does the individual act as a free agent or in a manner dictated by social structure?

The second key dimension is epistemological: 'What are the necessary and sufficient conditions of knowledge?' More precisely, we distinguish between the question of 'how the social world functions' (understanding) and the question 'what makes the world function?' (explaining). Understanding refers to the scholar's attempt to make us grasp what events mean. In order to understand an event, we must interpret it, put it into perspective, generally in starting the explanation from an actor's view. Explaining, on the other hand, refers to the attempt to explain the laws of nature: 'The crucial move is to insist that every individual works basically in the same law-like way, with individual varieties depending on systematic differences in, for instance preferences and information' (Hollis and Smith 1991: 4). A theory of knowledge thus tries to determine whether we can build up sufficient knowledge of the world (for example, via empirical observation) that will ever enable us to validate our hypotheses objectively. Or, conversely, is any observation based on a, at least partially, erroneous theory, as this theory will implicitly determine the responses that we hope to find in the empirical field? Both of these concerns are specifically discussed in the chapters on constructivism (Chapter 7) and sociological approaches to European integration (Chapter 8). Another way to frame the dimension of epistemology is to distinguish between positivist and post-positivist perspectives: A positivist theory of knowledge argues that causalities, i.e. relations between cause and effect (explaining), are out there just waiting to be found, whereas post-positivists refer to a value-laden social reality, only coming to light through individual interpretation (understanding).

A third dimension concerns the explanatory functions of subdivisions in the social sciences more generally. This book primarily concentrates on political science and sociological approaches and, thus, offers a rather homogenous view as compared to theories developed in legal studies, history or economics. At the same time, the different sub-disciplines of political science such as political theory, public policy, comparative politics or international relations raise also different questions, which in turn lead to different answers in European study research. Thus, international relations approaches until the 1970s were mainly concerned with identifying those factors that encouraged states to pool their sovereignty at the European level, whereas more general comparative politics approaches questioned the consequences of European integration for policies as well as for the citizens of European member states.

The fourth and last dimension concerns the scope of the theoretical approach. Can we explain a political or social system in general, in time and in space, and thus develop a so-called grand theory, or should researchers strive to explain a particular context, an attitude that can be found in so-called mid-range theories? Thus, theoretical approaches vary not only in terms of objectives, but also in terms of scope. Analysing EU energy policy, for example, requires different tools, based on mid-range theories than those used to assess the EU as a political regime in its own right where we can find attempts to develop grand theories.

The structure of the book

The book is divided into three main parts: Part I groups together theories which attempt to explain the reasons behind regional and, more specifically, European integration and the direction this process took. Part II presents frameworks that explain the way the EU functions, an aim that has led to a gradual 'mainstreaming' of conceptual frameworks for studying the EU by using those designed to analyse the state ('bottom-up mainstreaming). Part III presents international relations approaches developed to analyse the variety of intergovernmental bargaining. A variety of these approaches, however, are not based on state-centred views, but deconstruct terms such as 'sovereignty', 'national interests' or 'power' ('top-down mainstreaming').

The consideration of the factors accounting for European integration, developed in the first part of the book, begins with what is widely called original debates on regional integration, such as functionalism, transactionalism and federalism (Chapter 1). As we will see in Chapter 1, federalism, in particular, will be presented as an evolutionary theory – from its origins to more contemporary conceptualizations. Originating as a largely normative approach in EU studies, federalism analyses cooperation between states, where cooperation leads, or is meant to lead, to the establishment of a new task-oriented body. Federalism gathered momentum again in the periods of evolutionary treaty negotiations, such as after the Maastricht Treaty in 1992 or the Constitutional, and then Lisbon Treaty, respectively, in 2004 and 2007. Thus, while empirically challenged at the EU level from the 1950s to the 1980s, it was reinforced again through a new set of empirical developments at the beginning of the 1990s and 2000s, to be challenged again after the rejection of the Constitutional Treaty. For nearly thirty years, until the beginning of the 1990s, neofunctionalist (Chapter 2) and intergovernmentalist approaches (Chapter 3) replaced federalist approaches. The critical analysis of these approaches is the subject of the first part of this book. The central question these theories try to explain is why states agree to join a regional bloc, and how this supranational organization developed or stagnated.

The second part of this book critically analyses conceptual frameworks in EU studies that stem from more general political science and comparative politics approaches. This new research did emerge at the beginning of the 1990s, with a call to mainstream European studies and a plea in favour of abandoning the project of conceptualizing the EU as a single case or as being *sui generis*. As developed above, this has meant the emergence of analytical frameworks proposing a greater use of comparative politics, public policy, political sociology or political theory in the study of European integration, mainly concentrating on policy areas linked to former pillar 1 policies. In this second part, the book will thus look in turn at different forms of institutionalism (Chapter 4) and governance approaches (Chapter 5), Europeanization and policy transfer studies (Chapter 6), constructivism (Chapter 7), sociological approaches to European integration (Chapter 8) and political theory (Chapter 9). The main objective of these academic concepts (and accompanying sets of literature) is not to develop frameworks for explaining *why* states join regional integration schemes in the first place (motives, rationale, costs/benefits), but to contribute to our understanding of *how* the European political system actually works in practice today, and how the EU has influenced and transformed domestic politics in the various member states.

In the third and final part, the book seeks to analyse how the EU can be interpreted by using international relations approaches: on the one hand, to examine how general international relations theories can be applied to European integration when coupled with more sociological interpretations of international relations (Chapter 10). This chapter will allow us to present conceptual frameworks for measuring the influence of sovereignty and national interests on the bargaining behaviour of member states, as well as the EU's role in the world, i.e. whether it can be seen as a normative power, a coherent international actor or whether its internal structure prevents it from influencing international relations.

On the other hand, comparative regional integration approaches turn, at least partially, back to initial questions such as why states agree to form regional integration schemes and how these regional integration schemes function, in studying forms beyond the European continent (Chapter 11). These conceptual approaches thus attempt to conceptualize international integration processes more generally, rather than concentrating solely on those concerning European integration.

The proliferation of theoretical and conceptual approaches for studying the EU allows us, on the one hand, to engage in a more detailed and nuanced analysis of the EU and its historical development. At the same time, however, they have also revealed signs of increasing fragmentation (Paterson, Nugent and Egan 2010). While most of the approaches and theoretical frameworks have avoided becoming too specialized, there is nevertheless a certain danger that, instead of bringing the whole picture of European integration back in, they increasingly concentrate on micro-subjects or issue areas. In other words, we currently observe the consolidation of a multitude of middle-range theories that do not set out to *explain* the reasons for integration, but, instead, enable us to *structure* our research in a coherent manner. That is not to say that these many different approaches are operating in complete isolation from each other. What we hope for, of course, is that the borders between these different approaches are broken down or become more permeable, to give way to more open debates on the advantages and disadvantages of each approach and their level of application (Manners 2009).

However, it does seem that we are at a point where contemporary theoretical frameworks should consider how they might be more ambitious, in an attempt to explain the structure and functioning of the wider system as a whole. This is essential if we want to avoid wallowing in a multitude of very detailed examinations of specific, yet isolated, policy studies. Further studies focusing on European society (Fligstein 2008) or the EU as a system (Bartolini 2005; Leuffen, Rittberger and Schimmelfennig 2012) would allow us to envisage the 'bigger picture' from alternative perspectives, and arguably, have more value for the community of Europeanists as a whole.

The aim of this book is not to present a history of European integration, to give precise accounts of specific policies, or to analyse the political system of the EU, for these endeavours have been carried out elsewhere with great success (Dinan 2004; Wallace, Pollack, and Young 2010; Hix and Høyland 2011). Instead, it seeks to provide the reader with critical tools in order to navigate through what is an increasingly complex and dense body of theoretical and conceptual literature. That said, the frontiers between the approaches presented in this book – where one begins and another ends – are sometimes not as clear-cut as one might expect. Sometimes approaches overlap or cross over because of what they focus on and how they inherently perceive the EU. This is due to the fact that concepts often develop simultaneously, influencing each other either through stark opposition or apparent complementarity. In turn, proponents of one concept or framework may react to the emergence of another by tightening up their own so it becomes more separate and/or distinct. Accepting this mutual dependency, throughout the chapters the reader might not find the authors where they expect them to be, but instead discover their horizontal influence upon, and/or relevance to several other conceptual frameworks.

Part I

Why Integrate? Theories of Integration

The study of intergovernmental cooperation is by no means a recent phenomenon. The question of why states cooperate is subject to different interpretations in international relations and can be traced as far back as the peace treaties of Westphalia in 1648. Academic attention to state cooperation in regional frames gained ground more systematically after the Second World War and, in particular, during the 1950s and 1960s. The first part of this book provides an analysis of the origins of, and recent developments, in those early theoretical approaches to regional and European integration. The main question was *why* sovereign states cooperated in international affairs at all, i.e. how did they do so, who were the central actors of cooperation, what was its bottom-line objective, what were the limits and constraints, the processes and procedures?

The theories analysed in this part are mostly concerned with the factors conducive to integration, as well as with the results of this process. This differentiates them from the approaches discussed in Parts II and III of this book, where the *how* question predominates. Conceptual frameworks dealt with in the latter parts of the book concentrate on specific developments of regional integration, and on processes and dynamics, but not so much on the question of why international actors search out and agree to be part of regional integration processes. The questions raised by the theories in Part I address issues such as why European states accept to gradually transfer powers to the European Parliament or the European Commission, how states organize their cooperation, what the consequences of integration are in terms of elite socialization, or why and how states use their veto power. The answers to these questions are multifaceted, but what they have in common is an attempt to address the reasons leading to the construction of a political union, either explicitly or implicitly.

Developed after the First World War, the first integration theories paid particular attention to the dangers of nationalism and economic protectionism. War was considered an essential characteristic of the international system, which divided peoples into nation-states and pushed them to fight to secure scarce resources. Federalist, functionalist and neofunctionalist accounts aimed to develop analytical models that could explain how international anarchy might be replaced by a system of international societies that regulate international relations. Alternatively, neorealist, intergovernmental and liberal intergovernmentalist theories argued, at different degrees, that international anarchy remained the driving force for state behaviour.

Albeit diverse, three characteristics are common to the theories studied in this first part (Eilstrup-Sangiovanni 2006: 17): first of all, the idea that the problems of contemporary society have reached such a scale that they can no longer be handled adequately at the level of the individual nation-state but require international solutions – which can potentially be found by state representatives through international cooperation. Secondly, these theories argue either in favour of or against the basic assumption that international institutions have the capacities necessary to develop solutions, which in turn help states cooperate with each other. Finally, scholars in that first period of integration research initially pursued a framework that went beyond European integration to study regional integration comparatively beyond Europe. Neofunctionalists, intergovernmentalists and federalists based their thinking on non-European examples of regional integration. Developments from the beginning of the 1990s onwards transformed those theories into EU-centred approaches with little or no interest in regional integration beyond the European realm.

Rather than limiting the debate on grand theories in EU studies to the three usual suspects – federalism, neofunctionalism and intergovernmentalism (see Wiener and Diez 2004, 2009; Chryssouchou 2008; Schimmelfennig 2010), the aim of this part is to trace the origins of these theories and to present more general approaches to state cooperation in the regional context.

Thus, the first chapter presents theories of international and regional integration that laid the foundations for classic integration theories – the so-called 'pre-theories' (Rosamond 2000; Eilstrup-Sangiovanni 2006): functionalism, transactionalism and federalism. These pre-theories profoundly influenced later mainstream integration theories, albeit implicitly. Europe is often used as a regional case study for identifying distinct features of regional integration processes.

Our examination of specific approaches to European integration begins in Chapter 2, with its focus on neofunctionalism. It is followed by a third chapter looking at intergovernmentalist approaches that developed as a result of empirical observation – specifically, after the Empty Chair Crisis triggered by the French government of General de Gaulle in 1965/1966. As such, both chapters hark back to the original attempts to explain regional integration, namely, why exactly states accept to pool their sovereignty.

All theories and theoretical approaches discussed here have strongly influenced the conceptual frameworks developed since the end of the

1980s to analyse European integration. As Part II will show, while some conceptual frameworks oppose the premises and hypotheses of this first generation of work on regional integration, later scholarship attempts to refine them by tightening up concepts and fleshing them out in greater detail.

Chapter 1

Original Debates

While regional integration studies are no recent phenomenon, they certainly gained in importance after the Second World War. The extent to which the world became organized according to regional logics increased steadily. Trade flows, direct investments or indeed the activities of international organizations were increasingly concentrated within 'regions' – often entire continents – as well as globally. With the end of the First World War, the prevalence of a system based on states with a tendency to engage in conflict was called into question – how to establish more effective balance of power mechanisms? In both academic and political circles the liberal idea of rejecting the state as an ultimate form of human governance emerged. Yet state conflict soon led to the subsequent horrors of 1939–45. International and supranational institutions were thought necessary to help overcome the antagonistic attitudes of states, in particular in Europe. On the one hand, these ideas were rooted in economic institutions created during the 1920s such as the European Customs Union and the International Steel Cartel which associated German, French and British steel producers. At the same time, the rise of American political and economic power triggered fear among the European elite that the continent would lose its central position in world affairs. On the other hand, philosophical ideas found their way back into political debate. The intellectual origins of European integration can be found in the Kantian idea of a European federation or Winston Churchill's United States of Europe. The vocabulary and ideology of federalist movements emerging at the beginning of the twentieth century were forged on the eighteenth-century philosophy of Immanuel Kant. In the 1920s Richard Coudenhove-Kalergi developed the Pan Europa idea with his call for a federal union of European states centred on France and Germany. While this discourse, these actions and ideas do not qualify as theories in the social science sense, they are nonetheless important in terms of providing an intellectual basis, and set of alternatives for political debates on how to practically 'reorganize' the European continent.

In order to contextualize the current conceptual tools used in EU studies, it is therefore important to return to the origins of theoretical approaches to regional integration more generally. This chapter does so in three steps, with a first section presenting functionalism as a pre-theory to neofunctionalism. A second section then presents transactionalist

Table 1.1   *Original debates in brief*

Perspectives	Main assumptions
Functionalism	International organizations, governed by experts, are needed to guarantee peace. National elites are too interested in re-election to make efficient and good decisions
Transactionialism	Communication is the key variable determining the social engagement in communities (security communities)
Federalism	The theory or advocacy of federal principles for dividing powers between member units and common institutions

perspectives, focusing on the construction of a regional identity through cooperation in the field of security. A final section discusses federalism, which is not only an analytical toolbox, useful for explaining why and how states integrate into a larger territorial entity, but it is also a normative approach in the sense that it argues in favour of greater integration. Contrary to the two other theories, federalism has, since the 1980s, been further explored and refined. The aim of these conceptual developments was to better understand recent European integration phenomena. It is essential to grasp how these pre-theories intellectually underpinned early developments in regional integration, even if much academic enquiry in contemporary EU studies has now shifted to focus more on governance processes and thus took the so-called 'governance turn' (Pollack 1996: 454).

Functionalism

Functionalism led to a new and influential understanding of why states agreed to establish international organizations. Functionalist approaches and, in particular, the account developed by David Mitrany, are considered as the cornerstones of classic integration theory. As a precursor to the neofunctionalist approach (Chapter 2), functionalism had been central to the study of international relations and was part of the liberal-idealist movement which spanned Kant to interwar liberals such as Woodrow Wilson. This movement developed ideas on how to guarantee peace among nations. The conceptual framework of functionalism emerged as one of the first to directly question state-centred approaches. Through its arguments that allowed for the including of other actors in international relations, such as experts, civil servants or international organizations, it paved the way for the so-called interdependence approach(es) by Robert Keohane and Joseph Nye (Keohane and Nye 1977) or the 'regimes theory' of the 1980s (Krasner 1983).

The founding father of functionalism, David Mitrany, was very much an exception among the authors whose works are analysed in this book. Mitrany studied at the London School of Economics (LSE) but did not subsequently embark upon a university career. As a journalist, adviser and foreign-policy analyst (Claude 1964; Pentland 1973; Navari 1995), his work had a more normative character than those of his colleagues. For him, the idea was less to establish a refutable theory and more to develop a conceptual framework conducive to promoting conditions that would put an end to situations of war – a framework that curried considered intellectual favour in the 1940s. Mitrany's objective was to propose specific factors that might lead to the establishment of permanent international organizations guaranteeing peace, and not to retreat into the quick-fix, enthusiastic idealism of the interwar period. As Ben Rosamond points out, Mitrany's starting point is not to identify an ideal form of international society, but to pinpoint the essential functions that such a system should be able to deliver (Rosamond 2000: 32).

At the heart of this approach is the belief that the political game *per se*, i.e. politics, stands in the way of the creation of favourable social conditions for all. Ideological positions harboured by states are a powerful factor working against the collective wellbeing and which can also, *in fine*, lead to war. According to the functionalist conception, as entities, nation-states are therefore the least suited to nurturing the fundamental development of their citizens. Public policies are encumbered by politics' (and its politicians') quest to optimize individuals' needs. As a result, powerful supranational institutions are needed to exercise the function that rational individuals attribute to them, hence the notion of functionalism.

Through their political elite, governments create situations in which the acquisition and exercise of power overshadow the pursuit of the common good. Politics also prevents the state from acting creatively when faced with public policy challenges. Their inflexibility, due to their ideological nature, creates a need for institutions and international or transnational agencies. Thus, according to Mitrany, in order to achieve certain objectives, it is better to ignore the constraints of territory – and national territory in particular. The creation of such entities is thought to have two consequences. First, citizens or populations in general will transfer their loyalties to newly created institutions. The second consequence of the creation of such institutions is a marked reduction in the probability of armed conflict. The application of the rational and technocratic approach is therefore the basis of a sustainable, peaceful system (Mitrany 1943). The functionalists' key idea is that the *form* (the institution to be created) is the consequence of the *function* that this same institution is required to accomplish – form follows function. Since the state – and political actors more specifically – cannot govern in a flexible manner, the need for transnational institutions arises. If distinct governmental forms arise for different functional needs, however, the predicted outcome is not a single regional body like the EU, but a 'cobweb' of organizations with different functions and memberships.

It was in the complex interwar period of the 1930s that Mitrany pursued the idea that the state should not be the centre-point of internationalist reflection (Mitrany 1933, 1943). Three areas of critique emerged. First, the state should not be considered as an entity independent of others, nor indeed should it be considered sovereign. Mitrany was the first to use the notion of 'material interdependence' – a term subsequently adopted by Robert Keohane and Joseph Nye and extended through the development of regime theory (Keohane and Nye 1972, 1977). Secondly, Mitrany considers the state as ultimately archaic, precluding any constructive or innovative reflection. In his view, international and transnational institutions are the only antidote to this reigning inertia. Finally, and particularly apposite in contemporary debate, Mitrany considers the state as a poorly suited and rather inadaptable structure for resolving the problems of complex interdependence, one of the characteristics of contemporary public policies (Papadopoulos 1995). Only the proliferation of transnational organizations and institutions could lead to interests being pursued to meet the needs of humanity effectively. These institutions should be numerous and specialized, while remaining profoundly independent. The result of this process could be a network of overlapping institutions that differ according to their functions.

Critiques

Some of the observations developed in functionalist theory have been taken up in more recent conceptual frameworks in EU studies, such as in the governance literature (Chapter 5), or normative theories of European integration (Chapter 9) – for example, the inability of states to deal individually with specific transnational issues such as environmental protection, trade or, more recently, financial regulation, which arguably need transnational institutions to regulate their relevant policy fields. However, the functionalist approach in general has been widely criticized on the grounds of its normative and teleological nature, the minimal importance it has attached to the political nature of decision-making, and the absence of any sociological analysis of actors working within transnational and supranational institutions.

With regard to the normative and teleological issue, functionalism is criticized for not sufficiently explaining the notion of 'human need'. These needs are legion and often contradictory, while the notion of rationality is particularly relative in this context. There is no guarantee that supranational institutions will apply a rational approach or that individuals will be convinced of functionalists' arguments referring to 'human need' in their day-to-day affairs.

Secondly, and more importantly, by insisting on the technocratic nature of the organizations to be created, Mitrany fails to take the permanent and unavoidable presence of politics into consideration. No public policy management can be purely technocratic. Politics is not necessarily always an ideological or partisan game, but fundamental power-play in any process of bargaining exists when it comes to the public interest. Thus, even experts and civil servants – considered as neutral – will defend the interests of the group they represent.

Finally, it is not clear which actors Mitrany believes should manage functionalist transnational and international institutions, nor what their selection criteria should be. The abstract category of 'experts' is too broad to be operationalized in empirical research.

Neofunctionalists (Chapter 2) took these critiques seriously and transformed the conceptual and normative frame of functionalism into a fully-fledged theory.

Transactionalist perspectives

The process of regional integration between the end of the Second World War and the end of the 1960s gave rise to a substantial body of theoretical studies. While some developed into fully-fledged theories, based on a coherent set of assumptions, such as neofunctionalism and intergovernmentalism, others such as transactionalism somehow got shelved and forgotten. Implicitly, however, it very much influenced subsequent studies on socialization and cultural learning in EU studies.

With its focus more centred on the security of a set of countries than political or economic integration, the main exponents, Karl Deutsch and his colleagues, looked at the conditions required for a regional security regime to emerge. For Deutsch and his research team, integration was defined as the creation of stable, secure communities in a region or group of states. The EC was not the research object, but the North Atlantic Community. The objective was to develop 'the means by which individuals will one day be able to abolish war' (Deutsch et al. 1957: 3). Effective integration could thus be measured through the radical reduction of states' resorting to violence. Being both a specialist in international relations and political sociology, Deutsch's aim was to study the link between the creation of nations and the communication between individuals using newly developed computerized data-gathering methods. His central assumption was that communication is the key variable determining the social engagement of communities. These communities precede the emergence of nations.

Through the notion of 'security communities', the author and his colleagues referred to groups of people who became integrated within new political entities. Communication would lead to the establishment of a 'we-feeling', created psychologically through a devotion of individuals of this community to some symbol representing the community. This feeling of community would give rise to stable institutions and mutually acceptable practices, facilitating a transformation to peaceful coexistence. The authors went on to make a distinction between 'amalgamated' security communities and 'pluralistic' communities. Amalgamated security communities merge smaller units – states – into a bigger unit, thereby creating a new institution that is very much in line with federalist arrangements. Pluralistic security communities are communities in which individual states retain their sovereignty. They need three factors to exist: compatible values, a peaceful approach to internal conflict resolution by all participants, and the ability to predict the social, political and economic behaviour of the other members of the community (Deutsch 1968; Cobb and Elder 1970).

The central idea of the *transactionalist* approach is that the degree of community between states will be a consequence of the level of communication and the existence of a network of transactions between them. Only a high degree of communication and transaction will lead to a cognitive adaptation of all actors at the expense of the singular existence of one institutional elite – a criticism that Deutsch made of the functionalist and neofunctionalist approaches. Deutsch was more specifically interested in issues of identity and government within such security communities and states that agreed to form these communities than in external factors such as economic or security imperatives. Through this process, he directly defied realist and neorealist hypotheses which refused to open the 'black box' (the state) and which considered citizens as a negligible variable. Karl Deutsch and his colleagues stressed, on the contrary, the importance of the feelings of the individuals that constituted these security communities (for a more recent application see also Kaiser et al. 2005; Adler and Barnett 1998). This sociological approach led the authors to take only a very limited interest in the formal institutions of regional integration or, indeed, those of the member states. Their main study perspective was communication and transactional procedures between individuals. European integration *per se* was merely one example among others worthy of research investigation.

Limits of transactionalist perspectives

David Puchala (1981) drew attention to several difficulties in this perspective, of which two in particular were crucial. The first was the operationalization of the specific research question, i.e. the possibility of transforming transactionalist hypotheses into measurable variables.

While a longitudinal and historical study was deemed the most suitable method, there remained the problem of knowing how to measure change in feelings of 'belonging'. While Eurobarometer statistics, or indeed, the *European Values Survey* are useful tools to measure the we-feeling or the sense of belonging to a community such as the European Union, tools that are at our disposal today, they were not around in the 1960s. A second difficulty, also methodological, concerned the issue of under-standing how to recognize that a change or cognitive adaptation had taken place. In work by the transactionalists, cognitive adaptation certainly exists, although no proof of such a change is produced. Indeed, it seems clear that through an increasingly high degree of communication and transactions, ideas and/or behaviour can change, but how can we be sure that such change is due to learning instead of the strategic attitude of a given actor? (Jacquot and Woll 2004b; for a stimulating debate see also Hayes-Renshaw and Wallace 2006 as well as Chapter 6).

Federalism

Among the grand theories seeking to explain why states integrate into regional organizations, federalism occupies an important place. Based on assumptions from comparative politics and international relations, federalism is a theory explaining the principles for dividing powers between member units and common institutions (Dosenrode 2007a).

As a theory, federalism provides an analytical toolbox for explaining why and how states integrate into a larger territorial entity. It is, at the same time, also a normative approach advocating greater integration to overcome national interests that lead to war. There is indeed a rather striking interdependence between the political ideal of federalism and its institutional output (Beaud 2007). In spite of its hybrid nature – some-where between a normative approach requiring that the union created is a federation, confederation or consociation, and an analytical approach which proposes tools to systemize the study of the integration process – the role of federalism in European integration theory is crucial. Just like neofunctionalism (Chapter 2) from the 1950s onwards, the federalist idea has been a constant in political discourse and academic debate. If we compare historically the varied experiences of establishing federations, such as Germany, Austria, Belgium, the USA, India or Canada, or the ongoing processes of devolution in countries such as Spain, Italy, France and the UK, we can pinpoint certain common features. These features suggest why states might agree to join a regional integration project and what the consequences of this project might be.

Federalist scholars argue that the political will and the interests of states making up such a supranational federal entity are essential. However, even though states remain the key actors of regional integration, a central federalist assumption is that part of their sovereignty is transferred to new centres, such as the Commission or the Council of Ministers. For federalists, a real centre of power – a government, in a manner of speaking – is, or must be, established at the supranational level.

Definitions

In the most consensual definition, federalism can be perceived of as a form of government based on a *convention* (*foedus*) combining separate and equal political communities, which act together while retaining their identity (Reuter 1956; King 1982). A confederation, on the other hand, is an association of sovereign member states, linked by a *treaty* that establishes common institutions to which the states have delegated a number of competencies in order to coordinate their policies in a number of areas. The relationship between the states forming this confederation can be of varying natures: some confederations can be similar to intergovernmental organizations, while tighter confederations may resemble federations.

From a judicial point of view, the difference between a federation and a confederation lies in the extent to which powers are transferred to the new centre. Whereas membership of a confederation can be reversed, membership of a federation cannot simply be abandoned with a decision by the concerned member. Thus, a confederation is an institutional arrangement bringing together sovereign states into an organization that unifies without completely absorbing the centre. A federation or a federal state, on the contrary, is a type of sovereign state characterized by a union of partially self-governing states united by a common government. Its status is usually constitutionally defined and cannot be altered by a unilateral decision. From a legalistic point of view, the constitution or constitutional agreement is at the heart of this arrangement. Whether the EU is a confederation or a federation is subject of intense debate. Indeed, the EU is not based on a constitution, does not tax its citizens directly – its main revenue source is a levy on the gross national income of member states – and member states retain individual membership in intergovernmental bodies such as the United Nations (UN) or the North Atlantic Treaty Organisation (NATO). It does not seem to qualify as federation under these circumstances. At the same time, however, the citizens of the EU's member states are also citizens of the Union, the European Court of Justice adjudicates disputes between levels of government, as does the US Supreme Court, and the EU public policies have direct and immediate impact at the EU level (Menon and Schain 2006; Weiler 2002; Nicolaïdis and Howse 2001).

Finally, a consociation is an institutional arrangement allowing for diverse social groups to govern collectively. Consociations are commonly sub-state structures, but their characteristics can be applied to the EU, as we will see later.

While these definitions form the cornerstones of political debate on the nature of the EU, they are not as clear-cut at they might seem (Burgess 2004; Beaud 2007). For instance, is a treaty a form of constitution in the context of the EU, as argued by the ECJ in 1986 ('Les Verts', Case 294/83; 23 April 1986)?

But even so, they are central to political and ideological debates in the context of EU studies; why this is so becomes clear when we look in more detail at the origins and uses of European federalist ideas.

Federalist ideas in the European construction
The influence exerted by the federalist idea on political action in Western Europe can be traced back to the sixteenth-century writings of Jean Bodin (see Burgess 2000, 2004). The contemporary understanding of federalism, however, was marked by three events at the beginning of the 1920s: (1) the 1923 publication of Richard Coudenhouve-Kalergi's work, *Pan-Europa*, and (2) the publication of the pan-European manifesto in 1924. The 1926 Pan-European Congress defined the broad brushstrokes of a future European federation: the guarantee of equality, security and confederal sovereignty, military alliance, the progressive creation of a customs union, sharing of European colonies, a single currency, respect for national cultures and the protection of minorities, and Europe's collaboration with other groups of states within the Society of Nations. The culminating point is generally seen to be situated in the years immediately after the Second World War and the 1948 Hague Congress, when federalist movements were particularly active. Three logics of federalist thinking linked to the later European construction can be distinguished (Burgess 2004): the war experience, the debate between the 'Founding Fathers' of European integration over what form this new project should take, and, finally, national federalist movements.

The first logic refers to the conception of the postwar period based on the experience of war itself. All over Europe, not least the UK, federalists put their case for the best way to establish a European federation (Dinan 2004). In Winston Churchill's Zurich speech of September 1946 he invited European countries to form a United States of Europe. It was actually among the anti-fascist resistance fighters that the federal idea of a future unified Europe was born, and the victory over Hitler was thought to be but the first step towards a new European political order. This idea can be found in most pan-European movements created during the Second World War. It is important to emphasize, however, that conceptualizations of what a future Europe would look like were anything but unified and homogenous – in fact, many competing and contradictory beliefs were subsumed under the notion of 'federal' Europe.

The second idea can be found in the key federalist publication during this period: the *Manifesto di Ventotene*. Drawn up by a group of Italian federalists, and led by Ernesto Rossi and the future member of the European Parliament, Altiero Spinelli, the document brought together a set of ideas, attitudes and assumptions about a federalist future for European integration. Spinelli's influence as an adviser to the Italian Government as General Secretary of the Italian Federalist Movement was particularly important during the first half of the 1950s, despite the failure of both projects he helped set up (the European Defence Community, EDC and the European Political Community, EPC). Nonetheless, it was Jean Monnet's economically-driven vision of Europe that subsequently replaced Spinelli's. The one key element of the Spinelli project that did come to fruition was the creation of a European Parliament. Spinelli's idea, called 'democratic radicalism', led to a parliamentary assembly, which now plays a central role in European decision-making. However, beyond Spinelli's democratic radicalism and Monnet's rampant integrationism, a third logic emerged: the establishment of individual federalist movements at the national level under the heading of the European movement. Based on diverse ideological foundations across different European Economic Community (EEC) member and non-member states, the objective was, and still is in today's EU, to decentralize the decision-making process, to involve civil society in the reflection and management of European affairs, and to create a truly federal EU with a federal government and a federal governance system (Pinder 1992). European movements continue to be extremely active in campaigning to promote these ideas at the national level.

Parallel to these normative perspectives, analytical approaches to federalism in European integration emerged. However, they only gathered momentum at the beginning of the 1990s when the empirical developments of European integration reintroduced questions of levels of government.

Conceptualizing the EU as a federation in EU studies

After a period of relative disinterest among EU scholars, federalism made a comeback in the 1990s with the Maastricht Treaty and questions over the future and aims of the European project. This gave rise to more sophisticated and differentiated federalist approaches, which were incorporated into other theories and concepts of European integration. Federalist perspectives in particular influenced the literature on governance (Chapter 5), and liberal intergovernmentalism, which emerged partly in response to federalist perspectives (Chapter 3). More generally, federalism helped link the analysis of the EU more closely to general political science, thus playing an important role in the 'mainstreaming' of European studies (see Introduction).

Comparative federalism

Modern-day comparative approaches to federalism are less characterized by their focus on the best way of governing a multi-state entity such as the EU, but to help us to understand how actors situated at different levels of government cooperate and manage political affairs (Scharpf 1988; Sbragia 1991; Weiler 1991; Dehousse 1991). Comparative federalism encountered new research enthusiasm after German Foreign Affairs Minister Joschka Fischer's federalism speech in May 2000. In his speech, Fischer argued in favour of a federal structure for the EU, reigniting the theoretical and conceptual debate. What followed was the framework of the European conventions (the 2002–03 European Convention on the Future of the European Union, often compared to the American Convention of 1787, and the European Convention on the Charter of Fundamental Rights of 1999/2000), which put comparative federalism back on the agenda (see Nicolaïdis 2004; Magnette and Nicolaïdis 2004; Magnette and Lord 2004).

The form, dynamics and consequences of political government at different levels of a political system is at the heart of comparative federalist studies in EU scholarship. The notions of devolution, decentralization and 'subsidiarity', which gained importance in the 1980s, were clearly influenced by earlier debates in federalism (Menon and Schain 2006).

Comparative federalism is a vast conceptual field. In order to clarify its specific tools used to understand European integration it is possible to distinguish between three areas of study:

(1)   polity- and democracy-related aspects, referring to the structure and the constitutional characteristics of the EU,
(2)   policy aspects, and
(3)   studies analysing the political features of the EU, concentrating mainly on parties and elections, and the political game more generally.

Polity considerations

Questions of democracy and the supposed democratic deficit have attracted more and more interest from analysts of comparative federalism from the end of the 1990s onwards (Nicolaïdis and Howse 2001; Menon and Schain 2006; Kelemen 2006). Comparative federalist approaches concentrating on polity considerations question the origin of various forms of legitimacy in a political context in which diverse levels of government and governance interact. These questions prominently concentrate on forms of representation.

The nature of democratic representation in federal states is based on a dual understanding. One house represents the people and the other the member states of the federation, leading to a balanced system. The German political system is an illustration: the Bundestag (assembly) represents the people and the Bundesrat (senate) represents the Länder.

Comparative federalism has shown that in federal systems, territorial representation is the starting point of political organization and remains predominant over a long time (Sbragia 1991: 280). While in most federal systems, in particular in the USA, Germany, Switzerland or Austria, the two logics clearly become interdependent, the EU remains anchored in a system whereby territorial representation seem to prevail through the Council of Ministers, and, in a certain sense the European Council, representing the heads of state and government. This analysis applies despite the constant strengthening of the European Parliament through an enlargement of its prerogatives.

Linked to the debate on representation is that on political account-ability, which became increasingly interrelated during the 2000. Several authors (in particular von Beyme 2005) argue that, due to complex deci-sion-making and the institutional structure of the EU, competitive feder-alism broadly explains citizens' Euroscepticism and the system's perceived lack of legitimacy (Christin, Hug and Schulz 2005) as a result of the extension of the federal powers of the EU. The shared political competencies between state and supranational levels has led to a situa-tion where the federal government can limit member governments' room for political and economic manoeuvre (Kelemen 2003; Kelemen and Nicolaïdis 2007). On the basis of both rationalist and constructivist logics, Kelemen (2003) argues that the transfer of authority from the national to the federal level can be explained by the opportunities that federal institutions offer.

Empirically, this is difficult to observe (see also Majone 2005). Due to an increased variety of state interests (cultural, social, institutional and economic) and new decision-making methods (such as the Open Method of coordination), the EU cannot provide the degree of accountability the European citizen may take for granted. In this sense, Majone suggests that a postmodern confederal model, based on market integration, offers the only viable project both for governing citizens and for playing an effective joint role in the international community. Here, however, the size of the regional entity again becomes a problem: for Majone, the EU is too big to allow for close contact with citizens and has little capacity to identify their needs and desires. What precisely is meant by 'too big' remains unspecified. In this context, Majone is very close to Montesquieu's idea of a Republic. Montesquieu advocated a small republic, since it allows for close contact with citizens and provides a greater capacity to identify their needs and desires. In this model, greater emphasis is placed on the constituent polities as these polities are led to protect individual liberties inside their borders.

Policy frames

A second, theoretically equally important, tradition of contemporary federalism studies can be found in European public policy. Scholars consider how elements such as decision-making structures can best be analysed in a federal system such as the EU. Decision-making in federal systems very often leads to situations whereby the final decision taken reflects the smallest common denominator. Applying this insight from German federalism to the European system, Fritz Scharpf (1988) showed in his seminal article that in systems where member governments directly participate in unanimous decision-making, this process will systematically lead to sub-optimal policy outcomes unless a problem-solving style of decision-making can be maintained. According to Scharpf, huge tensions (or 'joint decision-traps') are created in a federal system, and in the EU in particular. In the EU, European institutions identify problems and suggest solutions, which are then blocked by member states using their veto rights, on account of political conflict and disagreement among themselves over which course of action to take. The reason member states continue to participate in this system is very much linked to the fact that both disintegration and greater integration (centralization) are considered suboptimal outcomes.

Scharpf indicates three conditions under which a joint decision trap occurs: (1) when the decision rule requires (quasi) unanimous decision-taking, (2) when the decision style is bargaining and (3) when the political preferences are fixed and divergent, and imported from the domestic level. Joint-decision systems generally lead to sub-optimal policy outputs (Scharpf 1988: 258). This is due to the initial difficulties of agreement on a European policy between member states, but also because European policies, once in place, are equally resistant to reform and constrain the independent action capacities of the constituent units – the member states.

These decision traps can be found in a large number of policy areas, not at least in the field of the Common Agricultural Policy (CAP) or the EU budgetary process after the Lisbon Treaty. The outcomes are also suboptimal because based on the lowest common denominator existing amongst member states.

In a later, revisited version of the 'joint decision-trap', Scharpf (2006) added the role of the ECJ to his analysis. In cases where the Court is called upon, its decision must be applied to all member states, and no negotiation process is theoretically possible. In the field of legislative harmonization, this supranational, hierarchical governance system is based on the fact that, even the mere threat of Court action would greatly increase the willingness of all governments to accept the minimum harmonization directives proposed by the Commission (Scharpf 2006: 853). Thus, Scharpf argues that attempts to avoid sub-optimal outcomes encourage member states to continue their participation in a joint system, while acknowledging and accepting the Commission's monopoly on legislative initiative in most policy fields (see also Dehousse 1998; Halberstam 2008; Falkner 2011).

Kelemen (2004) makes a similar argument. He argues that the development of EU regulatory policy can only be understood by viewing the EU as a federal system – one which mediates conflict and imposes common regulations aimed at harmonizing standards and practices. The paradox is that while the EU's central institutions exercise less control over its member states than governments of federal polities, they are nevertheless able to impose 'detailed, inflexible rule making and litigation enforcement that constrains state discretion' (Kelemen 2004: 2). A counterintuitive hypothesis results from this: that the greater the fragmentation of power in the structure of a federal government, the lower the discretion granted to state governments in implementing federal laws. Fragmentation of power is the result of a high number of veto players. In other words, the larger the number of competing institutional power-holders, the greater the mistrust, and the stronger the incentives to contest it. In order to make sure that EU laws are respected at the national level, European institutions must reduce member state level discretion.

While these studies develop a general framework for policy analysis using federalist approaches, in which the main question is how competencies and instruments are allocated across different vertical layers of the administration, other studies concentrate more specifically on distinct policy areas in federal systems, such as fiscal federalism, environmental policy or economic integration, comparing the EU political system with the USA, Switzerland, Canada or Germany. The EU's lack of fiscal federalism is probably the area in which the EU least resembles other federal systems. Comparisons with the US federal system illustrate this aspect, in particular since the European Monetary Union (EMU) crisis at the end of the first decade of 2000. A central principle of US federalism is that states are sovereign in their macroeconomic management. That means that while states receive federal funding, the federal government cannot mandate spending cuts or tax increases. States cannot declare bankruptcy and the federal government does not guarantee state debt. At the same time, the US Federal budget allows for massive intervention into state governance when action is perceived necessary. The EU, on the contrary, cannot do that. It is not foreseen that the European budget provides stimulus by spending money (Alves 2007; Begg et al. 2004; Schelkle 2012).

Politics and federalism

Finally, comparative federalism research also centres on the question of politics and elections. Anchored in political sociology, this theoretical branch analyses the functions of political parties in a federal system. It sees the emerging party system at the EU level as being constructed in a confederal manner. The consequence of such a construction is an extremely heterogeneous party system where national ideologies and interests overlap, sometimes clashing with pure party ideologies or interests. The reasons for this are twofold. First, there are a large number of national political parties operating outside the strict ideological logic of the main families of European political parties. Secondly, certain parties have emerged within the framework of European elections alone (Thorlakson 2003, 2005). By using the tools of comparative federalism, research has shown that constructing a system of integrated parties at the supranational level raises major challenges. Subsequent enlargements have brought new political divisions to the party system, which has yet to achieve the level of coherence of a national federal system. Comparative research on the functioning of European parties and their voting patterns in a federal system differs, or even contradicts, analyses by scholars using rational choice institutionalism (Chapter 4), both in approach and findings. Contrary to comparative federalists who insist on the influence of nationality and country size, institutionalists argue that parties in the EU system act only according to a (crude) left/right cleavage, and that national interests do not play a role (Kreppel 2001).

The EU as a consociation

Undoubtedly, the most marginalized approach to analysing the EU as a form of federation is, according to Alex Warleigh-Lack (1998), that of consociative democracy. Developed in the 1960s, the approach is based on comparative research carried out on consociative federal countries, i.e. the Netherlands, Austria or Switzerland. These domestic political systems share the possibility of stable, longstanding governments, in spite of major segmentations on religious, linguistic, ethnic or ideological grounds. The basis for this work is Arend Lijphart's research into the Netherlands as a consociation (Lijphart 1968, 1977). He emphasizes that the construction of institutions, and development of a consensual political culture between the elite, can be sufficient to govern a society effectively, despite major cultural divisions.

The model of the consociative decision-making process argues that, in societies with major segmentations, a major coalition government allowing each constituent elite to exercise its veto is more stable than a majority government. Power must be shared proportionally between the elite according to the size of the population represented. The consociative model has been useful for describing the functioning of the EU since the segments (states) cooperate either on a unanimous or proportional basis in order to take decisions (Lijphart 1999; Warleigh-Lack 1998; Costa

and Magnette 2003; Chryssochoou 1994, 2008). The system is characterized by the existence of sovereign peoples, each with a national identity, political traditions, a social structure and a distinct civic culture. The
aim of this approach is to help explain the dilemma in which EU member
states regularly find themselves (Taylor 1996, 1998). In particular, they
must consolidate contradictory demands similar to those which confront
the elite at the domestic level, i.e. reinforce the effectiveness of management at the supranational level and, at the same time, ensure that the
interests of their national systems are sufficiently represented at that
level. More recently, the consociational idea has been used to argue in
favour of a non-contentious mode of politicizing the EU (see Chapter 10;
Magnette and Papadopoulos 2008). Instead of fostering the role of mass,
competitive and partisan politics in the EU as a way of strengthening its
democratic character, this approach argues that any efforts to do so must
take into account the EU's consensual decision-making processes.
Participation in the EU does not occur along a left/right division, given its
political structure based on compromises and cooperation. This
approach allows for 'globalization losers', such as acutely Eurosceptic
citizens and anti-system political entrepreneurs, to be integrated (Kriesi
et al. 2008). In this sense, the EU can be understood as a 'bargaining
democracy' with mechanisms for direct participation.

Criticism

Although among the first theories developed to study and actually politically construct European integration, federalist approaches to European
integration are generally found today on the margins of EU studies,
replaced instead by multi-level governance agendas (Chapter 5). While
the idea of the EU as a highly asymmetric federation is relatively widely
shared (for a debate see Dosenrode 2000b), the continued use of this
approach is comparatively rare. A first obstacle seems to be the ever-
present normative nature of federalist analyses. Using federalism to
justify national and international integration projects seems to delegitimize them in the eyes of analysts of the integration process.

A second obstacle, while less central, is the highly heterogeneous nature
of federalist approaches in question. Although designed as a theory, most
applications of federalism have not focused on a set of hypotheses that
need to be validated or, conversely, refuted. It is more a 'descriptive
theory' – but a theory nonetheless, because it develops explicit, albeit
diverse and sometimes contradictory hypotheses to understand the nature
of a political body, which is based on inter-state foundations.

A final obstacle seems to be empirical. The most recent European
treaties have appeared to reinforce the power of the member states
against that of the Commission. The member states remain stronger than

the supranational level of institutions, with the Council of Ministers enjoying the power to prevent policy developments in areas where member states object. As Dosenrode underlines (2007b), the picture of the EU as a centralized polity seems widely exaggerated. Nevertheless, it is possible to see in the EU a club of states with a number of federal characteristics. Conceptual tools developed by federalist scholars have enabled us to develop a better understanding of these processes and

Table 1.2   *Perspectives on original debates*

Perspectives	Main assumptions	Authors
Functionalism	'Form follows function': since political elites cannot govern in an efficient manner (their search for re-election hinders them from doing so), the need for transnational institutions arises	Mitrany 1933, 1943
Transactionalism	Central assumption: communication is the key variable determining the social engagement in communities (security communities)	Deutsch et al. 1957 Cobb and Elder 1970
Federalism	The theory or advocacy of federal principles for dividing powers between member units and common institutions	Pinder 1992 Burgess 2000, 2004 Beaud 2007
Comparative federalism	Compares EU federalism with other federal systems – mainly USA, Canada, Germany	Scharpf 1988 Sbragia 1991 Dehousse 1991 Menon and Schain 2006
• Polity considerations	Compares constitutional frameworks of federalist organizations	Nicolaïdis and Howse 2001 Kelemen 2003, 2006
• Policy frames	Compares the policy-making processes in federal systems. Identifies possibilities and limits ('joint decision-trap')	Scharpf 1988, 2006 Kelemen 2004 Begg et al. 2004 Falkner 2011
• Politics	Compares political parties and elections in federal systems	Thorlakson 2003, 2005
The EU as consociation	Scholars compare EU with consociation: characterized by the existence of sovereign peoples, each with a national identity, political traditions, a social structure and a distinct civic culture	Warleigh-Lack 1998 Costa and Magnette 2003 Chryssochoou 1994, 2008

reminded us constantly of the power game in which European member states, sub-national actors and the European institutions operate. However, the evolution of the EU cannot be put on the same footing as that of state federations: no European government exists to exercise its own political legitimacy, distinct and/or superior to that of the member states; there is no exclusive domain of constitutional jurisdiction, but rather the EU has shared legal competences with national constitutional courts since the early days of the Community.

Conclusion

The analysis of these original debates addressing the reasons for regional integration is necessary in order to grasp the scope and development of subsequent theories and of the approaches discussed in this book. The questions raised by these different perspectives were taken up and developed later by analysts of European integration. We find them in particular in the subsequent chapters of Part I: Which factors lead to regional integration? What political processes can be observed during this period? And what are the implications for international affairs more generally? Identifying different factors that lead to integration was the original concern of regional integration theories, but scholars have subsequently broadened the research agenda, which has come to question the influence of European integration on domestic politics, the role of different actors on integration, and the normative consequences of regional integration. However, none of the pre-theories presented here (functionalism, transactionalism, federalism) developed into one coherent regional integration, as was the case later with neofunctionalism (Chapter 2) and intergovernmentalism (Chapter 3). They most certainly paved the way for further analysis and thus were crucial forerunners.

Chapter 2

Neofunctionalism

Neofunctionalism is one of the best-known and 'basic' theories of European integration. Closely associated with Ernst B. Haas, who developed the notion at the end of the 1950s as part of his Ph.D. research on the European Coal and Steel Community (ECSC), neofunctionalism is today one of the most commonly referred to theories of European integration, either through counter-arguments attempting to refute it as convincing theory (more often than not) or recognition of its contribution and attempts to broaden its scope (more rarely). Like the conceptual frameworks analysed in Chapter 1, neofunctionalism seeks to establish why states accept the idea of being part of an international or supranational organization. However, it also attempts to go beyond this question by analysing the process leading to regional integration. While functionalism was profoundly anchored in normative thought, espousing conditions designed to bring about a more peaceful and fairer world, neofunctionalist approaches to integration are analytical, seeking to understand the reasons for, processes leading to, and consequences of, regional integration.

The aim of this chapter is to critically analyse the development of this approach, from its origins to later revisions and its application as a theory. These revisions can be seen as answers to the cyclical challenge of the theory. Real-world events – in the case of neofunctionalism, the 1965 decision of the French President de Gaulle to recall the French representative in Brussels stating France would not take its seat in the Council until it had its way – the so-called 'Empty Chair Crisis' – put the theory under stress and let to its temporary demise (see below). The general relaunch of European integration at the end of the 1980s allowed for a revival of the theory. Phenomena such as enlarged powers of the European Commission, the establishment of a single market which increased the number of policy areas dealt with at the European level, all contributed to the comeback of neofunctionalist frameworks. As stated in the Introduction to this book, these cyclical challenges lead to a refinement of the theory, and to a higher capacity to explain new empirical phenomena.

The chapter looks first at the assumptions and principles of neofunctionalist theory. Two notions are central in this context: *spill-over* and *transfer of loyalty* to a new regional organization. The second section then offers a critical overview of new hybrid though mainstream approaches that attempt to revive neofunctionalism by adopting a new research focus and revising existing concepts.

The founding theory of European integration

Convinced of functionalism's basic usefulness, but accepting its limitations, neofunctionalists sought to deepen and broaden the premises of the earlier theory. Neofunctionalism emerged in a particular political and scientific context: the adoption of functionalist theses by political and administrative actors, such as Robert Schuman and Jean Monnet, coincided with the emergence of the behaviourist movement in the USA during the late 1940s and early 1950s. This paved the way for the development of one of the first European integration theories. At the time, behaviourists were attempting to make the study of social phenomena more scientific through verifiable hypotheses, with the empirical observation of facts validating or refuting them. There are, therefore, undeniable links between the political speeches and actions of the Europeanized elite at the beginning of the 1950s and the scientific paradigm of the day (Dinan 2004).

Neofunctionalist ideas were most clearly expressed in 1958 in the key work of Ernst Haas, *The Uniting of Europe* (Haas 1958, 1968, 2004), followed by a plethora of other publications including, most significantly, Leon Lindberg's *The Political Dynamics of European Economic Integration* (Lindberg 1963), Stuart Scheingold's *The Rule of Law in European Integration* (Scheingold 1964), Ernst Haas's *Beyond the Nation-state: Functionalism and International Organizations* (Haas 1964) and the edited volume by Lindberg and Scheingold entitled *Regional Integration, Theory and Research* (Lindberg and Scheingold 1971). In these publications, neofunctionalism is constantly refined, adapted and retested, in other words, 'cyclically challenged' (Paterson 2010) and reinforced. One of the characteristics of neofunctionalism is its search for permanent adjustment to correct conceptual errors and inaccuracies (Ruggie et al. 2005).

Neofunctionalism started as a critique of functionalist and interactionist approaches. It proposed a study of domestic factors in order to explain regional – but more specifically European – integration. It was based on an in-depth analysis of the political systems and administrative structures of the founding states of the EC, focusing on political elites – parties, governments and interest groups – and on employers' associations and trade unions. It was clearly opposed to the dominant international relations paradigm of the time – neorealism – which explained regional integration by looking at exogenous causes, i.e. the existence of an external enemy and the desire of small states to join forces with larger ones in order to increase their influence.

According to functionalists, the key factor encouraging actors to create supranational political communities was not David Mitrany's 'technocratic automatism', but rather the rational action of a political and administrative elite seeking to defend its own interests. 'The decision to proceed with integration or to oppose it rests on the perception of interests and on the articulation of specific values on the part of existing political actors. Rather than relying on a scheme of integration which posits "altruistic" or "idealistic" motives as the conditions of conduct, it seems more reasonable', argues Haas, 'to focus on the interests and values defended by the major groups involved in the process, experience showing that these are far too complex to be described in such simple terms as "the desire for Franco-German peace" or the "will to a United Europe"' (Haas 1968: 13–14). Deepened integration, however, will change the perceptions and opinions of political elites: 'As the process of integration proceeds, it is assumed that values will undergo change, that interests will be redefined in terms of a regional rather than a purely national orientation at that the erstwhile set of separate national group values will gradually be superseded by a new and geographically larger set of beliefs' (ibid.).

This quotation bears all the elements of the neofunctionalist theory of European integration: it is clearly opposed to the authoritative or idealistic elements of functionalist approaches; it underlines the complexity of variables leading to political decisions; and finally, it highlights the consequences of integration processes, i.e. the change in values, beliefs and interests. Like his predecessors, Haas argued that the ideologies and politics of actors played a secondary role in integration, while emphasizing that the integration process is a competitive joust between different actors. Indeed, it is not ideologies that push for deeper integration, but functional necessities. Thus a customs union (a free-trade area with common external tariffs) could operate with greater efficiency if the participant states would create stable exchange-rate parities. Exchange-rate coordination would then imply the need for wider cooperation in monetary policies, and this, in turn would then lead to the establishment of an economic and monetary union (Rosamond 2000: 60). This spill-over hypothesis suggests that integration is a linear, progressive phenomenon. Once started, a dynamic would be set in place that would continue the momentum.

According to neofunctionalists, administrative as well as non-state actors carry these functional demands. This understanding positions neofunctionalism very close to the pluralist hypotheses developed in social sciences during the same period. In a pluralist political system, the state fields demands from social groups. It takes on a more or less neutral arbitration role over the activities and policies exercised by those groups. Thus, long before the international debate on the usefulness of taking concepts that had emerged from the analysis of the state and then using

Box 2.1   *Core neofunctionalist assumptions*

1 Relevant actors are economically rational beings. While their capacity to learn exists, their attitudes are based on interest. Therefore, when transferring loyalty to a new power centre or transforming beliefs and values, these actors choose their options rationally.

2 Once taken, decisions have unintentional consequences, more often than not leading to new decisions in other policy fields. This conceptualization of unintentional 'spill-over' shows that neofunctionalists did not believe in any preconceived grand design for European integration. Once launched, it seemed rather difficult to see where the progress was heading (Haas 1971).

3 Institutions created under this logic take on a life of their own. They are not only secretariats in the service of member-state preferences, but become independent actors pursuing their own agenda. The High Authority, later the Commission, influences the interests and beliefs of both public and private actors participating in the integration process.

them to analyse and theorise European integration (see Part III of this book), the neofunctionalists were already espousing this idea in the 1950s and 1960s.

Neofunctionalist core actors: interest groups and administrations

Economic interest groups are indeed the central actors of this approach. Driving the process by lobbying national governments and administrations for greater integration, they can also be considered as a variable in the transfer of actor loyalties from national to supranational levels. Thus, according to neofunctionalists' own perception of competence transfer, a shift of loyalties occurs to such an extent that interest groups cease to represent their interests to national governments and turn instead to the new supranational authority – more precisely the High Authority, the predecessor of the European Commission. This assumption has, at least implicitly, been explored many times by researchers working on collective action (Mazey and Richardson 1993; Schmitter and Streeck 1991; Schmitter and Traxler 1995).

Neofunctionalists argued that those who trigger spill-over effects are more likely to be non-state actors than sovereign states. National societal interests encourage greater political integration in order to promote their own economic or ideological interests. In parallel, the European Commission, or High Authority, as the Commission was called until 1958, seeks to increase its powers to heighten the influence of European institutions on political outcomes (or on public policies). The important technocratic capacity of supranational institutions to find solutions to specific problems explains why, according to neofunctionalists, societal actors were willing to transfer their expectations, political practices and allegiances to the Community level. Thus, for neofunctionalists, European integration would lead to the reformulation and reconstruction of social and sectoral interests, in particular, for those actors most directly affected by European policies. This shift in emphasis, in turn, would lead to the formation of transnational interest groupings, with a transformation in the allegiances and identities of those actors mobilized. Over the longer term, the European integration process would lead to a European identity and specifically new European forms of political representation. Non-state actors would communicate their pro-European interests to their national governments which, in turn, would influence national technocratic actors. This influence would result in a heightened awareness of national political actors, who recognized the benefits of cooperating and networking at the European level. The tangible outcome would be an increase in support for European integration within national political systems. In addition, it would become easier to negotiate integration agreements and to transfer some state sovereignty to a supranational authority.

In early neofunctionalist readings, two processes are advocated as being more or less automatic in this chain of events: first of all, economic integration leads almost automatically to a high level of transactions between economic actors in the region. Secondly, this high level of transaction provides major opportunities to these groups to create new forms of organization at the supranational level, such as employers' federations or trade unions.

More generally, four prerequisites are necessary for achieving regional political integration (Lindberg 1963). First of all, the main institutions and policies (economic, political, social) must be present at regional level. Secondly, institutions should have the capacity to initiate economic and social programmes, thereby superseding those of conventional international organizations. Thirdly, the tasks of supranational institutions should be extendable: integrated policies create pressures for integration in other areas by involving more and more actors in the decision-making and implementation of the resulting public policies. And finally, member states engaged in regional integration should have shared interests and perceptions.

This important role of the supranational administrations explains why neofunctionalist approaches became central to analyses of the European Commission as a political entrepreneur in the 1980 and 1990 (Nugent 2000, 2001; Cini 1996). These studies showed how crucial the Commission's role has been in enlarging the competencies of the EU and controlling the implementation of policies; they also exposed how difficult life is for the Commission when it finds itself weakened for various reasons – owing perhaps to changes in leadership and internal politics, accusations of fraud and the wider economic and political climate in the member states.

Neofunctionalist core assumptions: spill-over and transfer of loyalty

Spill-over

The notion of spill-over is certainly the best known of all neofunctionalist concepts – it is the key driving force behind all integration processes. Lindberg defines spill-over as 'a situation in which a given action, related to a specific goal, creates a situation in which the original goal can be assured only by taking further actions, which in turn create a further condition and a need for more action and so forth' (Lindberg 1963: 10). Initially it concerned economic sectors that would enhance the economic power of the ECSC on the world stage and which had the obvious potential to foster political integration. It was held that economic integration in one sector automatically leads to the integration of others, to the extent that the problems which emerge through the experience of the first sector can only be resolved by integrating the second as well.

This spill-over, analysed empirically by Haas in the context of the ECSC, means that member states' economies need to be relatively interdependent prior to the integration process. 'There is no circumventing the need for stating the initial demands and expectations of relevant elites, and to sort them with respect to identities, oppositions and convergences' (Haas 1968: 286–7). In this sense Haas argues that 'the acceptance of ECSC is best explained by the convergence of demands within and among the nations concerned, not by a pattern of identical demands and hopes' (ibid.).

However, a transnational authority is needed to implement this process. At the transnational level, it was the High Authority and later, the Commission, which was responsible for accelerating the degree of economic integration by technocratic means and, in particular, through more rational, optimized public management.

It is here that the link between the empirical development of European integration and theorizing by the neofunctionalists reached its pinnacle. Monnet and Schuman headed up this process with a profound belief in the '*de facto* solidarities' upon which the integration process was based. Hence, integrating one sector after another, slowly but surely, was the key, because the elites involved would recognize that only increased integration would truly allow them to resolve national economic problems. According to neofunctionalists, initially two kinds of spill-over existed: a functional and a political one. Functional spill-over refers to the interconnection of various *economic* sectors or issue-areas, and the integration in one policy-area spilling over into others. Political spill-over is the creation of supranational governance models, such as the EU or

Mercosur (Southern Common Market) (Groom and Taylor 1975; Caporaso 1998).

While spill-over remains the central argument of neofunctionalist theory, it was this concept in particular that was widely criticized – criticism which was later acknowledged by neofunctionalist scholars themselves. In the long preface of the second edition of *The Uniting of Europe,* Haas attempted to answer the questions raised by an empirical event that seriously challenged the theory: General de Gaulle's Empty Chair Policy from 1965 to 1966. De Gaulle believed that national governments should be the motors of integration and disagreed with the Commission's attempt to create a shift towards supranationalism. The Commission's strategy was very much influenced by neofunctionalist ideas: deeply convinced that economics were more important than politics, it actively contributed to create the necessary condition to make spill-over work. The Commission's attempt met its paroxysm in 1965 with General de Gaulle's fierce opposition in the budget negotiation of the CAP. While de Gaulle supported the creation of the CAP, he disagreed with the Commission's budget proposals for financing it. De Gaulle made it a condition that majority voting with a right to veto must exist if France was to participate in the EC. When de Gaulle was not granted a veto right, he left the Council of Ministers. This event was not resolved until the Luxembourg Compromise in January 1966.

The consequences for neofunctionalism – and the Commission – were harsh. Neofunctionalist ideas were so intertwined with the Commission's ideology that the defeat for the Commission became a defeat for neofunctionalism. Haas recognized that political will certainly precedes economic spill-over (Haas 1968: xix). He acknowledged furthermore that the difficulty of establishing a correlation between economic and political spill-over had not been resolved in a satisfactory manner. Neofunctionalists themselves acknowledged at that point the possibility of 'spill-back', in the opposite direction to 'spill-over' (Lindberg and Scheingold 1970).

The neofunctionalists very openly recognized that 'de Gaulle has proved us wrong': the European Commission, which had made the neofunctionalist main assumption its own, had expected to prevail in the crisis but was not able to do so. Its role and power was seriously challenged owing to the Empty Chair Crisis. The crisis was only solved by the 1966 Luxembourg compromise, which gave a de facto veto power to every member state on topics that were deemed to be very important national interests. It was agreed that should a topic of concern arise, members of the Council would seek to create a solution that all members could unanimously agree upon, regardless of whether or not the treaty required only a majority. This provision effectively created a short cut and weakened the Commission's capacity to foster integration even against the interests of specific member states. Thus, ten years after the publication of Haas's study, Europe was still not politically unified. Haas offered four reasons for this failure and suggested improving the initial conceptual framework on the basis of four variables (Haas 1968: xxii–xxiii).

First, neofunctionalism had ignored the changes in actors' preferences at the time of integration and new expectations emerging soon after membership. This distinction would have allowed for a more nuanced analysis of actor transformation and a better understanding of why spill-over is not a permanent and automatic phenomenon.

Secondly, Haas recognized that the absence of the 'ideology' variable – or more generally his assumption of the 'end of ideology' – was erroneous, because it led to the exclusion of national political considerations from the analysis. This led to an underestimation of political decisions, which could clearly bring integration to a halt when national interests were deemed to be threatened, as was the case with the CAP for France, and hence de Gaulle's firm stand.

The third factor is the external environment of European integration. Confronted with the absence of internal factors in realist explanations of regional integration, Haas admits to having pushed too far in the opposite direction. Understanding regional integration requires knowledge of member states' external relations with states other than those members of the integration scheme. He explains that, when changes in the international system are perceived both by the governmental elite and non-state actors, the limits of automatic spill-over are reached.

Finally, the fourth 'omission' of neofunctionalist theory was the massive transformation taking place in European societies and acknowledgement of differing political cultures and styles across the political systems themselves. Indeed, according to early neofunctionalists, transformations were taking place in parallel to, yet independently of, European integration. It has been shown recently, in particular through research undertaken by sociologists (Favell 2008; Diez Medrano 2003), how significant had been the change that European societies had undergone during the previous 50 years. At the same time, these transformations influenced the direction and the speed of integration processes more deeply than neofunctionalists had originally realized.

This self-criticism formulated in the 1960s was an impressive precursor of the issues that most integration theories and approaches would go on to face, even today: accounting for member states' domestic policies and their influence on the integration process, the importance of transnational and international relations outside the EU *per se* and the difference between Europeanization, globalization and state transformation – all of which have since become core issues in new approaches to the study of European integration.

In his foreword to the 1968 edition of *The Uniting of Europe*, Haas gives these critiques the benefit of the doubt, admitting that the spill-over function is not always automatic and that a spill-back situation can arise, given that the population or a part of the elite can reject the integration process, an idea analysed in European studies through the notion of Euroscepticism (for recent accounts see Harmsen and Spiering 2005; Szczerbiack and Taggart 2008; Gifford 2008; Chapter 8 in this volume).

Based on this recognition, Philippe Schmitter (1969, 1971), in particular, developed alternatives to the notion of spill-over: 'spill-around' (spreading integration to new areas, but not increasing the competences of the High Authority), 'build-up' (increasing the competences of supranational authorities without allowing them to exercise these competences), 'retrench' (increasing the level of joint deliberation, but outside institutions), 'muddle-about' (debating without making decisions at supranational level), 'spill-back' or 'encapsulate' (not reacting, or only reacting belatedly, to an ambient crisis) (Schmitter 1971: 242). According to Schmitter, spill-over is thus not automatic because joint decision-making involves costs. These costs can lead to conflict and therefore to the politicization of the decision-making process; a hypothesis which tends to partially correct the highly criticized neofunctionalist notion that, through integration, issues become apolitical and purely technocratic.

Transfer of loyalty

The second central assumption of neofunctionalism refers to the transfer of loyalty by elites participating heavily in the integration process. With little interest in citizens or the populations of member states in general, neofunctionalists concentrated their research on the political and economic elite; they were perceived to be the actors driving the dynamics of integration. However, the concept of loyalty re-establishes the relevance of European citizens as well, albeit vaguely. The idea went that citizens would also transfer their allegiances to the new supranational institutions and, in so doing, further drive the integration process (Haas 1964: 49), a process later characterized as 'ideational spill-over' (Risse 2005). Such a transfer was deemed to be necessary for the creation of a new political community. Since government would not be political but rather technocratic, politics would play a minor role compared to the efficient management of policies by bureaucracies. Pushing this idea yet further, beyond the conception of functionalists, who themselves were not interested in the normative aspect of European integration, one can also consider that the aim was to create a new political and public sphere through a movement or shift towards a new centre – something ahistorical and more effective than the nation; this development is the core idea of normative approaches centred on constitutional patriotism (see Chapter 9).

The difficulty of this assumption, however, remains its empirical observation. While spill-over and its diverse consequences have been observed, the transfer of citizens' loyalty was under-theorized and under-analysed by Haas and his colleagues. Concentrating on governmental, political, technocratic and non-state elites, the authors did not provide a model to *explain* the transfer process – in fact, only the transfer of loyalty by the national political elite, in favour of a technocratic supranational body, was originally envisaged.

Neofunctionalist hypotheses were, as mentioned earlier, not only applied to European integration processes but also formed the basis of a comparative research design. Comparative neofunctionalism, later criticized by neoregionalist approaches (Chapter 11), constituted a lively scientific community in the 1960s. It can be seen as one of the precursors for the 'mainstreaming' movement we observe in the 1990s in European studies.

Comparative neofunctionalism

Contrary to the current situation in regional integration studies, where the EU seems to have become the primary subject of analysis, neofunctionalist theories from the 1950s and 1960s were comparative in nature. Haas and Schmitter (1964), Sydney Dell (Dell 1966), Keith Griffin (Griffin and Ffrench-Davis 1965) and Miguel Wionczek (Wionczek 1970) studied Latin American integration. Schmitter compared the Central American and European integration models (Schmitter 1969, 1970). In a similar vein, Joseph Nye compared economic integration in East Africa, in the Arab League, in the organization of American states and in the Organisation of African Unity (now African Union) (Nye 1966, 1970). Indeed, the development of theoretical approaches did not exist outside the comparative model:

> At a time when common markets, free trade associations and specific regional arrangements are sprouting up in the four corners of the globe, the basic question of the implications of these efforts for the process leading to the construction of political communities is ever-present, both for the theorist and the practitioner. One means of linking these phenomena is an intensive *and* comparative study of the capacity of these common markets and free-trade associations to transform member states into a political union. (Barrera and Haas 1969: 705)

Amitai Etzioni proposed a comparative analysis of the United Arab Republic, the Federation of the West Indies, the Nordic Association and the European Economic Communities (Etzioni 1965, 2001; see also Chapter 11). The scope of this research is impressive, as is the operationalization of variables such as the security context, the nature of societies to be integrated and the relations of those states with external powers. According to Etzioni, the coherence and identification discourses of elites lead to greater integration. Reunifying messages are more likely to deepen integration than coercive power options. Furthermore, the stability of a regional union is threatened when the mechanisms of political representation are closed or malfunction. These assumptions about the dynamic aspect of integration power introduce a time factor. Etzioni argues that there are different phases of integration. In the first period of regional construction, the 'construction phase', the power of the elites needs to be greater than in the 'consolidation phase'.

These hypotheses were tested by using a rigorous and historically detailed comparative method, in order to explain how two of the four regional integration schemes on which the research is based – the United Arab Republic and the Federation of the West Indies – failed, largely because of external elites being unfavourable to the process, as well as the multitude and weakness of internal elites. The Nordic Union and the European Economic Communities were more successful thanks to a more homogenous, united elite, which helped them through the first extremely unstable 'construction phase' of integration where failure is much more likely.

Contrary to this research, contemporary analytical models used to study regional integration are almost exclusively interested in the EU or, to a lesser degree, North America and Asia, while constructing borders that are essentially sealed off between the different regions being analysed (Chapter 11). One of the reasons for this situation might be based on the fact that few regional trade agreements have gone beyond the stage of a free-trade agreement and customs union. The EU is a notable exception in this respect. This might be one of the reasons why the theoretical tools developed to analyse it are broadly used to study other regional integration projects (Jong Choi and Caporaso 2002).

The demise and resurgence of neofunctionalism

In the mid-1970s, however, despite numerous adjustments, Haas declared neofunctionalism obsolete. Contrary to a widely held belief, this was not to debase neofunctionalist theory (Haas 1971), but to nuance its explanatory power. While certain issues continued to help explain phenomena, such as the concept of spill-over, such as to elucidate certain developments in economic public policy, others, including those linked to state sovereignty and national interests, could no longer stand up satisfactorily. Nevertheless, according to Haas, neofunctionalist approaches had, just like the transactionalist accounts developed by Karl Deutsch, succeeded in systematizing studies into the causes of regional integration.

Empirically, the 1970s and 1980s can be considered as unfavourable years for neofunctionalist approaches. Criticisms were manifold, as this chapter has shown: scholars have questioned the inevitability of spill-over; the capacity of spill-over mechanisms to function in times of economic slowdown or even recession, given the fact that they were designed during a period in which the economy started to boom; the fact that neofunctionalists underestimate the impact of state interests and sovereignty; as well as the broader impact of international affairs on the process of integration (Hoffmann 1995a) – all of which pushed the neofunctionalists themselves to revise their theory (Schmitter 1970).

During the 1990s, empirical events – the deepening of European inte-gration through the increased use of qualified majority voting (QMV) in a large number of new policy areas, the transfer of new competencies to the European level, the reinforcement of the European Commission – led to the relaunch of neofunctionalist approaches. These phenomena could be explained by the reformulated neofunctionalist hypotheses – spill-over and transfer of loyalty. New conceptual accounts pointed to the close ties existing between neofunctionalism and newer theoretical approaches in European studies (see in particular Tranholm-Mikkelsen 1991), illustrating the idea developed in the Introduction according to which theories are 'cyclically challenged' and reinforced.

Schematically, it is possible to distinguish between four specific developments: legal integration theory; institutionalist approaches; constructivisms and sociohistoric accounts of European integration; as well as a revisited version of neofunctionalism itself, the so-called neo-neofunctionalism.

Legal integration theories

In the field of legal integration theories (Weiler 1981; Burley and Mattli 1993; Joerges 1996; Stone Sweet, Slaughter and Weiler 1998), scholars using neofunctionalist assumptions argue that the role of the ECJ is very similar to that of the Commission. According to this approach, a strong correlation exists between the activism of the ECJ and the passiveness of other EU institutions. The most important legal doctrines of the Court emerged between the mid-1960s and the mid-1980s, a period generally felt to be rather uneventful for the European integration process: 'direct effect' (Case 26/82 van Gend en Loos *v*. Nederlandse Administratie des Belastingen – 1963), 'supremacy' of European law of national law (Case 6/64 Costa *v*. Enel – 1964), and 'pre-emption', or the so-called 'norma-tive supranationalism' (Haltern 2004). During this time the EC clearly worked in the shadow of the Luxembourg Compromise of 1966 (in the aftermath of the Empty Chair Crisis); decision-making being based on intergovernmental consensus. The Commission seemed to have lost its role as central motor of European integration, to be replaced by the ECJ.

Institutionalist approaches

As a set of theoretical perspectives in their own right (Chapter 4), insti-tutionalism offers another refined account of how neofunctionalism might be enlarged through mainstream theories. Indeed, it is in this very context that the neofunctionalist paradigm would re-emerge by the end of the 1990s (Sandholtz and Zysman 1989; Stone Sweet and Sandholtz 1997; Sandholtz and Stone Sweet 1998; Stone Sweet, Sandholtz and Fligstein 2001; see also Transholm-Mikkelsen 1991; Mutimer 1989). This hybrid approach was severely criticized by Schmitter (2004) as being atheoretical in nature and 'devoid of any discrete and falsifiable hypotheses about where the process might be heading in the future' (ibid.: 45). However, Alec Stone Sweet and Wayne Sandholtz argue that by bringing certain core neofunctionalist assumptions and concerns into an institutionalist analysis, neofunctionalism could be made more effi-cient for analysing contemporary issues in European integration research. Thus, partly in opposition to Schmitter's system of assump-tions, Sandholtz, Stone Sweet, Neil Fligstein et al., in particular, put forward an approach conceptualizing the institutionalization of European integration – what they called supranational governance (Stone Sweet, Sandholtz and Fligstein 2001).

The authors argued that transnational trade, as defined by the neofunctionalists, generates pressures for regulation (harmonization) at the European level. Supranational institutions are created to provide EU regulations. The important element is the institutionalization of these regulations. Their establishment, however, creates demand channels, which bring non-state actors to increasingly mobilize at EU level. The main question of scholars of supranational governance is to understand how these processes create these channels. In this sense, the authors rein-terpret neofunctionalist theory in a specific form of institutionalist analy-sis (Rosamond 2000: 127). Here, institutions search for broadening and deepening regulations:

> We view intergovernmental bargaining and decision-making as embed-ded in processes that are provoked and sustained by the expansion of transnational society, pro-integrative activities of supranational organi-zation, and the growing density of supranational rules. And ... these processes gradually, but inevitable, reduce the capacity of the member states to control outcomes. (Stone Sweet and Sandholtz 1997: 299–300)

The authors conceptualize the varying institutionalization of suprana-tional arenas in terms of relative degrees of precision, formality and authority of rules and procedures, generally understood as informal stan-dards. In doing so, they insist on the central role that social interaction, structure and agency play in the coordination of complex processes.

Constructivist and sociohistorical approaches

More recent accounts of neofunctionalism are, however, closer to constructivist approaches, insisting on learning and socialization. The drawback of these approaches is that they sometimes stray from the early, sociologically sound neofunctionalist accounts, which questioned who the agents of learning and socialization were, something Haas himself pointed out (Haas 2001, 2004).

Constructivist and sociohistorical accounts particularly inspire neofunctionalist assumptions about the transfer of loyalty from the national to the European level. Constructivists use the neofunctionalist hypothesis on the transfer of loyalty in general terms (Schimmelfennig 2000a; Checkel 2001a, 2005; Risse 2005; see also Chapter 7) arguing that, as Haas emphasized, this transfer is possible without abandoning national identity. However, the transfer of loyalty is not only the result of material incentives, contrary to what the neofunctionalists say about the prerequisites of effective integration. 'Socialization into European identity works not so much through transnational processes or through exposure to European institutions, but on the national levels where Europeanness or "becoming European" is gradually being embedded in understandings of national identities' (Risse 2005: 291). The assumption of a transformation of citizens' loyalties towards their nation-state, as found in Europeanization research (Chapter 6), is that citizens in a federal state change their collective identity more rapidly than unitary and centralized states and are thus more predisposed to take 'Europe' and supranationalism on board.

The transformation of citizens' national identity, and thus the transfer of loyalty(ies) from their own nation-state to the EU, is a subject dealt with within constructivism. Recent socialization research on European elites is, however, more sociologically inspired, tackling the question of loyalty transfer head-on (Beyers 2005, 2010; Hooghe 2005; Egeberg 2006). These studies address the question of whether European civil servants have developed a specific form of Europeanness due to their longstanding socialization in Brussels or Strasbourg, and come to the conclusion that, while there has certainly been some influence, national patterns of behaviour remain prominent. The transformation of civil servants refers to the high degree of collective responsibility in finding solutions for policy problems acceptable to all European member states. Sociohistorical accounts also study the emergence of a specific status for the 'European civil service' (Gravier 2003; Cini 2007). Magali Gravier's approach, in particular, develops a model of analysis for studying the transformation of loyalty at the Community level. The idea is to consider the European civil service as an environment in which European civil servants are, above all, socialized. The idea is to try and map the civil service to identify how European institutions, since their foundation with the Treaty of Paris of 1951, have codified their loyalty expectations among their civil servants. To do this, Gravier uses a concept of loyalty that combines a rational logic ('mercenary loyalty') with a logic referring to identity ('identity-building loyalty'). Three historical periods can be distinguished. The first, after the creation of the ECSC, is the period during which the status of a specific European civil service developed. It is characterized by an institutional strategy emphasizing the loyalty of the mercenary: the loyalty of European civil servants is first and foremost stimulated by financial incentives. The second period, beginning with the foundation of the EEC and he European Atomic Energy Committee (Euratom), is seen as a period of consolidation: the European institutions continued to apply the same strategy of loyalty incentives. With the resignation of the Santer Commission owing to accusations of fraud, the period 1999–2000 saw a sea change, with a renewed emphasis on identity-building loyalty: European institutions focused on awareness-raising – sometimes with merely a reminder of the rules of the game – and on the morality and integrity of the European civil service. Hence, European institutions switched from a situation where the financial incentives were rather important, in order to develop a European identity amongst its civil servants, to one allowing them to demand standardized behaviour that corresponded to a particular ethic of the European civil service.

However, while this research is particularly clear in explaining the transformation of loyalties amongst civil servants in European institutions, it contributes to the increasingly compartmentalized nature of EU studies. While initial neofunctionalist accounts of loyalty aimed at describing the process of European integration as a whole, contemporary accounts concentrate mainly on the European elite (for an exception see White 2010), while failing to explain the larger, perhaps internationally embedded process of regional integration.

Neo-neofunctionalism

Finally, in an attempt to revitalize neofunctionalism as a general or 'grand theory', Philippe Schmitter (2004), Arne Niemann (2006), as well as Schmitter and Niemann (2009), develop three sets of hypotheses linked in particular to spill-over. These hypotheses include a number of known assumptions about interest groups, the Commission as entrepreneur (Cini 1996; Nugent 2000, 2001), and hypotheses about socialization, learning and deliberation. Based on these arguments, both authors argue that 'functional interdependencies are most likely to occur in areas of high issue density' (Schmitter and Niemann 2009: 58). Thus, formulated generally, the higher the number of policies debated and managed by the EU, the higher the functional spill-over between areas (Schmitter 1969; Pierson 1996).

Thus, (1) spill-over will occur if interest groups consider that the potential gains from European integration are high, that interest groups will benefit from EU activity, and that the policy area illustrates (an already, or de facto) high degree of integration at the EU level. On the other hand, (2) the Commission must have the capacity to forge internal cohesion, shape the agenda (also in areas where it has no or limited competencies), establish close relations with member-state governments, show abilities to build consensus and broker compromises, and know its own limits when acting as a policy entrepreneur. Finally, (3) long-term learning and socialization processes depend on the degree of issue-politicization: the more politicized – and according to Schmitter and Niemann (2009), the less technical – policy processes are, the more difficult socialization and deliberation processes become.

According to Schmitter (2004), neofunctionalism must develop a number of clearly testable hypotheses in order to resume its role as general integration theory. In responding to this challenge and relying on his earlier work, he offers eight clear-cut hypotheses on the reasons, process and consequences of integration, which have the advantage of taking both international developments and politics (such as resistance to European integration) into account, but are particularly tricky operationally. First of all, tensions arising from globalization influence the search for shared objectives (spill-over hypothesis). Second, alternatives found among national actors lead to institutional solutions that fit the lowest common denominator (encapsulation hypothesis). Third, the greater the tensions and contradictions between actors, the higher the number of associate actors in the decision-making process (politicization hypothesis). Fourth, this leads to a broadening of the audience or clientele who are interested and active in European integration. Fifth, the integration process begins with global politics, which exercise enormous influence on the regionalization process. Sixth, while external conditions can initially be considered as given, these external conditions are transformed by the global position of the institution created (externalization hypothesis). Seventh, actors' perceptions of their own respective interests become more complex as they participate in an increasingly elaborate integration process (additivity hypothesis). Finally, how change is perceived at national and Community levels is curvilinear or parabolic. Up to a certain point, the relationship is linear between change and consensus in favour of integration (more commercial transactions result in a more homogenous group). However, when changes become too rapid, actors are more likely to disagree or reject proposals and be against further integration (curvilinearity hypothesis) (Schmitter 2004).

While neo-neofunctionalism, as Schmitter called the revisited approach, addresses a number of criticisms voiced since the early 1980s, such as the automaticity of spill-over and the role of the nation-state, it

Table 2.1   *Neo-neofunctionalist hypotheses*

Type	Assumption
Spill-over hypothesis	Tensions arising from globalization influence the search for shared objectives favourably
Encapsulation hypothesis	Alternatives found amongst national actors lead to supranational solutions which fit the lowest common denominator
Politicization hypothesis	The higher the number of actors associated in the decision-making process, the greater the tensions and contradictions between actors
Widening hypothesis	The more areas the regional integration process covers, the broader the clientele searching for accession
Hypothesis of increasing	The higher the number of integrated mutual determination policy areas, the higher the chances that regional integration leads to a political community
Externalization hypothesis	The more integrated a regional community becomes, the less influential external conditions will become in the workings of the regional organization
Additivity hypothesis	The more elaborate the integration process becomes, the more complete the perceptions that actors have of their respective interests become
Curvilinearity hypothesis	When changes become too rapid, actors are inclined to readopt rejection attitudes towards integration

has also become, as the author himself acknowledges, less parsimonious. In attempting to become more reactive, revisited neofunctionalism is also in danger of becoming 'so indeterminate in its conclusions as to provide no clear direction for research' (Schmitter and Niemann 2009: 53).

Thus neofunctionalist research design as a coherent theory has been revisited and refined. At the same time, many neofunctionalist ideas have found their way into other conceptual and empirical studies since the

Table 2.2 *New perspectives in neofunctionalism*

Perspectives	Main assumptions	Authors
Legal integration theories	The role of the ECJ is similar to that of the European Commission: legal activism leads to functional spill-over	Weiler 1981 Burley and Mattli 1993 Stone Sweet, Slaughter and Weiler 1998 Haltern 2004
Institutionalist approaches	Transnational interactions such as trade generate pressures for regulation at the EU level	Stone Sweet, Sandholtz and Fliegstein 2001
Constructivist sociohistorical approach	Insistence on learning and socialization, new modes of transfer of loyalty	Risse 2005 Checkel 2001a Beyers 2005, 2010 Hooghe 2005 Gravier 2003
Neo-neofunctionalism	Renews and reformulates precise hypothesis on when regional integration occurs. Main assumption: 'functional interdependencies are most likely to occur in areas of high issue density'	Niemann 2006 Schmitter 2004 Schmitter and Niemann 2009

early 1980s. It might be relevant to ask whether neofunctionalism can and should be redeveloped as an individual theory, or whether its core assumptions have been so deeply integrated within other theories that it has dissolved. Schmitter's renewed conceptual framework might be an exception, as it goes beyond individual actors and beyond specific policy fields and offers, similarly to Bartolini's attempt, a theory of European integration processes in general (see Chapter 9).

Conclusion

While neofunctionalism emerged in the 1950s, research questions espousing its core theoretical concerns remain widespread in contemporary approaches of European integration: the influence of non-state actors in decision-making processes; the reasons behind the emergence of integrated policy areas; the entrepreneurial role of the European Commission; the European identity of elites and citizens; the influence of socialization and learning processes in European integration; the influence of European integration at the national level; as well as the impact of non-state actors' participation on the democratic system.

At the same time, there have been various attempts to revisit and refine neofunctionalism and to transform it, once more, into a leading theory in EU studies. Neofunctionalism is thus clearly cyclically challenged and reinforced through real-world events. Quantitatively, this attempt has met with limited success: the number of scholarly works referring explicitly to neofunctionalism remains rather low. Two reasons can be found for this phenomenon – one theoretical, the other empirical. On the one hand, integration theories attempting to address the integration process as a whole are considered to be unrealistic in contemporary research. The number of approaches and concepts has increased exponentially since the 'relaunch of European integration' in the 1990s, to address – with the exception of Bartolini (2005) and Fligstein (2008) – sectoral problems rather than the process as a whole. At the same time, neofunctionalism has not managed to give a clear answer to the main question, that is, 'why do and how did supranational integration processes come about?' The revised neofunctionalist account has become extremely complex to test, in particular, in a research context in which rational choice methods prevail.

Neofunctionalism is also confronted with an empirical problem: since the end of the 1990s in particular, European integration has been 'cyclically challenged'. A number of important political events have impeded any attempt to convince of the usefulness of concepts such as spill-over and transfer of loyalty: the extremely scope of reform provided by the Nice Treaty of 2001; the rejection of the long-debated constitutional treaty by French and Dutch voters in 2005, the Irish 'NO' to the revised constitutional treaty – the so-called Lisbon Treaty; the emergence of new modes of governance, such as the Open Method of Coordination (OMC – see Chapter 5) which, contrary to the Community method, do not require voting in the Council of Ministers and the Parliament; and the complex and uneven efforts of 'institutional engineering' in the field of European economic governance by the member states themselves, acting through intergovernmental mechanisms. While Schmitter's neofunctionalist account explicitly introduced a curvilinearity hypothesis – where negative attitudes increase once a certain high point of integration is reached – generally neofunctionalists have had difficulties explaining when the integration process will come to a standstill or is likely to slow down.

However, contrary to a number of approaches analysed in this book, neofunctionalism remains a pluralistic and open framework, whose founding fathers remain convinced of its usefulness, and whose successors attempt to refine it. The very fact that the initial limits of this approach have been repeatedly identified and 'chewed over' for more than fifty years of analysing the integration process, helps explain why it is so dynamic (Rosamond 2005a) – contrary to intergovernmentalism, addressed in the following chapter. Another reason that makes this approach so relevant to the study of European integration is that it has never considered what has occurred in Europe as singular and unique, nor as a *sui generis* process or an end in itself (for a critical analysis see Mattli 2005). This makes it particularly useful for contemporary debates on the EU as an institutional, political, legal and normative power in the context of globalization, and as a bloc that can be compared with other regional integration schemes (Chapter 11).

Chapter 3

Intergovernmentalism

Critiques of the neofunctionalist approach became increasingly elaborate during the 1960s. Two factors are able to explain this: one empirical, the other theoretical. The empirical variable refers to the 'Empty Chair Crisis' (1965/66) during which France refused to attend any intergovernmental meetings in Brussels, and the dual rejection of British candidatures in 1963 and 1967. More precisely, it was neofunctionalism's failure to explain General de Gaulle's policy of obstruction within the European Community that led to a renewed theoretical interest in European integration by intergovernmentalists in the mid-1960s. What emerged was a rather exaggerated intergovernmentalist account of the 1960s and 1970s as the decades of Eurosclerosis, when economic recession led to the rise of new non-tariff barriers to trade among EC member states. The establishment of the European Council in 1974, a regular summit meeting of EU heads of state and government, was furthermore interpreted as the strengthening of intergovernmental aspects of the Community. At the same time however, integration continued and the role of the ECJ expanded (Chapter 2).

The second factor is theoretical and methodological: from the beginning of the Cold War, studies of world politics adopted an increasingly state-centred approach. Along with this came the search for more 'scientific' enquiry in social-science research, based on the possibility of validating or invalidating hypotheses based on large statistical tools, and the rigorous construction of causalities. The use of modern computers in the 1950s has expedited large-scale statistical computation, and has also made possible new methods that are impractical to perform manually. The neofunctionalists' own self-critiques analysed in the previous chapter illustrate this phenomenon particularly well: falsifiable hypotheses were developed with increasing care in neofunctionalist approaches, which opposed descriptive or interpretative accounts of European integration processes.

However, while realists or neorealists such as Kenneth Waltz (1979), who are part of the broader intergovernmentalist school, were only marginally and rather lately interested in regional integration processes (from 1990 onwards), a small number of Europeanist scholars achieved considerable visibility in the intergovernmental field. Thus Stanley Hoffmann emphasizes the internal diversity of states involved in

Box 3.1   *What is intergovernmentalism?*

In a nutshell, the intergovernmental understanding of European integration is that of cooperation between sovereign states, who behave as rational actors and whose interactions are managed by the principles of authority and hierarchy. Cooperation, or pooled sovereignty, does not reduce the independence of states; on the contrary, it strengthens them by helping states to adapt to the constraints imposed by the international environment.

European integration processes as opposed to Haas's and Lindberg's assumption of a convergence of elites. Integration is the result of intergovernmental bargaining, which does not lead automatically to new policy areas being integrated. In the same vein as Hoffman, that is, concentrating on national interest and state action, historian Alan Milward shows how important the process of European integration was for the re-establishment of state sovereignty in the 1950s. Thus, national

Table 3.1   *Intergovernmentalism in brief*

Perspectives	*Main assumptions*
Conventional intergovernmentalism	States are central actors in international integration processes. Their behaviour is based on a rational cost-benefit analysis. Four specific perspectives: 1 analysing the attitudes of governmental elites 2 European integration as saviour of state sovereignty 3 neorealist accounts 4 two-level games
Liberal intergovernmentalism	International bargaining is a three-stage process: 1 the formation of national preferences driven by issue-specific, mostly economic, interests 2 inter-state negotiations based on asymmetrical interdependence between member states 3 the choice of supranational institutions which reflects an interest in securing credible member-state commitments

interests are the key to understand the ups and downs of the integration process, as shown by the third key scholar in this field, Andrew Moravcsik.

The aim of this chapter is to analyse the emergence and transformation of intergovernmental approaches. The idea is to illustrate the diversity of approaches, going beyond the simple common denominator of 'states as the sole actors of European integration' which is often used in a rather simplistic way to sum up the limits of intergovernmentalism. Two subsections address this issue in order to understand the wealth but also the limits of intergovernmentalist approaches in EU studies. The first presents conventional intergovernmental accounts of European integration. While softer intergovernmentalist traditions open the 'black box' of government, treating it not as unitary actor but a complex system of checks and balances, neorealists consider regional integration as possible only under certain circumstances. The second part looks at the emergence of contemporary intergovernmentalism, in particular, based on the work of the main representative of liberal intergovernmentalism, Moravcsik.

Conventional intergovernmentalism

Intergovernmentalism is rooted in the realist paradigm of international relations. According to realists, international actors – sovereign states – act according to established preferences and behave in a rational manner.

Four conceptual contemporary intergovernmentalist approaches have emerged in EU studies: a first group analyses the state in concentrating specifically on governmental elites and their actions, a second group tells the tale of 'saving sovereignty through European integration', a third represents classical neorealist thinking, and a final part refers to the influential approach of the 'two-level game' in international negotiation theory.

Analysing the attitudes of governmental elites

Contrary to neorealism, which treats states as unitary actors and therefore ignores the processes taking place inside states, conventional realists such as Edward H. Carr or Hans Morgenthau start from the assumption that elements of states' domestic policy significantly influence their external policy. This is crucial in order to understand the conditions necessary for the emergence of a balance of power. Only by examining the history, values and ambitions of European states and societies does it become possible to understand the reasons for regional integration. Conventional intergovernmentalists thus seem to combine international relations theory with area studies, which, as an academic field of study, is largely based on in-depth empirical analysis.

These scholars refute the hypothesis that the main interest of states is to survive; survival is just one of many objectives. Understanding the preferences of states means taking a closer look at the historical, political and economic foundations of states' foreign policies. It is therefore futile to generate grand theories in international relations, as only in-depth knowledge of a field offers new perspectives (Aron 1962). Cultural and historical studies of a state are thereby crucial analytical components for conventional intergovernmentalists, because they allow an explanation of different individuals' representations of the world and, in particular, of its leaders.

Stanley Hoffmann's work is particularly anchored in this perspective. As a former student of Raymond Aron, his accounts of France's foreign policy (in particular, General de Gaulle's) and its influence on European integration are based on an in-depth study of the cultural and historical foundations of French policy, which, in his view, had been unjustly ignored by neofunctionalist researchers (Hoffmann 1954, 1956). Hoffmann's analyses concentrate on the main political actors, i.e. heads of state and government, including ministers of foreign affairs, defence, economy and finance. Hoffmann's main criticism of neofunctionalists, in particular after the Empty Chair Crisis of 1964/65, is their sole focus on the integration process, meaning that they neglected the context in which the state, that is, the government, actually acts (Hoffmann 1964). The Empty Chair Crisis, triggered by French President General de Gaulle in 1965, who disagreed with the Commission on the financing of the CAP, saw France's representatives refuse to attend any further intergovernmental meetings of the European institutions. Such an episode provided scholars with a story, or empirical evidence, to *claim* the superiority of intergovernmentalism over neofunctionalism as a theoretical account; clearly it was the member states, not the supranational institutions that were 'running the show'. Neofunctionalism had not yet developed explanations for the unforeseen standstill in the integration process, and could not account for the fact that a single state's veto could bring political developments to a sudden halt – this flaw in the theory would be refined in the years to come (see Chapter 2).

[The state's] autonomy is either denied (the state thus becoming a mere receptacle and by-product), or limited to whatever is functionally necessary to defend the social order (the state as the guardian of the higher or long-term interest of the dominant class); or else the state is being reduced to a set of institutions somewhat decoupled from the rest of the society, yet still analysed primarily as the target or victim of social forces (the besieged state). The theory overlooked the *differential impact* of external countries (such as the two superpowers) on the various nations. Moreover it underestimated the ability of actors, especially the major nations, i.e. France, Germany and Italy, to promote or prevent the building of a central political system (the role of counter-ideas, if you like) and the ability of national bureaucracies to resist the transfer of power to the centre (the power of inertia). (Hoffmann 1995b: 215–19)

Conventional intergovernmentalism's core ideas in EU studies

Thus, Hoffmann seeks to develop an antidote to the way in which European integration is discussed. Two ideas are at the heart of Hoffmann's analysis and constitute an extension to the central hypotheses of realist approaches in international relations. First and foremost, there is the assumption that the international system produces more diversity than coherence between its central units, i.e. states. Since the situation of each state is unique in the world, cooperation between states cannot lead to an homogenous system, but rather to diversity, highlighted by intergovernmental bargaining in which individual leaders exert influence to various degrees (see also Beach 2009). On the basis of this hypothesis, Hoffmann distinguishes between *high* and *low* politics in international affairs in order to explain why integration is possible and not particularly controversial in certain technical domains, but in others is sensitive and complex, owing to concerns over government autonomy and state identity.

The second central idea concerns the assumption that there is no continuum between the economic domain and the political domain. In other words, according to Stanley Hoffmann, there is always a preponderance of politics over economy, hence the importance that the analysis of governmental power structures and political games has in European integration studies. Hoffmann argues that '[T]he self propelling power of the unifying process is severely constrained by the associates' view on ends and means. In order to go "beyond the nation-state", one must do more than set up procedures in adequate "background" and "process conditions". A procedure is not a purpose, a process is not a policy' (Hoffmann 1995a: 83–4). Conversely, there is an opposition between a *logic of integration*, as defended by Haas, and a *logic of diversity*, as favoured by Hoffmann. According to Hoffmann, each state has a unique profile of based on a specific configuration of economic data (rate of inflation, unemployment, growth) and political culture.

However, what Hoffmann proposes is not a theory, i.e. a system of causalities, but a list of factors, variables or, more generally, elements which must be taken into consideration when analysing the process of European 'construction', a term which he prefers to that of European integration. This slightly anachronistic approach in the 1960s – a time when the behaviouralist and scientific paradigms rose to the fore and imposed clear-cut research designs based on dependent and independent variables – implicitly influenced the study of foreign and security policy

Box 3.2 *Conventional intergovernmentalism*

Stanley Hoffmann's state-centred pluralist, structured approach, particularly developed in his *Reflections on the Nation-State*, was guided by four central assumptions:

1 The distinction between state and society is a necessary starting point and must be used as a compass to guide analysis.
2 The nation-state is a social system in which the state plays a decisive role (autonomy of the state, power of the state, effectiveness of the state).
3 Each state is specific and must be analysed according to structural, procedural and ideological variables.
4 The room for manoeuvre of each state is primarily limited by outside economic constraints.

research in European integration studies until the beginning of the 1990s. Hoffmann's approach, however, characterizes him more as a gifted commentator of European affairs than an integration theorist attempting to compete with the complexity and richness of neofunctionalist accounts (Rosamond 2000). Nevertheless, Hoffmann has introduced the important elements of governmental interests, governmental elite behaviour and the distinction between *high* (diplomacy) and *low* politics (economy) in integration research, which inspired later intergovernmentalist researchers, and not least his pupil, Moravcsik (see below).

European integration as saviour of state sovereignty

A number of Hoffmann's assumptions can also be found in Milward's historical account of European integration, which asserts that the evolution of the European Community since 1945 has contributed to the revalidation of the nation-state as an organizational concept of international relations. Without European integration, the nation-state could not have offered its citizens the same level of security and prosperity that it has done, in Western Europe at least.

After 1945, the European nation-state rescued itself from collapse, created a new political consensus as the basis of its legitimacy, and through changes in its response to its citizens, which meant a sweeping extension of its functions and ambitions reassured itself as the fundamental unit of political organization ... Interdependence is not, therefore, a phenomenon which has progressively and inexorably developed in twentieth century Western Europe. States, far from being its helpless prisoner, have actively sought to limit its consequences. (Milward 1992: 3–10)

Milward's central argument – that governments defend economic interests and not political wishes or ideologies in their attempt to build an integrated Europe – is similar to Moravcsik's liberal intergovernmentalist framework (see below). Hence, the economic, rather than political, integration of Western Europe illustrates the actual design and success of the European construction. Thus, the idea that transnational economic and political networks account for the main independent variable in explanations of European integration, as argued by another group of historians (Kaiser et al. 2005; Kaiser, Leucht and Rasmussen 2009; Kaiser 2010), is forcefully rejected by Milward. He offers a very detailed study of economic and political developments in Western Europe from 1947 to 1951. It starts with the economic crisis of 1947, whose origins the author finds, not in the end of the Second World War, but in the economic collapse of 1929–32, and goes through to the setting up of the Common Market and the CAP. In this understanding, the success of Western European integration stems from institutionalized economic interdependence between the nation-states. It was not the Bretton Woods system, nor idealistic, federalist or Atlanticist ideas that pushed Western European governments into integration, but rather, economic interests articulating the need for new political institutions.

> Previous writers have always entirely failed to show through what political mechanisms the idealisms which supported Western European integration actually influenced governmental policy making in the nation-states, unless it be through the vague suggestion that men like Adenauer, Schuman, Sforza, and Spaak, who themselves shared these enthusiasm, were able to override the massed cohorts of government and bureaucracy whose task it was and is to define and uphold the national interest before all else. (Milward 1984: 492)

Similar economic concerns existed in all Western European states: the decline in trade, the desire for a higher standard of living, dealing with inflation and a substantial dollar deficit because of the US currency being in short supply. Domestic economic policy objectives were diverse, but political ones similar: to rebuild their own nation-states. By the early 1950s, the Schuman Plan made this goal achievable.

Thus, Milward challenges the conventional views of European integration as a process destined to replace nation-states by a European federal political structure. In the wake of the Second World War, Western Europe's political leaders were preoccupied with rebuilding their countries as nation-states. Integration was therefore the conscious outcome of European governments' decisions to pool sovereignty in certain areas. It is not human idealism which led to European integration, but the self-centred realism of powerful governments.

Milward's meticulous research leads neofunctionalist (Chapter 2) and federalist (Chapter 1) accounts to be openly questioned. However, his historical method is based on governmental archives and economic statistics compiled by state bureaucracy (see also Rasmussen 2008). Given this method, it is unsurprising that he tends towards a very state-centred integration process. Nevertheless, the scale and wealth of his research make his account of early European integration a very precise and stimulating approach to theorizing the building of Europe.

Neorealist accounts

A third, and in EU studies rather neglected, theoretical account of intergovernmentalism is situated in a neorealist perspective. It is, however, true that neorealists themselves traditionally showed very limited interest for regional integration. In this theoretical tradition, regional integration is a contradiction in terms: states are independent actors, jealous of their sovereignty that must be defended by all means. There is no possibility for the creation of a world, or even regional, government: what emerge are alliances that states enter into out of self-interest. Only under certain circumstances does regional cooperation become possible (Walt, 1987; for an analysis applied to the European context see Mearsheimer 1992/1993; Talliaferro 2001/2002).

First of all, the existence of an external enemy, such as the Soviet Union during the Cold War, can lead to the establishment of a regional alliance (*balancing*). In this context, if a hegemonic power exists, states might be encouraged to cooperate, with the support of the hegemon (*bandwagoning*). The USA played this role with the Marshall Plan in creating the European Economic Cooperation Organisation, as well as in setting up NAFTA. It is, however, also possible for a regional union to succeed against the wishes of a neighbouring state, as illustrated by the examples of ASEAN with Vietnam, the Gulf Cooperation Council with Iran and Mercosur with the USA (Hurrell 1992; Crone 1993). *Buck-passing* is another possibility whereby states use the regional organization as an excuse to focus on a specific policy field, legitimizing the fact that they ignore others (Rynning 2006; Collard-Wexler 2006).

For a short time the end of the Cold War launched neorealist interest in European regional integration. According to neorealist assumptions, the end of the Cold War and the weakening, and finally disappearance of the main enemy – the Soviet Union – would slow down, if not completely put a stop to European integration processes. In fact, the contrary happened: the SEA of 1987 and the Maastricht Treaty of 1993 relaunched European integration. This puzzle needed explanation if neorealists did not want to lose face in academic circles.

Based on the above-mentioned hypotheses, neorealist Joseph Grieco (1988, 1995, 1996) argues that the relaunch of European integration by the end of the 1980s must be analysed as strategic behaviour, to counter the growing importance of the USA and Japan. However, the Maastricht Treaty also coincided with the end of the Cold War and the resurrection of Germany as a medium-sized power within Europe, which makes a distinction between causal variables more difficult. The attitudes of Italy and France in their support of the creation of an economic and monetary union is, according to Grieco (1995), more to do with *bandwagoning* than *balancing* an imaginary German security threat. When states bargain over new institutions and rules, they seek to ensure that these rules will give voice to their opposition.

This analysis corresponds to a past situation in the EU, in which small states had a tremendous influence in the bargaining process compared to big states (Panke 2011). When these opportunities are lacking, states have to renegotiate the terms of contracts or institutional arrangements, allowing them to reduce or withdraw their support for the organization in question. Thus, France and Italy's support for EMU should be interpreted as two countries seeking to influence the institutional structure of this organization and to shore up their influence therein.

In summary, it is possible to argue from this theoretical perspective that in regional integration schemes, states may advance their interests through non-coercive means by applying a strategy of cooperative hegemony. This strategy implies an active role in regional institutionalization and the use of various strategies such as side payments, power-sharing and differentiation (for a particularly well informed use of these arguments see Pedersen 1998, 2002). Nonetheless, a number of preconditions for regional institutionalization must be met in order to deepen regional institutionalization: the capacity for power-sharing and power aggregation and the commitment capacity of the biggest power in a region. This explanation particularly well explains the Franco-German relationship and its role as a motor of European integration: both countries' commitment to European integration allows them to aggregate their powers, a role the UK has difficulties in playing, given its reticence to commit itself to deeper integration.

The fundamental tenets of neorealists and intergovernmentalists are similar in the sense that states are central actors on the international scene. However, intergovernmentalist theories specific to EU studies put forward a slightly more nuanced account of regional integration than is normally found in neorealism (Legro and Moravcsik 1999), given that they open the 'black box' of the state and take state elites as well as economic forces into account.

Two-level games

In an entirely different geographical as well as theoretical context, far removed from integration studies, a movement emerged in the 1960s that was opposed to the then broadly accepted belief in international relations, that states would develop foreign policy on the basis of their military, economic and political capabilities. As with the approaches analysed above, this theoretical framework very much influenced liberal intergovernmentalist accounts of European integration that developed at the beginning of the 1990s. James Rosenau (1969), Wolfram Hanrieder (1967), Peter Gourevich (1978) and, in particular, Graham Allison (1971) argued, on the contrary, that national and international policies are closely linked. The two levels of analysis – national and international – are intertwined and not independent. However, while the approach was developed in the 1960s, it only became one of the more central hypotheses of international relations research some 20 years later. The beginning of the 1990s saw a mushrooming of such approaches (Jacobsen 1996), mainly based on an article published by Robert Putnam in 1988 in which he develops the 'two-level game' approach, upon which a large number of institutionalist theoreticians and multi-level analysts of European integration based their work, at least implicitly (see Chapters 4 and 5).

The two-level game is based on an assumption that the processes that occur within a state substantially influence the behaviour of that state at the international level. Thus states are 'chief negotiators' at 'two tables'. What happens at the international level in turn influences national policies. But how can this fairly plain statement be turned into an explanatory model?

In his founding article, Robert Putnam (1988) developed the idea of a two-level game of international negotiations based on an empirical analysis of the Bonn Summit in 1978 where Germany, Japan and the USA – the main economic drivers of the time – tabled a global economic recovery programme. The positions of these states were highly divergent: domestically, US President Jimmy Carter was facing Congress's opposition to the National Energy Programme; internationally, Germany and Japan criticized the USA for its voracious appetite for oil imports and poor management of the dollar exchange rate. After long and arduous negotiations, an agreement was reached: Germany agreed to a major fiscal stimulus package; Jimmy Carter agreed to oil price controls in the USA; Japan committed to 7 per cent growth.

How exactly did they secure this agreement, given the highly divergent discourses of the three countries beforehand? Putnam's explanation shows that during the bargaining process, the main state negotiators operated in parallel, both at home and abroad with their international counterparts:

- At national level (level I), groups protected their interests by putting pressure on governments to adopt their preferred policies,

and decision-makers tried to create coalitions between these groups to increase their power.
- At international level (level II), decision-makers tried to convince their diplomatic counterparts that the pressure from the domestic level made it impossible to accept the proposal on the table, while at the same time negotiating at the domestic level to convince groups that parts of the international agreement are acceptable.

Putnam recognizes three independent variables influencing the outcome of international negotiations: first, preferences and coalitions of national actors; secondly, the structure of national institutions; and thirdly, strategies adopted by national negotiators at international level.

According to Putnam, the broader or more all-encompassing the coalitions at national level (or win-sets, as Putnam calls it), the more likely it is that agreement will be reached at international level.

More precisely, (1) the lower the cost of non-agreement at national level, the more difficult it will be for the negotiator to find a beneficial agreement for its government at international level. Generally, there is no homogenous position at national level: it is important to find the strongest coalition and convince it to support the agreement negotiated at international level. However, it is possible that opposing groups at national level challenge the agreements (the banks because the economic recovery programme goes too far, the trade unions because the programme does not go far enough). These are trade-offs – situations whereby one thing will be traded for another. Subsequently, (2) the size of the win-sets depends on the structure of national institutions. For example, it is easier for a corporatist state to negotiate because actors are more open to compromise before international negotiations get under way. A pluralist state, on the other hand, is permanently dealing with opposition between different groups all seeking to influence decision-makers.

Finally, (3) it is in the interest of each negotiator to support the winning coalition in order to influence the negotiations favourably. The winning coalition's positions are complex: a state with a broad winning coalition will find it easier to impose an agreement, but it is also more difficult for the coalition to convince its co-negotiator that its hands are tied because actors – more precisely, voters at home – consider these any such agreement as a step too far. On the other hand, a state with a more restricted winning coalition can put more pressure on its international co-negotiator, but at the risk of the agreement stalling.

Two-level games at the EU level

Applied at EU level, scholars use the two-level game in two different ways. One group of studies concentrates on the interaction between national and EU levels in the bargaining strategies of the member states and the European institution. Here we find a large number of empirical studies applying the two-level game directly as a theoretical framework explaining the processes and the results of member-state bargaining. The specificity of these studies is to show how EU member states negotiate under the very specific institutional constraint they experience both at the domestic and the EU level. This is different from Putnam's initial framework insofar as his model did not conceptualize international negotiations as constraint by institutions at the international level. The studies on the EU deal with questions as diverse as the negotiation of EU treaties (Smith and Ray 1993), of EU labour law (Menz 2011), of the EU's budget (Dür and Matteo 2010), or the role of national parliaments in EU decision-making processes (Pahre 1997).

Another group of scholars look at international trade negotiations in which the EU intervenes as an actor in its own right. In this context, Lee Ann Patterson (1997) enlarged the initial framework of a two-level game into a three-level game in her study of EU bargaining in General Agreement on Tariffs and Trade (GATT) agriculture negotiations. In distinguishing levels I (GATT negotiations), II (EU negotiations) and III (domestic negotiations), she concludes that the variables of interest-group power and the heterogeneity of at various levels of the game influence the outcomes of negotiations significantly. However, she develops the approach further in adding the element of actor perception. According to Patterson, the real and perceived costs of reaching no agreement affect the degree of substantive reform. A three-level interactive strategy seems crucial in achieving an acceptable agreement at each level of the game.

Another rigorous attempt to apply and to further develop the framework of the two-level game can be found in Sophie Meunier's (2005) study of the EU's external commercial policy from the 1980 to the 2000. She analyses negotiations on two levels – the EU and the international level. At the international level, the Commission, instead of member governments, becomes the chief negotiator.

She starts from a paradox: if the EU speaks with a single voice on commercial matters, why does it have such difficulty imposing its will on international trade negotiations? While common wisdom shares the assumption that institutional rules allowing for more effective decision-making in Council and more autonomy for Commission representatives to present a unified front in external negotiations strengthened the EU's leverage in international bargaining with third parties, Meunier's study shows that 'the international bargaining power of the EU is not a linear function of its degree of integration' (Meunier 2005: 166). On the contrary, two key variables must be taken into account to understand the extent of the EU's external bargaining power: the degree of supranational competence – that is, the EU's ability to negotiate an agreement at international level – and the bargaining context in relation to the status quo. Distinguishing between a 'conservative' and a 'reformist' bargaining context, it is possible to understand the probability of reforms decided by the negotiation partners.

In the 'conservative' context, in which the status quo is to be upheld, the unanimity rule in decision-making makes the EU a very tough negotiator, which can be of considerable benefit to members of the EU. If the EU applies unanimous voting, it has more power to resist its opponents' demands and requests. In such cases, the EU's common position reflects the lowest common denominator. In this situation, it is impossible for the EU's opponents to divide the EU member states and to convince them to question the EU's position.

In a 'reformist' context, however, the EU seeks to change the status quo to which its adversary is firmly attached. In this case, only the rule of a complete transfer of competences from the Council of Ministers to the European Commission may lead to a more favourable outcome for the EU, as the Commission keeps a margin of manoeuvre which is not possible in the case of unanimity.

This conceptual framework is applied to four case studies of international trade negotiations: agricultural negotiations between the EC and the USA as part of the Kennedy Round (1964–67), negotiations between the EC and the USA during the Uruguay Round (1986–93), which are both considered as 'conservative', since they did not lead to substantial progress during negotiations. Conversely, the study of public procurement negotiations (1990–94) illustrates the EU's 'reformist' model. The demands of the majority of member states to open up access to American public contracts led to the signing of an agreement which was favourable to the EU. Finally, the fourth case study introduces a new model in which the states circumvent the common position and negotiate individually: 'Open Sky' transatlantic international aviation agreements (from 1992 to the present) represent a control case. Meunier's core claim is that centralization has variable effects on bargaining leverage, depending on institutional arrangements and the distribution of preferences relative to the status quo.

Approaches analysing interactions between the national and international levels in bilateral or multilateral negotiations have made intergovernmental analysis more thorough. At the same time, however, they remain distanced from what most conventional intergovernmentalists have tried to do, that is, explain the integration process in full. Nonetheless, this is the aim of a specific type of contemporary intergovernmentalism in EU studies: liberal intergovernmentalism.

Contemporary intergovernmentalism

Theories are the result of cyclical challenge and reinforcement, as the previous chapter on neofunctionalism has illustrated. Empirical events question a theory's main hypotheses. Subsequent empirical events then allow the theory to re-emerge and to be strengthened through new conceptual considerations. Contemporary intergovernmentalism is no exception in this context. It has emerged in its theorized form through an adaptation process (Pollack 2001). Theorists were confronted with a number of empirical challenges, such as the difficulty in understanding the relaunch of European integration by the end of the 1980s despite the disappearance of Soviet threat – the bipolar system had become unipolar – which intergovernmentalists and particularly neorealists had believed initially sparked European construction. The liberal interpretation of intergovernmentalism attempts to explain this continuity – the relaunch of European integration at the beginning of the 1990s – by two general factors: intergovernmental bargaining and national interests.

The movement's most influential scholar in the field of European studies is undoubtedly Moravcsik. Frank Schimmelfennig (2004: 75) formulates this particularly well: 'According to a bon mot among EU scholars, liberal intergovernmentalism (LI) is a theoretical "school" with no "disciples" and a single "teacher": Andrew Moravcsik.' Through a series of publications in the first half of the 1990s he sought to demonstrate that national preferences represented at international level had obvious national origins.

Based on the study of the behaviour of economically rational actors, liberal intergovernmentalists focus on political and social interactions in economic integration. On the assumption that states wish to reduce transactions costs in an open economy, liberal intergovernmentalists working on European integration consider European integration first and foremost as a collective action seeking to optimize gains for each state. Moravcsik's analyses take up where Keohane and Hoffmann left off (Moravcsik 1991, 1993a, 1995). His bargaining theory of international cooperation has three main characteristics: it builds on intergovernmentalism but offers more rigorous and sophisticated assumptions, it is a grand theory in the sense that it aims at explaining European integration as a system and not as specific cases, and its is a parsimonious theory in line with the requirements of, in particular, US social sciences since the 1950s (for a masterly analysis of liberal intergovernmentalism see Schimmelfennig 2004).

A rationalist theory of international bargaining

Liberal intergovernmentalism seeks to identify the dynamics of European integration and understand why sovereign states have agreed to renounce certain prerogatives in favour of supranational institutions, which progressively enlarged their powers to the point that they began to control domestic economic policy. For liberal intergovernmentalists, European integration is the result of a strategic calculation by member governments to promote their key economic interests, and of a series of rational choices made by national elites. This makes it very similar to Milward's historical account of European integration. Instead of a detailed, and very rigorous historiographic description, however, Moravcsik develops a positivist or methodologically analytical research design – a set of hypotheses which he then tests using qualitative methods. Liberal intergovernmentalism includes two conceptual frameworks in international relations: on the one hand, he presents a liberal assumption in a rationalist framework and, on the other, a theory of international bargaining. With regard to the first framework, liberal intergovernmentalism is based on the assumption that the fundamental actors in international policy are private, rational individuals and groups. While the state remains the main actor in bargaining at the European level, that state is only a representative defending the material and idealistic interests of members of civil society.

As a theory of international bargaining, liberal intergovernmentalism starts from the assumption that each state attempts to satisfy its own objectives, taking other states' objectives and the inherent obstacles into account. More specifically, interdependence between states, which is characteristic of the international sphere, produces externalities. These externalities can take the form of negative consequences (costs) or positive consequences (profits) for each state, if all states collectively pursue the priorities of a single state. In order to lower the transaction costs occurred in the pursuit of these objectives, states create institutions. In the context of the EU, institutions are thus agencies created by member states for the purpose of making inter-state bargaining more efficient.

In his key work, *The Choice for Europe* (1998), Moravcsik analyses five key periods in European integration: the Treaty of Rome (1955–58), the Common Market (1958–69), monetary integration (1969–89), the SEA (1984–88) and the Maastricht Treaty (1988–91). He argues that European integration was possible owing to the perceived economic benefits of cooperation and the commercial interests of member states, on account of the both the relative powers of those states and the credibility of the undertakings they made. According to Moravcsik, geopolitical, ideological and idealistic factors have undoubtedly influenced European integration, but only marginally, and therefore deserve less attention. To the contrary, he asserts that European integration occurred for reasons of economic interest – a possible economic boom and new markets with huge possibilities for expansion. Political decisions in the EC were thus based on economic interest and not on ideology. In practical terms, it was not for reasons of French supremacy that General de Gaulle opposed Great Britain's membership of the EU, but because of the price of French corn.

European integration: a three-stage process

At the core of liberal intergovernmentalism is the idea of international bargaining as a three-stage process: (1) the formation of national preferences; (2) inter-state negotiations and (3) the choice of supranational institutions.

The formation of national preferences

In the first stage, the formation of national preferences raises the question of what influence externalities such as security and commercial policy exert on national preferences – preferences which determine the shape of international economic cooperation. What is attractive about this approach is the idea that national objectives and interests are not fixed. On the contrary, a state's preferences are linked to a specific international and national political environment. In the context of the national political environment, individuals and social groups select a single representative to negotiate internationally – the state. Once a compromise is found at the national level, it is transformed into its official position. The state can then be conceptualized as a single, rational actor, pursuing coherent national strategies with maximum efficiency and speaking with a single voice, even though at domestic level national preferences are shaped as the result of confrontation between diverse actors. The decision to delegate sovereignty is based on a cost-benefit analysis.

For the author, two different notions of national preference formation come head-to-head: political and diplomatic vs. economic interests. The first supposes that national preferences reflect perceived threats against national sovereignty or territorial, military or ideological integrity. Security is therefore conceived of as a priority for states and economic objectives are subordinate to it. The consequences for economic objectives are therefore indirect, since European integration is conceived of in terms of security-based externalities, and the pursuit of economic goals is merely a matter of politics. As a result, cooperation can only be envisaged if the states share the same ideological and geopolitical vision and if this vision has the potential to engender positive diplomatic externalities. From this perspective, European integration should have led to a Common Defence Policy, but it did not, since the proposal by the French National Assembly was rejected in 1954.

Conversely, the second standpoint holds that economic interests have a direct influence on the formation of national preferences; international cooperation is seen as an effort to set up economic policies that will be to everyone's benefit. In other words, the idea is to eliminate negative economic externalities and generate positive ones, i.e. improve the competitiveness of national manufacturers by offering them new markets, or limit public spending by sharing costs. For Moravcsik, this second interpretation is the only valid one, for it allows us to understand the economic integration of the European continent since the early 1950s.

Intergovernmental negotiations

Once national preferences are formed, the second stage begins, when member states negotiate and agree upon mutually beneficial areas for cooperation. However, states' preferences are rarely compatible and harmonious; they are sometimes even totally contradictory. Here, Moravcsik applies the two-level game theory: states must be ready to make concessions in a given area in order to benefit from counter-concessions in others. Bargaining operates in two dimensions: *effectiveness* and *distribution of gains*. Again, two different perspectives come head-to-head: one focusing on supranational negotiations, the second one concentrating on intergovernmental bargaining. The former – neofunctionalism – which held sway for some considerable time, considers that supranational civil servants have an autonomous, essential role in obtaining compromises during negotiations and puts the emphasis on the notion of spill-over. Between single nations, transaction costs are too high in relation to the gains derived from agreements. Supranational civil servants are the only ones able to convert vague proposals into negotiations. This approach is based on the assumption that information is key and that leaders have privileged access to it. Thus, only they can manipulate information and ideas in order to find compromises. Key historical figures such as Jean Monnet and Jacques Delors, for example, seem to have played crucial mediation roles; without them, negotiations would have fallen short of their potential in a number of cases.

Moravcsik argues that the second approach, focusing on intergovernmental bargaining, is more pertinent since information is comprehensive and widely available; governments possess more and more precise information than the overworked und understaffed Commission could ever have. As for the effectiveness of negotiations, contrary to what neofunctionalist theory suggests, intergovernmentalists consider that states – and *not* supranational civil servants – act as political entrepreneurs. It is important to make a distinction between 'big states' and 'small states' in bargaining processes, because they do not carry the same weight. In fact, negotiations are non-coercive and states can reject agreements if gains are expected to be less than those potentially derived from a unilateral policy. However, states use diverse means to guide negotiations in their favour: the right to veto; the creation of alternative coalitions to avoid instruments such as military coercion, which would be too costly for European democracies; economic sanctions; and the threat of withdrawal. Since intergovernmental negotiations are a two-level game (see above), a state negotiating on the European scene is subject to dual pressures: those national interest groups who follow their own agendas and those of nation-state partners who defend their own national preferences. The author therefore establishes a theory on the governments' room for manoeuvre. To some extent, the EU increases the powers of states by allowing national political leaders to use the constraints of European cooperation and advance those inter-state commitments taken on that stage (upper level) that happen to be in line with government priorities, while avoiding certain domestic demands (lower level).

Institutional choice

The question is then raised as to why states seek to delegate their decision-making power to supranational institutions and do not hang on to them for future unilateral decisions. For Moravcsik, we are now moving into the third and final stage of European integration: the moment of institutional choice. Three theories offer different explanations to explain why states create international institutions: the federalist theory, the technocratic theory and the so-called 'credible commitments approach'. The federalist theory contends that recourse to supranational delegation varies, depending on the country, but not on the subjects addressed; divisions can be found between federalists and nationalists. The institutional formula resulting from this vision places the emphasis on democratic, or failing that, ideological legitimacy. Technocratic theory, on the other hand, asserts that delegation to supranational institutions applies particularly to technically, legally or politically complex topics, and is encouraged by experts, officials and sometimes social elites. The emphasis is not on democratic will, but rather, on achieving technocratic consensus in order to settle collective problems through central planning.

Finally, the theory of 'credible commitments' puts the emphasis on the need for political coordination: delegation and union are perceived as ways of committing governments to a series of decisions, removing any possibility of unilateral control while progressively increasing the costs of non-cooperation and non-decision. In this scenario, the support for institutions varies according to the countries and the objectives involved. Through the five periods of European integration studies, Moravcsik (1998) observes that governments have often opted for supranational institutions when they serve their own interests, irrespective of ideology. He also shows that there is no correlation between the legal or technical complexity of a topic and the level of cooperation it secures. He sees the theory of 'credible commitments' as the only pertinent one. In this scenario, the EU is considered as a set of institutions designed to facilitate the collective action of member states in a reciprocal approach to lowering costs and maximizing gains. States accept supranational institutions because they are a means of ensuring that their partners commit to a specific policy, the results of which may remain uncertain. States maintain a high level of control in spite of the existence of these institutions:

Box 3.3   *Regional integration: a three-stage process*

At the core of liberal intergovernmentalism is the idea of international bargaining as a three-stage process:

1   The formation of national preferences driven by issue specific, mostly economic, interests.
2   Inter-state negotiations based on asymmetrical interdependence between member states.
3   The choice of supranational institutions which reflects an interest in securing credible member state commitments.

unanimous voting and vetoes illustrate this because states can demand minimum commitment only. Furthermore, the forms that delegation to European institutions have taken show that supranational actors have never been perceived by states as neutral, and that they have always sought to limit their autonomy (Moravcsik 1999).

These elements prompted Anand Menon to speak of 'institutionalised intergovernmentalism', in which the state accepts that there will be winners and losers in the construction of supranational institutions and enters into it knowingly (Menon 2003). However, they cover their backs extensively 'upstream' and attempt to rewrite the terms of the contract 'downstream' if and when they have experienced significant costs or a loss of control.

Critiques

Moravcsik conceptualizes his approach as a *grand theory* to explain the reasons for integration, but does put forward three preconditions that must exist for liberal intergovernmentalism to be able to explain outcomes convincingly (Moravcsik 1995, 1998). First, the theory works best when it explains intergovernmental decisions taken unanimously, i.e. specifically intergovernmental negotiations in foreign and defence policy or, partially still, justice and home affairs. The renegotiation of treaties is also an area where liberal intergovernmentalism can be applied well. Secondly, Moravcsik considers national economic interests as the most influential element in the positions that member states defend. This is particularly visible in trade and agricultural policies. Finally, intergovernmental negotiations are most decisive when the transaction costs are low, when complete information is available and it is shared symmetrically (see also Schimmelfennig 2004).

Although systemic and complete, Moravcsik's theory has been fiercely challenged on several grounds: methodologically as well as empirically. Methodologically, critics have questioned his use of historical material as well as his approach to theory building. While he claims that he only used data stemming from primary sources, historians (Kaiser 2008, 2010; Rasmussen 2010) have criticized his research for predominantly referring to autobiographies and oral sources, instead of using research purely based on historical archives, as done by Milward. These oral sources are criticised as pro domo plaidoyers which are reconstructed *a posteriori* to justify a specific position. Based on such data, it is indeed difficult to put forward convincing evidence and establish causality because actors reinterpret the reasons for their actions in the light of the consequences they triggered. This raises the question of whether it is really possible to consider economic reasons as the predominant force driving integration, and whether it is appropriate to reject the ideological reasoning of the Founding Fathers altogether.

Furthermore, since liberal intergovernmentalism seeks to be rational, it becomes monocausal and, as a result, ignores many of the innovative aspects of European integration as a political and economic project. This is also true of critiques stemming from historical institutionalists (see Chapter 4) who argue that Moravcsik ignores the dynamic institutional aspect of European integration. In other words, the feedback loop of European integration – where every decision is anchored in a process that began often quite some time before – makes differentiating three steps (national preference formation, intergovernmental bargaining and establishment of supranational institutions) impossible, however heuristic the method might be (Bulmer 1993, 1994; Pierson 1996; Stone Sweet and Sandholtz 1997). On the contrary, European institutions (the Commission, the European Parliament, and the ECJ) are not simply agencies created by the state to enhance inter-state bargaining. Those organizations have their own interests and powerful informational resources, the capacity to generate ideas and intervene as independent actors in decision-making processes. This gives the institutions at the heart of a system, and in particular the European Commission, centralized policy management powers.

Finally, scholars defending alternative approaches, in particular sociologists and constructivists, criticize Moravcsik's conceptual framework for neglecting the domestic diversity of central governments, the nature of elites and their independent activities at EU level (Sandholtz 1993, 1996; Risse 1996; Lewis 1998; Checkel and Zürn 2005). While Moravcsik takes civil society interests into account, he only does so in the first step of his three-step model, more specifically, during preference formation. According to Moravscik, inter-state negotiations are derived from domestic bargaining between domestic societal groups. These groups compete to influence political decision-makers who, on the European stage, will defend the winning position that emerges from domestic debate. Thus, for the CAP, the farmers' unions saw their interests prevail. The French state simply served as a channel for their

Table 3.2   *Perspectives on intergovernmentalism*

Perspectives	Main assumptions	Authors
Conventional intergovernmentalism		
• Analysing the attitudes of governmental elites	Each state is specific and must be analysed according to structural, procedural and ideological variables. Difference between high politics (diplomacy) and low politics (economy)	Aron 1962 Hoffmann 1954, 1996
• European integration as saviour of state sovereignty	European integration processes have allowed Western European States to rebuild their economy and their sovereignty after the Second World War	Milward (critical perspective: Kaiser et al. 2005; Kaiser, Leucht and Rasmussen 2009)
• Neorealist accounts	States are independent actors, jealous of their sovereignty that must be defended by all means. There is no possibility for the creation of a world, or even regional, government: what emerge are alliances that states enter into out of self-interest	Mearsheimer 1993 Grieco 1995 Talliaferro 2000/2001 Rynning 2006
• Two-level games • EU level bargaining among states • Bargaining between EU and other states/ organizations	Processes that occur within a state substantially influence the behaviour of that state at the international level. Thus states are 'chief negotiators' at 'two tables'	Putnam 1988 Smith and Ray 1993 Dür and Matteo 2010 Menz 2011 Patterson 1997 Meunier 2005
Liberal intergovernmentalism	Based on the idea that international bargaining is a three stage process: 1 the formation of national preferences driven by issue specific, mostly economic, interests 2 inter-state negotiations based on asymmetrical interdependence between member states 3 the choice of supranational institutions which reflects an interest in securing credible member state commitments	Moravcsik 1991, 1993a, 1995, 1998

demands. But, as Moravcsik shows, a state negotiating on the European stage is subject to dual pressures: domestic interest groups pursuing their own competitive interests and other states defending their own national preferences. Thus, the author establishes a theory on governments' room for manoeuvre, not unlike Milward's descriptive analysis (1992): in a way, the EU increases the powers of states by allowing government leaders to use the constraint of European cooperation to circumvent claims formulated domestically. The concept of *blame avoidance*, so widely used in analyses of distortions in government behaviour between the national and community levels – and which political sociologists have used explain the rejection of the EU at national level – is clearly in line with this logic.

More generally, though, liberal intergovernmentalism suffers from its monopolistic position. It seems as if all other theories contradict its main assumption that states and governments remain the only significant actors influencing European integration in a rational manner; these other theories base their criticisms on case studies and don't generalize for the European integration process as a whole.

What is lacking is a rigorous debate between scholars who have sought to develop grand theories in recent years, but outside the liberal intergovernmentalist framework. While neofunctionalists seem to have abandoned the grand theory project and concentrate on case studies and comparative policy studies, sociological accounts such as those by Fligstein (2008) and Bartolini (2005) (see Chapter 9) challenge liberal intergovernmentalist accounts of European integration as a general project. Contrary to Moravcsik, however, these accounts are more complex and less parsimonious, as is the liberal intergovernmentalist approach; they are also arguably less attractive at present, partly owing to the positivist rational choice atmosphere that prevails in mainstream political science. Liberal intergovernmentalism, with its sole theorist, Moravscik, was for a long time the only theoretical framework that conceptualized the influence of the state and sovereignty, a situation that has changed with the arrival of social constructivist perspective in international relations (see Chapter 10).

Conclusion

The intergovernmental approach in European studies takes many forms. Designed partly as a forceful critique of 1950s functionalism, its different conceptualizations have continued to enrich it. As its name suggests, the essence of intergovernmentalism remains the action of the state in intergovernmental relations. Its objective is to explain why states, perceived as rational actors pursuing their own interests, actually accept the idea of shared sovereignty. While approaches diverge on the main factors to be taken into consideration, the premise remains the same: sovereignty is the cornerstone for explanations of how states function and relate to each other. More actors may be involved, but they only influence the details of negotiations and decisions between states. If national governments oppose higher levels of integration, no bureaucratic or administrative agent can counter it.

While the first movement against neofunctionalism in the 1960s was mainly descriptive and focused on intergovernmental elites, a second movement was more theoretical and conceptual. The two-level game theory, developed by Putnam and refined in the EU context by Meunier, was taken up by Moravcsik, who adopted a positivist research design and developed a series of robust hypotheses in liberal intergovernmentalism.

However, this contemporary attractiveness also faces major criticisms. Federalist approaches (Chapter 1), posit that state sovereignty is something to be overcome and even done away with; they advocate constructing a new political system in which competencies and sovereignties are shared between different actors and different levels of government. While mainly stemming from comparative policy and public policy approaches, as we have seen, critiques also come from the international relations discipline itself (Chapter 10). Thus, even though state sovereignty remains a key explanatory factor, it is important to consider it as socially constructed. Sovereignty as a social construct might be considered as something impossible to circumvent, abandon or ignore, precisely because it is part of every political actor's' *discourse* at the international level. Chapter 10 addresses this particular issue, and in so doing goes beyond liberal intergovernmentalist or federalist perspectives on this matter.

Part II

Mainstreaming European Studies

From the end of the 1980s, an increasing number of publications on European integration broadened out the themes dealt with in European studies. Instead of concentrating on the questions of why states abandon their sovereignty and the consequences of this process, scholars started to take an interest in the day-to-day of European policy-making. The 1990s thus saw the development of conceptual tools aimed at understanding European integration through lenses previously forged to scrutinize domestic policies and politics.

I call this reciprocal influence – between theoretical perspectives developed to study the state and those developed to study European integration – 'bottom-up mainstreaming' in European studies (see Introduction). The term refers to the use of conceptual tools developed within mainstream political science, as opposed to 'top-down mainstreaming' which brings in tools from international relations, with a view to studying European integration in a broader global context – and this is the subject of the third part of this book.

As noted in the Introduction, 'bottom-up mainstreaming' was launched initially by Bulmer's seminal 1983 article where he links domestic and European politics, and got under way in earnest in the middle of the 1990s when a number of scholars argued in favour of the introduction of comparative politics in EU studies (Hix 1994, 1998; Caporaso and Keeler 1995; Risse 1996). These scholars rejected international relations approaches in favour of conceptual frameworks developed by public policy and comparative politics to analyse the European political system and compare European integration to processes usually seen in domestic political systems. Instead of developing analytical tools that would require years of refinement and in-depth exploration, existing frameworks could be applied immediately to study in detail how actors and policies functioned within the EU. The EU, while not actually being a traditional European state, could be compared to one. The politics and government in the EU could thus be perceived as 'not inherently different to … any democratic political system' (Hix 1994: 1), an idea shared by all conceptual frameworks developed in this second part of the book.

One of the characteristics of the chapters dealt with in Part II is the concentration on middle-range conceptual frameworks explaining sectors of European integration, as opposed to grand theories attempting to explain the process as a whole. With the exception of rational choice institutionalism, none of the approaches studied here has aimed to develop a series of hypotheses to explain all the phenomena of integration. The approaches presented in this second part have enabled European integration to become a less unique research object (though no less distinctive).

However, mainstreaming has also led to a situation whereby the subjects of research became increasingly small. Even large-scale quantitative research designs often concentrate on a single, specific aspect of integration, such as decision-making in the Council, or domestic compliance in one specific policy area. While, on the one hand, theorizing clearly and testing falsifiable hypotheses in a smaller domain can be scientifically superior to unfalsifiable grand-theory musing on the future of European integration, it seems as if, on the other hand, contemporary mainstream EU studies have increasingly lost sight of the EU as a general system. This is partially due to the fact that studies have become more microscopic and close-up in their empirical analyses – alas, often not drawing out the wider implications, or asking, so what? Many studies trace minor empirical developments, which are out of date tomorrow. The international research structure in which scholars are embedded is partially responsible for this situation: individual scholars must constantly produce innovative research, proving earlier scholars wrong. We will see a number of those illustrations in the chapters that follow.

This part of the book is divided into six chapters. Chapter 4 focuses on four institutionalisms: rational choice, historical, sociological and discursive. Chapter 5 looks at governance approaches, which explain the European system through the overlapping of public and private actors present at different levels. Europeanization and public policy transfer are addressed in Chapter 6. Chapter 7 focuses on multiple forms of constructivism, based on a continuum of paradigms ranging from positivism to post-positivism. Chapter 8 focuses on the newly developed sociological approaches to European integration. Finally, Chapter 9 presents political and normative theory on European integration.

Chapter 4

Institutionalist Approaches

The EU is undoubtedly one of the most institutionalized political systems in the world, with a dense network of intergovernmental, supranational and non-state actors producing a set of laws – the EU's so-called *acquis communautaire*. From this point of view the self-definition of many European scholars as institutionalists is not surprising.

Despite this fact, institutionalist accounts of European integration are a rather recent phenomenon. Institutionalism emerged within the study of comparative politics more generally and had been imported into European studies by the beginning of the 1990s. One of the reasons that accounts for the central role institutionalists play today in European integration studies was the intergovernmentalists' obsession with governmental actors and the secondary role given to European institutions such as the Commission or the Parliament. The relaunch of European integration and the important role played by the European Commission in drafting the SEA, the single market as well as the EMU led analysts to refocus on institutions, understood both as actors and structures in which agency is embedded. Supranational institutions, such as the Commission, the Parliament, the European Council as well as the Council of ministers, the ECJ, but also the legal, administrative and political structures in which these actors acted became increasingly important to understand to make sense of this complex process.

Basic assumptions

Although a diverse group of scholars, institutionalists agree on the basic assumption that 'institutions matter'. Based on this premise, scholars countered the behaviourist paradigm prevailing in social sciences during the 1950s and 1960s, which saw the aggregated behaviour of social actors and, more specifically, the free interplay of their interests, as the main explanatory factor behind political processes. Institutionalists criticize behaviourists for ignoring the embedded structures of political life that make up the state (Evans, Rueschemeyer and Skocpol 1985; March and Olsen, 1984, 1989; Katzenstein 1986, Berger 1981, Hall 1986, North 1990) and themselves emphasize the way that political institutions structure political life and policy-making. The main argument is that these structures must be integrated into policy analysis as an independent or intervening variable when studying the preferences of social actors and seeking to explain the results of their interactions. At the same time, institutions are more than just agents facilitating exchange between actors, or instruments to lower transaction costs. They can act in their own right and develop their own action strategies, based on self-interest.

It is this that distinguishes neo-institutionalism or new institutionalism from the institutionalism that dominated political science before the behaviourist revolution of the 1950s and 1960s (for a debate see Thelen and Steinmo 1992). This old form of institutionalism, rejected by behaviourists, offered detailed studies of administrative, legal and political structures. The work produced in this framework is characterized by normative positioning and a juxtaposition of detailed descriptions of institutional configurations in different countries. Although useful for developing an understanding of political systems in general, old institutionalism does not define categories and concepts that can actually be used to construct explanatory theoretical frameworks; it describes but does not explain outcomes or results.

On the contrary, new institutionalism's main hypothesis, whether in its historical, sociological, rational choice, or discursive form, is based on the assumption that organizational forms of relations influence actor strategies. In general, researchers applying this concept to their work look at all state and social institutions, as bodies creating order and predictability, and thus influencing actors' interests.

Institutions: multiple definitions

The definition what an institution really is, however, remains somewhat vague, leading to a situation whereby every other publication adopts its own (Aspinwall and Schneider 2001). The majority of EU scholars base their research on an understanding that encompasses diverse forms such as organizations, formal and informal institutions, conventions, norms and symbols, political instruments and procedures (Bulmer and Armstrong 1998). Thus, at the most general level, institutions are 'formal rules, compliance procedures, and standard operating practices that structure the relationship between individuals in various units of the polity and the economy' (Hall 1986: 19). In a similar vein, two of the founding fathers of new institutionalism, David March and Johan Olsen, define institutions as 'a relatively enduring collection of rules and organized principles, embedded in structures of meaning and resources that are relatively invariant in the face of turnover of individuals and relatively resilient to the idiosyncratic preferences and expectations of individuals and changing external circumstances' (March and Olsen 2006: 3). Another way of defining institutions is to distinguish between, on the one hand, formal and informal institutions, and, on the other, organizations. Formal institutions refer to elements such as rules of the game, constitutions, laws and regulations; informal institutions refer to norms, conventions, beliefs and ideologies. While institutions are the rules of the game, organizations are the players. They are groups of individuals engaged in purposive activity (North 1990), such as the Commission, the Parliament, interest groups or diverse agencies.

These definitions allow us to consider institutions as dependent or independent variables, actors or arenas in which debates take place. When institutions are considered as dependent variables, institutionalist approaches analyse the emergence and establishment of organizations, such as the Commission, the Parliament, the ECB or independent regulatory agencies, as well as formal and informal institutional features such as norms, rules, beliefs or conventions. Understood as independent or intervening variables, they are seen as parameters creating elements of order and predictability. Here the research focuses on the impact of EU law, or more broadly, norms. More generally, institutions can also be understood as factors that influence the cultural and social frames influencing and transforming the behaviour of agents at the domestic level.

Finally, research on institutions as arenas concentrates, on the one hand, on institutions as mediators or facilitators – in short, as actors that

Table 4.1 *Neo-institutionalisms in brief*

Perspectives	Main assumptions
Rational choice institutionalism	Analysing the factors, which allow political actors to delegate powers to independent bureaucratic authorities
Historical institutionalism	Not only cost-benefit analysis but also historical rules and regularities influence the incremental transformation of policies and institutions
Sociological institutionalism	Informal institutions, identity, shared experiences, cognitive frameworks are the main objects of analysis
Discursive institutionalism	Discourses are 'carriers of ideas' and instruments of change. Research must focus on the content of ideas and the interactive process, which brings them to a head

help states decrease transaction costs in international bargaining. Researching institutions as purposeful actors, on the other hand, means identifying the role institutions play as independent agents in negotiations at the EU level.

These understandings of institutions can be found in all four institutionalist approaches discussed in this chapter. In order to distinguish more clearly between these four approaches in European studies, the next four sections detail the hypotheses and variables of the four most used institutionalisms – rational choice, historical, sociological and discursive (Peters 2005) – in their relationship with European studies, followed by a presentation of the challenges that these institutionalisms face today.

Rational choice institutionalism

Rational choice institutionalism originated in the North American political science community as a general approach to the social sciences. It fostered a large number of specific theories and falsifiable hypotheses concerning human behaviour (Pollack 2007; Snidal 2002). At the end of the 1970s, analyses of decision-making processes in the US Congress showed that political choices were unstable and wavered according to different majorities (McKelvey 1976; Riker 1964, 1980). However, studies noted that, in certain circumstances, Congress was capable of forming stable majorities around certain public policies (Shepsle 1979). The main variable explaining the emergence of these equilibria was a system of committees producing a structure-induced equilibrium by authorizing or, conversely, blocking certain political options. Thus, institutions were found to structure actors' behaviour as well as their veto and agenda-setting powers (Shepsle and Weingast 1984; Moe 1984).

On the basis of this research, two influential models emerged: the principal-agent model showing that, under certain circumstances, Congress delegates powers to independent bureaucratic authorities (Moe 1984), and the transaction-cost model showing that institutions reduce costs that emerge in any typical transaction between actors (Epstein and O'Halloran 1999).

Although initially formulated as part of research on North American political institutions, these models were extensively applied to comparative and international political contexts. Research on veto points and veto players was developed by scholars concentrating on public policies (Tsebelis and Garrett 1997; Tsebelis 2002) and, and more generally, those interested in the reasons behind the delegation of powers to independent agencies and judicial courts (Huber and Shipan 2003). Delegation in this research has both a functional and a dynamic character (Tallberg 2002a). It is best captured by a four-step model, which allows for analysing the reasons and consequences of delegation:

(1) Tasks are delegated to agents to allow for effective solutions to collective action problems.
(2) The institutional design of these delegations allows control of the agents who have to execute the tasks transferred to them by the principals.
(3) Control instruments exert influence on the degree of delegation.
(4) Delegation creates consequences through feedback loops.

This research led to a number of conceptual frameworks developed in international relations, but also, and specifically, in European studies.

Rational choice in European studies

Scholars in European studies seek primarily to understand why national governments consent to abandon or at least share their sovereignty at supranational level by creating supranational institutions; a process known as 'pooling sovereignty'. The key is to understand how member states manage to control institutions and what their relative share of autonomy is (Aspinwall and Schneider 2001). The central assumption is that state actors rationally pursue their own interests while transferring competencies to institutions. States understand perfectly well that the *ex-post* control of these institutions can be problematic. They nevertheless transfer competencies to the European level. Why? Because institutions help to decrease the uncertainty linked to the imperfect division of power between competing European actors. Furthermore, delegating powers to supranational institutions helps to reduce transaction costs involved in the decision-making process. States agree to act according to international agreements they have signed and benefit to this end from the expertise of supranational actors.

In exchange for delegating competencies, these supranational bodies provide the states with control instruments to implement policies decided at European level. However, if the rules of implementation are not respected, the European Commission refers cases to the ECJ. Thus, *principals*, meaning the states, accept to be controlled by *agents* – the Commission and the ECJ – to ensure that implementation is equally applied to all member states. Empirically, research concentrates mainly on four empirical areas: the European executive, the ECJ, decision-making processes and the influence of the EU on the domestic level. In each of these four domains, different theoretical advances have seen the light of day.

The EU executive

The central theme of this area of research is to understand how principals – the EU member states – react when agents – generally the European institutions – oppose their demands (Pollack 2003; Kassim and Menon 2003; Maher, Billiet and Hodson 2009). Research focuses on the *ex-ante* definition of the agent's preferences by the principal and on the control measures developed by the latter. Importance is attributed to the study of committees – bodies created by member-state representatives to control the Commission. From this point of view, delegation becomes the dependent variable in analysis.

Research starts from the assumption that European institutions behave broadly as agents of member states. Sometimes, however, they are strongly independent. This is due to the fact that the mechanisms put in place by the state in order to control institutions are costly, which discourages their extensive use by national governments. In this respect, four factors determining the relative influence of supranational institutions can be distinguished (Pollack 2003):

- The distribution of preferences between principals (member states) and agents (i.e. supranational institutions).
- The institutional decision-making rules on applying sanctions, overruling legislation and changing agents' mandates.
- The presence of incomplete information or uncertainty.
- The influence of transnational interests.

In studying the reasons for and conditions of delegation by governments to supranational bodies, this research analyses whether European institutions succeed in broadening their powers, thereby facilitating European integration and the creation of a European market. Through a series of case studies, scholars demonstrated how and under what circumstances European institutions can broaden their powers. These studies concerned institutions such as the Commission (Pollack 2003; Maher, Billiet and Hodson 2009), the EU Council Presidency (Tallberg 2003) or the ECB (Elgie 2002). Pollack (2003) in particular offers a number of comparative case studies on the Commission and the ECJ in which he develops an overreaching conceptualization of the principal-agent theory in EU studies. The first set concerns cases regarding liberalization and the creation of the European market. By examining three cases involving the role of the European Commission in foreign trade (Blair House Agreement), competition (De Havilland Affair) and case law of the ECJ on the free circulation of goods and services in the EU (Cassis de Dijon Ruling), his research shows that supranational institutions influenced European integration and promoted the introduction of a single market when the control mechanisms set up by the governments were relatively weak.

A second set of examples concern the case of the European market. Here, the analysis concentrates on the role of the European Commission in social regulation (the 1993 Working Time Directive), regional public policy (the reform of structural funds of 1988 and 1993), and ECJ case law on equal pay for men and women (the Defrenne and Barber rulings) (for an in-depth historical discussion of these cases see Dinan 2004).

Results were similar in both sets of case studies: the supranational organizations fulfil their regulation and rule-making role in the European market, but their power and room for manoeuvre is closely controlled by national governments. When the European Commission or ECJ acquired discretional power considered to be excessive by the major member states, the latter reacted by creating new control mechanisms or by limiting certain effects of their decisions in new treaties. An example can be found in the limits set by the Maastricht Treaty with regard to the retroactive effect of the Barber ruling of 1990 on the ECJ. Indeed, the Barber protocol was inserted into the Treaty with the intent of limiting the impact of the ECJ's *Barber v. the Guardian* ruling equalizing pension policies for men and women, and forcing the ECJ to base its decisions on existing case law, i.e. the legislation established before the Barber ruling.

Principal–agent approaches on the EU executive highlight the paradoxical relationships between governments and supranational institutions (Kassim and Menon 2003). Governments create institutions and give them their autonomy but then limit it again by creating complex control mechanisms. Rational choice institutionalism thereby argues that institutions are created with a rational objective of reducing the transaction costs generated by the creation and implementation of public policies. To a limited extent only, and under the constant control of member states, organizations succeed in broadening the scope of their competencies by promoting their know-how and expertise.

Rational choice institutionalism and agencies

At the beginning of the 1990s, the notion of delegation was broadened and applied beyond the Commission, the Parliament and the ECJ. The delegation of decision-making power to an increasing number of regulatory agencies became one of the most significant developments in the EU's administrative apparatus. Delegation of regulatory functions on the European level, however, is often done on account of specific problems usually not encountered in single nation-states, namely the challenge of coordinating public action across national governments – in other words, problems of collective action. This implies, first, that rivalry between governments is likely to undermine horizontal coordination. Secondly, governments sometimes try to evade their obligations, or renege on prior commitments signed up to in international regimes (Magnette 2004: 7). In this light, the study of regulatory authorities in the EU relates to the broader debate about the transfer/retention of sovereignty and institutional deepening in the EU. Wonka and Rittberger (2011), for example, argue that the degree of formal institutional independence enjoyed by regulatory agencies can tell us a lot about 'who governs' in practice. The authors point out that the level of influence regulatory agencies exert largely depends on their 'zone of discretion' (ibid.: 733).

Judicial politics

Rational choice institutionalism is also used when it comes to analysing the judicial policies of European integration. In this context, the role of the ECJ is of particular interest to scholars, many of whom question the degree of independence the Court has from the EU member states – is it an agent of the member states (Garrett 1992) that follows the wishes of the most powerful states in its decisions, or, to the contrary, is it an independent player, as foreseen in Montesquieu's separation of powers? According to the first hypothesis, the member states created the Court of Justice to resolve problems arising in the implementation of European legislation. The Court's duty is to rule on the compliance of national legislation. From a rational point of view, this means that states must accept the decisions of the Court, even when they are against their own national interests. The reason lies in their long-term preferences. One group of scholars argues that the Court does not hand down rulings that go against the interests of the larger states (Garrett and Weingast 1993; Garrett, Kelemen and Schulz 1998; Garrett and Tsebelis 2000). This hypothesis is strongly criticized by sociological and historical institutionalists, who contend that scholars of rational choice institutionalism overestimate the control mechanisms available to the most powerful member states. On the contrary, the Court has shown a penchant for independence and can take European integration much further than the combined interest of the states would seem to allow. The Court has succeeded to do just this on numerous occasions because circumventing strategies such as long-term noncompliance are too costly for states to use. The Court thus succeeds because it is too costly for states to try to resist over a long period. Furthermore, in its pro-integration stance, the Court has powerful allies in the national courts, which refer hundreds of cases per year to the ECJ (Mattli and Slaughter 1995, 1998; Stone Sweet and Caporaso 1998).

In responding to these criticisms, rational choice institutionalists agree with the limits of their explanation, adopting a more nuanced approach by testing hypotheses in the areas where the Court has most autonomy (Garrett 1998; Pollack 2003). New studies analysing the Court and legal integration emerged from these criticisms. They questioned the links between the ECJ and national courts, on the one hand, and the individual practice of the ECJ on the other. Studies have shown how actors use the Court as a resource to overcome obstacles they face at national level (Alter 2001, 2009; Conant 2002). These studies, largely based on historical institutionalism, show the importance of the EU relationship between the Court and the member states – a dynamic relationship influenced greatly by the historical context, and which cannot be understood as a simple principal-agent structure.

Decision-making processes

A third research area for rational choice institutionalists concerns the legislative process within the EU (Pollack 2001). Scholars are interested in the voting procedures within both the Council of Ministers and the European Parliament and, linked to that, the respective powers of the Commission and the European Parliament in decision-making processes (König 2008; Schmidt 2000), as well as the influence of interest groups (Schneider, Finke and Baltz 2007).

Voting procedures in the European Parliament have been the subject of extensive modelling since the mid-1980s. The supranational nature of the European Parliament and discourse on the *sui generis* nature of European integration contain assumptions widely criticized by rational choice institutionalists. Rational choice scholars show that the voting patterns of Members of the European Parliament (MEPs) hardly differ from those practised at national level. Despite the multinational nature of the European Parliament, MEPs follow the party line in their voting and therefore *do* put their party before their country. While the nationalist/supranationalist divide explains the behaviour of voters, MEPs adopt a more classical left/right attitude (Hix, 2001, 2002b, 2004; Hix, Noury and Roland 2007). Another group of studies analyses the powerful parliamentary commissions that deliberate on specific public policy issues, and shows that their behaviour is not necessarily very distant from that of national parliamentary committees (Kreppel 1999, 2001). This work has contributed to the mainstreaming of European studies and, more specifically, to the use of social science tools, more broadly developed in political science for analysing domestic political systems.

In a similar way, research on the Council of Ministers has focused on the puzzles of the relative weighting of voting and power among member states in the QMV systems (Hosli, van Deemen and Widgren 2002; Thomson et al. 2006; Schneider, Moser and Kirchgässner 2000; Tsebelis et al. 2001; Golub 1999). Such research questions the impact of the Luxembourg Compromise on Council voting behaviour. More precisely, does the Luxemburg Compromise, by allowing member states to use their veto power in the voting system, influence their voting behaviour in the Council? Or, on the contrary, is it the position of the member states on an issue compared to that of the Commission that determines their voting behaviour on a proposal? Quantitative research has concluded that the consensus model of decision-making used in the Council can be explained on the grounds that the Commission attempts to avoid a divided Council by initiating proposals that it *believes* all member states will favour, based on common support for policy change in the same direction. If this is not possible then the Commission searches for issue linkages, i.e. logrolling, which refers to trading of favours, such as vote trading by legislative members to obtain passage of actions of interest to each legislative member. These proposals either belong to the same policy domain or are negotiated during the same period (König and Junge 2009).

Finally, a group of scholars have investigated the influence of interest groups on legislative procedures. Two main questions can be distinguished here – on the one hand, whether national interest intermediation patterns are responsible for the degree of interest-group influence at the EU level, and on the other, whether alternative variables are statistically more significant. With regard to the first question, a group of rational choice institutionalists have sought to demonstrate that in EU lobbying, interest groups are more influenced by a statist model (whereby they lobby their own state, instead of directly lobbying European institutions, as conceptualized by liberal intergovernmentalism (Chapter 3)), based on the assumption that member states' political structures influence the behaviour of interest groups more than European structures (Schneider, Finke and Baltz 2007). More generally, research on interest-group influence based on rational choice institutionalism has shown that influence depends on the capacity of groups to establish a wide coalition based on diverse interests – the wider the coalition and more specific the demand, the higher the influence the interest group can exert (Klüver 2009, 2010).

Since the early 2000s, research has increasingly used both quantitative and qualitative methods to test rational choice institutionalist hypotheses in EU studies. This has led to substantial databases being set up, which are open for consultation and, in turn, also contribute to the expansion of rational choice institutionalism.

The influence of the EU at the national level

The influence of the EU at the national level is generally analysed by the conceptual framework developed in the Europeanization literature (Chapter 6). Among the scholars working with the conceptual tools developed in this realm, few are explicitly committed to rational choice institutionalism. One of the most salient, albeit soft, applications has been in enlargement research. The key assumption here is that the conceptual framework of rational choice institutionalism is empirically better suited to analysing the effects of enlargement than any other, given that the demand for accession is based on rational cost-benefit thinking. This is based on the understanding that the concept of conditionality presupposes rational action (Schimmelfennig and Sedelmeier 2004; Pollack 2004). The conditionality model places an emphasis on major European Council meeting declarations to analyse the process of EU enlargement, but also takes tensions among Directorate-Generals, interest groups, national bureaucracies or political parties into account. In order to explain progress in negotiations for EU enlargement (and the obstacles therein), it combines a cost-benefit analysis based on actors' preferences (member states, candidate states, European institutions), with the influence exerted by the EU institutional context. Thus, the instrument of conditionality does not automatically lead to a linear process whereby an emitting body (the EU) decides and a target body (the candidate state) accepts and adopts. Conditionally can lead to unforeseen outcomes. Indeed, legal, economic and political mechanisms of coercion influence the target political system (the candidate state), either directly through intergovernmental negotiations or by modifying the power game between domestic actors of the candidate state. At the domestic level, conditionality modifies political opportunity structures and can reinforce or, conversely, weaken the bargaining power of certain actors. The state is more likely to accept conditions imposed upon it by the European institution, i.e. the Commission, if the benefits of accession are considered greater than the costs of adaptation. Beyond the scale of benefits foreseen, the speed with which 'emitting body' transfers those benefits is also important – the quicker the transfer, the more likely it is that the recipient (governmental or non-governmental) will comply with the requirement(s).

The effectiveness of conditionality as an instrument depends on the number of veto players or veto points (actors and structures with the power to block decisions). Based on Tsebelis's veto-point research (Tsebelis 2002), this means that the more veto points and actors there are, the more complex and restricted that institutional transfer will be. As a result, for the *acquis communautaire* to be transferred to Central and Eastern European countries, the candidate country's political system needs to be relatively consensual.

The empirical conciseness of the rational choice institutionalist perspective on Europeanization, however, precludes any systematic analysis of the historical complexity of enlargement. It generally focuses on factors which – in the context analysed here – are considered fixed.

More generally, however, one of the more main limits in all rational choice approaches presented here refers to the premise that states act as individual actors (as the original theory principal–agent theory developed to study American domestic policy asserted). States possess their own features (they have vast resources and sovereignty), which make the nature of their interactions with international organizations qualitatively different from those that prevail when domestic political actors interact with national institutions. States can generate much greater resources than domestic actors. The expertise they can cultivate and draw upon is also much greater than that of international institutions or individual national political actors (Moravcsik 1993a). Thus, rather than arguing that relations between states and European institutions are a unidimensional power play, it is crucial to consider the influence of specific policies on power struggles between states. States as well as institutions do not act in the same way with regard to different public policies (Menon 2003).

Historical institutionalism

Historical institutionalism developed as a response to the functionalist and structuralist approaches of the 1960s and 1970s (Steinmo, Thelen and Longstreth 1992; Hall and Taylor 1996) in comparative politics. Historical institutionalism has been applied to analyse European policy-making and European state transformation more than it has been specifically developed in EU studies (Bulmer 2009). Thus, in order to understand historical institutionalism in European studies, it is crucial to focus on the basics that have been applied to the empirical context of the EU.

While the functionalist paradigm in comparative politics focused on the activities of groups in political systems and their competing for rare resources, structuralism favours deterministic structural forces over the ability of people to act. Both have been criticized for being ahistorical, that is, for not taking into account how the weight of history frames an actor's behaviour and shapes its preferences. Historical institutionalists, while accepting the structural premises of both structuralist and functionalist paradigms, reintroduce the historical embeddedness of actors and their decisions into the analysis. From this angle, research centres on how long-established economic, social and political structures frame public policies and, more particularly, tries to understand how actors enter into conflict when some are set to benefit to the detriment of others. The reintroduction of the 'state' variable in this research is central. The state, however, is not analysed in its capacity as a unified actor recording requests from its civil society, as the pluralist approach suggests. Nor is the state a functional response to problems, but rather, seen by historical institutionalists as a set of institutions which are in competition and capable of influencing the nature and result of conflicts between groups (Evans, Rueschemeyer and Skocpol 1985; Katzenstein 1978; Berger 1981). One of the main research areas of historical institutionalism concentrates on the analysis of macroeconomic structures. Such research attempts to explain how the state arbitrates between different demands by regulating access for trade unions and employers' associations in particular (Hall and Taylor 1996). Institutions are defined by historical institutionalists as 'official and officious procedures, protocols, standards and conventions which are inherent to the organizational structure of the political community or the political economy' (Krasner 1984; Pierson 1994, 1995, 1996).

The institutions thus defined influence along two perspectives: one strategic, another cultural. While the first perspective concerns the strategic use of institutions, which, although historically constructed and contingent, are also tools to defend interests, the second perspective considers the individual's vision of the world.

The central contribution of historical institutionalism is its focus on asymmetric power relations, unlike the pluralist approach, which argues that all actors have the same potential to influence political decisions. Actors have unequal resources; the state gives or refuses access to those resources. The state, in its historical embededdness, thus becomes a crucial variable to be taken into account in explaining actors' attitudes.

Historical institutionalism, as the name suggests, considers the establishment of institutions over time. It rejects the conjecture that the same forces produce the same results in all cases. Each specific context influences political processes, and those contexts are forged and historically institutionalized (Thelen and Steinmo 1992: 9). A central concept to understand this specific assumption is *path dependency* (Pierson 2000, 2004). Its aim is to explain how a set of present decisions is limited by the decisions made in the past, even though past circumstances may no longer be relevant. In other words, path dependency 'characterizes specifically those historical sequences in which contingent events set into motion institutional patterns or event chains that have deterministic properties' (Mahoney, 2000: 507).

More generally, historical institutions are able to transform the objectives and preferences of actors and, in so doing, structure political situations and influence the results of decision-making processes (Thelen 1999; Olsen 2009). Thus, historical institutionalism rejects the idea that actors have perfect knowledge of institutional influences. The consequences of their actions being framed by formal and informal institutions are not, on the face of it, perceived and known. Although institutions influence the context in which political and social processes develop, the actors do not control the consequences of their actions.

Historical institutionalism can be applied to specific policy case studies, or more general macro-sociological research attempting to explain political and social systems.

In a macro-sociological perspective, historical institutionalism involves arguments about points of critical juncture of institutional formation – moments that send countries along broadly different developmental paths. It also suggests that institutions continue to evolve in response to changing environmental conditions and ongoing political manoeuvring, but in ways that are constrained by past trajectories. Institutions certainly constitute 'intervening variables', but they also govern the wider context in which political action occurs. As a consequence, institutions also have the capacity to shape the goals and preferences of actors (institutional dynamic), and in so doing structure political situations and leave their own imprint on political outcomes (Thelen 1999).

Applied to European integration, this means that the establishment of European institutions and policies cannot be explained solely as a result of the rationally motivated preferences of actors. While these preferences certainly exist, the results are historically contingent (*path-dependent*), and lead to a range of unforeseen logics and consequences (Thelen and Steinmo 1992; Hall and Soskice 2001; Immergut 2006; Heritier 2007; Streeck and Thelen 2007).

Historical institutionalism in European studies

In European studies, historical institutionalism defends a rationalist, but at the same time historically contingent, explanation of institution-building and change. Studies concentrate, on the one hand, on the European institutions and European policies as such, and on the other, offer a comparative analysis of member states and/or their public policies.

With regard to research centred on European institutions, historical institutionalists study their influence on the action and attitudes of actors more than their supposed aim to reduce transaction costs, which is the hypothesis defended by rational choice institutionalists. Institutions become actors on their own account and constrain the margins of manoeuvre of individual actors (March and Olsen 1984, 1989). Historical institutionalism, contrary to rational choice institutionalism, considers institutions as central historical devices for structuring governance in the EU (Bulmer 1993, Armstrong and Bulmer 1998). In this context, historical institutionalism concentrates on the creation and transformation of EU institutions, in particular, the Commission (Egeberg 2006) and the Parliament (Lindner and Rittberger 2003; Rittberger 2005), as well on the establishment of governance institutions (Aspinwall and Schneider 2001). Institutions are seen in this respect as agents who make meaning 'routine'. They prevent or at least make it very difficult for states to break from path dependency in public policies and to reassert their sovereignty. As a consequence the imprint of the past would affect any political development, but without making change impossible. Pierson puts this particularly well in the EU context (1996: 123): 'Once gaps in control emerge (at the EU level), change-resistant decision rules and sunk costs associated with societal adaptation make it difficult for member states to reassert their authority.'

Simon Bulmer underlines how historical institutionalism has opened new venues for research in EU studies (Bulmer 2009), allowing us to understand how the political dynamics of major reforms as well as of day-to-day politics are essentially influenced by past decisions. This means that researchers have become increasingly aware of the weight of history – both national and supranational in decision-making processes.

Historical institutionalism has also shown that political systems, and the EU system in particular, have a complex network of veto points, defined as instances of institutional vulnerability where the engagement of actors can block, or conversely, trigger innovation (Pollack 1996). While veto points are generally stable and historically contingent, they are not permanent, and can shift when a change in the balance of power occurs. These changes can trigger their emergence, disappearance or movement.

This approach helps to explain how relational structures or networks between actors can be modified, in particular in the field of public policy reform, illustrated for instance by Susanne Schmidt's work on the Commission's role in the reform of telecommunications and electricity policies at the EU level (Schmidt 1998). Three factors seem to influence the modification of structural relations (Scharpf 1997). First, a change of political environment challenges existing institutional forms. Secondly, a change of actors or their power, after an initial institutionalization of relations between them, leads to the emergence of new actors. Thirdly, the degree and quality of information that actors have at their disposal modify the form the network takes. Generally, this means looking at how institutions filter political processes, and also how the impact of institutions is itself filtered by a broader political context.

With regard to the second field of research, centred on the comparison of domestic political systems and policy areas, this has focused predominantly on welfare-state reforms (Pierson 1996, Thelen 1999). Scholars argued that the attitude of governments is conditioned by previous decisions, the so-called *path dependency* of decisions, which *lock* them in. Change is purely incremental. Focusing on the effects of institutions over time, the approach studies the ways in which a given set of institutions, once established, can influence or constrain the behaviour of the actors who established them (Pollack 2005). This 'footprint' or 'weight' of the past seems to mark any political development. Thus, once a set of institutions are in place, actors adapt their strategies in ways that reflect but also reinforce the logic of the system. This implies a situation in which once a particular path is chosen, actors adapt to the existing institutions in ways that push them further along that trajectory, even if it does not create deliberate consequences at first (Thelen 1999).

As a number of scholars (Pollack 1996; Stacey and Rittberger 2003) emphasize, rational choice institutionalism and historical institutionalism are not fundamentally incompatible (DiMaggio and Powell 1991). In both frameworks, the central assumption is actor rationality, understood as being exogenous to the process being explained, but placed clearly in an historical process, which itself serves as the framework for analysis.

However, contrary to the rational choice variant, historical institutionalism does not only analyse the asymmetric characteristics of power linked to the genesis and development of institutions, but also analyses path dependencies and the unintended consequences of historical developments. Hence, it insists more strongly on the fact that actors' interests depend on the context in which they are conceived.

Sociological institutionalism

Elements of historical institutionalism are also present in the third type of neo-institutionalism: sociological institutionalism. In this approach, the emphasis is on the cognitive dimensions of institutions. Sociological institutionalism derives from the different conceptualizations of organizational sociology. One of the path-breaking publications is this respect is Paul DiMaggio's and Walter Powell's edited volume from the early 1990s (DiMaggio and Powell 1991), building upon Max Weber (1980), Émile Durkheim and Talcott Parsons. Parallel to James March and Johan Olsen's work (March and Olsen 1984, 1989), these authors have strongly influenced sociological institutionalist accounts of European integration. Three concepts are of particular importance in sociological institutionalism: *isomorphism*, the *logic of appropriateness* and the *logic of consequentialism* (Peters 2005). Isomorphism results from social processes of *emulation* and *diffusion*. Actors replicate organizational models collectively sanctioned as appropriate and legitimate (DiMaggio and Powell 1991). This idea is strongly influenced by Weber's argument on bureaucracy's tendency to converge around a rational legal format – the 'iron cage'. The authors identify three mechanisms of institutional isomorphic change: *coercion, mimesis* and *normative pressures*. Coercive isomorphism refers to pressures from other organizations, mostly the government via public subsidies, upon which institutions are dependent and to those exercised by cultural expectations stemming from society. Institutions conform with expectations from the outside. Mimesis occurs mostly through the migration of professionals from one organization to another, or through the influence of external factors fostering learning. In a context of uncertainty and limited rationality, institutions have a tendency to imitate one another. Finally, normative pressures are mainly linked to the institutionalization of specific attitudes. Norms are legitimized by institutionalization and imported to institutions by hiring professionals from the outside.

The concept of isomorphism is regularly used as a supporting concept in EU studies, in particular when insisting on the fact that institutions created at the EU level are influenced by those existing at the domestic level. This influence has been illustrated through studies on the impact of domestic regulatory agencies on those created at the European level (Thatcher 2011), the influence of French state bureaucracy on the original High Authority (later European Commission) or on the influence of the German Central Bank on the ECB.

However, the two logics mentioned – logic of consequentialism and logic of appropriateness – have structured EU studies even more significantly. According to the logic of appropriateness, cognitive dimensions offer frameworks, categories and cognitive models which allow actors to interpret social phenomena. These frameworks help them understand the appropriateness of their behaviour in a specific context and not simply which behaviour corresponds best to their individual interests (logic of consequentialism). Contrary to rational choice institutionalism, which focuses on the rational behaviour of actors (agency-centred), models developed by the sociological variant of institutionalism use the idea that the behaviour of actors is more influenced by structural conditions created by the social, cultural and institutional climate. Thus, while actors behave rationally to increase their power, the structure in which these preferences and interests are formed is of substantial influence.

In EU studies, this approach is similar to constructivism (Chapter 7) and is also part of the sociological perspectives of European integration (Chapter 8), hence its rather cursory treatment here. Empirical studies research focuses particularly on the European Commission (Cini 1998; Fouilleux 2000) and decision-making processes more generally (Jachtenfuchs 2001; Richardson 1996a; Christiansen and Tonra 2004). These analyses are based on case studies that pinpoint the cultural and cognitive links between actors. Institutions are defined primarily as standards and rules determining actors' preferences in processes perceived as endogenous. The main assumption of sociological institutionalism is that institutions evolve through cognitive processes linked to external events. However, while these events trigger change, they are interpreted by actors who are embedded in and thus influenced by collective and individual cognitive frameworks.

Discursive institutionalism

Finally, a fourth approach can be added to the three forms of institutionalism discussed, which has been summarized by Vivien Schmidt as discursive institutionalism (Schmidt 2008. For first conceptualizations see Fairclough 1992; Peters 2005). Discursive institutionalism refers both to sociological institutionalism and constructivism, investigating changes of paradigm and reference sets of public policies through ideas – with ideas conceived of as the main variable (Blyth 1997; Hay 2001; Hay and Rosamond 2002; Schmidt 2004).

Put simply, discursive institutionalism is based on four tenets. First, it considers ideas and discourses as central variables of research. These elements are thought to be the central elements that influence policy as well as political outcomes and must be studied primarily, and not only as a marginal or secondary factor mentioned in passing. Secondly, discursive institutionalism perceives ideas and discourses in their general context. This is very similar to constructivist research, which insists on the contextualization of variables (Chapter 7). Discourses do not have the same meaning and the same reception in all sectoral contexts. This is even more precise in the third element put forward by Schmidt: ideas refer to different meanings (i.e. sovereignty or environmental protection) specifically in different national contexts. For instance, the influence of Greenpeace on politics is extremely different in France and Germany. In the first case, the association's influence is low, in the second the association's proximity with the Green Party and the relative importance this party has in politics allows for environmental ideas to be more influential and to be taken more seriously than in France. Fourthly, the discursive institutionalism draws out the dynamic nature of the change analysed, which, according to its supporters, distinguishes it from the other forms of institutionalism that adopt a more static viewpoint.

These four tenets indicate the two central variables in discursive institutionalism: ideas and discourses. These are defined in precise terms. While ideas as a factor of change emerged in the early 1990s in the international relations literature (Goldstein and Keohane 1993), they are differentiated by discursive institutionalists on at least three levels (Schmidt 2008). The first level refers to ideas in specific public policies and, more particularly, solutions to problems raised by political and administrative decision-makers. Here, the use of ideas is rather micro-sociological and concerns specific issues.

The second level concerns ideas upon which general political programmes are based. In this context, ideas can be seen as paradigms reflecting the organizational principles that guide policy. The literature refers to these ideas via the notion of *référentiel* (Muller and Jobert 1987) or the notion of programmatic beliefs (Berman 1998).

The third and last level concerns common ideologies or, indeed, the deep core (Sabatier and Henkins-Smith 1993) and reflects a world-view (*Weltanschauung*) shared by a particular set of actors. Each of the three levels contains two types of ideas: *cognitive* and *normative*. While cognitive ideas explain the beliefs on which public policies are based, emphasizing the interest of agents and the need for action, normative ideas are the mechanisms that justify policies; they attach values to political action. However, even those ideas so clearly identified as mechanisms of political change require the existence of a vehicle that can be observed. It is here that discursive institutionalists refer to discourse as an instrument of change. In this logic it is important to focus on the content of ideas and the interactive process which brings them to a head: from the emergence of ideas, through their dissemination and finally their legitimization.

Discourses, the second element, are 'carriers of ideas'. They can be divided into two types: *coordinative* and *communicative*. Coordinative discourse takes place between a set of actors such as epistemic communities, advocacy coalitions or even mediators. This type of discourse can be found in the context of bargaining and negotiation processes involving European institutions, member states and non-state actors behind closed doors. Communicative discourse, on the other hand, is delivered to the public through communicative action. According to this approach, institutions are themselves tantamount to discourses; these discourses carry ideas. Discourses are not merely boxes in which ideas and interests of actors are embedded without being transformed, as argued by sociological institutionalists. At the EU level, the European Commission has attempted increasingly to build communicative discourses in its coordinative discourses, as a way of legitimizing its policies and reforms ever since claims of a 'democratic deficit' in the EU began to emerge in the early 1990s (Fouilleux 2004). For example, while the German and French capacity to reform their telecommunications policy was enforced by discourses that directly referred to EU institutional requirements, the reform of French immigration policy did not refer to European pressures, but was very much based on French internal political debates (Thatcher 2004; Geddes and Guiraudon 2004).

The problem that this institutionalist approach faces is to determine whether discourse really can be the independent variable. As with sociological institutionalism, establishing unidirectional causal links between different phenomena is extremely difficult. Discursive institutionalists therefore insist more on the existence of correlations between variables. Vivien Schmidt and Claudio Radaelli (Schmidt and Radaelli 2004) identify five factors that enable scholars to establish such correlations: the relative force of the cognitive argument; the interpretation of an argument at a given point in time; the appropriateness of information upon which the argument is based; the relevance or applicability of recommendations; and, finally, coherence and consistency of the discourse.

At the same time, one of the difficulties is to identify the carriers of these discourses and to measure their influence in a specific context. Discursive institutionalists agree that discourses do not exist independently of the agents who 'carry' them. Thus it is crucial, in adopting discursive institutionalism, to identify the actors who carry this discourse and to contextualize the latter in order to understand the influence the discourse has on policy outcomes. This brings discursive institutionalism close to actor-centred approaches (see Chapter 7, actor-centred constructivism).

Hence, discursive institutionalism, although considered by some as a subfield of sociological institutionalism (Peters 2005), is based on a number of tenets common to sociological and historical institutionalism. However, it seems less determined by the rationality of actors; instead it is ideas that allow us to explain why transformations take place (McNamara 1998; Parsons 2002; Schmidt 2002; Berman 2006).

Table 4.2 *The four neo-institutionalisms*

Perspectives	Main assumptions	Authors
Institutionalism	'Institutions matter'	Evans, Rueschemeyer and Skocpol 1985 March and Olsen 1984, 1989 North 1990
Rational choice institutionalism	Principal-agent model showing that, under certain circumstances, political actors delegate powers to independent bureaucratic authorities	Aspinwall and Schneider 2001 Pollack 1997, 2003 Tsebelis and Garrett 1997 Wonka and Rittberger 2011
• EU Executive	Transaction-cost model showing that institutions reduce costs that emerge in transaction between actors	
• EU agencies		Garrett 1992 Garrett and Weingast 1993 Garrett, Kelemen and Schulz 1998
• EU judiciary		Kreppel 1999
• Decision-making		Hosli, van Deemen and Widgren 2002 König 2008 Schneider, Finke and Baltz 2007 Hix, Noury and Roland 2007
• Enlargement		Schimmelfennig and Sedelmeier 2005

Historical institutionalism	Historical rules and regularities influence the incremental transformation of policies. The establishment of institutions and policies cannot be explained solely as a result of the rationally-motivated preferences of actors. These preferences certainly exist, the results are historically contingent	Thelen and Steinmo 1992 Hall and Taylor 1996 Pierson 1995, 1996, 2000, 2004 Bulmer 1993 Armstrong and Bulmer 1998 Lindner and Rittberger 2003
Sociological institutionalism	Informal institutions, identity, shared experiences, cognitive frameworks are the main objects of analysis. Change can be understood through cognitive processes that interpret reality	DiMaggio and Powell 1991 March and Olsen 1984, 1989 Fouilleux 2000 Jachtenfuchs 2001 Christiansen and Tonra 2004 Thatcher 2011
Discursive institutionalism	Discourses are 'carriers of ideas' and instruments of change. Research must focus on the content of ideas and the interactive process which brings them to a head: from the emergence of ideas through their dissemination and finally their legitimization	Schmidt 2008 Sherman 1998 Hay and Rosamond 2002 Muller and Jobert 1987

Conclusion

Since the 1990s, three institutionalisms, and more recently a fourth, discursive institutionalism, have become the dominant conceptual frameworks in the analysis of European integration. This is due to two factors in particular. First, institutionalist approaches overcome the division between neofunctionalists and intergovernmentalists in a constructive way. Instead of questioning the end goals or final destination of the integration process – i.e. the construction of supranational institutions and the transfer of loyalty versus the continued centrality of the nation-state – institutionalists are interested in processes: the modes of decision-making and institutional change. Secondly, institutionalists pursue theories and conceptual frameworks developed at the national level to analyse the state in an appropriate manner. This opens up the European studies community to comparative politics and allows us to introduce more general research questions and methods, as undertaken in political science. Furthermore, it makes it possible to apply conceptual frameworks to the EU that were originally developed for studying processes both at international and domestic levels.

However, the prominent position occupied by institutionalist approaches in EU studies also brings with it a number of drawbacks. Two are particularly significant in terms of the limitations they imply.

First, institutionalisms are designed to feature as middle-range theories. While this allows for an extremely detailed knowledge of a number of policies or actor strategies, it is rather less suited to explain and understand the European construction process as a whole. European integration studies is pluralistic but at the same time piecemeal, with scholars bringing in many different research designs. While the aim of new institutionalists was precisely to go beyond the functionalist-intergovernmentalist grand theory divide, its concentration on middle-range designs prevents it from offering tools that can help us understand the contemporary European integration process as a whole, its difficulties, its crises, its progress.

A second limit is the relative distinctiveness of the four groups of institutionalists. On the basis of the initial three 'i's developed by Hugh Heclo (1994) and taken up by Peter Hall (1997), an attempt was made recently to overcome the relatively strict distinction between rational choice institutionalists focusing on interests, historical institutionalists focusing on the historical contingency of institutions, and sociological/discursive institutionalists concentrating on ideas (Palier and Surel 2005). The authors assert that questioning which element – institutional structures, the interests of actors or ideas (three 'i's) –is most important is in itself not particularly worthwhile. They propose taking all three factors into consideration in order to analyse public policies effectively. By identifying all three in each of their case studies, they recognize the plurality of dimensions in policy analysis and the diversity of types/sources of influence on public action.

While this conceptualization has the great merit of allowing us to study the influence of formal and informal institutions horizontally, it is perhaps not yet ambitious enough. Insofar as one of the major weaknesses of institutionalism is its lack of interest in the causes and consequences of integration in general (for an exception see Olsen 2007), these approaches clearly offer a way to study integration as a set of procedures, even if they provide little or no analyses of the 'why' of integration. Rational choice institutionalism was the most ambitious in this respect, particularly in the way it conceptualized the interaction between principal and agent. The weakness of this approach, however, is its premise that rational actors seek to maximize gains, but without sufficiently taking into account the non-intentional consequences resulting from the action of an institution. Implicitly, sociological and historical approaches advance the hypotheses that integration can lead to new forms of state (*Staatlichkeit*), through path dependency or indeed the social construction of our European identity. However, these hypotheses are rarely explicit. This is even more the case with discursive institutionalism which looks more at the question of 'normativity' and how legitimation discourses are transformed through European integration. Neo-institutionalism's focus on institutional arrangements more generally has meant it has becomes distanced it from the workings of the system as a whole (as well as the logical and sociological coherence and comprehensibility of governance patterns), and as such it is not suitable for analysing the goodness of fit of a specific policy or polity, as Leca convincingly argues (Leca 2010).

In spite of these limitations, institutionalisms offer an important number of conceptual tools for analysing the forms and dynamics of European integration, all based on the central hypotheses that institutions count in a big way.

Chapter 5

Governance

While constructivist and institutionalist approaches have been applied to certain puzzles of European integration largely ignored by the 'conventional' theoretical approaches covered in the first part of this book, such as a European identity or the independent role of European institutions, research on the EU also started to investigate the general functioning of an increasingly integrated social and political system, spread over numerous levels of government and including a large set of both public and private actors.

Attempting to come to terms with the interplay of different levels of government, conceptual frameworks since the 1980s, both in political science and international relations, have increasingly referred to the notion of *governance* to describe the sociopolitical and economic systems of the EU. The SEA of 1987 and the Maastricht Treaty of 1993 introduced a denser network of legislation in all policy areas, a movement that continued until the second half of the 1990s. Policy fields such as JHA, or social and environmental policy, became increasingly integrated as competencies were transferred from the national to the European level. The linkages between private and public actors, and between the domestic and the European level, were duly reinforced. Simple causal explanatory models such as intergovernmentalism, which neglected the constant multi-level and multi-actor interplay of European day-to-day politics, were challenged by new conceptual frameworks. Governance became the key word for describing policy-making in the EU. The term is defined as a polycentric configuration, in which horizontal coordination mechanisms between social sub-systems prevail over notions of political authority and sovereignty (Bulmer 1983, 1994; Marks, Hooghe and Blanc 1996; Kohler-Koch and Eising 1999). Governments become one of many potential participants in the broader process of governance (Peters and Pierre 2009). A vast body of empirical, theoretical and political literature has sought to define governance – an academic enterprise that has unfortunately led to certain confusion as to what precisely governance itself represents. In this context, Volker Schneider correctly argues that the very vagueness of his definition in part contributes to its success (2004).

In order to clarify the different meanings and interpretations of this notion, the chapter is divided into two sections. The first section addresses the notion of governance through a 'genealogy' or family tree of governance approaches, i.e. by tracing their emergence over time. The second section presents the different applications of the study of governance at the European level, such as the regulatory state, multi-level governance, network governance and new forms of governance.

A genealogy of governance approaches

Governance approaches did not emerge through the transformation of European integration alone. Three separate, but interconnected, origins of the concept can be traced: one stemming from the literature on international relations, the second on comparative politics and, finally, studies concentrating on the political use of the term by international and supranational actors such as the World Bank, the IMF, the OECD and, indeed, the European Commission (see also Kohler-Koch and Rittberger 2007).

Table 5.1   *Three origins of governance*

International relations	Emerged through the process of economic globalization and the end of the Cold War. International systems needed to find solutions to global public policy problems. In international politics, governance entails the activities of governments as well as informal non-governmental mechanisms through which individuals and organizations act, satisfy their needs and, more importantly, achieve their objectives
Comparative politics	Negotiation and bargaining processes between public and private actors, which increasingly take place without the influence of clear-cut hierarchical structures. Two traditions: • German • Anglo-American
'Good governance'	Refers to the activities of international organizations to achieve sustainable financial management and administrative efficiency at the national level

The international realm

The notion of governance in the field of international relations must be understood as a reaction to the processes of economic globalization which, according to some authors, has led to 'societal denationalisation' (Zürn 1998). This refers to the limited capacity of national political systems to secure their political objectives due to the frontiers of social transactions increasingly taking place outside state borders. In international relations, the notion of governance emerged towards the 1990s when the debate on the end of ideologies, or indeed the end of history (the two being synonymous in certain academic disciplines), was in full swing (Fukuyama 1992).

The emphasis was on the capacity of governance systems to find solutions to problems of international public policy, contrary to more complex situations where intra-state politics muddy the waters, so to speak. Governance was considered a means of making cooperation work in what were otherwise anarchic international systems. Thus, according to a strand of international relations developed by James Rosenau and Ernst-Otto Czempiel, the notion of governance refers to an interdependent political and social system. From this perspective, international politics entails the activities of governments as well as informal non-governmental mechanisms through which individuals and organizations act, satisfy their needs and, more importantly, achieve their objectives (Rosenau and Czempiel 1992; Rosenau 1997). This conceptualization identifies forms of horizontal coordination between actors used to formulate and implement policy. In its wider interpretation at least, it does not appear to exclude the existence and even structuring role of conflict between actors, as some scholars have sometimes suggested (Smith 2004). However, the main source of conflict – the Cold War – is no more. According to Rosenau and Czempiel, these new forms of negotiation between actors at international level are no longer exclusively based on an East–West opposition, nor on ideological left–right cleavages. Rather, at the international level, the complex interplay between public and private actors, state and non-state actors, or economic, social or military interests, constitutes a system of governance searching for collective solutions to common problems. From this perspective, international relations is no longer a system where self-help prevails, as described by Hobbesian realists, but a space of governance in which public and private actors cooperate and interact.

The domestic realm

In the domestic context, the notion of governance similarly places the emphasis on negotiation and bargaining processes between public and private actors, which increasingly take place without the influence of clear-cut hierarchical structures (Mayntz 1987, 1998). Two traditions can be distinguished: a German or continental one, and a more Anglo-American one.

In Germany, the governance approach developed as a response to the critical analyses of the neo-corporatist system in place, voiced by Niklas Luhmann. The German sociologist argued that social sub-systems, which exist in fields such as employment policies, were undemocratic. He explained that through the fact that so-called representative groups – more precisely employers' federations and trade unions – negotiated the term of these policies behind closed doors, and thus under the exclusion of the wider civil society. According to Luhmann, this problem-solving governance system prevents politics from exercising its role as societal coordinator (Braun and Papadopoulos 2001). In reaction to Luhmann's, and later Offe's, critique of the German governance system, Renate Mayntz and Fritz Scharpf from the Max Planck Institute for the Study of Societies proposed a model to observe the interactions between political sub-systems without assuming a normative, or anti-democratic, bias. More specifically, they argue that negotiations in sub-systems without hierarchical influence are neither good nor bad for democracy. Influenced by research on neo-corporatism, these scholars suggest that four factors must be taken into account: regulation capacities deployed by the actors involved; the actors' power games and strategies; the resulting configurations of actors; and, finally, the institutional opportunities and constraints within which the actors operate (Marin and Mayntz 1991; Papadopoulos 1995; Giraud 2001). Taking these four factors into account, their research strategy would allow us to open up the 'black box' of relations in subsystems and to understand why these sub-systems were profoundly democratic. Thus, from their perspective, economic governance becomes a social fact, not an anti-democratic entity that must be abandoned in favour of parliamentary and participatory politics including all citizens. Sub-systems, or committees, existing in different fields of public policies, and most prominently in employment policies, bring together employers and employees under the mediating power of the state and participate in the effectiveness and the pacification of the political system.

In this vein, governance research continued to develop around two main questions: first, what allows a sub-system to self-regulate? and, secondly, why does the state have a major, almost exclusive, ability to regulate in other cases? In the theoretical framework developed by the German 'governance school', Mayntz and Scharpf argue that the legitimacy of collective actors to intervene in the regulation of a specific sector is established through their *capacity* to intervene in that sector and resolve its practical problems (Mayntz and Scharpf 1995; Giraud 2001). However, in a cooperative state, the distinction between governors and the governed or, better still, regulators and the regulated, is obscured.

This idea was developed on the one hand by Scharpf in a ground-breaking article in which he links German federalism and European governance in his efforts to explain how both systems lead to joint decision-traps owing to the multiplicity of governance levels and actors (Scharpf 1988) (see Chapter 1), and on the other, by Beate Kohler-Koch, who concentrated on the European system of interest intermediation, an analysis very much influenced by Mayntz and Scharpf's work on German neo-corporatism (Kohler-Koch and Eising1995). Kohler-Koch argued in this context that the European system of interest intermediation appears to be similar to that existing in the German system: European interest groups, both public and private, are close to administrative and political actors in Brussels and Strasbourg. These relations are framed by committee structures and networks in policies are developed and reformed.

While in Germany the debate on governance and regulation was very closely linked to theoretical developments in research on the state (Schneider 2004), US governance research was more strongly influenced by changes in public policy coordination and management. Interest in governance research can, to a large extent, be attributed to the financial crisis of the state and the development of new state-management mechanisms and instruments (Peters, Levine and Thompson 1990; Hogwood and Peters 1985). This decline in the state's regulatory capacity was accompanied by a transfer of activities from the state to the market, a change that took place particularly under the administrations of Ronald Reagan and Margaret Thatcher (Pierre and Peters 2000; Faucher-King and Le Galès 2010). This transformation is best captured by the notion of new public management (NPM). NPM refers to the idea that public

Box 5.1   *What is governance?*

The following definition captures these two origins of domestic governance particularly well: 'in governance we find ideas of behaviour, piloting and management, but without the primacy of the sovereign state. Raising the question of governance suggests an understanding of the articulation between different types of regulation in a country, in terms of both political and social integration and ability to act ... This entails re-examining relationships between civil society, the state, the market and their different combinations, where frontiers have become blurred. (Le Galès 1998)

The definition develops a clear distinction between government and governance in the sense that governance researchers no longer take an interest in government, that is, the existence of a clear hierarchy between state actions and actors, but, on the contrary, in possible bargaining mechanisms between different groups, networks and sub-systems, mechanisms that disturb and go beyond a clearly established hierarchy between actors and norms.

administrations can be governed and organized similarly to efficient structures existing in large companies: instruments of efficiency measurement, peer review and benchmarking became mechanisms for framing administrative activities. This understanding of governance has also strongly influenced European studies, as we will see later in this chapter (Rhodes 2003).

The use of 'good governance' by international organizations

Finally, the use of the notion of governance becomes normative in the context of the functions of the World Bank, the IMF, the OECD and the European Commission. Since the 1980s, the quest has been to define *good governance*, referring, through the activities of these bodies, and particularly ECOSOC's Development Committee, to sustainable financial management and administrative efficiency (see also World Bank 1997; OECD 2001). This normative definition gained support not just from those non-governmental organizations (NGOs) active in the implementation of policies decided by the World Bank, but also from donor countries. 'Benchmarking', as performance assessment in this type of literature is called, also very popular amongst the EU's political and administrative actors, was subsequently extended to include the *legitimacy* of the government in question, referring to the existence of a rule of law, a competitive market and a partnership between state agencies and non-state organizations. NGOs not only participated in the development and implementation of public policies, but also stimulated the more active participation of 'civil society' at the individual level (Weiss 2000). This interpretation of good governance was also adopted by the EU and provided the basis for the development of relationships between the EU and the ACP (African, Caribbean, and Pacific Group of States). In this context, the EU's aid and assistance to developing countries– the values that projected the EU on to the international scene – has, since the 1990s, been associated with a form of human rights diplomacy – *good governance*.

Good governance is also used with regard to internal EU policies. The 2001 publication of the *White Paper on Governance* (European Commission 2001) systemized the EU's interpretation of the notion in its official documents. It pinpoints principles such as *transparency*, broad *participation* of all actors and *efficiency* (Hooghe 2001; Føllesdal 2003). The notion of good governance was particularly linked to the debate on the EU's supposed democratic shortcomings, and even its legitimacy (Chapter 9).

European forms of governance

In light of the plethora of analytical and normative interpretations of the notion of governance, the development of governance research in the

Table 5.2　*Governance perspectives in brief*

Perspectives	Main assumptions
Regulatory governance	The European regulatory state illustrates the end of an authoritative and hierarchically structured state
Multi-level governance	European integration cannot be understood without taking into account the roles played by sub-national actors
Network governance	Analyses policy networks as the result of more-or-less stable cooperation between organizations in a complex environment
New forms of governance	Analyses the flexible nature of non-coercive processes based on evaluation instruments and guidelines established at the EU level

context of European integration studies is based on two characteristics. On the one hand, most scholars agree that the process of developing public policies seems to be characterized by the interaction of a large number of states and private actors, by the complexity of bargaining processes at several levels and, finally, by the relatively low level of formalization of decision-making procedures (Zahariadis 2008a, 2008b). Among the first to develop a framework taking these specifics into account was Simon Bulmer (1983), insisting on the linkages between domestic and EU tiers and criticizing the concentration, in most of the 1980s research, of the supranationalism vs. intergovernmentalism debate (see also Bulmer 1994). On the other hand, a more normative approach in the context of the EU system emphasizes the notion of governance as characterized by cooperation between all actors concerned and by learning (rather than competitive) processes. In line with this approach, hierarchical or subordinate relationships between actors allow for a system of exchange between equal actors all seeking a common solution to their problems (Kohler-Koch 1996, 1999).

Based on these premises, four partially overlapping conceptualizations of governance emerge in the context of European studies: the concept of the regulatory state, multi-level governance, network governance and, finally, 'new' forms of governance. Each is discussed in turn.

The regulatory state

Influenced by research undertaken on the internal transformation of the state, a specific understanding of the political nature of the EU emerged in the late 1990s: the Union was conceptualized as a 'regulatory state' (Majone 1996). While the EU plays a minor role in two of the three fundamental functions of a state – the redistribution of revenues and macroeconomic stabilization – it occupies a central place in its regulation of the market, and efforts to correct distortions. The SEA and the Maastricht Treaty have increased the number of policy sectors regulated by the supranational European level. The European regulatory state has been identified in the European literature (Majone 1996; Moran 2002) with the end of an authoritative and hierarchically structured state, and its transformation into a complex system where these structures coexist with ever increasing self-steering mechanisms.

In this sense, self-regulation means a wider use of independent regulators, or agencies staffed with experts. These agencies can be found across both public and private sectors. The aim of regulatory states is to correct market failure while redistribution and macroeconomic stabilization become secondary functions.

Independent agencies – both public and private – become key players in this context. This allows for politics to be isolated, which would appear to be particularly important in liberalizing markets and where governments often retain interests in key operators.

In this context and regarding the EU, scholars argue that 'the Union is not, and may never become, a state in the modern sense of the concept. It is at most a "regulatory state" since it exhibits some of the features of statehood only in the important but limited area of economic and social regulation. In this area, however, non-majoritarian institutions are the preferred instruments of governance anywhere' (Majone 1996: 287).

The debate on the regulatory state subsequently diverged in two different directions: one, concentrating on the democratic implications of such a development, underlined the difficulties of independent agencies remaining accountable to the general public (Dehousse 1997; Scharpf 1999; Héritier 1999; see also Chapter 8). Recently, Eberlein and Grande (2005) introduced the term 'regulatory regime' in this research. This concept identifies a dilemma for EU regulatory policy, in that, despite the increasing need for uniform EU-level rules in the internal market, the bulk of formal powers and the institutional focus of regulatory activities continue to be located at the national level. This results in a supranational regulatory gap – a gap that is partly filled by transnational regulatory networks, which offer a back door to the informal Europeanization of government regulation. These informal structures, however, also lead to unresolved problems of democratic legitimacy.

A second group of scholars focuses more prominently on the establishment, functions, promises and efficiency limits of agencies in governance structures, without explicitly questioning the democratic character of these regulatory states (Kreher and Meny 1997; Gilardi 2010; Wonka and Rittberger 2011; Chapter 4). The conceptualization of the EU as regulatory state has thus spawned a very rich literature, and further research questions on the role of the EU, its democratic structures and the link between law and politics.

Multi-level governance

Contrary to the literature on the regulatory state, which originates in the studies on the transformation of the role of the state as such, multi-level governance centres on the political system that emerges beyond the state. The concept of multi-level governance is associated primarily with studies by Liesbet Hooghe and Gary Marks (Marks, Hooghe and Blanc 1996; Marks and Hooghe 2000, 2001). Their work starts from the assumption that, in order to understand European integration, the roles played by regional actors need to be taken into account, along with the strategic, cognitive and normative variables that form and influence the European decision-making processes. In this context, researchers highlight the fact that neither member states nor European institutions are monolithic: European policies are constructed by actors of different origins who share the same objectives on a given topic (Kohler-Koch 1996; Kohler-Koch and Eising 1999).

The multi-level governance concept emerged from research undertaken on the EU's cohesion policy, and has implicit origins in federalism. In implementation, as well as in evaluation processes of cohesion policy, regional agencies, non-state actors and the central government are required to enter into a partnership process to reach a compromise which allows for the efficient functioning of this policy's instruments and mechanisms. This compromise does not exclude conflict or the asymmetric distribution of power, but means that different actors – and not just states – intervene in the long decision-making process at EU level. These actors can be found at the local, regional, national or European level.

To this extent, the EU resembles the German federal system since the decisions taken at the supranational level depend on approval from the domestic level. But while the German federal system is clearly hierarchical and overlapping, at EU level a member state can use the argument of being constrained by EU demands in order to free itself from the pressures existing at the domestic level (Grande 1996; Benz 2003). This form of horizontal and vertical interdependence (Box 6.2) was not previously conceptualized by theoretical approaches to European integration, which concentrated broadly on a trade-off between two traditional levels of inter-state relations – national and European.

Multi-level governance perspectives explain the often deliberate choice of national elites to delegate power to the supranational level and, at the same time, to the regional and local levels by the fact that they search to achieve political goals and strive to govern efficiently (Bache

Box 5.2   *Horizontal and vertical interdependence in multi-level governance*

Horizontal interdependence: Multi-level governance is based on the assumption that public and private actors are not entirely distinct actors. They are not differentiated by a hierarchy, in which public actors would politically prevail over private actors, but can be situated on the same horizontal level. Environmental policy can hereby be taken as an example: in a multi-level governance system, environmental associations, member states and European institutions such as the Commission interact and collectively develop environmental policy. The same applies for negotiations between trade unions, employer's associations and the state, in which the state is nothing more than a consensus broker, but does not impose policies unilaterally.

Vertical interdependence refers to the fact that in the European political system, interaction between actors from the local, regional, national and supranational level is needed to develop and implement policies effectively. No level alone can claim to implement European policies singlehandedly.

and Flinders 2006). This fairly functionalist approach is supplemented by a reflection on the member state's inability to refuse certain policies imposed upon it or suggested to it by EU institutions and, in particular, the European Commission. One of the oft-cited examples is the agreement of the British Prime Minister, Margaret Thatcher, to the expansion of QMV during the negotiations leading to the Maastricht Treaty of 1992. Trade-offs between various British interests led to a situation in which, the otherwise rather Eurosceptical head of government agreed to enlarge the number of areas where QMV applies (Warleigh-Lack 2006a).

Despite this fairly broad understanding of multi-level governance, the concept was widely criticized for having neglected, on the one hand, the role both of institutions (Peters and Pierre 2004) and non-state actors other than regions (Rosenau 2004), more specifically, NGOs and social movements. On the other, it is criticized for being more a descriptive notion than a conceptual framework that actually allows us to develop and test hypotheses.

Type I and Type II multi-level governance
Confronted with such criticisms, Marks and Hooghe responded in an article in 2004 (Marks and Hooghe 2004), which developed future research programmes. Contrary to the criticism raised with regard to neofunctionalism or intergovernmentalism, theories that where also challenged and reformulated in depth based on empirical developments which first questioned the theoretical assumptions and then allowed its re-emergence (see Chapters 2 and 3), the challenge here was theoretical

rather then empirical, but nevertheless led to innovation and refinement in the framework.

Defending the central notion of multi-level governance, Marks and Hooghe developed the idea that multi-level governance would be normatively superior to the monopoly of power exercised by domestic governance, both on the basis of increased efficiency and greater involvement of non-state actors. Policies resulting from such a process reflect the interests and preferences of 'civil society' better than decisions taken unilaterally by state elites.

According to the authors, multi-level governance can thus take two forms, referred to as Types I and II. Type I refers to a hierarchically structured system in which competences are clearly defined. It can be understood as a definition of government, where responsibilities and abilities are precisely explained and distinguished. Type I organizations are determined by a territory and a feeling of community. The political system is based on politics; policies taking both redistributive and regulatory forms (Marks and Hooghe 2004: 28).

Type II multi-level governance is not based on hierarchical politics, but on regulatory policies. The only means of exerting pressure is not through elections or protest but by getting up from the bargaining table and walking away ('exit'). Jurisdiction of its courts is specific and does not concern all policy areas to the same degree: the EU's Common Foreign and Security or Defence Policy, for instance, are excluded from the ECJ's jurisdiction. Participation and levels of governance are encompassing, and thus include actors from the regional, national and European level. Policy-making is not based on hierarchically distinguishable decision-making procedures, or at least not to the same degree as in governmental systems. Institutions include actors on a flexible basis: beyond core groups, different public and private actors are regularly associated. However, the we-feeling among people participating in this governance system is low, as we can see when analysing the existence or better absence of a European identity. Finally, Type II multi-level governance systems refer mostly to market construction and regulatory policies and less to redistributive policies.

The authors conclude that, whilst Type I multi-level governance can be found in the majority of EU member states, the EU itself only presents the characteristics of Type II governance. According to the authors, this form of multi-level governance is particularly well suited to explaining how groups of actors act independently of their national representatives at the European level (Marks and Hooghe 2004).

Beyond this specific understanding of multi-level governance, specialists on international governance and cooperation outside the EU have extended the debate on multi-level characteristics of various governance systems and proposed several other conceptualizations of governance: hierarchical, non-hierarchical and heterarchical (Neyer 2002; Risse

Table 5.3   *Marks and Hooghe's Type I and Type II multi-level governance*

Variables	Type I	Type II
Jurisdictional inclusiveness	General	Specific
Participation	Sectorial	Intersectoral
Levels of governance	Clearly distinguished	Encompassing, interdependent
Inclusiveness of institutions	Systemic	Varied and flexible
Feeling of belonging to an integrated system	High	Low
Preferred behaviour of actors	Votes	Exit
Political fields concerned	Politics	Market construction

2004a). The first is the notion of hierarchical control of power from a single decision centre and, in fact, constitutes a form of government; the second analyses the emergence of political management forms between public and private actors without any stable decision centre; the third requires coordination mechanisms between several decision centres and calls for vast deliberation mechanisms in order to make the EU more democratic (Joerges and Neyer 1997; Kohler-Koch and Eising 1999). In broadening its scope, it transforms governance into a form of normative production and attribution of values, which creates political authority. This form involves the creation of public policies through different forms of democratic mechanisms – derivative, procedural, normative and communicational. Governance can therefore be distinguished from government in that it characterizes relationships between a set of public and private institutions and actors, rather than the activity of a body centralizing executive authority (Balme and Chabanet 2002: 108). One of the most promising developments in this field is to see governance and government as distinct but coexisting at the EU level. While they are intertwined, the analytical distinction allows for understanding the nature of their linkages and their reciprocal influence (Héritier and Lehmkuhl 2008).

Multi-level heterarchical governance opens up a somewhat forgotten perspective in this research movement: it combines reflection on the efficiency of systems and democratic legitimacy. This normative turn in European studies, more broadly analysed in Chapter 9, goes beyond the analysis of the day-to-day policy-making found in the EU. On the contrary, the approach raises the issue of new forms of accountability generated by multi-level governance. This perspective in governance studies emphasizes the weakening of territorial state power and effectiveness, and the increase in international interdependencies that serve to undermine conventional governmental processes (see Piattoni 2010). At the same time, this democratic understanding of governance suffers several shortcomings that can be found in empirical research on this matter (Eberlein and Kerwer 2004; Benz and Papadopoulos 2006; Papadopoulos 2003, 2007). In particular, there is a lack of transparency concerning the networks of actors active within the governance system. The multi-level governance system seems to be closed to the influence of citizens. Finally, the control of networks remains in the hands of members or those close to them (Papadopoulos 2007, 2010).

Network governance

The concept of network governance in political science is similar to that of multi-level governance. However, network governance does not place multiple levels of bargaining and decision-making at the heart of its analysis, but instead focuses on interaction between different types of actors (Peterson 2009). The network approach is the result of studies focusing on the creation of public policies in a system in which more and more public and private actors are involved. Hence, the concept of networks is first and foremost a descriptive tool. The network approach is thought as a means of explaining and assessing the influence of phenomena considered to be on the rise in contemporary politics: interdependence between a greater number of different actors, sectorization and fragmentation of the state, the growth of informal regulations in official debate and management arenas, the density of relations between public and private actors and the internationalization of action contexts threatening the specificity of each model.

Origins and conceptualizations of network governance
The networks approach emerged in the USA in the 1950s. Scholars stressed the existence of regular contacts between individuals in interest groups, bureaucracies and government, thus creating a sub-government or 'intermediate-level government' inside the state (Jordan 1990). The approach developed on the grounds of a critique of the prevailing pluralist model in American political science, whereby all interest groups were considered to have equal access to decision-makers, notwithstanding the differences in the financial or social resources they might possess (Freeman 1965). The network approach argued, on the contrary, that close relationships between the executive, the parliamentary commissions of the US Congress and only some, but by no means all, interest groups were established, leading to specific, tightly linked

networks, so-called *iron triangles*. These intermediate-level govern-ments were considered as groups of individuals taking routine deci-sions in specific political areas without referring to either the government or the parliament. In this context, private interests 'capture' a governmental agency in order to defend their interests or make decisions. Private interests linked to the government at the inter-mediary level can thereby control members of the latter, rather than meeting their demands (Lowi 1969). Two traditions emerged with regard to the networks approach. While American researchers using the networks concept for their research were more concerned with the analysis of interpersonal relations, the 'European' version of the network approach looked at structural relations between groups of actors (Marsh 1998; Kickert et al. 1997; for a critical approach, Thatcher 1998). The hierarchical political system, characterized by competition between actors, was thought to evolve towards a system of cooperation between stakeholders and shared learning processes (Jordan and Schubert 1992; Kooiman 1993; Kohler-Koch 1996; Mayntz 1998; Radaelli 2008).

Networks: a continuum of relationships in EU studies
The great fluidity of actor participation in EU policies, the complexity of European and international institutions and the plethora of levels make this concept a very fertile one. In their most general sense, policy networks are the result of more-or-less stable cooperation between orga-nizations that know and recognize each other in a complex environment and which bargain, exchange resources and share norms and interests. A network comprises a group of actors who depend upon each other for resources such as information, expertise, access to decision-making and legitimation (van Waarden 1992; Marsh 1998). For example, a network in the CAP field at the EU would bring together representatives of the EU's farmers' unions, Commission officials, independent experts, consumer representatives and national civil servants from health, envi-ronmental and agricultural ministries.

Network governance approaches are based on three premises: first, these approaches assume that modern governance is non-hierarchical. Few policies are simply imposed by the authorities. Governance in networks results in relationships of interdependence between public and private actors. This idea is very helpful in order to explain the function-ing of the EU's regulatory system and, in particular, comitology, i.e. all the committees that work at EU level to prepare and implement the EU *acquis communautaire*. In parallel, it allows to account for the important role of experts in these same committees, whose participation is consid-ered to be depoliticized.

Secondly, network governance enables the disaggregation of the decision-making processes; the relationship between public and private actors varies from one sector to another. It is, therefore, not very helpful to attempt to characterize states as strong or weak, pluralist or neo-corporatist. In EU bargaining, these labels lose their relevance because negotiations bring different types of actors together – whether national, transnational, supranational, public or private, stemming from different states and thus influenced by different political cultures. The distinction between strong states and weak states clouds the complexity of these negotiations more than it helps to clarify its meaning (Atkinson and Coleman 1986).

Finally, while governments are ultimately responsible for decisions taken at the EU level, scholars of network governance argue that it is essential to take into account the vast array of actors' positions in the decision-making processes in order to understand the reasons that encourage actors to take one decision and not another. These networks of actors can modify national preferences and put new challenges on the agenda. Thus, according to policy network perspectives, conceptual frameworks such as intergovernmentalism, which base their assumptions on the idea that national preferences are the main factor for European integration processes, are mistaken.

Empirical examples of network analysis can be found in particular in the field of regional (Ansell, Parsons and Darden 1997; Bache 1998), social (Falkner 2005) and research policies (Bomberg and Peterson 2000), where the interplay between public and private actors and the establishment of different types of networks can be observed: we find national, sub-national and supranational actors as well as technocratic procedures in these specific policy fields. Peterson (2003: 16) also uses the example of the CAP to show to what extent the tools provided by the network approach explain the functioning of this specific policy (see also in particular Daugbjerg 1999). He shows that, as CAP decision-making is shared between networks of product-specialized officials responsible for managing specific markets on a day-to-day basis, and the Agriculture Council, which is one of the busiest and most insular of all versions of the Council of Ministers, the Commission and Council Secretariat together act as institutional nodes that facilitate communication and exchange within a broader CAP policy network. Furthermore, although the CAP is one of the EU's truly 'common' policies (similar to EU's external trade policy), it is in fact highly decentralized, with considerable discretion held by national agricultural ministries and ministers. Thus, powerful networks of experts are given autonomy to manage this specific policy. Peterson argues that this leads to the establishment of policy networks, which are subject to domination by national actors and intergovernmental bargaining. This applies even though they are configured horizontally and sometimes enjoy considerable autonomy from their national political principals. Finally, the CAP is regularly criticized by the general public and Eurosceptics, who cite its wastefulness, regressiveness and easy exploitation by corrupt transnational networks of criminals. Peterson (2003: 17) argues that 'In reality, of course, the main problem is a classic "pooled sovereignty, divided accountability" problem: national administrations, not EU institutions, are mainly responsible for spending controls and the policing of fraud.'

These empirical examples show that the analysis of day-to-day policy making in a number of public policy fields can be understood as the interaction of multiple actors, bound together by more or less tight networks. These networks shape policy outcomes insofar as they provide a stable framework in which actors interact and develop solutions to specific policy problems.

Promises and pitfalls of network analysis

Based on research enquiries such as: who has an interest in this political problem? How are these interests engaged with and organized? What is the rhythm and nature of their participation in the political process? (Richardson 1995), three dimensions of the public policy network approach are particularly pertinent in understanding the EU's political system: the disaggregation of actors, the end to the purely sequential analysis of public policies and the development of a typology of forms of networks.

The network approach puts an end to seeing the state or other actors – such as international organizations or non-state actors – as homogenous, monolithic entities, but as complex systems (ministries, administrations, directorate-generals, units, etc.). The analyses focus on the resources of national or international actors, their strategies, practices, interests, representations and the constraints weighing on them. As Mark Thatcher observes, in spite of his scepticism with regard to the network approach, the concept encourages an analysis of factors that influence relationships between (public and private) organizations and individuals, the resources of private actors and forms of interdependence between them (Thatcher 1995).

The approach also steers clear of an overly linear and sequential vision of European public policy. Although the sequential approach is a heuristically pertinent tool for analysing public policies, since it reveals the different stages of the decision-making process, it is also important to emphasize its limits. The public policy process in general and the EU's policy process in particular do not always follow a sequential logic of public action. The agenda setting, problem definition as well as negotiation processes often run in parallel, are overturned or influenced by decision-making processes at inter-governmental or 'macro' levels, which interrupt or sometimes enable decision-making at the 'micro' level. Finally, the approach offers a typology of networks, which, although not exhaustive, does allow types of actors involved in the decision-making process to be categorized.

Figure 5.1   *Network continuum*

Policy communities ◄─────────────────────────► thematic networks

Network governance scholars (Rhodes et al. 1996) differentiate networks on a continuum, which loosely ranges from highly integrated policy communities to less integrated thematic networks (Figure 5.1).

In the context of European integration studies, the network approach to governance has allowed us to conceptualize the interdependence and blurring of boundaries between public actors, i.e. national and European public officials, state representatives and Members of Parliament, and private actors, i.e. interest groups, 'civil society' and experts. These interactions, and the often informal character of the negotiations, are the central characteristics of the EU political system and its decision-making processes in particular. With regard to the last element, Thomas Christiansen, Andreas Føllesdal and Simona Piattoni (2003) opposed this form of network governance against highly codified decision-making processes in national democratic systems. They define informal governance as an interaction between networks of individual or collective actors working towards shared objectives. These networks lead to cooperation, structured relationships and public decisions through regular non-codified and non-regulated exchanges in the institutional context of the EU (Christiansen, Føllesdal and Piattoni 2003: 7).

However, one of the difficulties that remain is the impression that networks are mainly a metaphor and do not manage to develop clear hypotheses that can be used to structure research on the EU. König's (1998: 387) critiques illustrate this point:

A growing number of studies use the network concept as a metaphor describing the complexity of social and political life, but they have neither explained why private and public actors are mutually dependent, whether their dependency is restricted to the boundaries of specific subsystems and how this dependency affects public decision-making, nor generated testable hypotheses regarding the causal importance of policy networks for public decisionmaking.

Thus, the main advantages of the network approach – the disaggregation of actors, the end to the purely sequential analysis of public policies and the development of a typology of forms of networks – are also its main inconvenience. In insisting on the multiplicity of actors and their interdependency, the approach does not allow for developing testable hypotheses or establishing causalities between the behaviour of actors in networks and policy outcomes. At the same time, it insists on one of the central characteristics of the European governance system, its multiple and changing interdependencies amongst actors and the establishment of complex coalitions.

New modes of governance

In the mid-1980s, the emergence of new public management ideas at the domestic level gave rise to a body of literature on new modes of governance (Lebessis and Peterson 2000; European Commission 2001). Numerous publications emphasized the flexible nature of these non-coercive processes based on evaluation instruments and guidelines. In the 1990s these ideas were imported into European studies, both for empirical and theoretical reasons. Empirically, the Lisbon Agenda – decided upon by the Council of the EU in 2000 – called for a new form of decision-making that would not lead to enforceable EU law but to non legally enforceable forms of mutual learning. This so-called Open Method of Coordination (OMC) introduced terms such as *benchmarking*, *best practice*, *peer review* and *mainstreaming* into the policy-making process. Through collective deliberation, these instruments were meant to allow actors to agree on procedural norms, forms of regulation and shared political objectives, whilst preserving a diversity of solutions and local measures (Bruno et al. 2006; Citi and Rhodes 2007a, 2007b). The objective of these forms of governance is not to create legally binding norms with which all member states must comply, but to allow states to maintain their national specificities whilst ensuring they remain compatible with the political and economic priorities of the EU. Thus, the emphasis is not on regulations and directives, but on the use of 'soft law'. Soft law is a norm, which requires voluntary acceptance and cannot be enforced by a court. The new forms of governance are negotiated between public and private actors at different levels of the decision-making process, while actual political choice is left to the member states (Jordan and Schout 2006) a procedure more commonly known as 'subsidiarity'. More generally these procedures abandon command and control mechanisms for public intervention in favour of 'softer' forms of intervention (Mörth 2005).

These systems are very much efficiency-oriented. Instead of regulating sectors through legally binding rules, new modes of governance aim to introduce instruments that delegate the responsibility of effective implementation to concerned actors. The main factor of change here is learning based on non-coercive instruments (see also Chapter 6; Héritier and Lehmkuhl 2008; Dehousse 2011).

Initially focused on the OMC introduced by the Lisbon Strategy for growth and employment, this set of works highlights voluntary agreements, standards, labels and diversified financial and fiscal incentives (Dehousse 2004a; Borrás and Jacobsson 2004; Borrás 2009; Borrás and Conzelman 2007). The scope was broadened to include major economic and employment policy guidelines and objectives in other political domains. However, norms developed in this way are not directly applicable or transposable to domestic law. The national authorities simply agree to take them into account when forming their own policies.

As we have seen in other theoretical areas, these empirical developments also led to a number of conceptual studies on soft governance and/or new modes of governance in EU studies. The literature can be resumed under four headings (Citi and Rhodes 2007a, 2007b). A first

Table 5.4   *Governance perspectives*

Perspectives	Main assumptions	Authors
Regulatory governance • Normative approaches • Analytical approaches	The European regulatory state has been identified with the end of an authoritative and hierarchically structured state, and its transformation into a complex system where these structures coexist with ever increasing self-steering mechanisms	Majone 1996 Moran 2002 Dehousse 1997 Scharpf 1999 Héritier 1999 Grande 2005 Gilardi 2008 Wonka and Rittberger 2011
Multi-level governance	European integration cannot be understood without taking into account the roles played by regional actors, along with the strategic, cognitive and normative variables that form and influence the European decision-making processes	Marks et al. 1996 Marks and Hooghe 2000, 2001, 2004 Kohler-Koch and Eising1999 Piattoni 2010
Network governance	Analyses policy networks as the result of more or less stable cooperation between organizations in a complex environment that know and recognize each other and which bargain, exchange resources and share norms and interests	van Waarden 1992 Marsh 1998 Richardson 1995 Rhodes et al. 1996 Peterson 2003, 2009
New modes of governance	Analyse the flexible nature of non-coercive processes based on evaluation instruments and guidelines established at the EU level	Lebessis and Peterson 2000 Borrás and Jacobson 2004 Mörth 2005 Citi and Rhodes 2007a Borrás and Conzelman 2007 Borrás 2009 Dehousse 2011

conceptual approach seeks to explain why new modes of governance emerged, thereby linking the research to existing theories of European integration as well as institutional change (Schäfer 2004). Second, a strongly normative approach underlines the usefulness of this new method for collective learning (Sabel and Zeitlin 2003; Eberlein and Kerwer 2004; Peters and Borrás 2010). A third more empirical approach applies the concept to specific areas, and finally, a critical approach analyses the claims made on the new mode of governance as an effective and legitimate instrument of policy learning (Bruno et al. 2006; Kröger 2009). This critical approach shows the limited effectiveness of the OMC at the domestic level. Kröger (2006) in particular underlines that minimal conditions for supranational learning processes are rarely met at the domestic level, nor within the context of peer reviews. According to the author, this is due to institutional differences and the lack of political will both at the European and the national level. These scholars argue that a road map or a code of conduct, decided at the EU level, seems to have rarely any impact at all at the domestic level. Learning processes are scarce in absence of efficient control mechanisms.

New modes of governance research, in general, met with criticism, particularly by scholars who insisted on the longstanding existence of 'new' forms of governance. The roles of supranational actors such as the European Commission in the production and reformulation of public policy instruments (Dehousse 2004a, 2011), which take place outside the classical decision-making process, pose certain problems in terms of legitimacy. Finally, new modes of governance are also criticized on the grounds that they lack accountability.

Conclusion

The perspectives on European governance in the 1990s brought new research agendas into European integration studies. Questions interested in the nature and behaviour of actors in the context of day-to-day European policy-making finally came centre-stage. While the intergovernmental theory of integration was revived by Moravcsik (Chapter 3), one of the key elements to understanding the mainstreaming of European integration studies was the European governance approach. As discussed here, this new concept brought both contributions and limitations (Jachtenfuchs 2001).

First, the mainstreaming of European integration by governance approaches considerably broadened the scope of analysis and united researchers working on other political science subjects; in particular, political sociology, comparative politics, public policy and political theory. Thus, European integration became one of the many sub-disciplines of political science. It emphasized horizontal and vertical interdependencies and the complexity of decision-making procedures, thus contradicting the rational choice institutionalist approach, which departs from the assumption that actors defend their interests consistently. Interdependencies, however, both horizontal and vertical, question this interest linearity, and show that the number of actors as well as their interests may change in the process of policy-making.

At the same time, and for precisely the same reasons, at least two limits appear. First, governance approaches did not increase the capacity of theoretical construction in EU studies. Thus, it is almost impossible to distinguish between dependent and independent variables in governance research (Kassim 1994; König 1998). Governance approaches often are more of a descriptive tool than a theoretical framework allowing rigorous structuring of empirical analysis. Second, the way governance is conceptualized makes the approach often oblivious for power struggles between actors. Actors generally have interests and voice demands in negotiations and debates. These demands and interests are a consequence of a number of factors: their position in the system, their financial or social resources, the context in which they act. The insistence on the interdependence between these actors as well as between variables gives the impression that governance scholars place all of these actors on the same level. However, state actors do not have the same resources at their disposal as do interest groups, or regions. Both their symbolic and material resources are much higher and can therefore be more influential than those of supranational and non-state actors. While this seems to be accepted in the governance literature, it is not conceptualized as such. Thus, contemporary governance research often gives the impression that solutions to policy problems emerged through deliberation and not through hard bargaining. Goetz (2008: 258) argues in the same vein that, viewed historically, 'governance does not so much indicate a shift from government as towards government, as the core institutions of the state build up capacity to deal authoritatively and hierarchically with new governing challenges'.

Nevertheless, and beyond these critiques, the chapter has shown that governance frameworks open up several avenues. In particular, they allow public policy analysis to be linked to institutionalist arguments more generally. It also helps understand actors, not as unitary entities, but as complex systems. Finally, governance approaches have helped to link policy research to the normative debate on the forms that the decision-making processes of European integration take (Jachtenfuchs and Kohler-Koch 2004). It is from this angle that the governance approach illustrates the functioning and internal dynamics of the construction of a political system *per se* at the EU level: indeed, it opened the 'black box' of the EU's decision-making processes.

Chapter 6

Europeanization and Public Policy Transfer

The concept of Europeanization seeks to understand the influence of the EU and European integration more generally on political, economic and social change within each member state. The SEA and the Maastricht Treaty spawned new research interest at the beginning of the 1990s. The deepening of European integration and the legalization of new policy areas increased the pressure at member-state level to adapt to European norms. 'Europe' seemed to be everywhere: not a single ministry or agent at the domestic level could ignore the outcome of European integration. The way cheese is produced, a cucumber grown, the hunting season organized, a footballer recruited or toys sold are influenced by EU law.

In its most restricted interpretation, Europeanization refers to transformation processes at the national level, which are dependent on European integration (Goetz and Hix 2000). Since the first scholarship in this area, this basic definition has become more complex and fullbodied. The concept enjoyed considerable success, and was taken up in increasingly diverse research projects (Exadaktylos and Radaelli 2009). Such success makes the analysis of the concept's emergence, central assumptions and applications particularly demanding. This chapter takes up the challenge, and proceeds in two steps: the first part presents the debate on Europeanization and explains its origins and developments, looking at both definition and processes. The second part analyses the competitive and complementary concept of public policy transfer.

Europeanization: definitions and processes

The wealth of Europeanization studies, exponentially, has given depth and nuance to the concept. This chapter captures the complexity of the conceptual framework by identifying three central debates: definitions of Europeanization, the policy domains in which it has been analysed, and its main findings.

Definitions

In simple terms, three conventional definitions of Europeanization can be isolated: bottom-up (uploading), top-down (downloading) and circular Europeanization.

While coming up with a suitable definition is essential in any research enquiry, it is important to note that, in the case of Europeanization, definitions actually direct us towards new research questions and puzzles. When considering the diversity of existing definitions, the unsurprising conclusion is that these are not incontestable truths, but a set of contested discourses and narratives about the degree of influence that the EU exercises over national political change. These definitions have in turn launched new research programmes and academic debates.

From uploading to downloading

Until the end of the 1990s, national policies, rather than European policies or institutions, played the crucial role of independent variables in the majority of European studies on the European integration process. This means that scholars used to analyse national positions and interdependencies between domestic and European actors to explain how European policies and institutional patterns evolved at the EU level. This was sometimes labelled Europeanization, later understood as the 'uploading' perspective of this process. Questions were, for instance: is delegation of competencies determined by governmental preferences, which are dependent upon the interests of transnational actors? Or is the European institutional architecture the result of preferences of supranational agents? Little research has concentrated on the impact of European integration on national systems or, in other words, 'how delegation of competences to the Community level influences political results in the national arena' (Goetz and Hix 2000: 3–4).

Research on the influence of European integration on the domestic realm began, slowly but surely, in the mid-1990s. One of the earliest definitions of 'Europeanization' is by Robert Ladrech, who sees Europeanization as 'an incremental process reorienting the direction and shape of politics to the degree that EC political and economic dynamics become part of the organizational logic of national politics and policy-making' (Ladrech 1994: 69, 2010). Here European integration is considered as a causal factor, incrementally transforming national public policies. European integration becomes the explanatory factor for the changes observed in the functioning of national public policies. In other words, European integration is considered as the independent variable which influences the transformation of policies, defined as the result of European integration or the dependent variable (Goetz and Hix 2000).

Thomas Risse, Maria Green Cowles and James Caporaso define Europeanization in a more encompassing manner as *'the emergence and development at the European level of distinct structures of governance,* that is of political, legal and social institutions associated with political problem-solving that formalize interactions among the actors and of policy networks specializing in the creation of authoritative European rules' (Risse, Green Cowles and Caporaso 2001a: 3; original emphasis). This definition adds complexity because Europeanization becomes both the dependent and the independent variable: the process of European integration or European governance, on the one hand, and the influence this process exerts at the domestic level, on the other. In this, the definition is somewhat ambivalent and integrates both European integration, a phenomenon that scholars call 'uploading', and Europeanization, referred to as a 'downloading' process.

Circular Europeanization
This problem was tackled head-on by Claudio Radaelli, who argued that it is impossible to think about Europeanization without taking into account the processes that led to the establishment of those rules at the European level in the first place. He thus defines Europeanization as a 'processes of (a) construction (b) diffusion and (c) institutionalization of formal and informal rules, procedures, policy paradigms, styles, "ways of doing things" and shared beliefs and norms which are first defined and consolidated in the making of EU public policy and politics and then incorporated in the logic of domestic discourse, identities, political structures and public policies' (Radaelli 2000: 4). This multi-factor definition helps pinpoint the different levels, actors and instruments of change. It clearly indicates that Europeanization is not a linear process but a circular one, which also includes European integration and the process's influence at national level, which, in turn, influences European integration anew. This is also the perspective of Bruno Palier and Yves Surel's, who see in 'Europeanization all institutional, strategic and normative institutional adjustment processes induced by European integration' (Palier and Surel 2007: 39). Empirical studies in this context start generally with an analysis of the process that led to the establishment of a specific norm or rule at the European level, study the interaction and power games amongst concerned actors (or stakeholders) and then look at how this rule is incorporated in the domestic political context.

To summarize, therefore, there are three types of Europeanization (Börzel and Risse 2000): a first traditional – and today outdated – understanding of Europeanization, emphasizing the emergence of distinctly European governance structures, labelled as 'uploading' (Risse, Green Cowles and Caporaso 2001a); a second focusing more on the progressive integration of the European dimension in national practices (Ladrech 1994; Wessels and Rometsch 1996; Börzel 1999), named downloading;

Table 6.1   *Definitions of Europeanization*

Perspectives	Definitions
• Top-down	European integration is considered as a causal factor, incrementally transforming domestic public policies
• Circular	Europeanization is not a linear process but a circular one, which also includes European integration and the process's influence at national level, which, in turn, influences European integration anew

and a third focusing on the interaction between the two levels (circular Europeanization) (Radaelli 2001; Palier and Surel 2007; Saurugger and Radaelli 2008). The last two definitions are not necessarily contradictory, to the extent that in all two cases the idea is to measure the effect of European integration on the organization of structures at domestic level. At the same time, these multiple definitions can lead to contradictory use and to research programmes where the concept is too vast to be academically useful (Exadaktylos and Radaelli 2009, 2012). Given that the first definition refers to a relatively outdated understanding of Europeanization, the chapter will concentrate exclusively on the last two definitions.

Definitions: advantages and limits

The downloading approach is part of the three-phase model developed by Risse et al. (2001) whereby: European integration → pressure → adaptation. Here, the existence of European norms is necessary to induce change at the domestic level. The second research step is the measurement of the compatibility between European and national norms. This measurement is crucial. Its result is referred to in the literature as 'goodness of fit', 'fit' or 'misfit'. More specifically, the greater the compatibility – where the norms, structures or institutions at national level most resemble those at European level – the easier it is for the EU to influence the national level. A third phase of this research model is the analysis of domestic institutions. Here scholars analyse how national institutions mediate the pressure exerted by the European level. This domestic filter strongly influences the extent to which the domestic level is transformed (Héritier et al. 2001). This sequencing can be summarized in the following way (Dyson and Goetz 2003): the first element to consider when analysing Europeanization is the extent to which the power of the member states – understood as the subjects of European integration – determines the course of the integration project and the shape of European public policies. The second element refers to the constraints in the domestic political arena exercised by European integration on member states. Finally, the third element relates to domestic opposition to European integration, i.e. to the EU in general (i.e. Euroscepticism), but also to the sectoral norms and rules of European integration (see also Bache and Jordan 2006).

Conversely, the circular logic (Figure 6.2) shows how, at any point in time, the national and European levels interact. This interdependence constantly influences public policies as well as political and constitutional structures (polity and politics) at the domestic level. Distinguishing clearly between the dependent and independent variable becomes difficult. While this methodological ambiguity creates problems for research into causality, at the same time it allows us to be more accurate empirically, in a context where informal negotiations are being conducted at so many levels and often at the same time. In a political system where public and private actors, such as interest groups or NGOs, interact and are both adapting to and rejecting European pressures, an interdependence model helps to structure research more efficiently than a unidirectional model or one seeking to establish linear causality.

This understanding of Europeanization offers two distinct advantages: on the one hand, it allows for conceptualizing real interdependence, to the extent that analyses are not limited to the study of the effects of Europeanization, but tend to 'look at substantial developments at national level and at European level at the same time' (Palier and Surel 2007: 40). What is sought is an understanding of the institutionalization that occurs between the European and domestic levels. On the other hand, this definition allows for Europeanization research to help in the continued mainstreaming of European studies using comparative policy and public policy tools.

Thus, contrary to the downloading literature of the Europeanization, which considers structures and domestic institutions as filters, this conceptualization stresses the fact that the relationship between European integration and the Europeanization of policies, institutions, actors, ideas and national discourses is more dialectic than simply unidirectional. This reflects a progression from the sequential causal model (Figure 6.1) to an interdependence model (Figure 6.2), which is, however, much more difficult to operationalize.

Figure 6.1 *Risse, Green Cowles and Caporaso's (2001a) sequential causality*

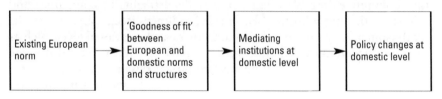

Figure 6.2   *Circular Europeanization*

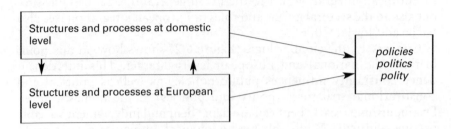

Areas of Europeanization

The question now is: what can be Europeanized? While contemporary Europeanization studies now look at every aspect of the state – policies, politics and polity, until recently, the majority of studies focused in particular on public policies and thus constitute the examples this chapter draws upon (e.g. Risse et al. 2001a; Featherstone and Radaelli 2003; Graziano and Vinck 2007). The Europeanization of politics and polities – that is, political systems, constitutional values or legal systems as a whole – have, with some exceptions, only more recently become research objects.

Politics
Politics refers to the study of social relations involving authority or power, and concentrates on the state and its executive, parliamentary or judicial system, as well as its public and private actors, and, more broadly, frameworks of thought structuring political processes at the national level. Europeanization in this field can take several forms. While in principle it affects all the elements of politics, i.e. actors, resources and instruments, it also influences the style or way in which the political game is played. The effects of Europeanization can take a direct or an indirect form. Direct effects include the creation of new structures, such as the EMU or, indeed, the ECJ. The establishment of these institutions at the European level led to a direct and immediate transformation of the domestic level. Indirect effects, according to Hix and Goetz (2000), distinguish between three different forms. First, European integration may strengthen existing processes by, for example, delegating responsibility to regional or local authorities. Secondly, it may act as a catalyst by creating new institutional forms at the domestic level, such as parliamentary committees for EU affairs or new departments in companies and ministries dealing with the EU. Finally, indirect effects can refer to the establishment of new opportunity structures at the national level, such as opening up venues for Eurosceptic parties. With regard to the Europeanization of political parties, empirical research has shown, for example, that European integration has had a significant effect on

national party elites (Ladrech 1994, 2010; Poguntke et al. 2007). Political cleavages have been clearly influenced by both European integration (pro-Europeans and Eurosceptics) but also, more largely, by globalization (the losers and winners of the process) (Kriesi et al. 2008; for a very good overview see Leconte 2010). Two groups of authors are generally associated with the analysis of Euroscepticism: Aleks Szczerbiak and Paul Taggart, and Petr Kopecky and Cas Mudde. Szczerbiak and Taggart differentiate between hard and soft Euroscepticism (2002). Hard Euroscepticism is a principled opposition to the EU and European integration, which takes the form of a demand to withdraw from EU membership. Soft Euroscepticism does not refer to a principled objection to European integration, but instead concerns specific policy areas, which are criticized. Kopecky and Mudde (2002) analyse the negative influence of European integration on European voters' behaviour in a larger sense as one of four ideal types. They differentiate between orientations towards the EU as current embodiment of the integration process (EU-optimists/EU-pessimists) and towards the general ideas of European integration (Europhiles/Europhobes).

Polity
Polity refers to the form or constitution of a politically organized unit. Empirical studies concentrating on the Europeanization of a polity thus concentrate on constitutional change, or more generally on the transformation of democracy at the national level (Schmidt 2006). This strand of Europeanization research illustrates particularly well that European integration does not only influence formal structures, but exerts influence on informal elements such as norms, values and dominant discourses within a member state. European integration can thus alter the legitimization of domestic policies, or even modify citizens' perceptions of a political controversy. This is the object of a number of studies carried out in discursive institutionalism (Chapter 4) and constructivist (Chapter 7) perspectives.

Sources of Europeanization

As we have seen above, the starting point for most Europeanization studies is, more often than not, attached to the common assumption of 'EU constraints'. The creation of rules and legal standards at European level has direct and indirect effects at the domestic level owing to the primacy of EU law over national legislation. In this regard, the constraint remains fairly formal and explicit. Sanctions applied in the case of member states or national actors failing to respect constraints have been analysed by numerous studies, and a typology of different states' adaptation levels established (Falkner et al. 2005).

Compliance with EU law

More generally, however, research into compliance and, specifically, non-compliance – effectively an expression of Euroscepticism by the back door (Leconte 2010) – started with the analysis of convergence between EU laws and their implementation at the national level. European directives and regulations were initially considered to be relatively apolitical, and the efficiency of implementation was measured in the same way that one would measure the efficiency of national administrative services: the quicker the legislative procedures, the more efficient the implementation of EU law. After a first group of studies emphasized, be it more or less implicitly, the convergence of different European national systems through European law, Europeanization and policy transfer studies began to show how differentiated the implementation of EU law is at the national level (for an overview of this research see Falkner et al. 2005: 14–17; Treib 2008). This differentiation becomes a dependent variable from the moment scholars consider the various national mediation structures or the differential match between EU and national-level regulations (Risse et al. 2001b). In this context, studies start from the assumption that the degree of convergence between a European law and the corresponding national policy depends on the degree to which the national political structures 'fit' the European demands. The more these structures (understood as historical institutional, economic, social, ideological or cultural mechanisms providing order) are similar to those existing at the national level, the easier adaptation will be. A major offshoot of the compliance literature has focused on the impact of the EU on the candidate and new member countries of Central, Eastern and Southern Europe (e.g. Dakowska 2003; Schimmelfennig and Sedelmeier 2005; Vachudova 2008; Sedelmeier and Epstein 2008; Schimmelfennig 2012; for a rational choice perspective, see Chapter 4). Europeanization of these states is measured by the degree of compliance with EU law, or the *acquis communautaire*. Compliance with EU law is the condition for accession of candidate countries. Conditionality refers to the fact that candidate countries must integrate the so-called *acquis communautaire* into their domestic law, to be allowed to join the EU.

However, the more the domestic and the EU level differ, the more difficult adaptation and change become. By the end of the 1990s, the concept of 'misfit' (or 'mismatch hypothesis') had paved the way for considerable research into resistance and non-compliance.

Non-compliance studies

A first group of studies concentrated on the evolution of the EU Commission's implementation policies (Börzel 2001). Here the studies on infringement procedures initiated by the Commission are central. In cases of member-state non-compliance, the Commission can initiate an infringement procedure with a letter of formal notice, which can be followed up by a reasoned opinion, a transferral to the ECJ and finally a ruling by the ECJ (art 226 ECT/art 258 TFEU (Treaty on the Functioning of the European Union). If the member state does not react to the ruling, a second infringement procedure can be initiated and financial sanctions imposed (art. 228 ECT/art.260 TFEU). Recently, studies in this area have become extremely systematic, testing a large number of data with routine research questions (number of veto players, degree of administrative capacity).

The most systematic research into the issue of compliance with EU law has arguably been conducted by three core research teams, dominated by German and Austrian scholars: one led by Gerda Falkner (Falkner et al. 2005, 2007, 2008), a second by Tanja Börzel (Börzel et al. 2010) and a third by Thomas König (König and Luetgert 2009). These teams have concentrated on three different EU directive databases, because directives enable us to observe the ease or difficulty of implementing EU law, given that directives must be incorporated into national law, whereas regulations are directly applicable at the national level and therefore do not offer a basis of observation about compliance processes. The studies examine the quantitative reasons for non-compliance and link Commission data to institutional aspects of legislative and administrative structures in the member states.

Falkner and her team argue that three elements are at least partially necessary for a state to be able to implement EU law successfully: administrative capacity, capacity to exert pressure, and the availability of information. Two phenomena, however, may lead to non-implementation: inertia (a paralysed implementation structure linked to an absence of societal activism) and stalemate (a situation of active opposition and the existence of strong veto points). Together these elements offer a systematic typology for causes of non-compliance. In line with Falkner et al.'s typology, these can be either intentional or unintentional.

Among the hypotheses explicitly rejected because they do not enable a causal relationship to be established is the misfit/mismatch hypothesis. Falkner *et al.* argue that they have found no correlation between different national and EU level normative frames and the speed or 'completeness' of compliance at the national level. The authors developed (Falkner et al. 2005, 2007) a rather problematic typology, differentiating between the worlds of *law observance, transposition neglect, domestic politics* and *dead letters*. Taking these multiple variables into account arguably helps the researcher focus more clearly and in greater detail on the procedures leading to compliance or non-compliance at the national level (see also Mastenbroek 2005; Versluis 2007).

The quantitative study undertaken by Börzel and her team (2010) was empirically based on a large quantitative dataset. It consisted of over six thousand official infringement procedures between 1978 and 1999,

Box 6.1   *Falkner et al.'s variables explaining non-compliance*

- 'Agency loss' refers to a phenomenon whereby national elites working in Brussels and Strasbourg have lost their understanding of and the political links with the national level. The higher agency loss in the decision-making phase, the higher non-compliance with EU law in the implementation phase at the domestic level
- 'Insufficient administrative resources' refers to the fact that poor administrative resources lead to inefficient compliance with EU law
- 'Parties matter'. This variable refers to the degree of politicization at the domestic level. The higher the politicization, the higher the level of opposition at the implementation phase at the domestic level. The 'parties matter' variable seems to be the most promising one in non-compliance research, and, in particular, in terms of identifying mechanisms that trigger resistance
- The central hypothesis with the strongest explanatory power according to Falkner et al. is the 'domestic issue linkage variable'. This variable refers to the phenomena in which the transposition of European norms is often linked to other political processes at the domestic level. In the majority of cases, these linkages lead to a delay in transposition

which start when the Commission issues a reasoned opinion and end with a ruling of the ECJ, after which the Commission can open new proceedings (which may lead to financial penalties if the member states still refuse to comply). In this context member-state compliance is a function of both power and capacity. Politically powerful members are most likely to violate European law, while the best compliers are small countries with highly efficient bureaucracies. Poor administrative capacities also tend to limit the degree of compliance in powerful member states. Thus, given the bureaucratic inefficiency and corruption reigning in Italy and France, compliance with EU law is very poor in these countries.

Contrary to Falkner et al., Börzel and her team start by developing a number of hypotheses that stem from three different conceptual approaches (see also Tallberg 2002b for a similar attempt): realists/power approaches (states do not comply when costs are too high), management theories/capacity approaches (states insist on capacity building) and, finally social constructivist/legitimacy approaches. Constructivists argue that the consequences of non-compliance – be they the naming-and shaming attitudes of the European Commission, ECJ judgements or financial penalties, do have an impact even if they create publicity and may foster domestic societal resistance (see Panke 2007).

Through a quantitative research design the authors come to the preliminary conclusion that an optimal combination of management and power can secure the best result, i.e. the highest level of compliance (see also Tallberg 2002b). This conclusion is also underlined in Treib's review article (2008) in which he argues that these two variables seem to be commonly accepted by implementation research.

Finally, the last study analyses failure and delay in transposing EC directives from 1986 to 2002. König and Luetgert's (2009) research is based on some 1600 directives in 15 member states across all policy sectors. This research design aims to reduce potential selection bias associated with studies on specific policy sectors, countries or national implementation measures. The study shows that notification failure and delayed compliance are more likely when three factors are present: first, a high level of conflict between member states during the EU legislative process; second, high levels of complexity linked to an increased use of parliamentary legislation; and third, the existence of more federalist and pluralist structures at the domestic level which increase the number of veto players in the implementation phase.

Limits of compliance studies

Although such research is not really aimed at describing simple passive public policy adjustments, the studies were criticized (with the exception of some by Falkner et al. (2005)) for neglecting the important roles played by individual and collective actors in applying EU norms. It is here that the concept of 'uses' of Europeanization might be able to overcome these limits, at least partially. The concept emphasizes the fact that Europeanization is an evolving and complex process. The researcher needs to dwell on the means and resources available to national and European actors in order to implement, or more generally, 'translate' European norms into domestic practice. While the current debate pinpoints structural elements or institutional pressures, it does so without specifying how they operate and what mechanisms they adopt in order to bring about change (Jacquot and Woll, 2004a, 2008, 2010). In their usage-based approach, Sophie Jacquot and Cornelia Woll emphasize two dimensions of Europeanization: first, the role of actors in the practical translation of the effects of integration and, secondly, the qualification of reasons to account for actors' actions – or more specifically, the interaction between the micro-level of the actor and the macro-level of institutions. The authors argue that actors can 'choose' and 'learn' free from institutional pressures, but that any social action within the European integration process also requires an understanding of the environment and the context. To be able to act, actors need to be able to interpret European institutions themselves and comprehend/cope with the pressures that those institutions bring to bear on them.

Beyond non-compliance: using European integration strategically

This sociological approach implies looking more closely at the role of actors as they interact, and recognizing the importance of their mediation. A sociological lens is required here because we are analysing how the actor and his interactive behaviour are constructed. Through their actions, individuals constitute the dynamics of adaptation, be it from a national context to a European context, and vice versa, i.e. they 'drive' Europeanization. More specifically, the idea is to study how actors manage to translate their social positioning (their institutional situation, interests, world-view) and the structures that frame their practices into power and influence.

Of course, usage supposes voluntary action. Whatever the nature of opportunity (political, institutional, symbolic, financial), actors must seize it and transform it into political practice. What makes this approach particularly interesting for the study of Europeanization is the observation that there can be conscious and deliberate action without the initial and final objective being identical, and without the final effects automatically being checked and controlled.

Thus, during the process, actors can be seen to-ing and fro-ing between the European and local, sectoral or institutional levels upon which they act or seek to act. Using the EU or European integration, however strategic it might seem initially, results in cognitive and normative adaptation in the medium-term, which, in turn, affects the actor behaviour and his/her social positioning in the longer term.

Three types of usage can be distinguished. First strategic usage, comprising the most commonly studied examples: interest groups and social movements usage employs both political and financial opportunities to sidestep the national level. This allows actors to advance their claims through alternative channels and to draw their governments into a two-level game. Secondly, cognitive usage is part of an interpretation and persuasion framework where each social fact needs to be interpreted in order to become an element of political debate. Finally, legitimization usage is where actors use EU politics as elements to legitimize or delegitimize political decisions at the domestic level.

Table 6.2   *Characteristics of types of usages (Jacquot and Woll 2004a: 23)*

	Elements used	Types of actors	Strategies
Strategic use	• Institutions • Instruments • Financing	• Institutional actors	• Bargaining
Cognitive usage	• Ideas • Cognitive frames	• Political entrepreneurs • Advocacy coalitions networks	• Argumention • Framing of political actions
Legitimation usage	• Public space • Discursive references	• Political representatives	• Justification • Deliberation

Scholars working with this approach have underlined that in order to make this research protocol operational, a longitudinal method must be applied, i.e. by conducting analysis over a long period.

The results of Europeanization

Europeanization leads to diverse changes at the domestic levels. Four possible results of these processes have been identified (Goetz and Hix 2000; Héritier et al. 2001; Featherstone and Radaelli 2003; Börzel and Risse 2000, 2003): *absorption, adaptation, transformation* and *inertia*. With regard to absorption, member states incorporate European policies and ideas and readjust their institutions accordingly. In adaptation processes, member states adapt their policies, processes, discourses and institutions without modifying their essential characteristics. Europeanization can also transform national policies when national actors replace policies, processes, institutions and discourses with new and substantially different ones. Finally, inertia refers to a situation where no change takes place. Paradoxically, this phenomenon is the least analysed in Europeanization studies, despite its apparent urgency, particularly in the light of citizens' resistance and lack of interest in their national representatives advocating greater integration or asking for increasing financial solidarity, a process that goes far beyond the phenomenon generally studied under the heading of Euroscepticism. While Euroscepticism is mostly based on large-scale surveys of citizens or parties, it appears from the results that resistance to European integration comes in the form of both individual and collective opposition to specific European policies, and less so to European integration in general.

The common thread running through many empirical studies on Europeanization in different research areas – public policies, national administrations, discourses (Schmidt 2001) and national actors, to name but a few – suggests that actors and national institutions play a filtering role in the influence exercised by European integration over political change.

Recognizing these different degrees of pressure stemming from the European level does not necessarily help us predict the result of norm implementation. Most case studies produce divergent rather than convergent responses. Thus, instead of identifying homogenization between member states' systems and policies, empirical studies have shown the importance of the past acting as a filter on domestic change. For instance, the structure of the energy sector is different in France and the UK, a difference based on the historical development of the policy area in these two countries. This emphasis on national and institutional historical landscape reflects an institutionalist-type analysis and, more precisely, the notion of *path dependency* as developed by Pierson (see Chapter 4) (Pierson 1996). More specifically, research on

Europeanization identifies five factors that condition the adaptation of national structures to European pressures: veto points, the existence of mediating institutions, political and organizational cultures, the reorganization of power relationships at the national level and, finally, learning processes. Thus, convergence can, at best, be partial. In other words, national political systems and the power relationships characterizing them are not fundamentally changed by Europeanization.

Conceptualizing in these terms has, however, remained largely focused on processes resulting from European decisions. The danger of this approach is to consider that all transformations observed at the national level are influenced by EU processes. It is here that the concept of public policy transfer might offer further avenues for investigation.

Enlarging the concept of Europeanization: towards policy transfer

One of the problems of the concept of Europeanization – and certainly not the most trivial – is that is does take European processes systematically as point of departure for changes at the domestic level. However, globalization, international organizations, state reform and/or diffusion of other state models also exert influence upon a political system.

How can we make sure that changes at the domestic level of European member states are not systematically perceived as being induced by European level developments? Several authors (Dolowitz and Marsh 2000; Radaelli 2000; Bulmer and Padgett 2004; Dolowitz 2006; Saurugger and Surel 2006; Börzel and Risse 2012) have addressed this puzzle and sought to reconcile the concepts of Europeanization and policy transfer studies. Despite the dangerous lure of concept-stretching, cross-referencing Europeanization and public policy transfer brings a comparative perspective to the analysis of transformations at national level, not as a linear dissemination of European norms, but as a complex series of processes of exchange and transaction determined by institutional and political constraints.

This idea has appeared in several studies on policy diffusion (Gilardi 2010; Gilardi and Mesenguer 2009; Shipan and Volden 2008; Marsh and Sherman 2009), and particularly in analytical proposals applied to the American system, comparative politics and indeed international relations (Graham, Volden and Shipan 2008), analysing the changes of associated public action in a given – generally national – context, with the more or less direct influence of other public policies carried out elsewhere.

Analysing policy transfer is particularly interesting during a period marked by globalization, the heightened interdependence of national economies and the increasing role of supranational organizations and institutions. Hence, the notion of policy transfer seems suitable for translating these dynamics as it focuses attention on the 'process through which knowledge associated with policies, administrative arrangements, institutions and ideas in a political system (past or present) is used to develop policies, administrative arrangements, institutions or ideas in another political system' (Dolowitz and Marsh 2000: 5; see also Dolowitz and Marsh 1996; Dolowitz 2000; Bennett 1991; Howlett and Ramesh 1993; Bennett and Howlett 1992). On this basis, the notion of public policy transfer could be broken down into several main dimensions, to fuel further analysis, such as that conducted by Dolowitz and Marsh on the basis of a number of questions: why do actors commit to public policy transfer? Which actors are involved in these processes? What are the purposes of transfer? What are the sources of transfer? What are the different forms of transfer? What are the factors that facilitate or restrict transfers? More recently, another question has emerged: if, and to what extent, transfers observed have resulted in failure or success.

Advantages of policy transfer studies

In general terms, it seems that the interest of this approach is twofold: first, it establishes an analytical framework for the multi-level games that characterize public action today (the influence of international institutions, development of local policies, dissemination of public action models, etc.); secondly, it synthesizes several notions and hypotheses associated with transfers and reforms, in particular concepts of institutional *mimicry* or institutional *isomorphism*. By dissecting the different mechanisms to which influences are attached, the notion of public policy transfer can potentially isolate the sources of change observed – and identify them as different means of those transfers.

More importantly, the concept of public policy transfer neutralizes one of the more problematic dimensions in Europeanization analysis, i.e. attributing the changes observed. Thus, in his analysis of transformations in telecommunications regulation policies in France and the UK, Thatcher shows how institutional developments cannot be attributed easily to European directives, but rather to tensions resulting from the technological revolution in that sector and the globalization of markets (Thatcher 2007). By questioning the objective sources of institutional transfers, this work brings the analysis of an often implicit dimension of public policy change to the fore.

Attention here is focused on three main dimensions of the notion of transfer, which help answer the question raised by Europeanization, namely, what are the sources of institutional transfers, the instruments of public actions engaged which finally can lead to the analysis of the consequences of institutional transfers as part of European integration?

Sources of transfer

The question of the sources of policy transfer can be broken down into two main dimensions: the vertical and the horizontal. With regard to the vertical dimension the question refers to the international sources of the policy transfer. Beyond transfer stemming from the international level, the second dimension refers to horizontal transfer. Here it is possible to distinguish between transfers enacted within a single national community and transnational transfers extending from one state to another (Dolowitz and Marsh 1996). The pressure exerted can also be global, i.e. perceived as the need to agree collectively on a compromise solution at international level, or horizontal.

The limits of focusing on formal sources of institutional transfers in Europeanization research have been detailed in a number of analytical public policy transfer studies (Dolowitz and Marsh 2000). The importance attributed to conventional institutional and judicial frameworks is questioned on account of the asymmetric and hierarchical nature of the processes studied – hence the hypothesis that sources of transfer are not only formal, judicial and financial, but can also be cognitive or discursive.

In addition to these considerations distinguishing between formal and informal sources of public policy transfer, it is important to differentiate between two specific motivation categories: on the one hand, the context and, on the other, the field in which the transfer takes place. Hence, in a period characterized by substantial political, social and economic stability, it is more likely that the transfer will take place voluntarily. Conversely, during periods of crisis, transfer will more often than not be coercive. Similarly, opposing this clear differentiation, Yves Dezalay and Brian Garth (2002) analyse the logics of influence exercised by the USA on Latin America, showing that they are less the result of individual identifiable strategies than the result of national competition mechanisms specific to certain public policies. The authors, therefore, take into account the resources and strategic choices of actors, according to the positions they occupy in the national system.

The instruments of transfer

In addition to the question of sources of institutional transfer, the policy transfer approach has the advantage of detailing the practical means of reforms undertaken, by pinpointing the role of the various public and private actors involved.

Through cross-analysis, the typology developed by policy transfer approaches clarifies the different elements involved in transformations at the national level. However, such a typology comes with two important provisos – one must avoid neglecting other active political contexts beyond or within the EU, and one must keep in mind the historical context in which these changes occur.

To analyse changes in public policies, institutions, or indeed cognitive frameworks at national level, it does seem important to understand the vectors of this influence, as well as their direction and nature. Recent reflection on government and governance instruments opens up an interesting avenue of investigation in this area. Instruments can be defined as

> a device that is both technical and social, that organizes specific social relations between the state and those it is addressed to, according to the representations and meanings it carries. It is a particular type of institution, a technical device with the generic purpose of carrying a concrete concept of the politics/society relationship and sustained by a concept of regulation. (Lascoumes and Le Galès 2007: 4)

The change processes are not linear but interdependent. Instruments, in this context, are considered not to be 'axiologically neutral and indifferently available tools. They are, on the contrary, sponsors of values, fed by an interpretation of social issues and specific conceptions of the form of regulation envisaged' (Lascoumes and Le Galès, 2004: 13).

The instruments developed by European actors – the European Commission in particular, as well as state and non-state actors such as foundations, national administrations, NGOs, interest groups and associations – whether they are legally binding or soft law instruments, must not be considered as a 'materialization' of an initial idea that has been refined and is ready to use, but rather as an often chaotic dynamic of adjustments and reciprocal learning. In this sense, EU instruments can be understood as institutions that structure public and political actions, in the same way that the behaviour of actors is based on cognitive and normative matrices. This suggests that political transfer instruments are not just problem-solving or legally constraining tools. Actors use these tools strategically, according to their individual or collective preferences. Thus domestic level adjustments are not random or gradual.

Accordingly, it seems important to base the analysis on a typology that makes the development of research protocols possible, and which allows us to distinguish between the different logics that underlie policy transfers. In other words, what form of incentives – coercive or soft incentives – trigger change at the domestic level?

Typology of instruments

Transfer by hierarchy

From the outset, all conceptual research into mechanisms concerning both public policy transfer and Europeanization distinguishes between coercive and voluntary instruments (Dolowitz and Marsh 2000; Radaelli

Figure 6.3   *Types of transfer (Bulmer et al. 2007)*

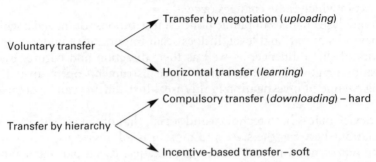

2000; Bomberg and Peterson 2000). More specifically, voluntary instruments are subdivided into 'transfer by negotiation' (uploading) and 'horizontal transfer' (learning) (Bulmer and Padgett 2004). Coercive instruments are grouped under the notion of 'transfer by hierarchy' (downloading), which can take two forms: compulsory (hard) and incentive-based (soft) (Bulmer et al. 2007).

These are not hermetically sealed categories, but part of a continuum that ranges from voluntary transfer to coercive transfer. However, coercive instruments remain central in Europeanization studies. Studies of the Europeanization of Central and Eastern European member states are no exception. Conditionality instruments (Schimmelfennig and Sedelmeier 2002) are considered in this context as practically exclusive explanatory factors of the enlargement process.

Voluntary transfer
Two other groups of instruments refine the research protocol somewhat. Thus, contrary to coercive policy transfer instruments, other vectors – learning and ideas – demonstrate that changes are influenced by ideology and cultural factors. The constructivist theoretical perspective applies more particularly to these two domains, to the extent that it focuses attention on the transformation of social identities, values and norms, much more than on material or institutional conditions, or indeed, the distribution of power between actors.

While these broad brushstrokes already clarify some of the problems of policy transfer, they do, nevertheless, need tweaking. First, there is the notion of learning. The literature on learning is particularly concerned with the sociology of elites who are likely to promote political and institutional transfer (Quaglia, De Francesco and Radaelli 2008). While the notion of interaction between exporters and importers of institutional, sociological or cultural models is central, the literature on learning through transfer also notes that the engagement of elites presupposes a certain degree of dissatisfaction with the prevailing system and knowledge of alternative solutions practised elsewhere. This literature insists that it is essentially the perception of the problem that leads to learning processes. Thus, benchmarking instruments are considered the most suitable mechanisms to allow for the triggering of a policy transfer. Institutionalized in the context of the EU by the European Council of Lisbon in March 2000 under the OMC heading, this instrument is tantamount to a systematic quest for comparison and knowledge (Chapter 6). As Renaud Dehousse observes, 'Apart from crisis periods, it is rare to see governmental structures, often prisoners of historical tradition, seeking to learn lessons from the experiences of other actors' (Dehousse 2004a: 333).

On the other hand, the transfer of ideas is more prevalent in the context of dialogue and argumentation. Argumentation and discourse sometimes switch preferences and/or construct or modify identities and norms, as Simon Bulmer and Claudio Radaelli illustrate (Bulmer and Radaelli 2004). In this context, learning is just one mechanism of political transfer or Europeanization, but the possibilities are much wider. It is more a process through which a group of actors develop a set of ideas and knowledge, which, through different means, will be integrated or, conversely, rejected by the actors 'receiving' them. This argumentation extends the work of Peter Haas and Paul Sabatier on epistemic communities and advocacy coalitions. Such communities are networks of professionals working in a specific field with the authority to make themselves heard (Haas 1992; Sabatier and Jenkins-Smith 1999). Policy transfer occurs via debating platforms through which the preferences of actors may, or may not, be changed. As well as there being a distinction between their coercive and voluntary nature, these instruments may also differ depending on the public policy domain: political and institutional, economic and fiscal, judicial and regulatory, informal and conventional.

However, two problems are raised in this body of work. First, looking at the different actors involved in public policy transfer it is clear that the differential nature of instruments, i.e. their restrictive or voluntary nature, is difficult to distinguish. Even though the norms might not be legally binding, the actors involved can – without using the threat of tangible sanctions – exert major pressure on national political leaders to encourage them to adopt a particular economic policy, as the much-cited examples of the World Bank and the IMF illustrate.

Secondly, it is important not to neglect the historical aspect of instruments used to make political transfer effective and to understand their origins in the political and institutional context of the EU. Thus, in parallel to judicial instruments, non-binding instruments have been developed and implemented by national elites to shift power distribution within a given political system – more often than not in their favour. Thus, the instrument adapts its cognitive and normative content and the networks of actors it weaves over time (James and Lodge 2003).

Table 6.3   *Europeanization/policy transfer perspectives*

Perspectives	Main assumptions	Authors
Europeanization definition		
• Top-down	European integration is considered as a causal factor, incrementally transforming domestic public policies	Ladrech 1994 Goetz and Hix 2000 Risse, Green Cowles and Caporaso 2001a, 2001b
• Circular	Europeanization is not a linear process but a circular one, which also includes European integration and the process's influence at national level, which, in turn, influences European integration anew	Radaelli 2000 Palier and Surel 2007
Sources of Europeanization		
• EU Law: Compliance and non compliance studies	• All policy areas	Tallberg 2002a Falkner et al. 2005 Börzel et al. 2007 König and Luetgert 2009
	• Europeanization of candidate countries	Schimmelfennig and Sedelmeier 2005 Sedelmeier and Epstein 2008
• Limits of compliance research	Strategic/cognitive/legitimation usage	Jacquot and Woll 2004a
Results of Europeanization	• Absorption • Adaptation • Transformation • Inertia/rejection	Börzel and Risse 2000, 2003 Héritier et al. 2001
Policy transfer	Helps to tackle one of the main problems of Europeanization: taking European processes systematically as point of departure for changes at the domestic level	Dolowitz and Marsh 2000 Radaelli 2000 Bulmer and Padgett 2004 Dolowitz 2006 Shipan and Volden 2008 Gilardi and Mesenguer 2008
Typology of policy transfer instruments	• Voluntary transfer (negotiation/ learning) • Transfer by hierarchy (compulsory/incentive-based)	Bulmer and Padgett 2004 Bulmer et al. 2007
Results of policy transfer	• Copying • Synthesis • Influence • Rejection	Bulmer et al. 2007 Radaelli 2000

The types of transfer

The literature on public policy transfer analyses the results of political transfer in a very similar way to Europeanization studies. Simon Bulmer and Stephen Padgett identify four types. First, copying the imported model is considered the most robust form of policy transfer. The idea is to borrow an almost complete political model and install it in the political system of the receiver state; a form of institutional mimicry. A second possible type of political transfer is synthesis through which two or more elements of two or more political systems are combined, and adapted to the national situation. Influence is the third model, whereby the foreign model is only used as an example or for inspiration, while the fourth type of policy transfer, rejection, occurs when a political or institutional transfer is blocked by the actors in the receiving state (Bulmer and Padgett 2004).

One of the biggest difficulties here is arriving at a clear distinction between types of change. As in Europeanization studies and institutionalist approaches (Chapter 4), the types of change overlap. One of the challenges of contemporary research is to go beyond small n-case studies in this field and to analyse transfer on a larger comparative scale.

Conclusion

Clearly, the lessons learned from Europeanization – the decisive influence of European integration, both through its material institutions and cognitive and normative frameworks – play a crucial role in explaining policy and political change at the domestic level. The Europeanization approach has enabled, to an even higher degree than institutionalist or governance approaches, the mainstreaming of EU studies, and for a link to be made in research on European integration with general questions pertaining to the transformation of political systems. Since its beginnings in the 1990, Europeanization research has taken important steps to conceptualize in increasing detail what European integration can – and to a lesser extent, cannot – produce at the domestic level. The sources, mechanisms and consequences of European integration have been typologies and causality principles have been developed. While Europeanization research was for a long time mainly based on comparative case studies, contemporary European studies concentrating on non-compliance with EU law – either seen as inertia or resistance – increasingly use large quantitative and qualitative databases to examine the reasons behind and consequences for European integration from a legal perspective. In this context, however, the danger of confusing the adoption of judicial rules and their actual implementation is high, as we have seen. Implementation is influenced not only by institutional structures already in place, but also by electoral issues or, more specifically, the domestic politics of each country. It is here that a more systematic comparison between variables encouraging and obstructing smooth transposition during policy implementation would be extremely useful (see also Toshkov 2010).

However, Europeanization research suffers from an important constraint: it concentrates on factors stemming from the European integration process, which makes it prone to either concentrate solely on the influence of the EU's legal output or to consider change at the domestic level as generally produced by European integration. It is here that policy transfer and diffusion studies can be considered as tools to broaden our understanding of the reasons for change in European states and societies. Concentrating on instruments of policy transfer and diffusion, and acknowledging that instruments are not neutral tools for problem-solving, allows us to conceptualize Europeanization both as the dependent variable that needs to be explained, and the explanatory, independent variable. The distinction between the model system (the exporter) and the client system (the importer) is not as clear as it might appear. EU negotiations show that changes occur in exporting systems.

Thus the interdependence between variables as well as the sources of change both remain as weak points in Europeanization research. The fact that actors from the domestic level are those who put an issue on the agenda, and are then again those transposing, implementing and experiencing these changes, makes it often difficult to distinguish clearly between top-down and bottom-up Europeanization, and to establish clear origins of policy change (see also Princen and Rhinard 2006). Attempts have been made to solve this problem. They have suggested adopting a policy-sequencing approach, or reintroducing the variable of the preferences of initial member states to explain whether states are more likely to reject European norms if they initially opposed the European law in Council negotiations (König and Luetgert 2009).

Finally, while there have been many analyses concerning the effects of change, work on resistance to or rejection of change is still somewhat underdeveloped and arguably needs more empirical and theoretical exploration. Further methodological work in these two areas may pay clear dividends.

Chapter 7

Constructivism(s)

Constructivist approaches to European integration emerged at the end of the 1990s. Initially developed in the disciplines of sociology and anthropology, constructivist approaches defend the idea that 'reality is socially constructed and that the sociology of knowledge must analyse the processes within which this occurs' (Berger and Luckmann 1966: 1). Constructivism concentrates on the question of how ideational factors (world-views, ideas, collective understandings, norms, values, cognitive schemes, etc.) dominate political action. In other words, how do norms shape political outcomes?

In the 1980s, this understanding of social phenomena made its way into international relations approaches, in particular, those developed by Nicolas Onuf and Alexander Wendt (Onuf 1989; Wendt 1999). This literature was key to bringing about the constructivist turn in EU studies at the end of the 1990s.

This chapter has a threefold objective: first, to identify the basic assumptions of constructivism in general. Second, to present the emergence of constructivism in the discipline of international relations before illustrating, in the third and final part, the uses made of this concept in European integration studies. It is crucial to understand constructivist approaches in international relations in order to grasp the research perspectives that these approaches have provided for European studies; in turn this enables us to identify the advantages and limitations of these approaches in the context of European policy-making.

It is important to note that constructivist approaches are extremely diverse, which makes any examination of this paradigm particularly challenging. Constructivism is positioned between a positivist and a post-positivist epistemology, or theory of knowledge. This means that positivist scholars develop causal explanations for social phenomena, while post-postivists reject the idea of testing hypotheses altogether. For example, while positivists would explain the establishment of the SEA as resulting from the strength of neoliberal ideas circulating amongst European leaders, post-positivists would argue that neoliberal ideas themselves are social constructs, which are too diverse and incoherent to be accounted for as a causal interference. The perceived influence of liberal ideas is thus in itself a social frame in which scholars are trapped owing to their prior socialization. In this sense, reality is neither objective nor subjective, but intersubjective, i.e. built through shared beliefs among actors. This rather 'uncomfortable' positioning makes constructivism particularly prone to criticism.

Constructivism-based principles

Resolutely interdisciplinary, constructivism was developed in sociology, philosophy and anthropology (Guzzini and Leander 2006). Constructivism, or social constructivism, as it is properly known, starts from the assumption that social reality is constructed and reproduced through permanent interaction between social agents. The idea here is that the material world does not present itself as a classified entity. The objects of our knowledge therefore do not exist independently of our interpretation and language. Constructivism links the production and reproduction of social practices and emphasizes their location in specific contexts.

Three ideas are key in social constructivism: contextualization, the co-constitution of agents and structures, and the endogenous construction of actors' interests.

The first key concept of social constructivism is *contextualization*. This means that, according to constructivists, individuals not only act according to a rational cost-benefit analysis. They are also embedded in social structures, i.e. they act as 'social agents'. These structures frame the actors' behaviour and make them act sometimes against their – externally perceived – interest. Constructivists hold the view that the building blocks of reality are ideational as well as material. Ideational factors have normative as well as instrumental dimensions and not only express individual but also collective intentionality. Finally, the meaning and significance of ideational factors are not independent of time and place (Ruggie 1988a: 33).

The second key concept is the *co-constitution of agents and structures* in constructivist approaches. According to this understanding, our social environment, or the social norms that guide our behaviour, constitutes who we are. At the same time, these social norms and frameworks are not stable. They are constructed and redefined through permanent interaction.

This leads us to a third key assumption of constructivism. Constructivists have a very different understanding of how interests change over time. For materialists (such as rational choice institutionalists in Chapter 4), actors' interests evolve as changes in their environment alter their situation. Actors' preferences are thus fixed and exogenous to the social environment. Constructivists, on the contrary, assume that interests change as agents alter their understanding of their changing world environment and recalculate their priorities (Béland and Cox

2011). They insist on the fact that the interests of actors cannot be understood as being established purely exogenously, or as deduced from any essential material structure. On the contrary, social, political and economic contexts structure these interests. It is important, first of all, to understand how they construct them. *Interests are thus endogenously constructed.*

The importance of this co-constitution is reflected in the widespread use of the notion of the *logic of appropriateness*, developed by sociological institutionalism (March and Olsen 1984, 1989, 1993) in constructivist literature. The literature argues that actors are more influenced by social norms in their actions and behaviour than by any weighing up of the costs and benefits of a particular course of action. It is more a question of behaving 'correctly', according to criteria established by a society or a group, than of maximizing one's preferences – an attitude known as the *logic of consequentialism.*

A third way to conceptualize the factors that influence the result of human interaction has emerged recently. In his *logic of arguing (or communicative action)*, Risse (2000) suggests considering the processes of argumentation, deliberation and persuasion as a distinct mode of social interaction, instead of opposing material (interests) and ideal variables (world-views) being central factors influencing actor behaviour and, subsequently, political outcomes. This logic occupies the middle ground between strategic bargaining and rule-guided behaviour. It starts from the assumption that human actors engage in truth-seeking with the aim of reaching mutual understanding. This, however, is only possible if actors are prepared to change their world-views, values and interests (Risse 2000: 1).

The logic of arguing must be understood as a conceptual continuum. On this continuum we find, on the one hand, the Habermasian idea of arguing as truth-seeking behaviour, and, on the other, the assumption that actors use arguments in a strategic mode in order to justify their

Table 7.1 *The three logics*

Logic of appropriateness	Acting according to a logic of appropriateness refers to correct behaviour in policy making processes, in line with criteria established by a society or a group
Logic of consequentialism	Acting to maximize one's preferences
Logic of arguing	Processes of argumentation, deliberation and persuasion are distinct modes of social interaction, influencing actor behaviour and, subsequently, political outcomes

Box 7.1   *Three constructivist core ideas*

Three claims sum up the core ideas of constructivism:

1   *Contextualization*: Individuals not only act according to a rational cost-benefit analysis, but are embedded in social structures, thus act as 'social agents'.
2   *Co-constitution of agents and structures*: Actors and structures are mutually constitutive: actors shape structures, which in turn shape actors.
3   *Interests are endogenously constructed*. The preferences of agents are constituted by structures which not only act as constraints but also shape the way in which actors consider what their interests are.

identities and preferences. From this perspective, actors engaging in 'rhetorical action' (Schimmelfennig 1998) are not ready to change their own beliefs due to a 'better argument'. Jobert's distinction between debates taking place in either forums or arenas illustrates this continuum empirically (Jobert 1998). In this regard, arenas are spaces of confrontation between divergent world-views, a sort of battleground where what matters is being convincing in your argument. Forums, however, are spaces of argument where institutional compromises are negotiated. Thus, strategic behaviour is framed and made possible by norms ('collective expectations about behaviour for a given identity' (Jepperson, Wendt and Katzenstein 1996: 54) – an idea we find in actor-centred constructivist approaches.

Constructivism in international relations

On the basis of these claims, the introduction of constructivism into international relations led to the emergence of a new paradigm in the late 1980s. A group of scholars, most prominently Richard Ashley (1982), Nicolas Onuf (1989), Friedrich Kratochwil (1989), John Ruggie (1998b) and Alexander Wendt (1992, 1999), used constructivist frameworks to explain international phenomena. These studies were also inspired by another generation of internationalists, more specifically Ernst Haas (1958) on European integration and Karl Deutsch et al. (1957) on international security communities. These authors were among the first to analyse international relations as historically and socially contingent phenomena: 'The structures of human association are determined primarily by shared ideas rather than material forces, and the interests of purposeful actors are constructed by these shared ideas rather than given by nature (Wendt 1999: 1).

More generally, it is possible to distinguish between three constructivist movements in international relations: *modernist/neoclassical* (Ruggie 1998a) or *conventional* (Checkel 2006), *interpretative* and *radical/critical*.

Modernist approaches are different from the two others on account of their 'conservative' or positivist research design, given the objective of explaining and understanding social reality. They introduce a language based on correlations, or even causal links, between the social facts observed. The objective of these scholars is therefore to discover the causal mechanisms and constitutive social relations that make international relations comprehensible (Adler and Barnett 1998; Finnemore 1996; Risse 2000; Onuf 1989; Kratochwil 1989). As Emanuel Adler argues, 'Contrary to positivism and materialism, which claim to study the world as it really is, (modernist) constructivism considers the world as an ongoing project – *becoming* rather than *being*' (Adler 2002: 95). The world is not only an ephemeral, discursive entity, but can be understood through the analysis of correlations between phenomena. In this respect, modernist constructivist perspectives add to other conceptual approaches, rather than replace them.

Interpretative constructivists explore the role of language in constructing social reality (Checkel 2006). This perspective does not consider change linked to causal variables but to a transformation of a specific cognitive frame, made visible through the study of discourses, media and literature. Based on inductive research designs, these scholars analyse the background conditions and discourses that make change possible in the first place.

A third group of scholars, referred to as '*radical or critical*' constructivists, represent a post-positive paradigm. These authors defy the idea that it is possible to achieve a certain level of knowledge in international relations. Material reality can never be truly represented. For this reason, their approach requires material reality to be ignored, and for attention to be paid only to discourses, narratives and texts, and to the researcher's own implication in the reproduction of the reality analysed. In this case, science is nothing more than another hegemonic discourse (Campbell 1992; Walker 1993). Knowledge should be used to emancipate society (Cox 1986; Linklater 1998). These scholars argue that a better understanding of the mechanisms at the base of social and political orders can lead to the emancipation of society. In other words, critical constructivists share a commitment to uncovering preconceptions about historical reality and the contextual nature of knowledge, and through this process they seek to change society. From this perspective, any theory is based both in *time* and in *space*. Hence the assumption that there is no theory *per se*, guided by the sole quest for scientific truth. According to Cox, 'a theory is always for someone and for something' (Cox 1986). Critical theories must be developed to question the process itself through which theories are produced.

Although epistemologically very different, these three movements – modernist, interpretative and radical/critical – take a particular interest in two objects: norms and interests. Norms and interests are also crucial factors in the context of constructivism in European studies. However, here constructivism is 'interpreted' through terms such as socialization, learning and identity building, as well as strategic action embedded in specific social contexts.

Norms and interests

According to constructivists, norms co-constitute actor behaviour. They do not simply frame them but make specific behaviour possible. Norms allow 'a space of inter-subjective meaning' to be shared. The emphasis is on the process of socialization and social learning in a community, which is essential to ensure the continuity of rules and norms, their development and use. The activity of any one individual is not sufficient to ensure the continuity of norms, rules and values in a coherent system. Any norm is embedded in a specific understanding, which prevails in a wider community. Thus, socialization and exposure to international norms result in these norms, values and rules being internalized by those within the community.

More generally, and according to social constructivism, norms and rules emerge through interaction between actors from different communities. Discourse therefore becomes the central vector in the creation of values, norms and rules. It is the instrument that enables actors, through interaction, to interpret – and in so doing themselves create – a social phenomenon. Political discourse is a forerunner to creating, defining and deliberating on the content of social norms (see also discursive institutionalism in Chapter 4) and thus creating 'intersubjectivity'. As such, it is difficult to analyse social norms exogenously, or to separate them from the social context in which they emerge, transform or disappear. Without acknowledging context, it is very difficult or even impossible to determine the influence of values or accurately interpret their content.

But what are norms? Constructivist approaches distinguish between two forms of norms: regulatory norms, which determine what states should and should not do, and constitutive norms, which create roles, identities and interests for states. For instance, sovereignty norms constitute sovereign territorial states as the primary actors of the international system. Constitutive norms are not legal instruments as such, although international law may formalize these norms.

Both types of norms have a dual quality. They are both stable and flexible, to the extent that they are constructed by social interaction and, at the same time, have a constituent influence on the behaviour of individuals and organizations. This dual quality of norms means that, in any research, international, transnational and national contexts may need combining. Constructivist approaches allow us to go beyond analysing the impact of European legal norms at national level. They open up the possibility of also studying the consequences and 'interpretations' of weak norms, such as through the use of 'soft law', or with regard to the voluntary nature of European programmes and efforts by the Commission at establishing benchmarks in the domestic realm (Wiener 2006, 2007). For example, the predominant, although not exclusive method of decision-making in the European Council of Ministers is via consensus – itself a norm constructed by social interaction; at the same time the use of this method influences the attitude of member-state representatives in EU negotiations.

The concept of interests is similarly challenged by constructivists: here too, constructivists question several tenets of rationalist international relations theories. In particular, their idea is to redefine the notion of state interest, which they see as being neither the sum of individual interests of national actors or national interest groups as a whole, nor the interests of an elite 'disconnected from the people', as found in the liberal intergovernmentalist theory of Andrew Moravcsik or Robert Putnam's 'two-level game' (Chapter 3). Moreover, constructivists reject the simple juxtaposition of interests and institutions. In their view, intersubjective arrangements constitute but also constrain interests. For example, according to constructivists, German interests in the Stability and Growth Pact established in 1997 through the Amsterdam Treaty can only be understood by combining the interests of German elites with the pressures perceived or actually felt by Germany's EU partners, and then recognizing that Germany will need to be seen to respond in an economically responsible way, in light of its general reputation as a prudent and cautious member state in the EU.

The features of constructivism in European studies

Using these epistemological bases, constructivists analysing the EU have developed three conceptual puzzles in particular (Christiansen, Joergensen and Wiener 1999): socialization and learning; the social construction of a European identity; and, finally, actor-centred constructivism, which is a specific approach resulting from one of the central critiques of constructivist approaches – the absence of considerations concerning authority and power (Checkel 2007). Empirical research in this field has brought three essential contributions to the study of European integration: first of all, the concept of the co-constitution of agents and structures has allowed for a deeper understanding of the processes of Europeanization and the transformation of states in Europe. Second, and along the same lines, the insistence on the co-constitutive

Table 7.2   *European studies constructivism in brief*

Perspectives	Main assumptions
Socialization and learning	Actors' preferences change due to learning and socialization
Social construction of European identity	European identities are intertwined and multi-dimensional. Socialization and symbolic politics influence the construction and reconstruction of identities
Actor-centred constructivism	Actor behaviour is influenced by beliefs and ideas framed by specific power constellations.

effects of judicial norms, rules and policies provides an opportunity to study how European integration forms social identities and shapes actor preferences (Christiansen, Joergensen and Wiener 1999). Finally, looking in particular at communication practices, researchers have been able to highlight how the EU is constructed in a discursive manner and how actors understand the meaning of European integration (Checkel 1999; Risse 2004b; Johnston 2005).

The three contributions to understanding European integration help to conceptualize the EU as a process, and not as a result (see Hix 1998). According to constructivists, other approaches ignore 'the arguably more important question of how the move from inter-state bargaining to politics within an emerging polity actually happened and where it might lead. Studying integration as *process* would mean concentrating research efforts at the nature of this change, asking to what extent, and in which ways, a new polity is being constituted in Europe' (Christiansen, Joergensen and Wiener 1999: 537). At the heart of constructivist research in European integration is the question of how to explain long-term social, political and economic changes.

Socialization and learning

A first constructivist perspective sees European integration as socialization and learning process. It triggers the internalization of norms, which are themselves defined through interaction (Risse 2004b). More specifically, member states' perceptions of their own political interests evolve due to an international socialization process (Schimmelfennig 2000b). Antje Wiener emphasizes that the starting point for the constructivist analysis of European integration was 'a link between the social construction of institutions and the success in implementing rules, norms and legal principles' (Wiener 2006: 54; 2008). This has allowed for a shared understanding of how the establishment of norms at the EU level leads to a higher level of norm compliance at the national level. The central methodological idea here is that processes are embedded in a specific context and that only an understanding of the overall context will allow us to comprehend the European integration process as a whole.

For constructivists, when precisely do socialization processes occur? Socialization occurs when norms, world-views and collective under-standings are internalized, and then subsequently codified by a group of actors (Schimmelfennig 2000b; Risse 2009).

Based on this assumption, a large number of analyses have been carried out into the socializing role of European institutions (see also Saurugger 2013). The main reason for doing so was the assumed inca-pacity of rational choice approaches to understand genuine change in actors' preferences. 'Constitutive dynamics of social learning, socializa-tion, routinization and normative diffusion, all of which address funda-mental issues of agent identity and interests, are not adequately captured by strategic exchange or other models adhering to strict forms of methodological individualism' (Checkel 1999: 545). The central research object here is not so much the construction of a European iden-tity in the broader sense. Instead, socialization research concentrates on the influence that the collective acceptance of certain standards of behaviour exerts on policy-making processes (Checkel 2001b; Tallberg 2002a).

Critiques of this research insist on the fact that learning and socializa-tion processes are not easy to prove. These phenomena must be rigor-ously studied in order to understand the moment at which a norm becomes a general reference and is not just an idea or ideological position of one single individual. For this reason, empirical research mainly concentrates on specific professional groups active in the EU realm such as European civil servants, COREPER and members of interest groups. A group of researchers have shown that socialization processes have taken place in working groups or European Committees (Lewis 2005, 2008; Checkel 2003). Others question this socialization process and present data that show how socialization processes are partial at best (Hooghe 2005; Beyers 2005). A new mode of governance, the OMC in particular, has led to a large number of theoretical and empirical studies. The constructivist branch of this field concentrates more specifically on learning processes. In its ideal form, the OMC is thought to have a poten-tial for learning at three levels (Radaelli 2008: 248): 'learning at the top' among EU civil servants, 'hierarchical learning' from the top to the domestic level and 'bottom-up learning' whereby non-state actors, regions and local governments participate in negotiations and diffuse their knowledge, thus triggering a change in actor preferences. In fields such as gender mainstreaming, lifelong learning, flexicurity, or activation (Zeitlin 2005), learning processes have occurred at all three levels. These policies, such as social policy, education or employment, are not legally binding but have triggered a change in discourse (Radaelli 2008).

This conceptualization of learning has two advantages. First of all, it shows that certain actors not only succeed in imposing their interpretation of social phenomena on others because they have the necessary authority. Their arguments are persuasive because they have managed to create a common understanding of a problem and, as such, they hold a legitimate position through the broader social context in which they are embedded (Jobert and Muller 1987; Dimitrova and Rhinhard 2005).

The second advantage is the ability to integrate one of the major challenges of research into European integration, i.e. thinking about the multitude of levels where reality is constructed. Reality is constructed by the individual, the group to which it belongs, the media or, more generally, by the messages transmitted on several levels: locally, regionally, nationally, Europe-wide or more internationally. However, it is precisely in relation to these two advantages that a problem arises: the disappearance of power as an element of change. If change in actors' preferences is based on learning and socialization, the hard constraints of power no longer seem to play a role. This criticism was put forward by a group of researchers known specifically as actor-centred or 'strategic constructivists', as we will see below (see also Zürn and Checkel 2005). Constructivist perspectives had a tendency, until recently at least, to underestimate the importance of asymmetrical power between actors; political problems could not only be solved through learning or the socialization of actors. Material factors, such as financial resources or social positions, influenced political results tremendously, even though strategic constructivists agree with the assumption that actor preferences do not solely reflect their material resources, but also take account of the social norms in which they are embedded.

Social construction of a European identity

A second conceptual constructivist approach emerged from the empirical question of whether, and if so, how, a common European identity had been established in the EU. Here, the starting assumption in constructivist analysis is very close to neofunctionalism: the process of European integration leads to the emergence of a transnational identity. The neofunctionalists and, first and foremost, Ernst Haas and Leon Lindberg (Chapter 2), envisaged a transfer of loyalty from the national level to the European level – a process that would take place, specifically, amongst the political and socioeconomic elite. However, constructivists broaden their analysis to European citizens as a whole, and highlight the multidimensional nature of identity (Rosamond 2005a).

The constructivist analysis starts from the assumption that a certain degree of identification with the EU is necessary in order to be able to consider the European political system as viable and legitimate: 'The support (of the European Union by its citizens) is the cornerstone of this citizenship since it represents an initial form of recognition of the legitimacy of the European and political system' (Belot 2002). However, instead of considering European identity in terms of a precarious balancing act, and presuming that the citizen can feel *either* European *or* national, the objective of the constructivists was to show the multiple levels of the notion of identity. Thus, both national identity and European identity have been conceptualized as 'imagined communities' (Anderson 1991), i.e. our different yet coexisting feelings of belonging are structured around specific issues, places or events.

In this context, the central issue is to understand how the different European identities are intertwined, how multidimensional these attitudes are, and what role socialization and symbolic politics play in the construction and reconstruction of identities (Risse 2001, 2003). Here, and in summary fashion, constructivists identify four forms of identity: first, an identity constructed in concentric circles. This refers back to the image of a central identity, which is, more often than not, regional or national, but also 'encircled' by several other identities such as European or international. Secondly, identities can overlap. According to this configuration, certain members of a group, though not all, can identify with another group; some young people may feel particularly European, but not all. A third conceptualization of identity is what Thomas Risse calls '*the marble cake*' (Risse 2001). According to this approach, the multiple identities of an individual cannot be clearly distinguished and/or identified. There are no separate identities within an individual: all identities mutually influence each other, become mixed and entwined. According to such reasoning, it is not possible to come up with a precise definition of what the notion of European identity means. This third interpretation of identity refers in some ways to a fourth one, close to strategic constructivism. Here, external phenomena such as globalization, an external enemy or a phenomenon perceived as a threat can be used to create European identity, as Rosamond shows in his analysis of European discourses on globalization (Rosamond 1999).

To provide these abstract interpretations of European identity with a more substantial sociological basis, political sociologists have identified a series of independent variables influencing European identity, such as gender, level of training, exposure to other Europeans or income levels (Belot 2002, 2010). On the basis of analysis developed from survey data (Duchesne and Frognier 1995, 2002; Cederman 2001), refined constructivist and sociological studies have emerged, taking power struggles and politicization among citizens (in particular, Europeanization's winners and losers) into account. These studies highlight the fact that the more citizens identify strongly with their home member state, the more they will also identify with the EU. For the constructivists, however, these variables can only be used as a basis for analysis. The aim is to understand their usefulness and the ways in which they might be used. For constructivists as well as for sociologists, it is crucial to analyse the diverse constructions of meaning. According to constructivists, European identity is not a fact, but rather a construction in a specific time and place, the content of which changes according to the political and social context in which it is embedded (Diez 1999). 'Europe' as a space of political organization and institutionalization has no clear boundaries. Moreover, differentiation between 'us' and 'them' – or 'othering', as constructivists call it – is context-dependent. Insofar as there is no fixed meaning of what Europe constitutes positively, there are no fixed European 'others' (Risse 2004a).

This understanding enables constructivists to take Euroscepticism into account (for an excellent overview see Leconte 2010). Identity construction is not peaceful, but conflictual. One of the results is the increase of opposition, not only to European integration but to specific policies (Risse 2010).

Actor-centred constructivism

In the two approaches presented above power relations and strategic behaviour of policy agents seem secondary in importance, however (see Checkel 2006).

Since the end of the 1990s a group of scholars have attempted to accommodate these limits of previous constructivist conceptualizations of EU politics. Although they agree with the general constructivist assumption that the individual ideas and beliefs of an actor are constructed, they emphasize the importance of taking into account the usage of ideas. More precisely, *how specific actors apply these ideas for their own purposes, and which specific power constellations influence these actors' ideas*. The central question to which actor-centred constructivism seeks to find an answer is: 'to what extent exactly do ideas shape policy outcomes?' Ideas are considered to be explanatory factors in their own right. But as Mark Blyth notes, constructivist perspectives have for too long opposed interests and ideas, and considered them to be radically different and unrelated concepts (Blyth 2002; see also McNamara 2006).

How do ideas frame interests? How can one describe the practices of actors through this framing process? When and why, for example, do European public officials evoke the neoliberal paradigm in their messages, and when and why does this idea not find its way into official documents and discourses? In other words: 'Since structures do not come with an instruction sheet, economic ideas make such an institutional resolution possible by providing the authoritative diagnosis as to what a crisis actually is and when a given situation actually constitutes a crisis.

They diagnose "what has gone wrong" and "what is to be done"'. (Blyth 2002: 10; see also Hay 1999, 2004).

In this approach, ideas influence outcomes significantly: they are used for strategic purposes. Hence the criticism voiced by 'actor-centred constructivists' that the purely rhetorical use of these notions underestimates the forms of mobilization and instrumentalization to which these frames have been subject (Surel 2000). It is, in a certain sense, rather trivial to say that these strategies are socially constructed. However, in saying that, we also understand that actors must create broad coalitions around common strategies in order to carry out major reforms.

This conceptual framework particularly inspired the research on European political economy. Scholars concentrated on the question why and how a convergence of beliefs around economic and political solutions to specific European problems has emerged (Hall 1993; Berman 1998; Blyth 2002; Abdelal, Blyth and Parsons 2010; McNamara 1998, 2006; Parsons 2002; Jabko 2006, 2010; Woll 2008; Meyer and Strickman 2011; Clift and Woll 2012).

Although these scholars develop different hypotheses, they all agree on the basic assumption that, even in an international environment that confronts political leaders with a set of challenges, actors do not automatically come up with the 'correct' or 'best' answer. Problems must be interpreted in order to be solved. It is here where we see how ideas influence actors. Different ideas lead to different interpretation of problems and the different framing of solutions. We can distinguish two different groups of scholars: on the one hand those who claim that, in order to be visible, ideas must serve the interest of the dominant actors by strengthening their position in the game (Hall 1993; McNamara 1998; Parsons 2002; Béland 2009). On the other, those who consider ideas as weapons that can be used quite independently from the position of the actor itself (Blyth 2002; Jabko 2006).

Hence, the difficulty of showing the empirical influence of ideas remains. One of the problems is to be found in the 'dichotomous (Janus-faced) nature of ideas' (Parsons 2002). Sometimes, the beliefs of actors guide their actions and sometimes perceived beliefs only rationalize strategies that may be chosen for other reasons. It is difficult to distinguish empirically between the two situations.

For this reason, actor-centred constructivism introduces sociological methods or process tracing, allowing a concentration on the study of individual actors or groups of actors. This helps to understand the power games that take place between actors in public policy. Craig Parsons, in particular, argues that, in order to observe the influence of ideas, it is crucial to consider the agenda-setting power of the actor in question. In his analysis of the success of integration ideology in relation to the confederal or intergovernmental model developed by the 'founding fathers' of European integration, Parsons offers a detailed study of French debates on this issue, as well as of the interactions between European partners in the 1950s (Parsons 2003).

Nicolas Jabko uses a similar research design in his analysis of the intensified European economic regional integration process starting from the 1980s (Jabko 2006). He studies European integration from the angle of economic governance. The dual economic and political change in Europe during this period is explained by the fact the European actors, and in particular the European Commission, defended a specific under-standing of 'market gain' that was subsequently shared by all European member states. The Commission's strategy was based on the idea of a common market, a concept which is sufficiently multifaceted to bring together all the European actors' ideologies around a single project: the construction of the single market and the establishment of an Economic and Monetary Union. This 'silent revolution' in Europe over time brought together a broad coalition of European actors. Through the use of what he calls 'strategic constructivism', Jabko emphasizes two para-doxical aspects of the EU: the parallel emergence of intergovernmental economic governance and the strengthening of powers at the European level.

Actor-centred constructivism attempts to tackle critiques expressed by opponents of constructivist approaches who claim that power consider-ations are absent in constructivist perspectives. Thus, research focuses on the one hand on the carriers of ideas and norms, and on the other, the influence of their power relations on policy outcomes. Actors' prefer-ences are brought back into the analysis. Agents are purposeful actors, embedded in ideational structures, which they use in line with their inter-ests. At the same time, this new generation of constructivist perspectives continues to include ideas and world-views as central causal factors in the explanation of decision-making processes. They continue to insist on the fact, however, that ideas, world-views or norms do not exist inde-pendently from the users of these ideas and are subject to the institutional conditions in which they are embedded. Thus world-views, norms or ideas 'do not float freely', as Thomas Risse-Kappen (1994) has so perti-nently observed.

One of the main problems here remains, however, the question of methodology. How ought the interdependence between ideas and inter-ests to be analysed, given that both of them are more generally embedded in specific world-views?

Although actor centred institutionalism mainly addresses the question to what extent ideas and world-views influence the process and direction of European integration, they also allow to deal with a crucial issue in contemporary European politics – the legitimacy of decisions taken at the European level (Saurugger 2013).

Legitimation strategies of actors in the EU

Actor-centred constructivist approaches are particularly well adapted to explain the legitimation strategies actors pursue in policy-making processes. This is important because in both political and academic debates the question of legitimate and accountable governance in the EU has become a crucial issue since the mid-1990 (Chapter 9). The influence of ideas, 'world-views, 'cognitive frames' or, more generally, representations, is central to such approaches. In this sense, European integration is understood as the result of the interaction between individuals whose interests are not only based on an instrumental cost-benefit calculation, but must be understood as something that is embedded in the specific social representations, values and norms in which the actor him/herself evolves. Constructivist approaches also aim at helping us understand why some proposals have more legitimacy in a debate than others at any given time:

> Politicians, officials, the spokesmen for societal interests, and policy experts all operate within the terms of political discourse that are current in the nation at a given time, and the terms of political discourse generally have a specific configuration that lends representative legitimacy to some social interests more than others, delineates the accepted boundaries of state action, associates contemporary political developments with particular interpretations of national history, and defines the context in which many issues will be understood. (Hall 1993: 289; see also Surel 2000)

This conceptualization does not exclude behaviour based on a cost-benefit analysis. However, cost-benefit analyses only occur when actors have chosen the instruments available to them in order to pursue a specific objective. Again, and this seems to take us full circle, these objectives are influenced through the cognitive and normative frames available to them. In this sense, 'actors always perceive the world through a lens consisting of their pre-existing beliefs' (Sabatier 1998: 109).

This understanding of ideas and cognitive frames allows the legitimacy of European integration to be conceptualized differently. Legitimacy is thus no longer an absolute value but must be understood in the light of a permanent framing process in which different ideas about legitimacy confront each other: the legitimacy of the integration process becomes the process of legitimating the policies this integration process produces (Jobert and Muller 1987). This research field has gained in importance since the beginning of the 1990s, when the debate on the democratic deficit of the EU became an important issue. Why European and domestic actors adopt positions in the European debate was analysed in the light of their understanding of the European democratic

Table 7.3   *Constructivist perspectives in European studies*

Perspectives	Main assumptions	Authors
Socialization and learning	Actors' preferences change due to learning and socialization	Checkel 1999, 2001a, 2001b Risse 2004a Tallberg 2002a Hooghe 2005 Beyers 2005 Radaelli 2008
Social construction of European identity	Analyse how different European identities are intertwined, how multidimensional these attitudes are, and what role socialization and symbolic politics play in the construction and reconstruction of identities	Risse 2001, 2003, 2010 Cederman 2001
Actor-centred constructivism	Actor behaviour is influenced by beliefs and ideas framed by specific power constellations	Blyth 2002 Jabko 2006 McNamara 1998, 2004 Parsons 2002, 2003

space and not only as a cost-benefit calculation. Nevertheless, it is here where actor-centred constructivism encounters a limit: if ideas purely become a weapon (Blyth 2002) or a strategic tool (Jabko 2006), then the difference between strategic constructivism and rational choice institutionalism is a very thin one. At the same time, it is methodologically challenging to analyse the influence of ideas as a strategic tool and the influence of the political, social or economic context in which these ideas occur.

Conclusion

This chapter has illustrated the diversity of constructivist approaches. The differences transcend national boundaries, but it is nonetheless still possible to distinguish a rather European and a more American approach to constructivism. Thus, while constructivist approaches developed in the USA sought to supplement the shortcomings of realist and neoliberal approaches, European constructivist perspectives developed in critical response to positivist paradigms in political science and, therefore, adopt a more radical post-positivist posture (Risse and Wiener 1999).

However, the difficulties of operationalizing constructivist approaches have been pointed out time and again: how to establish a research design that allows for establishing causalities? While critical constructivists reject the idea of establishing causalities as an impossible endeavour, a number of constructivists in European studies themselves consider this a shortcoming. Hence, one of the main challenges of constructivist research is its relation to methods. These challenges are partially linked to the difficulty of making research methods explicit. It seems crucial to identify the discourse and world-view 'carriers', as well as the reciprocal influence of agents and structures through a rigorous research protocol (Mérand 2008a).

Research designs are sometimes patchy, based on examples that tend to illustrate assumptions rather than attempt to establish correlations. A number of constructivist approaches, and, in particular, actor-centred constructivism, attempt to do just that – arguing that in any given situation, such-and-such an *idea* counts more than such-and-such an *interest*. It is in this area that constructivism has contributed most. The conditions under which ideas matter, and who the carriers of these ideas are, are brought to the fore and given due attention by these actor-centred constructivism scholars, who advocate that the power structures in which central actors are embedded, as well as the alliances and coalitions they create, themselves allow for ideas to become influential.

Nevertheless, criticism provides us with an opportunity to look at the importance of thinking about ideas in relation to interests, or indeed discourse in relation to material realities. While the boundary between symbolic and material things is clear, according to constructivism, interpretation allows us to give it meaning. It is therefore important to take the hierarchical position of actors into account in order to understand the construction of a meaning, hence the academic interest in going deeper into the tenets of actor-centred constructivism. Constructivism is stronger when it takes into account the historical and sociological embeddedness of actors or carriers of meaning: 'The frequent a-historicism of US constructivist writing is almost as striking as that of the positivist mainstream that it seeks to critique' (Hurrell 2007: 134). Indeed, this is one of the main criticisms of sociological accounts of European integration (Checkel 2006; Favell and Guiraudon 2011; Saurugger and Mérand 2010). Tackling this shortcoming head-on should help to make constructivist accounts more convincing and influential.

Chapter 8

Sociological Perspectives on European Integration

Within the burgeoning body of literature on conceptual and theoretical approaches to the EU, a 'sociologizing movement' emerged at the end of the 1990s. In the *Handbook of European Union Politics,* an entire chapter is dedicated to the sociology of European integration (Favell 2007). While sociological approaches are not entirely new in EU studies (Middlemas 1995; Bach 2000), they have only recently come to be considered as potentially relevant for the analysis of the EU (Rumford 2002, 2009; Favell and Guiraudon 2011; Saurugger and Mérand 2010).

Two factors help us to understand the emergence of this new direction in European studies: historical developments on the one hand, and research interest on the other. As for historical developments, during the 1990s for the first time European integration expressed a true interest in society. The peaceful revolutions in Central and Eastern Europe and German Unification changed the way EU citizens perceived supranational integration. Indeed, European citizenship was established and Europe became a larger geographical and social space. European integration came to be seen as a central aspect for shaping the near future of both European peoples and European elites. Furthermore, the referenda in France, Ireland and Denmark to ratify the Maastricht Treaty, and the negative outcome in Denmark, which led to a number of Danish opt-outs from the Maastricht Treaty (see also Dinan 2004), showed that European integration could not be understood without taking society into proper account.

Concern about the supposed democratic deficit and the impact of market liberalization and integration on citizens' everyday lives triggered new academic interest in society. Thus, instead of focusing on solely political, institutional and economic developments, scholars needed conceptual frameworks that would enable them to broaden their research interest, in order to better understand the reaction of European societies to regional integration in general. As such, European integration theories had never really dealt with European society.

This interest in society provided an opportunity to establish a certain unity in European societies' different cultures, economies, social models and social identities. It also allowed scholars to concentrate on micro-

162

sociological questions such as the identities of certain societal groups, be they immigrants or European civil servants, in European integration processes.

Although conceptually heterogeneous, the various sociological approaches to European integration share the belief that European integration studies should concentrate primarily on actors' attitudes rather than on institutional structures. Their aim, bluntly stated, is 'to bring the actor back in' (Georgakakis 2008). The actor is understood both in its collective and individual form. Understood collectively, sociological approaches concentrate on European society, its attitude towards European integration and how European integration has influenced society in daily life. Analysed individually, the actor becomes the main protagonist of decisions taken at the EU level. Advocates of sociological approaches argue that this research design is necessary to understand how and why decisions are taken in the European realm. Not concentrating on the sociological attributes of agents, i.e. the training they received, the family background they come from, the socialization process they went through, would not allow for explaining their preferences in multiple policy-making processes at the EU level.

And yet, while studies on the EU based on sociological approaches have gathered pace, theoretical conceptualization has remained somewhat implicit. The aim of this chapter is to present the common assumptions of these approaches and to identify the main groups that have formed in this context.

It is important to emphasize that these approaches are just as heterogeneous as those referred to as 'mainstream' approaches, discussed in earlier chapters. Scholars using sociological approaches differ in their research interests (individual actors or European society as a whole), epistemology (positivist or post-positivist) and research methods (quantitative or qualitative). Thus we find, within approaches focusing on public policy, normative analyses based on fields such as citizens, identity and society, systemic approaches and, finally, critical approaches that borrow their conceptual tools from Michel Foucault, Pierre Bourdieu, Norbert Elias, Antonio Gramsci and Jürgen Habermas. Talking about a single sociological approach is thus an oxymoron. The notion of 'approach' suggests common standards or research identities. With regard to sociological approaches, however, this specific methodological or epistemological identity seems very difficult to locate; a dilemma that sociological approaches share with constructivist approaches, to which they are indeed very close (Checkel 2007; Christiansen, Joergensen and Wiener 2001).

This chapter analyses these approaches and is split into two parts. The first part focuses more specifically on the ontological (the objects analysed by the framework) and epistemological (what can be discovered through the approach) bases of sociological approaches to European integration. The second examines five different groups of research, all of which share the most basic assumption that 'actors matter': the sociology of public policies, normative analyses and legitimacy, systemic approaches, a critical or post-positivist framework, and critical political economy.

Sociological approaches: more than a just method?

Sociological approaches are at the heart of some of the seminal analyses establishing European studies (Favell 2007): Ernst Haas's (1958) work on elite socialization during the creation of the ECSC (European Coal and Steel Community); Karl Deutsch et al.'s (1957) research on the consequences of increased transnational interaction between citizens of European states, pinpointing these phenomena as the most propitious to regional integration; Amitai Etzioni's (1965) study on the role of elites in the integration process in four regional integration projects; and Stanley Hoffmann's essays in the sociological tradition of Raymond Aaron, on the influence of governmental elites on the European integration process (1995) (Chapters 1, 2 and 3).

Subsequently, however, these research subjects were partially abandoned by European integration scholars. An increasingly large portion of the studies were based more on formalization and abstraction, searching for conditions under which a politics of rationality could emerge, than on analytical reflexivity (for a debate see Gilbert 2008; Cafruny and Ryner 2009; Rosamond 2007). This was particularly due to the fact that scientific accounts of European integration were strongly influenced by ideological foundations about the sense and direction of this particular process (Milward et al. 1993). It is only since the end of the 1990s and the beginning of the 2000s that sociological approaches to European integration have once again gained favour, as the conceptual analyses of Adrian Favell and Virginie Guiraudon (2011), Chris Rumford (2009), Ian Manners (2007) and Adrian Favell (2007) have shown.

Although any exercise to define the precise boundaries of sociological approaches is a hazardous one indeed, the assumption here is that these boundaries are characterized by two dimensions: ontological and epistemological.

Ontological differences: what should be studied?

Sociological approaches argue that it is not the actions and attitudes of European institutions or states that should be taken as a starting point in European studies, but the interaction, the personal exchanges, the coordination mechanisms between individuals, as well as the training of groups and elites, the power games, and normative games and conflicts.

Thus, sociological approaches seem to focus more on individual actors and less on institutional structures. Their aim is to understand the changes under way in diverse sociopolitical contexts.

This can be done in two ways. Either they adopt a bottom-up perspective that concentrates on the exchanges and linkages between social, economic and political actors that constitute European society as a whole, instead of analysing institutional structures or institutions as such (Smith 2004). It is this particular vision that distinguishes sociological approaches from new institutionalisms (Chapter 4). While new institutionalists and sociologists are very critical when it comes to the descriptive analysis of institutional structures and functions as undertaken in previous institutionalist accounts, sociologists insist on the crucial role of actors *beyond* the institutional structures that constrain them. These sociological studies have taken a critical approach, rejecting both the opposition between interests and ideas and the state-centrism of so-called 'mainstream' approaches (White 2010). According to these sociologists, it is thus not possible to analyse only the economic rationality behind a German representative's position in the Council. It is necessary to study the social references in which he or she was embedded (the German trauma of the Second World War, the fear of both right-wing and left-wing extremism, the insistence on the importance of limiting inflation), and to link these elements to more individual positions, if possible (the university the actors has graduated from, etc.).

Or scholars take a data-driven approach in which large-scale databases on European society are analysed to understand the class structure, allegiances and specific behaviour of Europeans. Here, the idea is not to understand the policy process, but how European citizens live, work and structure themselves in the European space and in European welfare states (Favell 2008; Diez Medrano 2003; Ferrera 2005).

The focus is thus on actors, practices, structures and social representations. Overall, '(sociological) approaches are often perceived in terms of dynamics may they be institutional, cognitive, political, intersectoral …; they balance between an actor-centred sociology and a form of sociology which is more attentive to long-term sociohistorical dynamics, more interested in phenomena of structuration or genetic structuralism' (Bigo 2006).

This suggests an interest in a specific type of empirical data that has been left aside by other European integration research: sociological studies are based on the analysis of the role individual and collective actors play in European integration. This approach leads to both macro- and micro-sociological works. Thus, not only are power relations between stakeholders in decision-making processes of interest – these power relations which are at the heart of studies of political science approaches – but also, and more especially, the transformations within societies themselves. In fact, sociological approaches recognize the construction and transformation of institutions and the results of this construction, i.e. the restructuring of social, political and public spaces at the national level (Ferrera and Rhodes 2000; Cederman and Daase 2003).

Is sociology different from constructivism?
These elements hint already at the differences between sociological approaches and constructivism, with which sociological approaches are often compared. However, while there is probably more that unites constructivism and sociological approaches than separates them, as most contemporary sociologists would agree, based on the rather trivial statement that 'social facts' do not exist independently of interpretive schemes and institutions (Searle 1996; for a debate see Saurugger and Mérand 2010), significant differences exist nonetheless. Although both traditions emphasize the production and reproduction of social practices and insist on the situated character of social action, sociological approaches criticize constructivist research with regard to two particular elements: on the one hand, the limited empirical interest of constructivism, which focuses almost exclusively on identity and socialization, and where actor rationality is absent, and on the other, the creation of false dualities such as the opposition between interests and ideas, or values and preferences (Mérand 2008b; Jenson and Mérand 2010).

1   Who are the carriers of ideas?
    With regard to the first criticism voiced, sociologists argue that concentrating on socialization and identity in general terms does not allow us to identify who the carriers of identities or cognitive frames are. On the contrary, constructivists (Chapter 7) explain the emergence of common beliefs, standards and identities as the result of an interaction between agents at European level. To know who the carriers are, is, however, decisive because cognitive frames and values do not float freely (Risse-Kappen 1994). According to sociologists, they are purposively used by actors to create a feeling of belonging, and establish a certain context in which actions become possible. One of the main objectives is, therefore, to identify the actors and track the process by which shared norms and identities develop. Based on Paul Dimaggio and Walter Powell's (1991) sociological institutionalism (Chapter 4), sociologists advance the assumption that repeating interaction can lead to the creation of common rules that primarily support the dominant actors in a given political sector. These developments are not natural phenomena: these norms are far from being homogeneous, but permanently redefined and reinterpreted, based on power struggles between actors.
    Sociologists therefore insist that good social science must, by definition, be pluralistic. While they share this idea with constructivists, they distance themselves from them through their desire to develop

rigorous empirical research protocols, contrary to the constructivist research agenda, which some sociologists often criticize as vague.

2   False dualisms?

With regard to the second criticism, Niilo Kauppi (2010) suggests that the main difference between constructivism and sociological approaches in EU studies has to do with ontology. Taking a close look at influential constructivist publications in EU studies, in particular at Jeffrey Checkel's research, he argues that most EU constructivism is based on an exclusive ontological framework that reproduces false dualisms, such as objective/subjective, socialization/calculation, interest/norm or reason/culture. An example of this false dualism is the sequential model, in which norms and interests are said to operate at different moments in social action (Jupille and Carporaso 1999). This norm/interest dichotomy is rejected by many sociologists, including those in the tradition of Pierre Bourdieu, Norbert Elias and Luc Boltanski, for whom there is a single, but contextual, logic of action. This inclusive ontology, Kauppi acknowledges, introduces 'shades of grey' into the analysis – and that is probably the reason why many EU constructivists have thought it wise to stick to dualisms (Parsons 2010).

Epistemological characteristics: how should we study European integration?

Epistemologically, the differences between sociological and political science approaches to integration might be more significant. Contrary to political science, sociological approaches to European integration are characterized by a more or less radical questioning of rational choice approaches. In this sense, sociological perspectives cover a vast metatheoretical area, across a continuum between rationalist and reflexive poles (Keohane 1988). While some frameworks, such as the sociology of public policy, the systems approaches in this field or parts of the normative approaches are based on a positivist paradigm, all of them underline the difficulties of adopting a strict language of causality. Critical approaches even go a step further and openly question the distinction between dependent and independent variables. These approaches insist on interlocking and overlapping phenomena and processes where effects and causes become mixed up. In parallel, the challenge that sociologists share is to identify how to measure and observe the behaviour of actors in the political and social system of the EU. Their aim is not to avoid abstract theorization, but rather to use empirical studies that contribute inductively to a better understanding of the Union's political and social system. A number of sociological approaches to European integration, therefore, go beyond a materialist research approach to show that the EU is also an evolving construction through its discourses, symbols and social representations. These critical approaches refute the idea that the world could be understood as it is, i.e. that there is a means to describe the world as it really is. Instead, all one can do is to describe the world as one sees it through a specific and individual lens. The world becomes relative. In other words, dominant theories are, therefore, not dominant because they best explain the social phenomena analysed, but rather, because those scholars that defend these theories have more resources than the others.

In this research context, the fact remains that the construction of refutable causal claims is considered difficult, and that the distinction between dependent and independent variables is clearly a problem. Nevertheless, their differentiation is considered a necessary heuristic tool and premise that must be continually questioned in order to show the empirical links existing between social phenomena. Thus, 'political formalization [is] not useless, it is also important to get as close as possible to the research object, to immerse oneself in it, to familiarize oneself with the social practices that underpin it, while keeping the distance that is necessary to contextualize what social actors comprehend as their "common sense"' (Mérand 2008: vii–viii).

The mosaic of sociological approaches

While approaches are heterogeneous, it is nevertheless possible to distinguish five groups of more or less coherent fields of research within the sociological analysis of European integration: the sociology of public policy, normative and legitimization frameworks, systemic approaches, critical sociology and critical political economy (see also Saurugger 2009).

The sociology of public policy

The sociology of European public policy distinguishes between the roles of policy-makers, on the one hand, and the framing capacity these same actors have when they participate in policy-making processes, on the other. This leads to two research agendas: first, research on the identity of social and political elites at the European level, as well as of those located at the margins of this transnational space (the movement of jobless or protest movements more generally) and, secondly, studies on European policy-making processes in general that analyse the attitudes and preferences of agents.

European elites
The first attempts to study elites and marginalized agents in the European integration process focused on the individuals and organizations that

Table 8.1   *Sociological perspectives in EU studies in brief*

Perspectives	Main assumptions
Sociology of public policies	Policy-makers do not only act according to their preferences and economic interest but also according to their social background, which frames and predetermines those interests
Normative analysis and legitimacy approaches	The analysis of actors and their legitimacy games shows that the EU is not technocratic or depoliticized
Systemic approaches	European studies need to analyse European society as a whole
Critical and post-positivist framework	Search for explanations for political conflict and competition • Actors monopolize resources • Existence of dominant parties to the detriment of the dominated
Critical political economy	The EU cannot be analysed independently from its underlying economic – neoliberal and capitalist – paradigms.

constitute, and contribute to shaping, this new political space (Guiraudon 2000, 2006). Its aim was to enable the analysis of collective identities, action repertoires, processes of framing and political opportunity structures open to actors in Brussels. This set of literature empirically analyses the socioprofessional trajectories of different actors before they moved to Brussels, Luxembourg or Strasbourg and their socialization process got under way. These approaches identify the competencies sought by European institutions, interest groups and companies and the process of constructing the role that specific actors play in the European policy-making arena. The purpose of the research is to better understand these roles and the influence they have in the production and development of public policies. The starting point, then, is not public policy *per se*, but the power game at play between actors as public policy is developed. Empirical research in this area concentrates on individual and collective actors, such as the European Commission and European civil servants more generally (M. Bach 1999; Ross 1994a, 1994b, 2008; Georgakakis and De Lassalle 2004; Shore 2000), members of the European Parliament (Marrel and Payre 2006; Navarro 2009), social movements and interest groups (Balme and Chabanet 2008), as well as on actors working in specific policy fields in particular such as foreign, defence and security policies, for example (Buchet de Neuilly 2005; Mérand 2006, 2008b). The majority of these studies analyse the influence of factors such as gender, education and political experience on political careers and collective action. In this context, the EU is a specific power structure in which agents evolve according to their sociological background. These studies are thought crucial in order to understand how policies are made:

> To understand the EU as a distinctive form of social organization and power structure, its influence and the effects of its policies, one has to 'get inside politics'. On must identify who the individuals and groups making up the EU are, where they come from, what kinds of resources and networks they have access to, how they perceive reality – their roles, the institutions in which they work and, more broadly, the social world around them. (Kauppi 2011: 150–1)

Some of these studies, in particular those concentrating on European civil servants, have been criticized for the way they concentrate on describing actors' attitudes, at the expense of analyzing what should be the main research question – how to explain European public policies through actors' attitudes.

Actors' roles in public policy
The second theme investigated in sociological approaches remedies these shortcomings by referring to the *influence* of actors' attitudes and strategies on public policy outcomes. By 'sociologizing' constructivism to a certain extent and developing a strategic constructivist approach (Chapter 7), a number of authors, in particular Kathleen McNamara (1998), Craig Parsons (2002) and Nicolas Jabko (2006), reintroduce politics into their European public policy analysis. In their work, they stress the key role of actors in the production of ideas and cognitive frameworks which, when they are used strategically, lead to reformed public policies. Their research recalled and inspired Sophie Jacquot and Cornelia Woll's (2004b) work on usages in Europeanization processes of public policies for strategic means (Chapter 6). European integration is used to either increase one's powers or legitimacy at the national level, or to circumvent the domestic level and to intervene directly at the European level. These authors focus on the role of ideas and perceptions in institutional development, while emphasizing actors' strategies in decision-making processes. This idea is also developed in studies aiming to link sociology to neo-institutionalism (Mérand 2008a; Jenson and Mérand 2010). These studies underline the fact that new institutionalisms – in particular those with a historical and sociological background – share the sociologist's concern for the empirical analysis of social

action, systems of meaning and patterns of conflict. At the same time, they agree with constructivists that systems of meaning embedded in norms are extremely relevant when seeking to account for actors' attitudes. In this vein, Mérand (2008b) and Bickerton (2010) analyse the Common Foreign and Security Policy (CFSP) as a process made possible by progressive socialization between relevant European actors. Stefan Goetze and Berthold Rittberger (2010), for instance, borrow from this school to address the issue of institution-building. The authors identify the factors that have pushed governmental elites since the 1960s to grant the European Parliament more powers, and for this process of conceding powers to be articulated on the grounds of eliminating the democratic deficit of the EU. The authors argue that political and social elites framed the legitimacy of the European Parliament and established it as a 'cognitive script'. In an attempt to connect sociology with constructivism around a critique of rational choice theory, their study advocated adopting a historical approach in order to understand which discourses have come to dominate the policy agenda in institution building. Thus, when studying cognitive frames, it is crucial to do so in conjuncture with the social structures that produce them. It is particularly important not to downplay the social dimensions of strategy and the conflict-ridden nature among actors engaged in norm construction (Kauppi 2010). As ideas and values, norms do not float freely. Their establishment, development and maintenance imply constant strategic calculations.

Actors' roles and Europeanization

Research on the influence of European integration on national public policies and societies – so-called Europeanization research (Chapter 6) – also has a sociological branch. These studies have shown that, in spite of the pertinence of identifying a European initiative as an initiator of political, economic and social change at the domestic level, Europeanization processes are more complex. Several recent works have investigated the intertwining and overlapping of local, domestic and European levels to understand transformation processes within the spheres of public and political action.

Using Radaelli's (2001) definition (Chapter 6), several studies stress the complexity of Europeanization processes (Jacquot and Woll 2004b; Palier and Surel 2007). Assessing the precise influence of European integration at the domestic level is more difficult if EU and member-state institutions are not considered as two separate and independent systems, but an institutionally and cognitively interlinked one. This rich strand of research has highlighted the challenges that exist for researchers with regard to the clear differentiation between top-down and bottom-up approaches in Europeanization. Instead of choosing between them, two research attitudes are necessary: first, putting the actor and not the institutional structures at the heart of the analysis; and, secondly, paying more attention to the reasons behind actors' behaviour. The authors advance the assumption that actors can 'choose' and 'learn' independently from institutional pressures. They suggest the existence of contradictory pressures, on the one hand recognizing that European integration does not systematically trigger public policy change, while at the same time asserting that the analysis of change in actors' attitudes at the domestic level needs to be made linked to decisions taken at the European level.

Closer to critical sociology, a series of studies looks at the socialization processes and reappropriation approaches at the domestic local level by European integration (Baisneé and Pasquier 2007). The authors see Europeanization more as a tool for emphasizing a series of transformations in European societies. The main criticism of these studies is that so-called 'mainstream' Europeanization approaches do not seem to recognize the multiplicity of actors involved and the constant interdependence between levels of governance. On the contrary, according to this research, European institutions participate in the production of global cognitive matrices within a broad scope of social frames, which affect a wide variety of structures and sociopolitical groups (Weisbein 2008). To better understand the processes of *reception* and *appropriation* of European norms, these sociological approaches question the dynamics of change generated by European integration and its effect on the self-representation and practices of domestic political and administrative elites. Micro-sociological analyses of these mechanisms of being exposed to and, thus, socialized with, European norms (management of European programmes, development of European projects, specialization in EU law, etc.) are considered a better way to illustrate the effects of European norms on domestic political systems (central and devolved administration, local and regional authorities) and the role of political and administrative elites (Pasquier and Weisbein 2006). These studies are characterized by the authors' deliberately 'microscopic' research design, based on a very small number of micro-sociological and detailed case studies, as well as on the analysis of a limited number of actors and small groups.

This research suggests that 'mainstream' Europeanization studies focused primarily on institutional frameworks, while neglecting the full range of actors, strategies and political configurations involved. Learning and socialization phenomena, however, have been present in many of the Europeanization studies since the start (see also Börzel and Risse 2003; Saurugger and Radaelli 2008; Mérand 2008a). The embeddedness of actors in domestic structures, and their permanent interaction with European structures, have been forcefully insisted upon by earlier studies on European integration.

Sociology of public policy in a comparative perspective

A final group of sociological studies on European policy processes adopts a resolutely comparative perspective and focuses on the challenges faced by the welfare state today (Ferrera 2005; Crouch 1999; Crouch et al. 2004), on industrial relations (Crouch and Traxler 1995; Traxler, Blaschke and Kittel 2001; Erne 2008) and on cities and regions (Le Galès 2002). Its authors do not concentrate on one public policy in particular, but on the influence of European integration on people's perceptions of social boundaries and the links between individuals, groups and territories in welfare states. Thus, by pointing out that European integration and globalization have transformed the context in which welfare states operate, the authors show that the boundaries of the welfare state itself are changing.

This specific strand of research makes connections with the other transformations in European integration induced by globalization and national politics. European integration is just one of several factors that have pushed agents to modify their preferences, cognitive frames and strategies. These comparative politics approaches are very much linked to mainstream political science and sociology frameworks existing outside European studies.

Normative approaches

In the field of normative approaches to European integration, sociologists stress the asymmetric distribution of power. The emphasis is placed on power and legitimacy games and, through this, the ability to link politics to policies. Scholars question the general assumption that European integration leads to increased depoliticization or technocratization of politics. Two approaches can be distinguished here: on the one hand, social theory, which concentrates normatively on the necessity of a European public sphere, on the other, studies that adopt an empirical approach for assessing the democratic character of the EU. Contrary to normative and mostly conceptual social theory, empirical sociologists are interested in gathering data through fieldwork projects of varying magnitudes.

Social theory

Social theory approaches to European integration are part of a normative logic that calls for the construction of a cosmopolitan area (Habermas 2001, 2003; Delanty 2005; Delanty and Rumford 2005; Beck and Grande 2007). According to cosmopolitanism, as defined by Rumford (Rumford 2008), the policy of public and discursive arenas is not necessarily framed by state borders. From this perspective, the transformation of Europe is primarily social rather than political or institutional. Europe, or the EU more specifically, is characterized as a post-Western or post-national system where loyalty towards the national realm transcends the nation-state. Patriotism becomes post-national (see also Chapter 9). The particularity of this literature is its focus on the social construction of identity – an argument used in a normative way (contrary to constructivist arguments on the same topic) to create a new cosmopolitan identity for Europeans, called constitutional patriotism (Habermas 2003; Delanty 2005). Ulrich Beck and Edgar Grande (2007) explain that seeing Europe as a community of nation-states reproduces the socially constructed boundaries of European integration that have characterized political action in the EU. They argue that taking another point of departure, namely concentrating on what unites people in Europe, would allow us to understand European integration differently, and more specifically, as a cosmopolitan space. For theses authors, cosmopolitan Europe is not a utopia but a reality, and must be analysed in studies of European society. In other words, the EU is not simply the particular moment at which, in contemporary states, elites are supposed to take decisions, execute laws and conduct policies; it involves actors who tend to organize and direct life in society.

Empirical sociology

Empirical sociology is based on radically different premises. Two assumptions are fundamental in this context. First, the EU is not only an institutional arrangement but a power configuration in which several public and private actors participate in the formulation and resolution of public problems. Secondly, the European public sphere does not reflect the 28 states that make up the system, but is a socially and territorially fragmented patchwork that transcends national borders. It is precisely this fragmentation that challenges both the solution to public problems and the legitimization of the actors involved in solving them.

In this sense, to understand the logics of power and how legitimacy is at stake, three issues have to be addressed (Smith 2004). First, it is important not to consider European institutions or individual actors as monoliths. Political, social and cultural representation processes – i.e. the contextualization of phenomena analysed – must be at the heart of any empirical analysis of the European integration process. Secondly, sociological approaches can help uncover the differences between resources of actors in negotiating, bargaining and deliberating in the EU. This focus on resources also ends the distinction between public and private actors, and between local, regional, national, supranational and international levels. In fact, there is a permanent overlap between these different spheres. The third and final issue refers to the question of the legitimacy of the Community's political system itself, long ignored by political sociology, which has seen it as too normative and producing a considerable analytical bias. The new-found interest in this topic focuses on the effort to critically demonstrate how an EU government is slowly emerging.

Two assumptions are developed in this context: First, the way in which European problems are constructed reveals and contributes to the low level of socialization of European government actors and their audience. Secondly, the institutional structure of the EU comprises few arenas for inter-sectoral mediation, such as debates taking place in widely read mass media instead of high-level journals and small-scale discussions in think-tanks. Public debates could bring about more decisions taken in the general interest, as Olivier Costa (2001) as well as Berthold Rittberger (2005) show in their analysis of the construction of the European Parliament. In Rittberger's research on the establishment of the Parliament, the author analyses the reasons that have pushed national governments of EU member states to create and to endow the European Parliament with supervisory, budgetary and legislative powers. Rittberger presents three variables to explain how the European Parliament acquired its status and why it acquired this specific status: First, the relationship between domestic perception of a democratic deficit at the European level and the decision to establish democratic control through the form of a parliament at this level. Second, the divergent views of domestic political elites on the democratic deficit at the EU level. Finally, the construction of beliefs and collective representations at the domestic level that make the establishment of the European Parliament possible and legitimate.

The hypothesis of the importance of national frameworks appears in research on European public space in particular (Koopmans et al. 2003; Foret 2008; Trenz 2011), characterized by an anonymous political personnel, the absence of political symbolism, disparate original mechanisms for the distribution of powers at national level, with those issues debated by elites seen by many as too distant from the daily concerns of European citizens.

Studies show that the European public space is extremely fragmented. It is, therefore, important to address it, not only by looking at support for the European political system among citizens, but also the type of support preferred, and the different visions of what European citizenry should look like (Belot 2002; Duchesne and Frognier 2002). Juan Diez Medrano (2003) has analysed variations in German, Spanish and British citizens' opinions of the EU. The author uses historical and ethnographic conceptual tools to show continuity in the existence of national action repertoires and how representations are promoted by the media. He argues that political identity equates to political self-understanding. And this self-understanding not only refers to the citizen's identification with the EU, but also has a multidimensional nature (Diez Medrano 2009). It covers three dimensions in particular: the self-understanding contained in documents that shape a polity, the self-understanding that shapes the identity of those interpreting these documents, and finally, the dimension Diez Medrano is particularly interested in: the political self-understanding that transpires in public discourse. His account (see also White 2010) presents the self–representation of the EU in everyday life. He shows that there seems to be a mismatch between the elite consensus and citizen division, particularly on social and cultural projects developed in the EU sphere.

Recent studies on European identity reflect this understanding. Identity construction in the EU is a process of diversity – and specifically, diversity in appropriating European integration (Duchesne et al. 2010; Belot 2010). Studies stress that identification with Europe is extremely context-dependent. Research on European citizens' mobility in the EU shows how complex the identity production of free-moving European is in day-to-day dealings (Favell 2008). Favell investigates migration within Europe, focusing on Western Europeans who have left their countries of origin to live elsewhere in Europe. Why, given the freedom of movement provided by the EU, do less than 2 per cent of Western Europeans live, work and settle in European states other than their own? Based on 60 interviews with these 'Eurostars' in three European cities – Amsterdam, London and Brussels – Favell shows that most of these 2 per cent of free-moving Europeans are educated and highly skilled individuals. Their identity is a multi-dimensional layer of values, interests and ways of living that can not be subsumed by one coherent European identity; it is also still deeply entrenched with the organization of life in the nation. Thus, asked whether she feels French or British, a Frenchwoman living in London explained that she feels French in Britain and British in France. Favell's study suggests the continuing power of national cultures despite the flows of capital, culture and persons across borders.

Research in these contexts emphasizes the multi-dimensionality of citizens' attitudes, the persistence of social variables and the importance of the national context, recognizing the fact that citizens identify with Europe, but maintain strong albeit complex relations with their nations.

Systemic approaches

A third group of research focuses on European political systems and European society as a collective actor, quite in contrast to the focus on actors found in other sociological approaches to European integration.

One of the outstanding names of the movement, Neil Fligstein (2008, 2011), adopts the premise that a specific form of European society is in the process of emerging via horizontal and vertical relationships between citizens and elites. According to the author, this will doubtless lead to a socially divided Europe, where those who participate more in European integration will feel more European than those who do not. Thus, he shows the contradictions of European integration: the more advanced integration becomes, the more it leads to politicization and conflicts at the heart of the integration project itself. At the same time, absence of conflict does not mean that there is a generalized movement of loyalty towards the EU. Absence of conflict might refer to the existence of *polite indifference* between Europeans. It is also possible to see that possessing a feeling of belonging to the EU does not necessarily mean that one will feel close to it, or have a positive attitude to other European citizens. One might agree with European integration for economic reasons, but reject the idea of a common European identity.

This analysis enlarges Fligstein's economic sociology approach, which perceives the EU as a specific economic system based on a particular form of capitalism. Here, Fligstein and his colleagues (Fligstein and Mara-Drita 1996; Fligstein and Mérand 2002; Fligstein and Stone Sweet 2002) question how markets emerge, stabilize and are transformed in the EU. The emphasis they place on the social construction of judicial frameworks in the single market is what differentiates this approach from historical institutionalism. In the sociological approach, these norms become variables that need to be explained and are no longer considered as simple data.

This argument is at the centre of sociological approaches, which seek to show how actors deliberately construct politics and markets through social conflict. This market construction very much influences the dynamics of European society. Fligstein (2008) argues that, the initial economic issues, which seemed to be the basis of European integration, are slowly transformed into political debates: 'Over time, trade increases and becomes more focused upon politics. This has been true not only in the 1970 and 1980s as the EU went from six to nine to fifteen members, but in the past ten years as the countries in Eastern Europe applied for membership' (Fligstein 2008: 23). In analysing the investments of European multinationals, Fligstein shows that that they became less national and indeed more European. Not only does he base his research on the market but he investigates three policy areas in depth: the European defence industry, telecommunications and European football. In these three areas the author illustrates how cooperation between domestic and European actors led to deregulation, allowing for the opening up of the markets to foreign as well as other European firms. Through this market building, the middle class of European member states was greatly transformed into European citizens: they increasingly feel European. This transformation, however, also led to the emergence of new conflicts – mostly between rich and poor social classes, as emphasized above (Kriesi et al. 2008).

From a rather different, yet at the same time equally systemic perspective, combining the conceptual frameworks of Stein Rokkan and Albert Hirschman (1970) to explain the formation of a state and the exit strategies of citizens and their representatives, Stefano Bartolini (2005) offers a sociohistorical approach of European integration. Contrary to Fligstein's study, it is based less on the analysis of the European economy, and more on political strategies. By adopting a macro-historical perspective, Bartolini retraces the trajectories of modern integration by situating the European integration process in a new historical phase of Europe's development. More precisely, the EU is seen as the sixth crucial phase in the development of the nation-state in Europe, one that challenges the idea that a political territory must have a certain degree of cohesion. The political construction of the EU is seen here as a boundary-building and boundary-removing process. The EU is based on four interrelated macro-elements: external territorial consolidation and relations; external boundary-building; internal hierarchical order (centre formation, loyalty, system-building, voice, political structuring); and finally, exit, as well as entry options (Bartolini 2005: 4). This allows Bartolini to analyse political and social as well as economic boundaries of European integration; this differs sensibly from the usual approach, which considers borders from a geographical perspective. These boundaries are studied from different angles: the coercive role of the EU with its party-political system, and, to a lesser extent, the establishment of a European market. The removal of boundary controls led to significant consequences for domestic political structures and agencies. These transformations took place at the EU as well as at the domestic level and thus permanently modified the terms of political exchanges.

Although methodologically different, these studies are similar. The main question is how to explain the political, social and economic system of the EU, while taking both social elites and structures and institutions into account. The idea is not to exclude institutions in order to focus only on individuals through macro-sociological studies. On the contrary, these generalist attempts use a broad spectrum of methods, focusing on the establishment of social structures between individuals. In other words, 'European integration has opened up a new phase of wide-ranging expansion of social practices that breaks up the three layered coherence between identities, practices and institutions, or ... dismantles the coincidence among the different types of state economic, cultural, political-administrative and coercion boundaries' (Bartolini 2005: 369).

Critical approaches

The fourth approach – post-positivist, or critical sociology – questions human capacity to objectively describe and effectively control what exists. This approach finds its origins in radical approaches in the social sciences more broadly: Scholars argue in general terms that scientific knowledge cannot be objective, i.e. philosophically or culturally neutral. They insist on the fact that academic methods to grasp reality cannot be limited to organizing facts around hypotheses, because the way these hypotheses are formulated depends on the position of the researcher and on academic fads, i.e. the funding of research projects depends on its accordance with a specific paradigm that is shared by a majority of researchers. Post-positivists, in other words, refuse to separate the subject from the object of their research. This refusal is based on two arguments: on the one hand, theory is not independent of reality and on the other, reality is not external to the theory that it is analysing.

The authors in this field are inspired by critical philosophers and sociologists such as Foucault, Bourdieu or Elias, who explain actors' attitudes through their embeddedness in constant political conflict and competition (Bailey 2006; Cafruny and Ryner 2009). The main subject of their research is the scope of power in European integration. Political activism is considered as a strategy within a given social field 'in which actors seek to monopolise resources, reproduce the benefits of the dominant parties to the detriment of the dominated, control sociopolitical actors' access to the Commission and to Parliament, and dominate weaker actors in a discursive way through the strategic use of ideas and values' (Favell 2007: 127; Manners 2007).

The European political arena is analysed critically by looking implicitly or explicitly at knowledge-building in the EU: how is a European law made? How is EU law accepted as the principal criterion against which the degree of integration is measured? Or indeed, how should the official history of European integration be written? The objective here is to put get some critical distance from the traditional uses of diplomatic or institutional categories of European integration.

The studies of Didier Bigo on police forces (Bigo 1996), of Niilo Kauppi on Members of the European Parliament (Kauppi and Rask Madsen 2008) and Antonin Cohen and Antoine Vauchez's work on judges (Cohen and Vauchez 2007) are exemplary in this context. For example, in their work on judges, Cohen and Vauchez highlight the fact that the ECJ does not only interpret EU law and ensure its equal application across all EU member states. The Court has managed to become an influential actor participating in the government of the EU not because it is legally authorized to interpret law, but through the strong interpersonal relations between national and European judges as well as their participation in the same professional associations (see also Alter 2009). For this reason it is impossible to study European law separately from the study of the lawyers who produce this law. According to Vauchez, law alone has no importance: the social and national background of lawyers and their legal training must be analysed in order to explain the symbolic power of the European legal system and thus the European judicial system as such (Vauchez 2008).

Niilo Kauppi and Michael Rask Madsen (2008) develop the issues and hypotheses surrounding critical approaches to European integration even further. Their reflexive sociology can be contrasted with two approaches to European integration studies: the institutional approach and the normative approach. Their central critique questions the objectivity of institutional studies using institutional structures as data while, according to the authors, systematically ignoring the crucial role of individuals and groups that (re)produce these institutions. In other words, the political reality cannot be treated as an objective fact that can be observed, but rather as a subjective construction. The interpretation of political reality is offered by the very actors that contributed to its establishment. The reflexive sociology approach allows scholars to 'break with these visions by focusing on two crucial aspects of political power in the European Union: first, the political practices of individuals and groups in the dynamic and generally structured context of the European Union today; secondly, the representations that these groups and individuals make of their own political activities' (Kauppi and Rask Madsen 2008: 87).

This analysis partly reflects the work of sociological institutionalists (Chapter 4) who place even more emphasis on individual and collective actors as the premise for, and focus of, empirical research.

Critical political economy

Last but not least, critical political economy perspectives centring on European integration take the debate on into the economic arena. Their assumptions are similar to those of critical sociological approaches (Cafruny and Ryner 2009): an economic system such as the EU cannot be analysed independently from the underlying economic – neoliberal and capitalist – paradigms.

This tradition in EU studies was partly introduced by the literature on the 'varieties of capitalism' (Hall and Soskice 2001) which gave prime position to the role of agency in the European economy, but, contrary to critical political economy perspectives, avoided conceptualizing neoliberalism as a global norm and a pure plot of powerful economic elites. Based on the assumption that national varieties of capitalism develop, critical political economy has gone a step further. It situates the political environment within the broader structure of social power relations and thus relates developments in the EU to the constraints and opportunities of capitalism. In this context, scholars argue that transnational capital is the main agent linking global and European processes of change. It distinguishes two different kinds of *agency* in transnational business: on the one hand, *traditional activities* such as lobbying and formal interest representation, and on the other, a *'higher form'* of political agency that transcends mere corporate interests, and is oriented towards the articulation of a more 'general capitalist interest', in terms of securing a general institutional and policy framework in which capital can operate (van Apeldoorn 2002; Pistor 2005).

According to critical political economists, supranational institutions have not been the key driving factors of European integration. Instead, they have mostly played the role of successful mediators of the interests and strategies of the dominant national, regional and transatlantic forces (Cafruny and Ryder 2007, 2009). Bastian van Apeldoorn, in particular,

Table 8.2   *Sociological perspectives in EU studies*

Perspectives	Main assumptions	Authors
Sociology of public policies • Policy-makers	The analysis of socioprofessional trajectories of European elites is crucial to understanding the preferences and the attitudes of European institutions (Commission, ECJ, Parliament)	Favell 2009b, 1999 Ross 1994a, 1994b, 2008 Shore 2000

• Actors' roles in policy-making
  ○ Actors' roles and Europeanization
  ○ Comparative sociology of public policy
	Policy-makers do not only act according to their preferences and economic interest but also according to their social background, which frames and predetermines those interests	Jacquot and Woll 2004a
		Mérand 2008a
		Bickerton 2011
		Radaelli 2001
		Ferrera 2005
		Erne 2008
		
		Le Galès 2002

Normative analysis and legitimacy approaches	The analysis of actors and their legitimacy games show that the EU is not technocratic or depoliticized • Social theory • Empirical sociology	 Habermas 2001 Delanty and Rumford 2005 Beck and Grande 2007 Rittberger 2005 Foret 2008 Trenz 2011
Systemic approaches	European studies need to analyse European society as a whole	Fligstein 2008, 2011 Bartolini 2005 Diez Medrano 2009 White 2010
Critical and post-positivist frameworks	Search for explanations for political conflict and competition • Actors monopolize resources • Existence of dominant parties to the detriment of the dominated	Favell 2007 Manners 2007 Kauppi and Rask Madsen 2008 Cohen and Vauchez 2007
Critical political economy	The economic environment of the EU is situated in the broader structure of capitalist and neo-liberal power relations. Class agency is the driving force of European integration	Cafruny and Ryner 2007, 2009 van Apeldoorn 2002

designates the latter as '*class agency*'. His objective is to determine its content and, through it, identify the *social purpose* underlying European integration. Hence, his approach counters the established trend in integration literature to focus solely on institutional outcomes of integration, that is, the *form*, and the relative power of states versus supranational institutions, disregarding what actually fuels change, i.e. *content* (van Apeldoorn, 2002: 7).

The main framework for interpreting this critical approach is a revised form of historical materialism. Thus, neo-Gramscian transnationalism focuses on relations of production rather than forces of production, with these relations seen as being largely determined by ideational structures (i.e. laws, rules, norms, ideas) that allow capital to exploit labour (van Apeldoorn 2002: 18). Unlike orthodox Marxists, neo-Gramscians consider that *structure* and *agency* have equal weight and determine each other mutually. Agency presupposes structure because action is always embedded in social relations, which help construct the agent's identity and interests. At the same time, structured properties of social systems are both the medium and outcome of agency, of human activity. Furthermore, agents are considered to be reflexive, knowledgeable and purposeful actors. This understanding contradicts both classical Marxist theory, which sees them as mere 'bearers' of a structure, and rational choice approaches, which frames them as utility maximisers.

Such research questions in the field of the EU's economic structure have the potential to be relaunched by the current post-2008 world recession which has huge implications for the EU. This can be seen as another example of the cyclical development of European integration theories, regularly reinventing themselves by drawing on empirical events (Paterson 2009).

Conclusion

One of the main common characteristics of sociological approaches is that they are not interested solely in the analysis of the EU as a unique organization. They 'insert' this European integration process within broader social issues. This clearly makes them part of the 'mainstreaming' movement of European studies. The traditions presented here are based on the conceptual frameworks developed by sociologists such as: Charles Tilly and Norbert Elias on state construction; Max Weber's analyses of bureaucracy, forms of legitimacy and links between expertise and politics; Georg Simmel on intersubjective communication within societies (1955); and the critical approaches of Pierre Bourdieu, Michel Foucault or Antonio Gramsci.

These conceptual frameworks illustrate the complexity of European integration, not only as a process of economic and political integration, but as a transformation of national and transnational societies. Sociological approaches offer the most innovative research in two areas: first, by opening up the black boxes of European institutions and deconstructing their social representations similarly to the main research agendas of sociological institutionalists, and second, by focusing on the transformation of societies through European integration and globalization.

Despite the plethora of sociological approaches in European studies, one challenge remains: to understand how to address the intergovernmental nature of the EU. In areas where governments have exclusive or even shared competencies, and where decisions are taken unanimously, it is important not to confuse the behaviour of states with the behaviour of individuals. A similar problem exists in the case of rational choice institutionalism. Criticism has been aimed at the principal/agent approach on the grounds that it confuses individuals' and European institutions' behaviour (Chapter 4). It would seem a promising project to try to integrate sociological approaches of international relations within sociological studies, since international relations perspectives conceptualize power, sovereignty and international norms partly as social constructs (Chapter 10).

Chapter 9

Political Theory

Political theory appeared at a relatively late stage in European integration studies, both as a subject of analysis and as an approach to analysing the process of European integration. The aim of political theory is a normative one: it draws up the standards required to create and maintain the legitimate political order necessary for the good functioning of institutions and policies. European political theory develops frameworks to understand the formation of a political entity or, more precisely, the creation of a *demos* at European level. Political theory covers a wide range of research objects: democracy, fairness, justice, citizenship and virtue (Leca 2001). The theoretical perspective questions the 'stateness' of the EU as well as its democratic character. What are the consequences from a normative point of view when the member states of the EU do not have complete sovereignty? To what extent does the EU exhibit the features of a (single) state? Must the EU be judged by the same standards as any other state would be (MacCormick 1999; Føllesdal 2007a, 2007b)? Reflecting on the fundamental principles of political life in the 'new Europe' is as relevant and necessary as it is for considering any national political system. Normative considerations of the form that a union between European citizens and a union between nations should take is in itself not new, as is shown in the first part of the chapter. However, the 'normative turning point' in European studies (Bellamy and Castiglione 2003) is more recent and focuses on trying to understand how European institutions should be governed – and this is very much the subject of the second part of the chapter.

During the second half of the 1990s, one key question dominated the normative debate: the EU's perceived legitimacy deficit. Indeed, the difficulties of ratifying the Maastricht Treaty in France and in Denmark, as well as the debates surrounding its ratification in Germany, which led to the German Federal Court ruling of the compatibility of the treaty with German constitutional law, seemed to bring the so-called era of 'permissive consensus' to a close (Lindberg and Scheingold 1970; Key 1961; Hooghe and Marks 2009). This term implied that European political elites had long been able to pursue their own policy interests because of general support of citizens or, indeed their benevolent disinterest in European integration processes. It allowed member states to cooperate without investing much thought in the democratic character

184

of the supranational organization to which they belonged. In the 1990s, however, these debates allowed for the development of a theoretical and political perspective that questioned the so-called 'legitimacy or democratic deficit' of the EU, and which is the subject of the third and last part of this chapter.

Political philosophy and the construction of European ideas

Deliberations on the form that a union between European peoples should take are not new. Indeed, the debates date back to the seventeenth century. Early debates concerned various projects meant to encourage the integration of the European continent, leading to the increasingly widespread idea of a European federation at the beginning of the twentieth century. However, the difficulties in ratifying the EU treaties since the beginning of the 1990s have reopened theoretical puzzles at the heart of the Europeanist literature. Attempting to go back to the (normative) origins of European integration in the widest sense might seem to be a waste of time. Nevertheless, I would argue that these earlier ideas are the cornerstones for contemporary political arguments in favour of European integration (deepening as well as widening), and have spread into current political philosophy on the European construction process. It is thus important to go back to the origins of myths and ideas tied up with questions of European identity and integration, before turning to contemporary political philosophy.

Archaeology of the idea of a union between European peoples

Charlemagne, as the founding father of an integrated Europe, was a myth promoted by Victor Hugo in the nineteenth century, and recently strongly contested by Jacques Le Goff (2003). In fact, it is possible to date the first political debates about a union between European peoples back to the first half of the seventeenth century. Henry IV proposed the creation of 15 European states of equal size and power which would meet together in the 'very Christian Council of Europe' – a Council excluding Russia. The structure of this Europe was to be composed of six Provincial Councils and a General Council. The main idea was to limit national sovereignty through the Council, which would take executive decisions. In the eighteenth century, the peace plan of the Abbot of Saint-Pierre, the plenipotentiary French minister at the peace conferences at Utrecht in 1713, was published in three volumes under the heading 'Project to ensure perpetual peace in Europe' and 'Project to ensure perpetual peace between Christian sovereigns'. His peace plan was to allow states to join a confederation set up to quell rebellions. These proposals, however, failed to meet with Jean-Jacques Rousseau's approval in his 1762 *Social Contract*. The philosopher's version of a united Europe contained several conditions: all major powers should be members; the confederation's standards should be binding; its armed forces should be more powerful than those of any member state acting alone; and secession would have to be illegal. He went on to argue that without a common army to enforce the union the Abbot's plans were essentially incompatible with the nature of the international system, which showed the state as selfish entities, unwilling to abandon their prerogatives. It was Saint-Pierre's opinion, however, that any change of rules should be decided unanimously.

Voltaire also developed projects to unite European peoples. In his 1745 *Discours préliminaire sur le poème de Fontenoy*, he states:

> The peoples of Europe have humanitarian principles not found in other parts of the world; there are greater links between them, they already share similar laws; all the houses of kings are related; their subjects travel continually and maintain reciprocal relations. Christian Europeans are the same as the Greeks were: they war between themselves but in these dimensions, they maintain such good-will … that often when a Frenchman, an Englishman and a German meet, you might be forgiven for thinking that they were born in the same town.

The projects of David Hume, Immanuel Kant and John Stuart Mill in the eighteenth and nineteenth centuries, and Saint-Simon and Pierre-Joseph Proudhon in the second half of the nineteenth century, returned to the task of designing democratic institutional structures and abandoned the difficult issue of European identity as previously conceived by Rousseau, Voltaire and Victor Hugo.

Thus, in his *Idea for a Perfect Commonwealth* (1752), Hume recommends a federal arrangement to allow deliberation between regional and national governmental entities. The regional authorities would have delegated powers and participate in national decision-making processes, but their laws could always be superseded by the decisions of the federal entity. Kant, in *Perpetual Peace: A Philosophical Sketch* (1795), defends the idea of a confederal cooperation between free states. For Kant, law is the best foundation for peace. Mill defends a similar idea: a confederation should facilitate transnational trade. Finally, in 1814 Saint-Simon published *On the reorganization of European society*, which was concerned with the need to bring the peoples of Europe together in a single political body, while allowing each to retain its national independence. The central idea is that of a Grand Parliament, made up of trading partners, scholars, magistrates and administrators.

Finally, Proudhon proposed a federal organization of Europe in his *Principe fédératif* of 1863: 'A federation is a political contract through

Table 9.1   *Ideas on Europe and its integration*

Theorist	Form of integration	Period
Henry IV	Very Christian Council of Europe (15 European states of equal power, excluding Russia); federal structure (provinces and states)	1620
Abbot of Saint-Pierre	Project to ensure perpetual peace in Europe	1712
Jean-Jacques Rousseau	Confederal Europe – including all European states – establishing binding standards	1761
Voltaire	European peoples share certain specificities: humanitarian principles leading to a common identity	1745
David Hume	Idea for a perfect Commonwealth based on deliberation between regional and national governmental entities	1752
Immanuel Kant	Confederal Europe based on a cooperation between free states	1795
Claude Henri de Rouvroy, comte de Saint-Simon	On the establishment of a European society	1814
Pierre-Joseph Proudhon	Federal Organisation of Europe	1863

which autonomous units agree to one or more specific objectives recip-
rocally and one to another, falling exclusively under the auspices of the
delegates of the federation.'

After the philosophical and institutional debates of the seventeenth
and eighteenth centuries, and the myth-making of the nineteenth century,
the twentieth century was characterized by theoretical and normative
reflections increasingly led by politicians. Beyond the idea of creating a
United States of Europe and the federalist and confederalist movements
that emerged in the 1920s (Chapter 2), the question of democracy implicitly found its way back into economic and security-related concerns
during the establishment of the supranational High Authority in 1951,
the precursor of the European Commission. Already at that point, the
fear of a 'government of experts' existed in the minds of the Dutch and
Benelux officials (Rittberger 2009).

Contemporary political theory of European integration goes down
two more distinct, albeit interrelated, paths. The first is concerned with

the more general question of good government and good *governance* at the EU level. The second relates to the question of the legitimacy deficit, and brings the citizen back in, both as an individual and collective actor.

Classifications of good government and good governance in Europe

As we are reminded by almost all analytical undertakings, any attempt at classification is a perilous exercise. However much of a 'caricature' (Lacroix and Magnette 2008) such an exercise risks being, it is important to demonstrate the context and inherent logic of normative conceptualizations of both good governance and good government (Chryssouchoou 2009). The main aim of this literature is to classify the 'European thing', the EU as not completely a state, nor entirely an international organization or empire. Two analytical approaches are applied to demonstrate the hybrid nature of the Union: the first focuses on central analytical variables of political theory by proposing research that links normative approaches with empirical research; the second theoretical perspective aims at classifying abstract normative political orders that scholars use to illustrate the Union. While the first group is transversal and more interested in policy analysis, the second is concerned with more general questions such as the different democratic features a political order of the EU should possess.

Empirical political theory

Empirical political theory on the EU broadly distinguishes between four key normative issues (Føllesdal 2006, 2007a, 2007b): the legitimacy and roles of certain institutions; the institutions' ability to resolve conflicts; the fundamental principles of the political order in question; and, finally, the political borders of the EU.

Studies on the legitimacy and role of certain institutions look at: the relationships between the ECJ and national courts (Lodge 1994; Dehousse 1999; Joerges and Dehousse 2002); the role of committees in deliberative procedures for decision-making at Community level; and, more broadly, deliberation between public and private actors (Joerges 1999; Héritier 1999; Bellamy 1999). Research on the need for greater accountability of the EU's political and bureaucratic actors to citizens completes this overview (Costa et al. 2001; Majone 1998; Magnette 2000; Lord and Beetham 1998; Mény 2002; Moravcsik 2002; Schmitter 2000). Scholars examine how 'institutional engineering' might allow for a greater transparency of decision-making procedures. This notion is based on the assumption that when institutions become accountable to citizens,

citizens will start to accept and trust them. However, the literature focuses on the citizen in a rather abstract way, and is very influenced by research published on accountability at the end of the 1990s. At the same time, it is questionable whether the networks created and confidence established among state and non-state actors of the EU will remain truly open to all actors and thereby allow equal access to agenda-setting (Abromeit 1998).

A second group of scholars analyse the EU's institutional capacity to produce effective results and, more specifically, to resolve political problems. In this literature, control mechanisms are perceived to be better suited to the institutional structure of the EU than conventional parliamentary instruments. These instruments would make the Union more democratic. Faced with an increasingly complex and fragmented executive, in competition with other public and private actors, and which frequently delegates and decentralizes powers, political theory has been used to look at the mechanisms controlling such dissemination of power. At the EU level, much has been written on bodies such as the Court of Auditors, the anti-fraud office (OLAF), the European ombudsman and expert committees involved in auditing, criminal law and politics (Costa et al. 2001).

Debates on the regulatory character of European public policies also fall under this heading. Characterizing the EU as a regulatory state, and borrowing from the American model, Giandomenico Majone considers independent agencies to be essential bodies for introducing such regulation (see also Chapter 5). From both a theoretical and constitutional-normative point of view, the literature on the regulatory state suggests that the delegation of regulatory powers to non-majoritarian institutions stabilizes short-term political commitments and reinforces the credibility of programme-based ones. Majone's conception is very close to that of Edmund Burke, as analysed by Hanna Pitkin: while citizens have a *real interest* in what they know very little about, the representative is allowed to represent what he thinks is best for his citizens, even if this is contrary to the citizens' wishes. However, this notion has a democratic bias in that, when this logic is extended even further, we are confronted with a situation whereby the 'neutral' expert decides the technical questions and 'takes charge of' the ignorant masses, just as a parent takes charge of a child (Pitkin 1967; Majone 1996).

Experts are used extensively in European policy-making processes – hence the idea of neutral agencies helping public policies to work properly. According to the literature on the regulatory state, experts, through their consultative bodies, guarantee the neutrality and rationality of opinions in managing European public policies. This partly concurs with those studies suggesting that the efficiency of political and administrative leaders in guaranteeing the democratic nature of a political system is a sufficient, or at least non-negligible, factor (Scharpf 1999) for making a system democratic. This presumed neutrality, however, in particular in technical and scientific areas (Habermas 1968), is somewhat opposed to the idea that experts could represent specific preferences in their arguments. The normative idea behind the use of experts is to consider that these actors might arrive at consensus through deliberation. The Union is analysed in this context as a paradox: instead of leading to total paralysis, the EU as a system is loaded in favour of consensus or, if consensus is not possible, to make attempts to subterfuge in order to avoid paralysis (Héritier 1999).

Political order and fundamental principles

Issues relating to the legitimacy of values and ideals that are at the foundations of the European integration project feature in studies on fundamental political principles, such as the welfare state, public participation and the state of law. For example, should the EU project include social policies with a redistributive character or even create a common European police force? Can the benefits of a European welfare state apply to individuals who do not share the same nationality and culture (Bellamy 1999; Schmitt and Thomassen 1999; Miller 1995; Scharpf 2002)? In this group of research we also find the debate on social justice beyond the state. Given that delivering social justice requires the state allocating resources generated by the market, the questions of how these markets are regulated, as well as what political strategy should be pursued to do so, are crucial (Lehning and Waele 1997). Again, this question is not new. Transferring resources from richer to poorer groups of European citizens was and still is the object of regional (cohesion) policy. Studies into horizontal transfers over the life cycle of an individual, however, cannot be found at the EU level. Yet, such questions on social justice are at the heart of the debate on social Europe, whether explicitly or implicitly. For many citizens, 'good government' means fulfilling the role of a welfare state; these mechanisms are still managed solely by member states alone, even if the EU's redistributive policies (agriculture, cohesion, etc.) have clear welfare objectives.

Finally, research on the nature of the political community established by European integration looks at the question of EU borders, and in particular, the identity question linking empirical fieldwork and normative approaches. This work, along with Joseph Weiler's, contends that

> the conceptualization of a European demos should not be based on the construction of real or imaginary trans-European cultural affinities or shared histories nor on the construction of a European national' myth of the type which constitutes the identity of the organic nation. The decoupling of nationality and citizenship opens the possibility, instead of thinking of co-existing multiple demoï. (Weiler 1995: 252)

Table 9.2   *Normative theories on the EU as a political community*

Theoretical perspectives	Main argument	Main authors
Civic nationalists	– Democracy stems from the nation-state – It is impossible to transfer principles and values to the supranational level cultural anti-Europeanism)	Miller 1995 Canovan 1996 Manent 2006 Gauchet 2005
Republican federalists	– Transfer of national democratic thoughts to EU is necessary – Creation of transnational solidarity	Eriksen and Fossum 2000 Nanz 2006 Walker 2008
Liberal post-nationalists	– EU is a set of procedures, rights and norms which influence national democracies	Weiler 2002 Bellamy and Castiglione 2003
Kantian cosmopolitanists	– The transnationalization of European nations lays foundations for the development of a shared civic culture – The EU is a shared world of values and meanings beyond the state	Habermas 1981, 2001 Lacroix 2009 Ferry 2006

More conceptually, the cosmopolitan ideas of Habermas, Francis Cheneval (2005), Jean Marc Ferry (2000, 2005) and Étienne Balibar (1992) are in opposition to those who support a strictly identity-based definition of the EU. Recent work on the way in which religion can act as an identity builder and normative resource at the supranational level in a secularized Europe is of interest in this respect (Schlesinger and Foret 2006; Foret 2007).

The very rich literature on the relationship between identity and a supranational regime can be distinguished along four lines, based on Lacroix's (2008) extremely useful differentiation: civic national (a telos-oriented Euroscepticism), republican federalist, liberal post-nationalist ('the dreamed-of Europe') and post-nationalist republican ('the missed Europe').

Civil national approaches

The civic national approach is particularly critical of European integration (for an indepth analysis see Lacroix 2008). According to scholars adhering to this line of thought, it is impossible to transfer principles and values to the supra- or transnational level since democracy stems necessarily from the nation-state. According to these theorists, democracy and, by extension, any legitimate democratic order, cannot be transposed into another framework when neither the language nor the belief system is shared by all the individuals of the larger political sphere. In this context, European integration is considered as a set of decisions taken by non-legitimate leaders on behalf of citizens who are themselves distanced from national social and political concerns (Manent 2006; Thibaud and Ferry 1992; Miller 1995; Canovan 1996). According to these authors, functionalism has clear limits; it is not enough to share the same interests and the same values. In order to create a political body, the EU needs a political will to affirm its identity internally as well as externally. According to Marcel Gauchet, this identity would need to be based on a constitutive relationship with the past (Gauchet 2005).

These Eurosceptic political theorists offer a nuanced and extremely pertinent vision of Euroscepticism. For them, Euroscepticism is not a homogenous term, as its use by the media would suggest. On the contrary, different 'varieties of Euroscepticism' exist, a specificity that has also been emphasized by scholars in political sociology (Leconte 2010; see also Hooghe and Marks 2007; Chapter 8 in this volume). In political philosophy, Euroscepticism takes four forms: utilitarian Euroscepticism, referring to scepticism about the gains to be derived from European integration; political Euroscepticism, which refers to a principled opposition to the establishment of supranational institutions; a value-based Euroscepticism, whereby it is held that EU institutions interfere unduly in matters where the nation-state governs; and, finally, a cultural anti-Europeanism, where the idea of a common European culture or common European values is rejected, either on the grounds that this culture threatens national values or because it is deemed that no such thing exists. These different varieties of Euroscepticism can be controversial for different reasons, and one must recognize that many citizens may choose to reject a particular aspect of European integration (e.g. a new treaty) while remaining, on the whole, a fervent proponent of the wider social and political process.

In political theory, Euroscepticism can be argued on the grounds of (a lack of) legitimacy as well as on the basis of its (flawed) rationale (Morgan 2005). While legitimacy claims refer to the legitimate right of European institutions to issue binding demands (a claim that political and value-based Eurosceptics, as well as anti-Europeanists, reject), rationale refers to the aims and goals of the European integration project. In this sense, the notion of justification is similar to Neil Walker's idea of 'polity legitimacy', which refers to 'the overall support for and the stability of the polity in question of a self-standing political community' (Walker 2001: 13). Goal- or project-centred Eurosceptics argue that 'no matter how transparent the process, no matter what institutional tinkering with the product, a more politically unified Europe is flatly undesirable' (Walker 2007: 56).

More specifically, it is possible to distinguish between two types of project-centred Eurosceptics, both arguing against supranational integration based on nationalist or, better, state-centred arguments (Morgan

2005: 56–8). On the one hand, there are conservative Eurosceptics – or 'civic national philosophers', as Lacroix (2008) calls them – such as Manent (2006) and Gauchet (2005), for whom a European supranational entity threatens national identity. On the other hand, there are social democratic or socialist Eurosceptics who argue along similar lines, but instead of bringing to the fore the national identity issue, underline how welfare identity is threatened by neoliberal and postmodern tendencies (Offe 2000; Miller 1995). This second argument has been increasingly visible in national debates, in particular surrounding the Dutch and French referenda on the Constitutional treaty of 2005. This clearly project-oriented Euroscepticism is aimed at creating a more egalitarian redistributive citizenship (for a discussion see Morgan 2005: 66). Where the two forms of project-based Euroscepticism meet up is in their rationale based on the nation-state. On the one hand, only the nation-state is thought to be able to maintain the political and – by conventional wisdom wrongly assumed – national coherence of the State. Conservative Eurosceptics argue that each supranational institution threatens the identity of the nation. In contrast, social-democratic Eurosceptics argue that only a national community secures social justice, as only this community is able to create the feeling of loyalty necessary for redistributive policies to become possible.

Republican federalist approaches
For republican federalists, the EU is untrodden democratic terrain. The standards required for a supranational democracy to emerge, and for it to exist in parallel to national democracies, should be inspired by the democratic thought developed in the domestic realm. To create a European public space, a written constitution is necessary, as is a charter of rights, a parliamentary regime and a set of shared fiscal, budgetary, economic and social policies to allow for the creation of the transnational solidarity needed to secure a shared political culture (Eriksen and Fossum 2000; Bobbio and Viroli 2003; Nanz 2006). Critics of this approach, above all Moravcsik (2005), argue that taking constitutionalism beyond the state in order to create a democratic government must be seen as a 'casting error'. To sum up critical objections, Walker states that the opposition to the idea of constitutionalization stems not only from 'the idea of a sovereign and so autonomous, self-contained and internally integrated legal and political order, but also the notion that for each sovereign political order there is a distinct "society" or "demos", as well as a dedicated collective agency – whether "nation", "people" or even the "state" itself' (Walker 2008: 521; 2007). In being closer to the republican federalist movement, albeit adopting a slightly critical perspective, Walker suggests the use of constitutionalism as a framing mechanism, differentiating between juridical, political-institutionalist, self-authorizing, social and discursive frames. Although these frames make the debate about a

European constitution possible, in insisting on the multiple types and debates when talking about the constitution, Walker underlines – in what is the 'critical' attribute of his approach – the limits of this understanding. These limits lay in the incapacity of the concept, understood as post-state constitutionalism or 'multi-level constitutionalism' (Pernice 1999), to break sufficiently with the normative properties of the Westphalian state, most particularly state sovereignty. State sovereignty is not considered in this literature as static but as a dynamic concept used or adjusted by European and domestic actors, according to their preferences.

Liberal post-nationalist approaches
The authors of the third movement – the liberal post-nationalist movement – see the EU as a set of procedures, rights and norms which influence national democracies and make them more democratic. This process takes place through the participation of member states in a European deliberation process. Member states must make their positions public and accessible, with European citizens treated in the same way across the entire European territory. This European democracy of the future is legitimized by the rights of individuals (human rights) which apply to all member states of the EU (Weiler 2002; Bellamy and Castiglione 2003). In fact, deliberative democracy places the emphasis on seeking better solutions through discussion and the confrontation of ideas. The fundamental idea is to switch from a logic of 'bargaining' to a logic of 'deliberation'. Deliberation is considered to be leading better democracy. Through the free exchange of ideas and arguments, the aim is to obtain the best decision possible. While the former is characterized by a quest for compromise through concessions between actors with stable preferences, the latter is more an exchange of rational arguments to secure a broad agreement (Habermas 1981). Deliberative democracy has enjoyed wide exposure in European negotiations where bargaining and deliberation are key features of the decision-making process (Cohen and Sabel 1997; Magnette 2004; Kohler-Koch and Rittberger 2007).

Kantian cosmopolitanism
The fourth and final approach is inspired by Kantian theory and referred to as Kantian cosmopolitanism. Its major proponent, Jürgen Habermas (2001), argues that the de-partitioning and transnationalization of European nations lay the foundations for the development of a shared civic culture, without converting it into a state. The normative strength of the EU resides primarily in the fact that it challenges this 'national–EU' equation by inviting each to dissociate their membership of a judicial and political framework with a universal scope from their membership of a 'shared world' of shared values and meanings (Lacroix 2009). The notion of constitutional patriotism somewhat confuses the issue, as Jean-Marc Ferry notes:

As much as we have pondered the association between the words 'patriotism' and 'constitutional' to see that if they match, how they do so and what meaning emerges, the expression remains difficult to understand. The problem is that the European Union has nothing else at hand to unify the European peoples. Despite the insistence on common spiritual heritage, and because there is no substantial, unchallengeable political project, the multiplicity of national cultures means that fundamentally only shared values can cement the Union and frame its action according to a given set of principles: recognition, reciprocity, non-discrimination, cooperation, tolerance, transparency and participation. (Ferry 2006: 6)

One of the applications of this particular philosophical strand is the idea of the EU as a public sphere. It is understood as a 'space or arena for (broad, public) deliberation, discussion and engagement in societal issues' (de Vreese 2007). In this understanding, informed conversation must take place between rational individuals who must resolve their difference by non-coercive means. Most of the authors, however, underline that it is simply not possible to transfer national models of public spheres, which are culturally relatively coherent, based on the same language – or at least a language that every participant can understand – as well shared values, to the European level. No transnational media system exists so far (Chapter 8), allowing for even the most rudimentary exchange among all European citizens. Currently, the exchange takes place among a very limited number of elites, as is the case today (Schlesinger and Kevin 2001). From a normative point of view, however, studies insist on the necessity to create such a transnational dialogue – one that transcends national and cultural divergences in order to practise European citizenship (Nanz 2006).

While all these studies at least in part look at the democratic shortcomings of the EU, they do tackle the problem in a broader context. These debates go beyond those reflecting on the democratic deficit of the Union, confronting the question of the aims and goals of European integration head-on, and are thus at the heart of the normative debate.

The research discussed in the next section of this chapter concentrates more on institutional engineering and links the theoretical debates to empirical research on contemporary European integration.

The European Union's democratic deficit: institutional engineering

As we have seen, the issue of the democratic shortcomings or lack of legitimacy of the EU is a recent one. Debated from different angles, it has not secured unanimity among researchers, political actors or indeed citizens. It is important first to understand the link between the legitimacy crisis and the ratification of the treaties before going into more detail on the theoretical, but also increasingly empirical debate.

Legitimacy crisis linked to the ratification of treaties

During the period broadly stretching from the 1950s to the 1990s, European integration advanced without any real normative debate on the implications of such a process for democracy and its legitimacy as abstract notions. As mentioned above, decisions are taken by political, economic and social leaders under a 'permissive consensus' (Lindberg and Scheingold 1970). The absence of debate and demonstration is taken as tacit agreement from European citizens, for whom European questions do not seem to have been very visible. During this period, there was little that was controversial about economic integration in an increasingly globalized market. Very few researchers openly questioned the basic tenets of the European Community.

During the 1980s, these questions began to become more prominent for lawyers. Eric Stein and G. Federico Mancini questioned the need to draw up a constitution in the context of European regional integration in order to reinforce the shared values of its member states (Stein 1981; Mancini 1989). This came at a time when the idea of a constitution appeared repeatedly on the agenda of a number of European actors, but without the impact that the convention on the future of Europe had when it was launched at the beginning of the 2000s.

Widespread concerns about the legitimate functioning of the EU first emerged in connection with national ratification procedures for the Maastricht Treaty (Keohane and Hoffman 1991). Referenda on ratifying the treaty in France and Denmark meant broad debates on the objectives and direction that the European integration process should be taking. While the French referendum led to ratification, Denmark rejected the Treaty (51 per cent against 49 per cent in favour). The Treaty was only accepted a year later, when Denmark was allowed to opt out of the single currency. At the same time, Denmark and Germany continued to contest the Treaty, but on legal grounds. While both constitutional courts agreed on the constitutionality of the Maastricht Treaty, the German Constitutional Court insisted on its duty to protect fundamental rights and to revise the decisions of European institutions when they go beyond their remit, as discussed earlier in this chapter. The German Court ruled against the unlimited transfer of the Bundestag's powers to the European institutions. Indeed, according to the Court, transfers of power must not reduce citizens' democratic influence over state authority. The idea emerged that citizens' influence should be secured, either through national parliaments or through a European parliament with extended powers. Contrary to the German Court, the Danish Supreme Court ascertained that the Maastricht Treaty was compatible with the Danish constitution if transfer of sovereignty occurred only in specifically defined areas. Any extension of these powers would require a unanimous Council decision, allowing the Danish government to use its veto. However, in 1998, the Danish Court ruled that national courts could determine the constitutionality and therefore the applicability of European laws in Denmark.

The failure to ratify the constitutional Treaty in France and the Netherlands in 2005, and the Irish referendum's rejection of the Lisbon Treaty in 2008, reopened the debate on the normative foundations of European integration. While the legitimacy deficit includes the idea of interpretation of a political process, the notion of democratic deficit refers to a more or less explicit understanding of what democracy is and why there is a substantial (formal) deficit in the EU (Føllesdal 2006; Smismans 2006). If this is so, what are the symptoms, diagnoses and prescriptions? Do we need a 'European identity' in order to have a legitimate and democratic EU? Do European citizens share the same values, traditions and rights, and so, for instance, should Turkey be refused membership? Since the beginning of the 1990s, these issues have been raised even beyond the confines of academic study, increasingly attracting the attention of political, social and economic actors.

Beyond the specific issue of a lack of legitimacy and democracy being linked to the question of whether Europe needed a European constitution, broader debates on the proper institutional engineering of the EU have emerged among political theorists.

Theoretical conceptualizations and empirical studies on the legitimacy deficit

As discussed earlier, bargaining within the European Community at the end of the 1980s in the run-up to the Maastricht Treaty introduced a political and academic discourse on the 'democratic deficit' of the EU. Initially, the focus was on the weakness of the legislative powers of the European Parliament, the lack of transparency in policy-making processes and the absence of European identity, allowing the creation of a European *demos* (Chryssochoou 1994; Gabel 1998; Costa and Magnette 2003). At the beginning of the 2000s, the debate on the democratic deficit of the EU increasingly focused on issues of accountability, diffuse control, legitimacy through outputs and, importantly, the efficiency of political processes (Majone 1996). More recently, Andreas Føllesdal and Simon Hix (2006) defined the EU's lack of legitimacy through five factors also partly found at national level: increased powers of the executive and reduced parliamentary control, the general weakness of the European Parliament, the absence of 'real' European elections (elections based on transnational lists of parties), the gaping divide between the EU and its voters and, finally, a change in political preferences that put sociodemocratic values to one side, and became associated with neoliberalism. There is also the weakness of the EU's symbolism, despite the presence of a single currency, of the European Parliament's vote, of a European festival and a European hymn, of statistics specifically drawn up for the EU and, more generally, the absence of a centre that gives any meaning to this European integration (Foret 2008). In short, Euroscepticism took a more hybrid form in debates on political theory.

What is legitimacy?

However, there are other positions on this question. Whilst Moravcsik rejects the very idea of the existence of a democratic deficit, arguing that governments that make up the EU are democratically elected and, therefore, that this sufficiently guarantees the EU's democratic status, Vivien Schmidt's analysis is more qualified. She explains that the perception of the EU's democratic deficit is linked to a phenomenon of low or non-adaptation by national elites and their people to the meaning given to democracy at the European level (Schmidt 2004, 2006).

One of the reasons for the contradiction in these analyses is the difference in the theoretical conceptualization of legitimacy and its legitimation process. To structure this debate, therefore, it is important to rigorously conceptualize the issue from a theoretical point of view (Kohler-Koch and Rittberger 2007). Cross-checking the analyses of Andreas Føllesdal with those of Christopher Lord and Paul Magnette produces five conceptions of legitimacy in the EU (Lord and Magnette 2004; Føllesdal 2006). All five conceptions are normative types of legitimacy, measured in terms of some ideal good identified by normative theorists, and not sociological definitions of legitimacy that might be measured in terms of actual, empirical levels of public support.

Legality

First, legitimacy can be understood as *legality* or *indirect legitimacy*. In this respect, the EU derives its legitimacy from the legitimacy of its member states. Since the member states are legitimate, the EU is too, hence the indirect vehicle of legitimacy. The democratic member states transfer parts of their sovereignty to the Community level and thereby form a *de facto* legitimate constitutional order to better achieve their objectives via coordinated actions (Weiler 1991). The authority of the EU is only illegitimate if it goes beyond its legally circumscribed competences.

Compliance

A second conception of legitimacy touches on the *compliance* of the actions of the member states and social actors with the EU's legal frameworks. Here, however, compliance could be interpreted not as a form of acceptance or legitimation of a process, but as a form of apathy (Abromeit 1998). At the same time, however, the compliance of states with EU law seems to be diminishing. Empirical phenomena such as Euroscepticism, and of contesting, resisting and sidestepping Europe (Lacroix and Coman 2007; Costa, Roger and Saurugger 2008), are increasingly prevalent and raise the normative question as to legitimation through compliance.

Effectiveness

Thirdly, European legitimacy is sometimes conceptualized by the results achieved in European policies. This technocratic legitimacy is based on the resolution of problems – what Fritz Scharpf called 'output legitimacy' (Scharpf 1999). Here, Scharpf distinguishes legitimacy through outputs from legitimacy through inputs. Legitimacy through inputs being a form of citizen participation, it is the only legitimate source of power according to the representative democracy model, articulated around the need to justify the majority's exercising of power. Output legitimacy differs from this vision of 'government for the people' since it derives its legitimacy from its capacity to resolve problems that individual actions or the market cannot. The essential criterion in this context is the effectiveness of policies implemented.

However, the purpose here is to identify the problem of the mismatch between the expectations of citizens and what the politicians can offer. In this context, the framing of results plays a significant role in the perception of this technocratic legitimacy. Scharpf's research on input and output legitimacy finds its way into a more recent, and – given the economic and social crisis the EU goes through – extremely timely debate in political theory concentrating on questions of social equality and solidarity in the EU. The main questions asked here are what principles of social solidarity should apply in the relations between European citizens and the European member states, and what norms of socioeconomic justice should be developed by the emerging European polity (in particular, Sangiovanni 2013; also Schimmel, Ronzoni and Benaï 2011; Van Parijs 2011).

Procedures

A fourth conceptualization refers to normative or procedural legitimacy. Here, legitimacy is about the justification of laws between equal individuals (Rawls 1993; Habermas 1995). Laws can be legally legitimate when they are adopted according to certain procedures (transparency, equal representation of all interests, proportionality and consultation procedures).

Representativeness

Finally, a fifth conceptualization refers to representation. From this angle, the legitimacy of a political system is based on the relationship between the representative and those represented within the system (Pitkin 1967; Manin 1995). The notion of political representation is generally linked to that of representative democracy. It is tackled from the point of view of institutional and social provisions or will even refer to the understanding of mechanisms through which a group of actors monopolizes access to positions of power. From this standpoint, elective representation is at the heart of any understanding. The main actors are parties or, better still, representatives of the political parties who manage to give their audience a sense of identification. Political representation from this standpoint seems to pose a problem in the European context for at least two reasons. First, whilst representation is only linked to the notion of elected representation, the analysis is limited to three objects: the European Parliament, since its members are elected representatives and have the right to direct representation; the Council of Ministers and European Council; and, finally, the Committee of the Regions as well as the Economic and Social Committee, which are characterized by indirect representation of the citizens of the Union's member states.

Secondly, research on public opinion shows that even institutions with direct representation – and the European Parliament in particular – struggle to awake feelings of belonging among European citizens, although this representative role of the European parties can be seen as a quasi-constitutional requirement (Mair and Thomassen 2010).

From this analysis of the limits of representativeness, a literature has emerged that argues in favour of other forms of representation, such as direct-deliberative polyarchy (Cohen and Sabel 1997), participatory or associative democracy (Kohler-Koch 2000, Kohler-Koch and Rittberger 2007), anchored in contemporary forms of pluralism. In parallel to the fundamental role given to elites in the political representation system, the traditional pluralist conception places the emphasis on power flows, on the complex organization of social groups and on the multiple affiliations of individuals (Dahl 1961, 1970).

Hence, empirical studies of interest groups and social movements at European level show that, contrary to the desire to reinstate a system of direct representation by including individuals or citizens more forcibly in the national political process, it reproduces a form of elitism within the system. This is because the most competent individuals are selected and become the privileged contacts of the public authorities – and hence a reproduction of the masses–elites divide at the European level (Bellamy and Warleigh 1998; Saurugger 2008).

Interest groups and, through them, citizens, possess unequal resources, meaning that not all groups can participate in the political process with the same intensity. This associative democracy, inclusive of groups both during the agenda-setting as well as implementation phase, is vulnerable to the interests of those who hold the most sought-after resources – more often than not financial and social. Therefore, far from the pluralist ideal according to which competition between all interests allows balanced representation, the most influential private interests will prevail over those which have neither the financial nor social resources needed to represent their interests within a multi-level Community system. One other criticism refers to the participation of a small number of individuals in the political process: delegates and representatives. Finally, critics point out that lumping together different types of representation modes cannot guarantee good representation if any of four conditions are absent: first, the Kantian principle of self-legislation, aiming at correcting the shortcomings and inefficiencies of formal representation (and thus referring partially to the proposals of associative democracy); second, the Weberian requirement of democratically controlled public administration; third, holistic public reason; and, finally, the existence of institutional features intended to regulate ways in which representatives combine (Lord and Pollak 2010).

Faced with such problems, certain authors propose the creation of forms of direct representation on a European scale: European referenda (Grande 2000), among other suggestions, as a further guarantee of transparency in the political process (Héritier 1999).

Inherent problems of representativeness

It is important to stress, however, that the successive results in Denmark and Ireland, where national governments have twice used referenda to decide upon the ratification of the treaties, show how the referendum is an inefficient instrument for adopting a European treaty, and one that lacks transparency. European negotiations, as well as the treaties, are the result of a complex compromise among 28 member states. The referenda on European integration seem, on the contrary, to lead citizens to answer questions of national importance and not of European importance – the same goes for European elections, considered as second-order elections (Reif and Schmitt 1980).

This debate is reflected in an argument on politicization between Simon Hix and Andreas Føllesdal, on the one hand, and Stefano Bartolini, Paul Magnette and Yannis Papadopoulos, on the other (Føllesdal and Hix 2006; Bartolini 2005; Magnette and Papadopoulos 2008. For a discussion see Rittberger 2010). In this debate, Hix and Føllesdal called for the increased politicization of European politics, both at the European and domestic level. Political competition among party groups in Brussels must be fostered, according to their argument. Bartolini, as well as Magnette and Papadopoulos, on the contrary, questioned this call for more left/right polarization, but on different grounds. Bartolini argued that the EU has already entered a period of contestation, which places the traditional legitimation of the state under severe pressure, as can be seen with the national referenda and in the field of non-state actor protests – contentious politics – against European integration, mostly at the national level (Imig and Tarrow 2001). European integration had already led to destructuring (Bartolini 2005) as well as restructuring (Kriesi et al. 2008) of previously rooted political structures and systems of representation. According to Peter Mair, the domestic parties imposed a 'gag rule' on themselves to keep EU issues from appearing in electoral debates (Mair 2007). Magnette and Papadopoulos went beyond electoral considerations, referring to the EU as a consociational system. In this sense, the Union's *raison d'être* is to create compromise out of opposing views, as occurs in the Swiss or the Dutch political systems.

As such, 'increased contestation is thus originally an effect of the ever deeper penetration of the EU into the interstices of domestic life, where it comes to collusion with deeply rooted interests and cultural values' (Paterson 2010: 413). This reflects empirical research undertaken by van der Eijk and Franklin, according to which 'the pro/anti-EU orientation, despite its apparent irrelevance for political behaviour in the domestic sphere, constitutes something of a "sleeping giant" that has the potential, if awakened, to impel voters to political behaviour that ... undercuts the bases for contemporary party mobilization in many, if not most, European polities' (van der Eijk and Franklin 2004: 32)

Table 9.3   *How can we analyse legitimacy in the EU?*

Concept	Puzzle
Legality	Is the EU a legal structure, since its member states are legitimate decision-makers, which therefore make decisions taken by the EU legitimate as well?
Compliance	Is the degree of compliance with EU law and norms an indicator for the EU legitimacy? Or is it a sign of apathy?
Effectiveness	Is the EU legitimate because it is effective and efficient? Does it allow for solidarity among the people?
Procedures	Is the EU legitimate because it follows legitimate procedures?
Representativeness and its inherent problems	Who represents citizens in the EU? Is representation enough, or must there be politicization and contestation?

Conclusion

As discussed, scholars of political theory took a belated interest in European integration. Once they did, however, they did so clearly, with a mainstreaming logic, adopting tools developed to analyse national political phenomena in order to study the EU from a normative point of view. The use of conceptual tools developed at the national level is not new: works on transnational cosmopolitanism are based on the works of Kant who, in his *Perpetual Peace,* called for a federation of free states between countries with republican constitutions. Just as in the case of every conceptual framework analysed in Part II of this book, analytical frames developed in political theory concentrating on the internal workings of the state have been imported into EU studies.

In the context of political theory on the EU, this movement seems to have a bright future. Since European integration is a process, the best form that this political regime could take is subject to change: 'The citizens' preferences concerning legitimacy will change over time, depending on the political domains concerned and the political structures in each member state. As a result, any reflection on the legitimacy of the EU means taking four factors into account simultaneously: the positions of the elites on the objectives of European integration, the different levels of governance (European, national, regional, local), legitimacies through outputs and inputs and the different conceptions of democracy itself' (Warleigh-Lack 2003: 125).

However, these pages have also emphasized the heterogeneous nature of studies so far, ranging from the analysis of theoretical conceptualizations on the best way to construct a *demos*, a government or governance system, to more hybrid studies, which combine normative approaches and empirical analysis – all of which helps to explain the multiple meanings of the EU and the possibilities for enhancing its democratic nature.

Part III

The European Union and the World

The central argument of this book is that theoretical approaches to the EU have increased their explanatory capabilities by way of 'mainstreaming'. The deepening of European integration in the 1990s, the increasing number of actors associated with policy-making, or simply the influence of European public policies on the domestic level, seemed to be better captured through mainstream political science approaches, developed to study the state. Thus, tools and theoretical perspectives originating in public policy, comparative politics, sociology and political theory have been used to minimize the exceptional nature of the European integration process and have enabled scholars to compare integration with other political phenomena associated with the State. One of the implications of the use of these perspectives is that the European integration processes can no longer be understood by international relations analyses alone, which are primarily interested in inter-state or intergovernmental relations (Hix 1994; Pierson 1996; Pollack 2005).

Comparative politics and international relations scholars agree that the EU's role in international affairs, such as its attempt to come up with a common position towards the 'Arab Spring' in 2010–11, its role in international commercial negotiation in the WTO (Wold Trade Organization) framework, its positions towards the newly emerging powers, or BRICS (Brazil, Russia, India, China and South Africa), or simply, the intergovernmental negotiations taking place in the current economic and financial crisis striving for establishing a – mainly intergovernmental – economic government, cannot simply be analysed with the tools developed to study the internal politics of a state, but need tools developed by international relations approaches. They disagree, however, on the extent to which these international relations perspectives are needed to understand the European integration process as such. Contrary to comparative politics scholars, a first group of international relations specialists argue that some of the processes occurring *within* the EU cannot be understood without considering the wider environment in which they operate, including processes of globalization, the creation of norms by other international organizations that influence the EU, or comparisons between different regional bodies. These processes involve concepts such as sovereignty, national interests or the framing power of national political and economic structures more generally. The study of these phenomena must thus associate tools developed by international relations scholars.

They argue also that member states continue being the institutional and cognitive reference that promotes further integration or, conversely, causes the European integration process to stagnate. These phenomena cannot be captured entirely by bottom-up mainstreaming approaches, which analyse member states as if they were a specific ministry, interest group or region at the EU level. Conceptual frameworks stemming from international relations seem better suited to explain two sets of issues: the role of sovereignty in intergovernmental negotiations taking place in the EU arena and the role played by the EU as an actor on the international scene (Chapter 10).

A second group of scholars looks more closely at the question of regional integration schemes and the relationships between the phenomena of globalization and regionalization. Rich in conceptual tools stemming from IPE approaches, this movement re-emerged at the end of the 1980s with the end of the Cold War and renewed scholarly interest in regionalization processes (Chapter 11).

While the opening premises of these two debates differ, they both seek to mainstream European studies by reintroducing tools previously developed to analyse international and transnational systems. Thus, this third and final part of this book argues that conceptual frameworks linking comparative politics approaches to those of international relations are extremely promising tools for studying European integration. Chapter 10 explores several avenues, taking the problems of intergovernmental negotiations into account, along with the role of the EU in the world. Chapter 11 then presents 'new' regionalism approaches and its critiques. The idea here is to go beyond the focus on European integration as the only case of regional integration – the so-called n=1 problem – and to compare it with other intergovernmental integration phenomena. The purpose is to better understand the processes of world politics and compare prevailing phenomena of globalization and regional integration.

Chapter 10

International Relations and European Integration

This chapter is based on the assumption that European integration cannot be understood without reintroducing international relations perspectives into mainstream theoretical frameworks of EU studies. On the one hand, this concerns the internal aspect of intergovernmental bargaining between – at least partially – sovereign states. The positions of member states in negotiating directives and regulations must not only be understood as similar to those of federal member states such as the *Länder* in Germany. In the EU, the member states' 'positions' are formulated as those of sovereign states, representing 'national interests'.

On the other hand, reintroducing international relations perspectives into mainstream theoretical frameworks of EU studies also refers to the external character of the EU as an entity in the international system, i.e., to the EU as an actor in international negotiations. The EU is an actor in international bargaining processes, be it as member of the WTO, as a partner of the Latin-American regional organization Mercosur, or as an actor more generally influencing non-member states trough its human rights norms or asylum policies.

Following this distinction, the first section of this chapter will analyse the notion of 'national interest' of member states and their sovereignty in bargaining at the EU level. The second section will then concentrate on the role of the EU as an international actor, a research question that has been analysed extensively in recent EU studies.

The intergovernmental dimension of European bargaining

In most theoretical perspectives to EU studies, state sovereignty, seen as a phenomenon gradually established since the Westphalian Treaty (1648), no longer seems to have the function of structuring inter-state relations in EU negotiations (Hooghe and Marks 2009). The dual sovereignty of the State, combining, on the one hand, the capacity of a state to set its own objectives, priorities and ways achieving them externally and, on the other hand, the domestic authority of the State, seems to have disappeared in EU studies. The difference between internal politics, driven by the supremacy of government (hierarchy), and foreign policy, based on the formal equality of governments (anarchy), acting at the international level without a hierarchical power reining them in (Biersteker and Weber 1996: 2), is neglected. Under the label neo-medievalism (Bull 1977; Waever 1995; de Wilde and Wieberg 1996) or postmodernism, international relations are viewed as being organized through non-overlapping centres of authority and multiple loyalties (Zielonka 2006). Thus, the post-modern state 'acts in an increasingly complex and interdependent network based on a blurring distinction between internal and external policy, increasing influence on the state's domestic affairs, increasing transparency and the emergence of a sense of community guaranteeing collective security' (Wallace 1999: 503). This is referred to as 'pooled sovereignty', negotiated by a large number of actors and their committees and controlled by the authority of regulations and judgements of the ECJ, illustrated by a political system that could best be analysed through comparative politics approaches.

While the premises of this 'bottom-up mainstreaming' shift are helpful, insofar as they allow us to conceptualize the EU not as a *sui generis* phenomenon but as a set of political and policy processes that can be compared to those taking place inside a state, they do raise a major challenge. By almost systematically omitting the intergovernmental nature of European integration, they make it practically impossible to reflect on the reasons for increased integration of the European continent, or on the contrary, for the increasingly significant resistance to European integration. It also makes it difficult to understand the relative respect for national sovereignties that we still find when analysing negotiations within the European Council and Council of Ministers of the EU.

Taking this challenge seriously, a number of scholars have argued that the EU could be characterized as an entity somewhere between an international system and a state (Hurrell and Menon 1996, 2003; Risse-Kappen 1996; Caporaso 1999). It is different from the national system because its forms of regulation are imperfect (it has no broad social redistributional policies (except in the field of agriculture and regional policies), no common police force or a common army that would defend the European borders under a supranational authority structure). However, it is more than a simple intergovernmental system, because its political authority overrides that of its member states in common policy fields such as the internal market (Aalberts 2004).

The purpose of this chapter is to present conceptual approaches beyond liberal intergovernmentalism or neorealism (Chapter 3), which both take the intergovernmental nature of bargaining among European member states seriously. Accepting this idea, however, does not necessarily mean returning to the neorealists' conceptual tools and the premise of the centrality of the state in an anarchical global system. While the

State continues to have considerable resources in public order, defence and diplomacy, it cannot be analysed as a unified actor, and treated as a 'black box'. It is crucial to analyse the power of the State and its action at the international level, not only through its agents, but also through the ideas and myths promoted by those same agents (see also Aalberts 2004, 2012; Adler-Nissen 2008, 2009). In other words, this section takes a critical look at the tools contemporary international relations perspectives employ in order to study the role of the State in EU policy-making processes. Contemporary approaches in international relations, as diverse as they may be, share the premise that international phenomena have to be interpreted as social facts. In this respect, these different approaches share a parallel interest in actors and structures much more so than classical neorealist accounts.

A first important dimension of European integration, and one not covered well by 'bottom-up mainstreaming' approaches, is the intergovernmental character of internal negotiations in the EU. Two notions are crucial in this context: national interest and sovereignty. Both notions should not, however, be taken for granted, but manifest themselves through social interaction.

National interest

Among the first studies making the connection between state action and norms is Martha Finnemore's (1996) research on national interests in international society. Her approach goes beyond the opposition between ideas and interests and develops a conceptual framework to help us understand the interests and attitudes of states by analysing international structures through meanings and social values. States are part of transnational and international relational networks, which form state actors' perceptions of the world and shape the role these actors play. According to Finnemore, in the international context, states are socialized to defend certain interests and not others. The interests of governmental representatives are constructed through social interaction. Thus, far from being static, interests and values supported by international actors change in what are shifting normative contexts. This normative construction is greatly influenced by power games between the actors involved. Like Finnemore, Judith Goldstein and Robert Keohane (1995: 13) argue that norms and ideas can be institutionalized as well as instrumentalized, thus reflecting the power of certain ideas and the interests of the powerful: 'These social structures may supply states with preferences and strategies for pursuing these preferences.' Similarly, Stephen Krasner (1993) argues that the origins of the international system show that certain norms or institutions – not unlike sovereignty – were initially institutionalized because they served the interests of powerful actors, but have since become independent of those interests.

Several factors influence changes in the norms guiding actors' behaviour, including the legitimacy sought and expertise provided (Haas 1990; Finnemore and Sikkink 1998). Numerous studies on the EU have implicitly or explicitly returned to this hypothesis (in particular see Boswell 2009). Applied to another empirical study, namely the World Bank, Martha Finnemore and Kathryn Sikkink show that expertise

> usually resides in professionals, and a number of studies document the ways that professional training of bureaucrats in these organizations helps or blocks the promotion of new norms within standing organizations ... Studies of the World Bank similarly document a strong role for professional training in filtering the norms that the bank promotes. In this case, the inability to quantify many costs and benefits associated with antipoverty and basic human need norms created resistance among the many economists staffing in the bank, because projects promoting these norms could not be justified on the basis of 'good economics'. (Finnemore and Sikkink 1998: 899–900)

Similarly, Nicolas Jabko shows that the divergence between actors seeking to promote the domestic market through different instruments must be seen as a resource for those actors seeking to reform the European system in the 1980s (Chapter 7). Jabko's premise is that 'these tensions are very important for understanding institutional change, because they represent opportunities for reform-seeking actors. The existence of tensions creates room for the emergence of political strategies and, ultimately, for institutional change' (Jabko 2006).

This does not mean that all national interests can be reformulated based on shared ideas and discourses. As Scharpf (2002) argues, it is also important to take account of the fact that certain political domains are, not surprisingly, much more difficult to integrate than others owing to differing national interests: a high political salience at the national level, linked to the conflict-minimizing practices – the famous consensus-based decision-making – at the EU level, according to Scharpf, leads to highly salient opposition at the national level. It transpires that the areas least likely to achieve unanimity at European level are tax harmonization, budget and certain areas of social policy. Any attempt at regulation in these domains comes up against coalitions of divergent national interests, making it impossible to achieve broad agreement on common European rules. The author observes that

> over recent years ..., the European Council has increasingly often bypassed the Commission's prerogatives in law-making by defining certain elements of the European political calendar during its summer meetings – elements which must then be developed through legislative channels or *ad hoc* intergovernmental arrangements. In all these

instances, national governments can use their veto if they need to fiercely defend their narrow or short-term national (or economic) interests, or indeed common European interests or derive longer-term benefits from enhanced political cooperation and coordination. (Scharpf 2002: 615–16)

To succeed, however, these countries must find a way of protecting democratic legitimacy, even if some of the above-mentioned adjustments come up against well-established interests. Thus, the national interest is not predetermined; rather, it comes about through interaction and is presented as such during intergovernmental negotiations. The national interest, defended in the name of state sovereignty at the European level, is considered by sociological approaches as an institution: 'Even our most enduring institutions are based on collective understandings, ... they are reified structures that were once upon a time conceived ex nihilo by human consciousness ... [which] were subsequently diffused and consolidated until they were taken for granted' (Adler 1997: 322). Furthermore, in countries where institutions are fragmented and thus offer a large number of veto points, a successful change of political strategy requires a convergence of cognitive and normative orientations.

Tackling the interests of actors or nations using the socioconstructivist tools of international relations allows the dynamics of, and opposition to, European integration to be interpreted. Hence, an interest becomes a social construct, just like a national interest – which leads us to the Wendtian reflection on the construction of anarchy in international relations (Wendt 1999).

Power and sovereignty of the state in the EU

Generally conceptualized as a set of capacities primarily beheld by the state, power is considered by sociological approaches of international relations as a relation. This fits with the Weberian definition, where power is the capacity of an actor to encourage other actors to do what they would otherwise not do. Power, therefore, is not only a set of material capacities, but also idea-based capacities. It is profoundly relative and differentiated, according to historical periods and international actor constellations. Rather than being an all-encompassing thing, power is broken down into a series of dominant positions in diverse political sectors. Thus, power is observed when an actor can switch easily from a dominant position in one sector to a dominant position in another (Berenskoetter and Williams 2007). Susan Strange (1988, 1996) suggests looking at power in four areas – military, research and development, production and commerce and finance. Joseph Nye (1995, 2004) adds the power of cultural and ideological influence (soft power), though not in the ineffectual sense, since it can give rise to a potential instrument of domination (Bially Mattern 2005). This differentiation makes the notion of power more dynamic and renders it adaptable to various conflicts and bargaining situations.

In the European integration context, the bargaining power of states is regulated legally by the weight of their vote. However, this often means that academics resort to a rather sterile analysis comparing major and minor states. Constructivist approaches, on the contrary, look more closely at those factors determining the bargaining power of states – factors that change depending on the negotiations in hand. Given that decisions are generally taken consensually, despite the QMV rule, the capacity of countries to influence their partners may be based on an infinite number of factors, depending on the political issues at stake. Thus, the risk of analysing the political power relationships of the EU through rational choice tools is that the power of the EU is being conceived of as an attribute of equal actors, that is, states.

On the contrary, it seems important to look at how member-state representatives in the EU behave in the arenas and forums of negotiation. Jeffrey Lewis, in his work on COREPER (Lewis 2000, 2005), analyses the permanent representatives' socialization process within the Council. Here, the notion of power is addressed sociologically, confronting it with actual discourses and attitudes during intergovernmental committee negotiations and debates. Lewis argues that national representatives share the conviction that they can be more influential if they can come up with common solutions. This idea is shared by Uwe Puetter (2006, 2012) in his study on the Council and the Eurogroup, demonstrating how a small circle of senior member-state decision-makers shapes European economic governance through a reutilized informal policy dialogue. He explores how the intergovernmental European Council has emerged as the forum for policy debate in the field of economic governance. Puetter argues that the increased high-level intergovernmental policy co-ordination reflects an integration paradox inherent to the post-Maastricht EU. While policy fields have become more and more integrated in some areas, such as the EMU, member-state governments have resisted the further transfer of formal competences to EU institutions. They aim for more policy coherence through intensified intergovernmental coordination, which Puetter labels 'deliberative intergovernmentalism'. Likewise, Rebecca Adler-Nissen argues that 'the very construction of a national position takes place as part of a struggle for distinction and dominance in a field where the stakes have already been defined' (Adler-Nissen 2009: 132).

According to Adler-Nissen, if power is primarily seen as a political tool, sovereignty was, from a legal but also constructivist point of view, always a possible weapon to block or, on the contrary, to reinforce European integration, particularly since the use of the French veto power during de Gaulle's Empty Chair Crisis, or the German chancellor

Helmut Schmidt and the French president Giscard d'Estaing's idea to establish a European Monetary System in 1979. However, from the SEA of 1987 onwards, there is evidence of new sovereignty arrangements that allow for its flexible use. Thus Article 100a (4) of the EC Treaty (now Art. 114 TFEU) allows member states to opt out of single-market harmonization measures 'on grounds of major needs' relating to public morality, public policy, public security, public health, protection of the natural environment and the working environment, and a range of other public interest grounds. The 1992 Maastricht Treaty develops the theme of sectoral flexibility. Alongside the narrow 'case-by-case' flexibility exemplified by Article 100a(4) (now Art. 114 TFEU), two other forms of flexibility are introduced: 'predetermined flexibility', where an area of flexibility is defined in advance; and 'enhanced cooperation', where member states are empowered to make their own additional cooperative arrangements over a broad policy spectrum.

A comparison of these opt-outs illustrates how states use their sovereignty (Adler-Nissen 2008). During the negotiation of the Maastricht Treaty, the UK and the Danish governments refused to participate in the EMU as well as in JHA. These opt-outs had two functions at the domestic level: on the one hand they created an image of national unity and established the idea of a unified public space, despite the disagreements that exist in other domains. These positions allowed the perception of the state as an entity, which exercised a political-legal authority over its population, its territory and its money. On the other hand, these opt outs presented sovereignty as a state attribute, which cannot be removed. These understandings of sovereignty clearly refer to a legitimation usage in a strategic context.

In the field of JHA, the UK negotiated an opt-out, with some possibilities for partial and temporal opt-ins. This allowed the government to maintain the control of its borders and to develop and later implement its own immigration policy. The Danish government, however, only decided to use the opt-out recognized by the Maastricht Treaty from 2001 onwards, when the liberal conservative government came to power. This new government replaced Danish immigration policies, which figured amongst the most liberal in Europe, with a stricter and more severe asylum and immigration policy than that of other member states.

However, at the EU level, the Ministers of Home Affairs participated and cooperated systematically in negotiations concerning JHA. Participation remained confined to the ministerial level. The population was not informed, as it was perceived to be hostile to any European cooperation in this field. The Danish government, which, contrary to the British government, had no legal possibility of joining its European partners, negotiated individual and bilateral agreements with the Commission. This allowed the government, at the same time, to use its sovereignty as a legitimation tool vis-à-vis its population ('see, we do not participate in this policy and are thus totally sovereign in this matter'), and to play a cooperation game vis-à-vis its European partners, while sometimes referring to sovereignty as a strategic tool ('here we will not continue to cooperate as these dispositions are contrary to our independence').

The implementation of the Stability Pact is yet another illustration of sovereignty games being played. The norms of the Stability and Growth Pact (SGP), albeit precise, were interpreted rather freely by a number of member states. Several targets of the SGP were indicative only (Hallerberg 2010). If a member state ran a budget deficit in the medium term, the Council of Economic and Finance Ministers (ECOFIN) could issue a recommendation for corrective action. The member state, however, could not be excluded from the EMU; it was not subject to a pecuniary fine, nor was under a legal obligation to follow the recommendation (Hodson and Maher 2004: 799). This flexible interpretation of the Pact gave more room for fiscal manoeuvre to states, but made it more difficult for ECOFIN to measure compliance. The German and French decision to allow a higher budget deficit and debts level, arguing that they remain sovereign countries, is an illustration of this case.

It is precisely in these contexts that we see how sovereignty is constructed, through the interaction of diplomats playing a particular role, but at the same time adjusting to outside pressures. In the constructivist sense, sovereignty is understood as an historical concept and not as a timeless legal principle. It links authority, territory, population and recognition in a unique way, and in a particular time (Biersteker and Weber 1996; Aalberts 2012). In order to understand this social interaction, it is necessary to analyse both the transformation of the concept and the carriers of its meanings, i.e. actors, be they public or private. In other words, 'It may be that the "speech-act" of sovereignty is more complex to perform in an era of globalization and constitutional pluralism, yet it remains an essential political tool in constituting the functional national and international legal orders in which power politics are played out' (Adler-Nissen and Gammeltoft-Hansen 2008: 7; Walker 2003: 19–25).

Due to their heterogeneity and epistemological conception, sociological approaches to international relations propose a broad analytical framework to address the link between capacities and power within the EU, insofar as they allow us to take into account the discursive and not solely legal criterion of state sovereignty as applied to EU negotiations (see also Walker 2003).

The external action of the EU

It is in the field of the EU's external action that conventional international relations approaches have most strongly influenced theoretical reflections. The first part of this book presented realist, neorealist, intergovernmental and liberal intergovernmental accounts of the EU's intergovernmental relations (Chapters 1 and 3). While the first three accounts explain the political and diplomatic forms of the EU's external relations more generally, or predict the difficulties these forms encounter (Howorth 2007), liberal intergovernmentalism has been interested both in intergovernmental relations in the EU (negotiations between EU member states) and in the external action of the EU as an organization (in particular, common commercial policy) (Moravcsik 1998; Meunier 2005).

Since the 1990s, studies of EU external relations have developed more specifically, though only rarely linking the questions treated in this context to more general subjects dealt with in EU studies. A large number of these studies have concentrated on the EU's role as an international actor. In this context, the EU's role is conceptualized as a producer of norms, more than an active intervening organization – and this despite the introduction of a new EU foreign minister (officially: High Representative of the Union for Foreign Affairs and Security Policy) whose role is to coordinate the EU's international diplomatic policies. A first subsection will thus present the theoretical approaches more generally dealing with the former second pillar of the EU (the CFSP). This will be done rather succinctly, since this part of the book provides a resumé of elements discussed under the theoretical headings in other chapters. In EU studies focusing on external policies, sovereignty is generally considered as a given fact.

A second subsection then turns to the role of the EU as external norms provider, where both sovereignty and the intergovernmental character of

Table 10.1 *Contemporary international relations in EU studies in brief*

Perspectives	Main assumptions
Intergovernmental dimension of EU bargaining	National interest is constructed through interaction (role-playing), strongly influencing bargaining in the EU. Power and sovereignty are tools in EU bargaining ('sovereignty games'), having both a legal and a political basis

The external action of the EU	Two distinct approaches
	• Conventional theories of EU foreign and security policy
	• The EU as an international actor
	  o Normative Power Europe (NPE)
	    – Normative/ethical
	    – Regulatory

the integration process are either implicitly or explicitly seen as a social construct. It is here where policies from pillars one and three (common policies and JHA) provide the majority of case studies, as we shall see.

Classical theories of EU foreign and security policy

Studies on EU external affairs, most commonly referred to as an issue of 'high politics' (Hoffmann 1966), started to emerge at the beginning of the 1980s when the member states aimed at establishing collective European diplomacy, the so-called European Political Cooperation (EPC). These studies have shown how and under what conditions the member states developed an informal framework for intergovernmental cooperation in this particular field (Allen, Rummel and Wessels 1982; Ginsberg 1989; Holland 1991; Nuttall 1992). With the establishment of a CFSP under the second pillar through the Maastricht Treaty in 1992, research on this subject started to mushroom, without convening around one particular theoretical stance. Most scholars adopted an analytical-empirical approach, analysing the functioning as well as effectiveness of CFSP compared to the foreign policies of the member states. As Knodt and Princen (2003: 2) stress, two debates have been central in this analytical-empirical field: 'First, "the coercion to act", which refers to the fact that Europe has to face challenges that can only be coped with in a common foreign policy. Second, "the logic of development", which describes the history of the CFSP as a natural process towards an ever closer cooperation.'

Among the few specifically theoretical approaches to CFSP, Christopher Hill's capability-expectations gap occupies a central place in the debate (Hill 1993, 1998). The assumption here is that CFSP is based on the smallest common denominator between member states, reflecting on the different political preferences internal to them (Hill 1998). Linked to this liberal intergovernmentalist approach, a number of constructivist explanations have been developed that underline the importance of socialization in identity building (Tonra 2001, 2003; Irondelle 2003), roles (Aggestam 2004) and discourse (Larsen 2004), most recently enlarged by sociological approaches. It is in this field where we find research on power structures between actors leading to a common strategic culture (Mérand 2008a), or the use of resources in this particular field (Foucault and Cochinard 2007).

From the 1998 Franco-British Summit in Saint-Malo in 1998, during which the French and British governments decided to equip the EU with an autonomous defence capacity, based on credible military forces, interest in the Common Security and Defence Policy (CSDP) increased considerably. Although the number of publications in this area is impressive, it is again interesting to note that few studies adopt a specific theoretical approach (Knodt and Princen 2003; Howorth 2007; for an exception see

Kurowska and Breuer 2011). Three subjects dominate the research: first, the origins and the modes of cooperation in the field of European defence; second, the policy-making processes in this particular field; and thirdly and finally, the impact of CSDP. While studies on the first two issues are strongly characterized by an intergovernmentalist (Gegout 2010; Rynning 2003a; Hyde-Price 2006) and supranationalist (Smith 2003; Howorth 2004) divide, the third group of studies concentrates on the EU's crisis management (Terpan 2004), adopting a more governance-based approach.

The EU as an international actor

It is in the field of research on the EU as international actor that the theoretical debate is probably the richest. While the EU was long characterized by the absence of legal personality and continued institutional fragmentation, the Lisbon Treaty's establishment of a EU 'Foreign Minister' in 2009, and its emphasis on member states for decision-making, nevertheless confirmed what many observers had argued, i.e. that the EU had to be seen as an international actor, in particular because it was recognized by third states both as an actor influencing other states and international organizations (Caporaso and Jupille 1998; Ginsberg 2001; Smith 2002; Bretherton and Vogler 2006), as well as being influenced by them in return (Costa and Jörgensen 2012a). The entering into force of the Lisbon Treaty and the merging of the pillars effectively made the European Community disappear, replaced by the EU. This conferred on the EU a legal personality, and brought it new rights, such as concluding international agreements and joining international organizations and conventions. While this legal approach is crucial to understanding what the EU is or is not supposed to do on the international stage, Bretherton and Vogler's behavioural approach (2006:16) offers an avenue that does more than simply designate the units of the system. It implies an entity that exhibits a degree of autonomy from its external environment and from its internal constituents. It is in this field that not only CFSP or external policies more generally were discussed but also the external aspects of an internal policy, such as environmental policies or JHA.

Studying the EU's actorness

Linking different research strands together, Bretherton and Vogler (2006) offer a conceptualization of the EU's actorness based on the inter-relation of three distinct variables: opportunity, presence and capability.

Opportunity refers to the external environment of the EU, which is constituted both by ideational and material elements constraining or enabling actorness. This conceptualization of opportunity allows for associating both structural elements and perception. Thus it is not only the fact that the EU can intervene or add to an international debate that counts, but also the expectations of the EU's partners, the fact that they perceive the EU's activity as relevant and necessary that contributes to its actorness (Ginsberg 2001). 'Opportunity' allows for a better understanding of the 'capability-expectations gap' (Hill 1993): 'while opportunity might be discursively constructed, the process of construction cannot be divorced from material conditions'. The situation of Central and Eastern Europe after the end of the Cold War is an example, which illustrates this interplay of discourse and material possibility. Central and Eastern European states expected the EU to open its borders, and, together with a number of EU elites, created a discourse allowing this thought to bloom. At the same time the structural context was favourable: the EU was resourceful enough to allow new member states to enter the Union. A counterfactual reasoning might help here: would it be possible, in times of huge financial and economic turmoil, in which Greece, Spain and Portugal are saddled with economic difficulties, to enlarge the Union towards the East?

The second variable refers to *'presence'*. Presence is the ability to exert influence externally, based on the one hand, on the character and the identity of the EU, and on the other, the external consequences of the EU's internal policies. The presence of the EU can be seen in external public policy fields such as the CSDP or Common Commercial Policy, but also in domains such as the CAP, the Single Market or the EMU. Thus, the Eurozone, equipped with the second largest currency after the US dollar, influences forcefully the macroeconomic situation of the world economy. The crisis touching this particular zone has had a large impact on the stock exchange beyond EU borders. JHA is equally concerned by the factor of the EU's 'presence' in the international arena. Similar to CAP or EMU research, JHA, as an internal policy, was for a long time analysed mainly by conceptual frameworks presented in the second part of the book such as constructivism, governance and sociological approaches. These approaches have, however, neglected to take the specific intergovernmental character of EU policy-making into account.

While this is problematic, as we have seen in the first part of this chapter, it becomes even more complicated when internal policies are infused with an external character. JHA is a prominent case in this respect. When JHA is linked to external affairs as such, as in the field of the fight against corruption, human rights, the cooperation in the Mediterranean Union, to quote but a few, it is considered to be an issue in which the EU becomes a more or less coherent external actor with 'presence' (see in particular Lavenex and Wallace 2005; Lavenex and Wichmann 2009; Lavenex 2010; Wolff, Wichmann and Mounier 2010; Kaunert and Leonard 2011).

Internal security issues influenced by external security questions such as EU counter terrorism became an important area of research after the

September 2001 attacks on New York's World Trade Center. Starting from the observation that the EU's ambitions and heightened activity in the field of counter terrorism offered a useful test case for assessing the quality of the EU's 'actorness', an important number of publications applied the concept of 'actorness' to shed light on the EU's behaviour in global counter-terrorism activities (Brattberg and Rhinard 2012; Kaunert 2010, 2012). A different argument can be made in asylum policy, a subfield of JHA, where the EU is equally influential. Traditionally a core aspect of state sovereignty, asylum policy has gradually become an integrated European policy (Boswell 2003; Lavenex and Wallace 2005). Currently, most asylum and immigration questions refer to the realm of EU external relations. This means that they concern the external borders of the EU and are subject of discussion with the EU's neighbours, discussions that are led by the EUand not by member states individually (Lavenex 2006; Trauner 2009). This literature interprets the decision to transfer sovereign rights at the European level as a strategy to maximize the gains from integration, in making the norms diffused by the EUmore coherent and thus reinforce the EU's *presence* at the international level.

Capability is the third variable that explains the EU's actorness in international affairs. It refers more precisely to the internal context of the EU's action or inaction. It is based on structural and material elements (the legal or financial ability to act) and the political willingness of European actors to engage in an activity. The EU must possess the possibility to identify priorities (consistence) and to formulate policies (coherence). For instance, while this capability is generally high in the field of the external commercial policy (Meunier 2005; Jacoby and Meunier 2010), it is less so in the fields of economic sanctions in the context of joint actions under CFSP (Portela 2010).

These approaches to the international actorness of the EU have insisted on the evolving practices of the complex and dynamic process that is the EU. While these perspectives remained largely analytical, a prominent approach –NPE – adopted a more prescriptive stance on this question.

Normative Power Europe (NPE)

In social constructivist approaches, research on social representations at the international level concentrates on the cognitive frameworks and action repertoires that actors call upon to make sense of their actions (Parsons 2004).

Understanding the normative aspect of European integration by applying the toolbox of constructivist approaches in international relations helps us to understand the effects of European norms on EU partners. The aim here is to conceptualize more specifically which actors, which cognitive frames and which instruments are vectors of the change induced by European norms.

Research on the influence of European integration outside the realm of the European Community emerged in the 1970. The literature on the notion of 'civilian power', introduced by François Duchêne, emphasizing functional and economic cooperation, allowed the adoption of a more specific perspective on what actors such as the EU, or European Community back then, could be expected to achieve in the international realm. This particular approach was interpreted as an anticipation of contemporary criticism of realist principles in foreign policy (Duchêne 1973). 'Civilian power' thereby referred to political cooperation within the European Community, whose influence on other regions and states of the world should be understood as a civilian form of power (Whitman 1998; Smith 2005; Sjursen 2006; Aggestam 2008). This idea was strongly criticized by Hedley Bull (1982), who saw in it a contradiction, since no power could have influence without its own military capability in a world system that is clearly not civilized. Bull's critiques, however, attracted rather limited attention from liberals or constructivists.

Duchêne's idea was adapted and further developed by Ian Manners (Manners 2002, 2006, 2008, 2009, 2012), who drew attention to its heuristic value. Manners deepened Duchêne's analysis, circumscribing the notion of civilian power by emphasizing the influence of human rights and democracy norms. In his view, the EU became a *normative power*, a power whose influence was intrinsically positive and morally good. This power is based on persuasion, naming and shaming, not on the action or creation of structures of change. Power in this case is a discursive form. It refers to the legitimacy and the coherent nature of an argument.

In his analysis, Manners highlights the cognitive impact of the identity and international role of the EU: it is normatively different from other international organizations, insofar at it is internally more coherent than organizations such as NAFTA or ASEAN. This – relative – coherence allows the EU to promote universal norms and principles in its relation with non-members more efficiently (Lerch and Schwellnus 2006). The EU's hybrid political system and a politico-legal construction has contributed to the commitment to place universal norms and principles at the very heart of its foreign relations.

Two claims are at the centre of Manners's approach to NPE. The first refers to the normative difference of the EU: according to Manners, the nature of the EU is conditioned by its commitment to certain constitutional values and norms, identified by EU treaties, treaty provisions and declarations. The commitment to universal rights and principles is what makes the EU different from other polities. The second claim concerns the nature of the EU's normative power. This consists in a power of opinion; in other words, the ability to reshape conceptions of what is 'normal behaviour' in international politics. Manners distinguishes six instruments of norm diffusion: contagion, informational diffusion, procedural diffusion, transference, overt diffusion, and the existence of a 'cultural filter', a typology influenced by the literature on policy diffusion (Chapter 6).

Richard Whitman's understanding of NPE points in the same direction. He argues that the EU's normative power derives from three sources (Whitman 2011: 5): historical context (particularly the legacy of two world wars), hybrid polity (the EUas a post-Westphalian order) and political-legal constitutionalism (treaty based legal nature of the EU). The EU as a normative power has its origins in its historical development: the establishment of the European Community in 1951 was based on a double objective: to create a peaceful European continent and to relaunch European economic growth after the Second World War. These two aims did not frame the newly created regional integration bloc as a defence community, but as a liberal powerhouse whose preferred activity was trade in order to foster development, both internally and externally.

In this respect, the EU has a tendency to reproduce itself, leading to 'external projections of internal solutions'. It therefore becomes a normative power, rooted in an historical context. The concept of NPE describes the process through which the EU is able to impose norms with a relative absence of physical force. The conflict-prevention policy developed by the EU, especially from 1970 to the mid-1990s, is noted by the author as one which embodies this particular notion of NPE. Nevertheless, the progressive implementation of a 'Brussels-based military-industrial simplex' and the existence of several actors and interest groups in this field contributed to develop a security strategy based on 'preventive engagement', which weakens the normative power of the EU. This evolution is considered to have an influence on the political form the EU has and will take in the future (Manners 2006; for an overview see Whitman 2011).

The normative power of the EU is interpreted somewhat differently by Zaki Laïdi (2008) and Lisbeth Aggestam (2008) in particular, who analyse how European regulations exert power by influencing international debates. This understanding of the EU's normative or regulatory power is slightly different from the normative approach. While Manners and Diez's perspective argues how the EU should be, reflecting the EU's refusal to commit to conventional power on the ground, based on physical domination, in favour of an idea of developing post-Westphalian norms (peace, freedom, human rights) on an international scale (Diez 2005), on the contrary, Laïdi and Aggestam concentrate on the regulatory impact of the EU beyond its borders. Laïdi and Aggestam's conceptualization of the EU as international norms producer brings the advantage of opening up the EU's external relations to issues beyond former first- and second-pillar issues (CFSP, CSDP and external trade relations), and allows the analysis of the external dimensions of internal policies. It allows us to study the EU's role in environmental or development policy matters, human rights or immigration and asylum policies. The EU as norm producer thus offers the possibility for horizontal analyses in international relations: 'the EU amongst its peers'. As an extension to this debate there is, of course, the notion of 'soft' power (Nye 2004). Contrary to civilian power, soft power is not based only on a strengthening of cooperation between actors, but on a transfer of cognitive norms and values in the discourse and actions of third-party actors (Orbie 2006).

Limits of NPE

However, while these analyses of European norms triggering transformation in other parts of the world are very stimulating, they do raise at least three challenges. The first is the shortage of empirical analyses. More fundamentally, the debate on Europe and norms confuses different types of European norms: more specifically, norms referring to the EU's regulation of globalization, norms that are being institutionalized, such as those pertaining to international criminal justice, and, finally, long-standing universal norms, such as human rights (Sjursen 2006).

Second, there is also confusion between political norms and legal norms, the latter being part of EU and international law.

The increasing consensus around the idea of the EU as 'normative power' on the international scene would require a distinction between political norms promoted by the EU, but hardly recognized at international level (the multi-functionality of agriculture, for example); norms consecrated by European law, but not with such clarity by international law (the precautionary principle); and norms whose jurisdiction at international level is linked to the engagement of the EU and its member states (to varying extents, depending on the case). This would include international criminal justice, International Labour Organisation (ILO) social norms and 'cultural diversity' recognized by the United Nations Educational, Scientific, and Cultural Organization (UNESCO). (Petiteville 2006: 214).

The third problem is linked to a neorealist interpretation of the EU's external power. In the neorealist understanding, the emergence of the EU's 'actorness' in foreign policy is linked to bipolarity and systemic changes in the structural distribution of power (Hyde-Price 2006). This has led to the development of the EU as a 'collective hegemon', shaping its external environment by using both *hard power* and *soft power* mechanisms. In this regard, the outcome or effectiveness of norm diffusion is determined by the willingness and capability of powerful states. This can be seen in all policy areas, but most clearly in the field of human rights, where, according to neorealists, international human rights regimes have only impact when powerful states enforce principles and norms. As for

Table 10.2   *Contemporary international relations in EU studies*

Perspectives	Main assumptions	Authors
Using international relations to understand internal and external EU policies	European integration cannot be understood without linking comparative politics to international relations approaches	Hurrell and Menon 1996, 2003 Risse-Kappen 1996 Caporaso 1999
Intergovernmental dimension of EU bargaining		
• 'National interest'	National interest is constructed through interaction (role-playing), but strongly influences bargaining in the EU	Finnemore 1996 Finnemore and Sikkink 1998 Jabko 2006 Scharpf 2002
• Power and sovereignty	Power and sovereignty are tools in EU bargaining ('sovereignty games'), having both a legal and a political basis	Walker 2003 Bickerton et al. 2007 Puetter 2006, 2012 Adler-Nissen 2008, 2009 Aalberts 2012
The external action of the EU		
• Conventional theories of EU foreign and security policy	External action of the EU is an intergovernmental playing field, confronted with a 'capability-expectations gap'	Allen et al. 1982 Ginsberg 1989 Holland 1991 Nuttall 1992 Hill 1993, 1998 Tonra 2001 Mérand 2008a Menon 2000 Hyde-Price 2006 Howorth 2004 Terpan 2004
• The EU as an international actor	Actorness of the EU must be analysed through three elements: • Opportunity • Presence • Capacity	Ginsberg 2001 Bretherton and Vogler 2006
• NPE o Normative/ethical	The EU, given its peaceful history, exports/must export democratic values to the world	Dûchene 1973 Manners 2002, 2006, 2008, 2009, 2012 Diez 2005 Sjursen 2006
o Regulatory	The EU, as a regulatory power, influences international norms and non-member states	Hyde-Price 2008 Laïdi 2008 Aggerstam 2008

the EU as a normative or civilian power, neorealists argue along three lines.

First, they assert that the EU is not a unitary actor on the international stage but rather 'an instrument for the collective economic interests of those states in the context of global economy' as well as 'an instrument for collectively shaping the regional milieu' (Hyde-Price 2008: 31). Consequently, the economic and strategic interests of individual member states, the real key actors, are at the heart of EU's foreign and security policy.

Second, they claim that EU member states are fully aware of the structural distribution of material capabilities, and, as such, will not act irrationally by pursuing the second-order human rights agenda at the expense of their crucial national interests.

Third, they see member states as 'systemic factors [that] either enable or constrain political choices in international politics' (Hyde-Price 2008: 37); exerting EU influence effectively requires favourable structural circumstances as well as the material power to react. European norms take on various forms and are built in different ways; as such, their effects and uses outside the EU require a more systematic analysis.

The conceptualization of the normative influence of the EU through these approaches offers exciting avenues for research, as both the intergovernmental and transnational nature of European integration can be seen as a social construction with extremely real effects on the debate. Thus instead of considering the EU as a legal norm producer either lacking influence or succeeding to exert influence, based on its legal status, perspectives conceptualizing norms allow us to perceive the interaction between actors as a power game whose players are not only acting to raise their benefits (or the benefits of the organization they represent), but are at the same time constrained by their role.

Conclusion

The different approaches to international relations, as diverse as they may be, allow us to address the EU, not only as a state-like body, federation or international organization, but also as a transnational, regional integration bloc where sovereignty, national interests and intergovernmental arguments play a role. Without denying the contributions of comparative politics perspectives, referred to here as 'bottom-up mainstreaming', it has to be said that their conceptual frames tend to generally neglect the intergovernmental nature of European integration.

Sociological and constructivist approaches in international relations allow the international as well as intergovernmental dimension to be addressed without forcing the researcher to have to accept liberal intergovernmentalist or realist assumptions (Puetter 2012; Aalberts 2012;

Bickerton et al. 2007; Sassen 1996; Bierstecker and Weber 1996). Sovereignty and power is not an undisputed attribute of member states or even the EU. Different types of power exist and their perception varies amongst the actors concerned, be they the EU's member states, non-member states or other international organizations. These approaches allow us to analyse state sovereignty not just as a concept that is eroded through the European integration process.

> Rather the application of sovereign power takes new creative forms as states play sovereignty games. The main argument brought forward is that states and other political and legal actors are not just observing passively how economic flows transgress their borders or how the national legal order is subjugated to international and supranational EU law. Instead they engage in new practices and modify understandings of their own sovereignty, which paradoxically may end up strengthening their position vis-à-vis other actors not only in Europe but on a global scene. (Adler-Nissen and Gammeltoft-Hansen 2008: 16)

Furthermore, work on transnational elites, the symbols and discourse of legitimization and judicial and soft norms, could breath new life into such research. Ignoring power and sovereignty in intergovernmental games in the European context, or leaving it to political commentators, prevents mainstream approaches to European integration from contributing to key debates beyond micro-objects, such as single institutions, single policies or single cases, however pertinent they may be.

Chapter 11

Comparing Forms of Regional Integration: Beyond European Studies

This final chapter returns to the question raised at the beginning of the book, i.e. the extent to which European integration could be analysed as a unique or *sui generis* phenomenon, in the language of European studies specialists. It argues that European integration theories would benefit from situating themselves in a broader perspective, i.e. regional integration, in general. While this perspective was central in the 1950s and 1960s, this trend waned somewhat, until the middle of the 1990s, when comparisons of regionalization once again appeared on the academic agenda. This renewed interest was the result of an empirical phenomenon: the emergence of a new regional dynamic with the renewed launch of European integration processes and the transformation of the European Community into the EU, the creation of NAFTA, Mercosur, APEC (Asia-Pacific Economic Cooperation), and the relative strengthening of ASEAN.

Just like 'old regionalism', the 'new' version that emerged remains within the domain of international relations but has influenced mainstream EU studies in a very limited way (Warleigh-Lack and van Langenhove 2010; Warleigh-Lack et al. 2011). However, instead of analysing institutional frames, common values or the process of elite socialization as scholars did within 'old' regionalist approaches, new regionalism is more generally situated within international political economy (IPE) broadly speaking. It offers an opportunity to compare the European integration process with other regional integration phenomena and to identify differences and similarities in political and economic structures, as well as processes. At the same time, however, the notion of integration is somewhat problematic insofar as it is considered by 'new' regionalist scholars to be too close to neofunctionalist vocabulary.

One of the central aims of new regionalism is to get around the n=1 problem of European integration studies. This refers more specifically to the problem identified in the Introduction to this book whereby the European integration process is considered as unique, and cannot be compared to other regional integration processes. Conversely, new regionalism scholars advocate that European integration *should* be regarded as but one instance of regionalization among others. This leads to the broader question of whether the phenomenon of regionalization can be analysed as a territorial form of globalization. From this perspective, regionalization and globalization are just two manifestations of an economic integration process taking place at two different levels, and which lead to greater interdependence (Katzenstein 1996; Warleigh-Lack 2004; Rosamond 2005a). Thus, since regionalization seems to be a universal phenomenon, it can only be interpreted by a comparative study of its various aspects.

On the basis of the issue raised in early studies on regionalism, i.e. 'why sovereign states accept the idea of uniting in a regional bloc and abandoning their prerogatives', the scope of new regionalism has extended further to include relations between different levels of government, and comparative studies of different policy areas (such as macro- and micro-economy or security), thus clearly going beyond the traditional focus of European integration studies, concentrating on governmental elites or an abstract state.

The purpose of this final chapter, therefore, is threefold: the first part analyses the establishment of regional organizations in comparative perspective; the second part presents the debates surrounding the conceptualization of 'new regionalism' and illustrates the difficulties of approaching European studies from this angle; and the third part looks more specifically at how scholars have conceptualized the link between globalization and regionalization.

Regions in comparative perspective

While the relaunch of the European project in the 1990s led to a renewed theoretical and conceptual interest in European integration, regional integration as a global phenomenon has brought about a number of theoretical concepts in the postwar period since 1945. Understanding the reasons for these processes is important if we are to grasp the origins of regional integration theories, beyond those developed by European integration scholars.

Definitions and historical developments

Pinpointing the beginning of the process of regionalization historically is difficult because the 'feeling of regional belonging' (Fawcett 1995) seems to pre-date the construction of regional entities in the political or economic sense of the word. Joseph Nye's definition, whereby an international region equates to a 'limited number of states joined together by a geographical proximity and a degree of mutual interdependence' (Nye

1968: xii), seems sufficiently encompassing to include both Fawcett's 'imaginary' regions and formal organizations.

However, in the context of an analysis of regional integration theories and, more specifically, those of European integration, the notion takes on a more institutional meaning and has more specific contours. In this context, it is difficult to talk about regional organizations before the end of the Second World War. With the exception of the inter-American system and the highly institutionalized European continent, very few regional groupings existed prior to 1945. The first regional integration projects were embedded in the economic crises and domestic politics that had led to the Second World War, and thereafter, the expansion and transformation of organized security globally, with the creation of the UN (Claude 1964).

The Second World War effectively divided the continent into two opposing spheres in which the two hegemonic powers sought to establish their influence. As Fawcett (1995) emphasizes, integrated regions, as a unit of analysis, became increasingly central, both in the collective imagination of political and economic elites and as a research topic. This specific focus emerged at the end of the Second World War, as Stanley Hoffmann described: 'One of the consequences of post-WWII policies was the division of an enormous, heterogeneous, international system into a world of sub-systems in which forms of cooperation or conflict management became more intense and less elusive than those of global systems' (Hoffmann 1987: 293). Emerging regional blocs, such as the inter-American system, the Commonwealth, the Arab League or, indeed, NATO were considered as agencies primarily created to settle conflicts between their members. Other regional integration projects, such as the EEC, were originally aiming to create an integrated economic zone. It is thus possible to distinguish between two main forms of regional integration: on the one hand, micro-economic organizations leading to formal economic integration and, on the other, political organizations focusing on conflict control (Nye 1971).

Peace through regional integration
Parallel to these developments the UN emerged as an actor promoting peace through regional integration. The main idea was based on peace promotion through cooperation in a variety of areas such as economic and social development, education or culture. Inis Claude had considered the UN, certainly over-enthusiastically, as a primordial element for the development of regional integration (Claude 1968). The UN perceived regional integration projects as an integral part of this formalized objective at the Dumbarton Oaks Conference in 1944. Thus, Chapter VII of the United Nations Charter on regional agreements stipulates that 'No provision of this Charter is opposed to the existence of regional agreements or bodies designed to settle affairs that require

regional action and concern peace-keeping and international security, on condition that those agreements and bodies and their activities are compatible with the principles of the United Nations' (Article 52, §1). Furthermore, the Security Council relies on 'regional agreements and bodies for the application of coercive measures taken under its authority' (Article 55, §1).

From the Cold War to the end of bipolarity
The experience of international cooperation during the first years of the Cold War seemed to suggest that states were rational, unitary actors seeking to bring about security by various means in an otherwise anarchical world. Peace was, however, not always the result. On the contrary, some of the regional blocs were involved in the East–West conflict, or even subordinate to the broader demands of the two major powers – the USA and the Soviet Union: the Warsaw Pact, NATO or the Organisation of American States – the latter often considered as the spokesperson and channel for North American interests. Moreover, the European institutions created after the Second World War were seen partly to protect Western Europe from the Soviet Union, or so it was widely held. The only exception seemed to the European Community, which received the 2012 Nobel Peace Prize for guaranteeing peace on the European continent for over 60 years. Other organizations such as the Arab League and the Organisation of African Unity, so called pan-movements – as their establishment was based not on economic or social interests but on the perceived existence of a common identity – faced different problems. These organizations whose *raison d'être* was based on a shared ideology came up against difficulties of cohesion (Fawcett 1995: 13).

At the same time, we also observe the creation of regional blocs by non-aligned developing states. Opposition to the East–West conflict, and North–South relations in particular, resulted in just such a coalition of southern powers, the Group of 77 (G77), a movement, which, among other things, led to the development of the dependency school (Willits 1978). The emergence of sub-regional security organizations such as ASEAN in 1967, the Caribbean Community (CARICOM) in 1973, the Economic Community of West African States (ECOWAS) in 1975, the Southern African Development Community (SADC) in 1980, the Cooperation Council for the Arab States of the Gulf (GCC) in 1981, and indeed the South Asian Association for Regional Cooperation (SAARC) in 1985, are all evidence of attempts to create security-oriented organizations without the support of global powers. However, given the unstable climate at the time, these initiatives did not have a very significant influence on global or regional politics, with the exception of ASEAN (Fawcett 1995).

The emergence of these regional groups at the time led to research focusing on factors that influenced this regionalization of the world, and

Table 11.1   *The establishment of regional organizations*

Association of South-East Asian Nations	ASEAN	1967
Conference on Security and Cooperation in Europe/Organisation for Security and Cooperation in Europe	CSCE/OSCE	1973/1995
Caribbean Community	CARICOM	1973
Economic Community of West African States	ECOWAS	1975
Southern African Development Community	SADC	1980
Cooperation Council for the Arab States of the Gulf	GCC	1981
South Asian Association for Regional Cooperation	SAARC	1985
Common Southern Market	Mercosur	1991
North American Trade Agreement	NAFTA	1994
Union of South American Nations	UNASUR	2008

on the consequences of the phenomenon (Nye 1968; Cantori and Speigel 1970). While the neofunctionalist approach developed in the context of European integration (Chapter 2) is indeed the best known regional integration theory, other theoretical and conceptual schemes did emerge and, be it often implicitly, went on to influence subsequent approaches to European integration, such as constructivism (Chapter 7), sociological approaches (Chapter 8), or, more recently, 'new regionalist' conceptual frameworks, as analysed in this chapter.

However, by the end of the 1960s, the hopes pinned on regionalization had increasingly led to disappointment. Regional integration schemes seemed to have run out of steam, with internal conflicts increasingly visible between members and common projects met with suspicion. European integration studies even saw one of its main theorists, Ernst Haas, declare that integration theory was obsolete in Europe, although still useful for the rest of the world (Haas 1975). It was at this moment that regionalism researchers started to take an interest in new issues: the challenge of interdependence between actors and the role of emerging international regimes (Nye and Keohane 1972, 1977). These regimes established a looser set of interdependence schemes, which, although often legally binding, concentrated on single policy areas such as human rights protection, environmental issues or the law of the sea, to mention but a few, and were not confined to a specific regional area.

At the end of the 1980s regional organizations were reformed and new regional blocs created; the demand for the 'regional organisation of the world' to support the UN at the end of the Cold War increased sharply (Rosecrance 1991; Ohmae 1993). GATT's recurrent difficulties at the beginning of the 1990s, and those of the WTO's today, plus the increasing importance of economic integration (economic and financial globalization in particular), ongoing processes of democratization and, consequently, the emergence of new democracies, have all encouraged scholars to take more interest in the question of regional integration.

In the 1990s, academic observers emphasized that conditions, both within states and internationally, were more favourable for the emergence and efficiency of regional integration. This situation was based on four factors: the end of the Cold War, economic change, the probable end of the 'Third World', and democratization.

- The end of the bipolar system led to new attitudes towards international cooperation. In particular, on several occasions, the UN called for regional organizations, not only in Europe but also in Africa, Latin America and South-East Asia (Roberts 1993). Devolution, which also followed the end of the Cold War, led to the reform of a number of regional organizations both in Europe, such as the reform of NATO, and the transformation of the CSCE into the OSCE; and in Asia, where ASEAN's involvement in the peace process in Cambodia is one of the more significant examples.
- Economic change and, more specifically, economic and financial globalization contributed to more profound cooperation in several regional blocs. Among these were the European Community and its transformation into the EU, Mercosur, UNASUR, created in 2008, and NAFTA.
- Finally, the end of 'Third-worldism' (Gilpin 1987) meant the G77 saw its powers of persuasion reduced. The heterogeneity of members and the absence of common institutions and objectives were largely responsible for this outcome. Democratization processes – in particular, in Central and Eastern Europe and, in the 1980s, in Latin America, Spain and Portugal – opened up new perspectives for debates on whether or not regional integration schemes were democratic.

Theoretical accounts

As we have seen, regional integration schemes were heterogeneous, and still are. The theoretical accounts developed before the end of the Cold War to understand these schemes reflected this heterogeneity. At the same time they were permanently searching for general explanations that went beyond single case studies. Neofunctionalism was one of the most important perspectives, offering comparative research designs to study regional integration (Chapter 2). Other, less well-known approaches, such as interdependence and elite-centred frameworks (Russett 1967;

Etzioni 1965), offered hypotheses to understand why regions emerged, insisting on the degree of interdependence or the depth of identification elites had with integration schemes. Thus, according to Etzioni (1965, 2001), coherence and discourses of elite identification were sufficient to account for deeper integration. Reunifying messages were considered more likely to deepen integration than coercive power options. This explains how two of the four regional integration schemes on which Etzioni's research is based – the United Arab Republic (UAR) and the Federation of the West Indies – failed: unfavourable external elites and the weakness and plethora of internal elites led to an incoherent message that did not convince the concerned citizens. The Nordic Union and the EEC were more successful, thanks to a more homogenous, united elite that helped them through the first extremely unstable phase of integration where failure is much more likely. Implicitly, elite-centred interdependence theory argued that while economic integration might trigger the establishment of integrated political institutions, regional integration cannot be attained by economic or political spill-over alone. A shared legitimacy and shared sense of belonging must be developed, which would emerge on the basis of political and economic interdependence.

Table 11.2   *Comparative regionalism in brief*

General perspectives	Specific approaches
Old regionalism	• Neofunctionalism • Interdependence and elite-centred approaches
New regionalism	• IPE • Constructivism • Rationalist approaches to comparative political economy
Beyond the old–new regionalism divide	Regionalization is dependent on three main factors: • the context of the genesis of regional integration • its functionality • the degree of socialization reached
Globalization and regionalization	Regionalization and globalization processes are intimately linked to a single phenomenon of global transformation, which can be just as complementary as they can be contradictory

These theoretical accounts influenced a number of studies during the 1970s, but then slowly vanished from the academic world. It is neofunctionalism that served as starting point for criticism and reflection, leading to a 'new comparative regionalism' movement during the 1990s.

'New' regionalism

The end of the Cold War and new dynamics in regional integration led to new conceptualizations of regional integration studies. These 'new' regionalism approaches attempted to contrast with 'old' regionalism, considered to be mainly influenced by neofunctionalist assumptions. On this basis, new research designs developed. While these new regionalist approaches are generally based on IPE perspectives, constructivist and critical political economy traditions have been increasingly influential.

Beyond neofunctionalism

While new regionalism brings together a heterogeneous group of scholars and research designs, they meet in rejecting the main neofunctionalist hypotheses. They argue that regional integration does not directly lead from a customs union to a single market, that the increased efficiency experienced in the integration of one area does not directly lead to that of another (i.e. a common agricultural policy or free movement of persons does not lead to a common social policy), and that integration does not necessarily lead to a transfer of loyalty from the domestic to the supranational level. Examples abound in this respect: African and Asian regional integration schemes do not aim to create a common identity but seek to establish preferential trade agreements and/or security cooperation. The main assumption here is that the neofunctionalist logic would be too teleological in its analysis, and fail to identify key variables explaining the diversified forms of regional integration (Hettne 2003; Laursen 2003, 2010). Furthermore, scholars argue that neofunctionalist approaches focus too much on institutionalized integration, preventing research from performing a neutral analysis of incidences of regional integration without speculating, in particular, on the point at which they might resemble European integration (Acharya 2002; Schulz, Söderbaum and Ojendal 2001). Finally, new regionalists argue that the 'old' regionalists' approach is too dependent upon state actors to explain the pressures brought to bear on member states for greater integration and does not pay sufficient attention to the globalized economic system, and to state actors who are not members of the EU or even international organizations (Fawcett 1995). 'Neoregionalists' do not in any way deny the importance of state actors, but attribute less importance to the role of formal integration – i.e. to the pressure brought to bear by these actors on the state – than to informal phenomena, such as actor involvement in the commercial or immigration sectors. This argument can clearly be seen in Hurrell's work (Hurrell 1995: 39), according to which 'the most important driving forces for economic regionalization come from markets, from private trade and investment flows, and from the policies and decisions of companies'.

IPE approaches to comparative regionalization clearly fall under this third and last heading. Here economic factors are the central explanatory variable for regional integration. In seeking to explain the reasons for regional integration – or the absence of it – Walter Mattli (1999: 42) argues that in order for integration to be successful, 'the potential for economic gains from market exchange within a region must be significant ... [T]he demand for regional rules, regulations and policies by market players is a critical driving force of integration.' While this element is certainly correct, it is important to measure precisely *how* the influences exerted by political design carried by political elites lead to more integration (Mansfield and Milner 1999). The comparison between European and Asian integration is relevant in this sense (Sbragia 2008: 43). Alberta Sbragia argues that it made economic sense for the countries of Western Europe to increase interregional trade in the 1950s. In this sense, the EU is a case of 'closed regionalism' in that it is a customs union that unites many of the richest consumer markets in the world and whose internal agricultural policy plays a major role in shaping international agricultural trade. By contrast, in Asia, trade relations are much stronger with countries outside the region than within the region, so that the reasons for establishing a regional integration scheme lay in other areas. The APEC forum symbolizes 'open regionalism' characterized by unilateral activity, such as the unilateral lowering of tariffs and the liberalization of domestic markets.

For most analysts interested in new regionalism, theoretical and conceptual frameworks developed to analyse European regionalism are insufficient to structure comparative regional studies. This is for two reasons: first, in EU studies, neofunctionalism and its recent adaptations will always be identified as the main theory of European integration. It is, however, only well-suited to explaining a specific form of regional integration, i.e. a European one, without taking into account the possibility of disintegration or the slowing down of integration, a subject which is particularly interesting during the current decade in the EU. Secondly, the turning point leading to 'bottom-up mainstreaming', that is, the use of public policy, comparative politics and sociology to analyse political processes in the EU as if it were a quasi-state, is considered by 'neo-regionalists' as reductionist, insofar as these conceptualizations tend to exclude the intergovernmental logic from their analyses (Warleigh-Lack 2004, 2007). As a consequence, scholars of comparative regionalism increasingly embraced assumptions stemming from IPE. In this vein,

Andrew Hurrell (1995, 2007) argued that the second wave of regional-ization, which emerged after 1985, produced regional entities character-ized by many new factors, such as closer integration between the countries of the North and of the South, of which NAFTA is an example. These forms of regional integration were more distinct than earlier neofunctionalist studies on comparative regionalism suggested. Thus, one of the specificities of the new regionalist approach is the particular attention it pays to factors explaining the distinction between regional integration schemes – such as the differences between North American and Latin American integration, based respectively on a hegemon and on equal relations, without taking the European integration process as a template.

The distinction between old and new regionalism

One particular group of scholars (Hettne 2002; Hettne and Söderbaum 2000; Warleigh-Lack 2007) have suggested that differentiating between old and new regionalism comes down to changes in the global context: the global economy and the contemporary political system, which are extremely different from the postwar situation.

Three elements must be particularly taken into account. First, the end of the Cold War significantly encouraged the USA to take more interest in certain forms of regional integration, as illustrated by its influence in the reinforcement of European and Asian regional integration schemes. According to these authors, this influence merits more systematic analy-sis than is currently the case in European integration studies. Second, economic issues more and more override military or security concerns. Through their cooperation, states seem to be increasingly prepared to abandon parts of their sovereignty to gain influence over international public policies that particularly concern them. Thirdly, and finally, new regionalist scholars argue that instead of being sectoral, new regionalist integration is multifaceted. Regional integration schemes, such as the European Community, NAFTA, Mercosur or ASEAN stated at the outset that regional integration should be based on different policy areas. If trade relations were important, so was cultural exchange, social or foreign policy. This does not mean that all these areas were successfully integrated at the beginning, but the intention was there, and in some cases, plans did exist.

The distinction between an 'old' and a 'new' regionalism seems, however, to be slightly overemphasized: Regional integration theories have evolved since their establishment in the 1950s and 1960. Indeed, questions formulated in international relations during the 1940s or even before that time were revised and refined during the 1970s, and then from the end of the 1980s, as we have seen in the earlier chapters. In the field of regional studies outside European integration, on the other hand,

Table 11.3   *Old and new regionalism (Hettne 2003; Warleigh-Lack 2007)*

Old regionalism	New regionalism
Regions: • Are structured in a Cold War context • Rely upon the influence of an external power to exist • Are protectionist • Are sectoral/thematic • Make few or no challenges to sovereignty	Regions are: • Created in a multipolar and globalized context • Initiated and extended by member states and not by outside powers • Economically open • Multifunctional • Involved in the transformation of state sovereignty

a difference can be found insofar as the early debates were focused on the concept of regional integration and cooperation among states, with a rather strong normative dimension, as they sought to identify ways to establish permanent institutionalized cooperation schemes.

However, these developments have also made any attempt to define the notion of 'region' more difficult. Thus, researchers such as Frederik Söderbaum and Björn Hettne proposed using the notion of *region-ness*, meaning the 'degree of regionalization'. They distinguish between three degrees of region-ness: core regions, which are extremely structured and allow their members to play an influential role on the world stage; intermediate zone regions, which imitate core regions so as to compete with them in the global economy; and, finally, peripheral zone regions, where

Table 11.4   *Factors leading to a degree of regionalization*
(Hettne and Söderbaum 2000: 473–5; Warleigh-Lack 2007: 565)

Regionalization factors	Characteristics
• Regional space	• A geographical bloc linked by trade and conflict management
• Regional complex	• A bloc structured by very limited economic interdependence
• Regional society	• Shared rules, state and non-state actors, can become more institutionalized
• Regional community	• Shared norms, transnational civil society, recognized as a central actor
• Regional state	• Pluralist state in which state sovereignty is effectively replaced

political and economic situations remain fragile (Hettne 2001). These distinctions also refer to the neo-Marxist approaches of the 1960s in international relations, whereby the division of the international system between centre and periphery explained the structures of dependence between states. While neo-regionalists do not advance any teleological hypotheses on the future of regional integration, the classification system is close to this logic. The problem with this distinction is, however, its proximity to the premises of neofunctionalist approaches, to the extent that, once again, the central variable seems to be the degree of institutionalization, an idea strongly criticized by the neo-regionalists, as we have seen.

Conceptualizations of new regionalism

Beyond the general trend in new regionalist approaches described above, conceptualizations embedded in this recent movement adhere more specifically to one of the following three traditions in international relations: IPE; constructivism; and the rationalist approach to comparative political economy.

IPE

Scholars interested in the first approach focus in particular on the role of international institutions in regulating the relations between state and society (Schulz et al. 2001). Here, we find studies that show how problems resulting from collective action find – or fail to find – solutions through the activism of international institutions. It is certainly here that the works of Europeanists are the most influential, both because of their number and their specialization. However, they also come up against major problems in the context of comparative regionalism: while in the European integration process, the increase and intensification of trade since the second half of the 1990s has led to an increase in the European institutions' power and competencies, the same cannot be said for Asia (Hurrell 2005) or other regional integration schemes, such as North and South America or Africa. This raises the question of the correlation between economic and political interdependence and the increasing powers and competencies of international institutions. Policy-making processes can furthermore change and diversify over time. An illustration can be found in European studies with regard to the opposition between the Community method, where the European Commission plays the central role of initiator (of legal proposals), and which is characterized by the decision-making process between Council and Parliament, and, on the other, the intergovernmental method which, as its name suggests, is based on a decision-making process that revolves around bargaining between member-state governments, excluding the Commission and the ECJ. Since the beginning of the 2000s, these two decision-making modes have been extended to include the use of informal policies and coordination mechanisms. The continuous debate for different forms of cooperation – deepening as well as widening integration – are not, however, specific to European integration, as analyses of the SADC and ASEAN have shown (Söderbaum and Shaw 2003).

Constructivism

Constructivists are more specifically interested in either the existence of a specific culture that leads to the establishment of a specific regional integration scheme (Katzenstein 2005) or the construction of collective identity within the regional bloc in question (Diez 2005; Hettne 2003; Slocum and van Langehove 2005). With regard to the first group of scholars, Peter Katzenstein (2005) plays a major role. He compares European and Asian regional integration in the framework of US power. These 'porous' regions, according to the author, are very much influenced by regional intermediaries – central states that through their cultural features influence the institutional form these specific regions take. While the American 'imperium' has had a very important influence on these 'porous regions' through actions that mix territorial and non-territorial powers, two crucial intermediaries – Germany and Japan – have imposed their cultural and specific capitalist features on the region – formal arrangements in Europe – informal arrangements in Asia. The Middle East, Africa and South America lacked these intermediaries – strong states, which are, while fundamentally independent from the USA, still sufficiently influenced by similar values.

The second group of scholars applies constructivist frameworks developed in European studies, but enlarges the geographical scope in going beyond European integration (Chapter 7). These studies do not offer a unified approach to identity-building, but illustrate the complexity of the issue by insisting on the multiple levels of identity existing in regions (for a critique see also Checkel and Katzenstein 2009). Studies analyse shared representations of the collective self as they are reflected in political debate, political symbols and collective memories. The aim is not to develop a coherent set of testable hypotheses but to analyse lived experiences: watching soccer or football clubs, meeting in regional social or business networks or 'shopping in supermarket chains increasingly organized on a continental scale' (Checkel and Katzenstein 2009: 2).

Rationalist approaches to comparative political economy

Finally, the third body of research is part of the rationalist approach (Taylor 1993; Mansfield and Milner 1999; Mattli 1999), bringing to the fore the reasons that push states to accept participation in such an integration process. These studies emphasize the importance of 'power' as a factor, as well as transaction costs – and their marked absence in constructivist approaches. Although the notion of power does exist in institutionalist approaches to IPE – framed as a factor in the battle between member states and institutions to define the latter's room for manoeuvre in exercising their responsibilities – the opposition between states is rarely analysed on the basis of their power attributes (Hurrell 2005). Thus, in the context of North and South American regional integrations with NAFTA and Mercosur, respectively, power imbalances between member states are largely responsible for structuring exchanges. The hegemonic roles of the US and Brazilian governments, respectively, in North and South American regional integration exert a crucial influence in the functioning of institutions: 'Weaker states have such an important stake in institutions and in keeping the hegemon at least partially integrated within those institutions that they are willing to accord deference to the hegemon, to tolerate displays of unilateralism, and to acquiesce in actions that place the hegemon on (or beyond) the borders of legality' (Hurrell 2005: 50).

The question that this analysis raises, however, is very similar to that found in Chapter 1: how can these multiple regional dynamics be analysed in a coherent manner?

In order to answer this question, realist perspectives on comparative political economy identify three variables: first, member states' perception of the need for integration; secondly, stability and continuity of intergovernmental cooperation linked to the degree of acceptance of institutional and political integration; and finally, economic integration.

Concerning the first variable, it is possible to distinguish between *endogeneity*, *bandwagon behaviour* and *strategic opportunity*. Endogeneity, in the absence of external pressures or threats, refers to a situation where all states perceive a necessity to cooperate with other states within a regional organization. 'Bandwagon behaviour' is qualified as the behaviour that states adopt when creating alliances with more powerful states, triggering a regional dynamic. Finally, the strategic opportunity model is understood as a situation whereby the state perceives regional integration as an instrument that will allow it to exercise greater strategic control over its environment. To these rational reflections, Mansfield and Milner add societal factors and conceptualize the influence of domestic institutions (Mansfield and Milner 1999: 602–8). The main assumption here is that it is not enough to solely concentrate on foreign policy behaviour of states; what is key is to understand how this foreign policy behaviour originates and which factors shape it. This allows for bringing politics back into regional integration. The assumption here is that political elites must strike a balance between the economic and political benefits stemming from regional integration, and must accommodate citizens as well as collective actors, since the support of both groups is needed to retain office. Similarly, although national political elites may favour joining a regional integration scheme to circumvent national resistance, they may also do so in order to engage in blame-shifting to other regional organizations.

Subsequently, stability and continuity in intergovernmental cooperation is measured more by the institutions for cooperation set up than by the political stability of its component members. Economic integration, finally, seems to be a crucial trigger for the creation of regional integration structures upon which legal and political structures are subsequently built. It is important to note here that this understanding of regional integration reflects the core assumptions of liberal intergovernmentalism (Moravcsik 1993a), which insist on the crucial influence that interest groups play in shaping national elite perceptions of the need for regional integration. In this respect, liberal intergovernmentalism might be a promising venue for rigorously conceptualizing the rational tradition of 'new' regionalism.

Horizontal perspectives

Going beyond a specific theoretical school, Alex Warleigh-Lack (2008) provides one of the most promising horizontal conceptualizations, however. In doing so, he differentiates between the dependent variable (regionalization) and three independent variables (the genesis of regional integration, its functionality, and the degree of socialization reached/its impact). Regionalization is defined as a dynamic concept, implying fluidity and movement:

> an explicit, but not necessarily formally institutionalised, process of adapting participant state norms, policy-making processes, policy-styles, policy content, political opportunity structures, economies and identities (both elite and popular level) to both align with and shape a new collective set of priorities, norms and interests at the regional level, which may itself then evolve, dissolve of reach stasis. (Warleigh-Lack 2008: 51)

Having thus defined regional integration as a dependent variable, Warleigh-Lack goes on to develop four independent variables influencing the outcomes of regional integration, based on Haas's (1971) neofunctionalist theoretical assumptions. The four variables can be summarized as follows:

- *Genesis*. In attempting to answer the question as to why states initially participate in an integration scheme and, in particular why they continue participation, Warleigh-Lack argues that states participate because they perceive a specific common interest in managing political, social, economic or cultural affairs. The importance of this hypothesis lies in the term 'perceived' interest.
- *Functionality*. The questions to be answered here are: 'Who is leading the integration process?' 'What kind of actors are they?', 'Where do

Box 11.1   *Warleigh-Lack's five types of regionalization*

1   *Structured regionalization* is based on a complex interdependence system with relatively strong regional institutions and high costs of breaking the rules – which would appear to be the case for the EU, and, according to Warleigh-Lack, for the African Union (for a different account see D.C. Bach 1999).

2   *Dominance regionalization* refers to an integration scheme where one member state exerts core influence over the political, and social but mainly economic integration processes, with the example of NAFTA clearly in mind.

3   *Security regionalization* describes an issue-specific regionalization scheme focusing on security issues in a broad sense, with examples being the Euro-Mediterranean partnership and NATO.

4   *Network regionalization* is a 'regional identity-driven response to globalization' (Warleigh-Lack 2008, 52). It is based on non-institutionalised or intergovernmental working methods, as can be found in the case of ASEAN.

5   *Conjoined regionalism* refers to links between an established regional integration scheme and other associated countries, such as the European Neighbourhood Policy and APEC.

they come from?' 'Which mechanisms are in place?' Here the hypothesis is that regional integration processes are discontinuous ('stop-and-go') processes led by the governments of the member states, with a tendency towards informal methods of decision-making.

- *Socialization.* Here the questions refer to the degree of integration and socialization as well as of legitimacy and trust. The hypothesis formulated in this context is that policy-learning and joint-decision-making are more visible than regional identities, trust or legitimacy questions both at the citizen and elite level.

- *Impact.* The question of impact addresses the levels of influence exercised by the specific regional integration under scrutiny – the global level, the internal functioning of the member states as well as other non-member states – in political, economic, or social terms. In this context the hypothesis is that regional integration processes have a significant structural impact on the member states.

While these hypotheses are sufficiently general to be specified in detail and in order to allow for a comparative research design for global regional integration studies, they still require a more general variable, which might be the global political structure, or, in other words, the link between regional integration and globalization. Thus, one of the main arguments put forward by comparative regional integration scholars is the still (benign) neglect of international or global structures in their

analysis of regional integration. New regionalisms attempt more specifically to study this link between regionalization and globalization.

Globalization and regionalization

One of the particular features of new regionalism is the emphasis placed
on the coexistence of globalization and regionalization (Telo 2007;
Hettne et al. 1999; Fawcett and Hurrell 1995; Farrell, Hettne and van
Langenhove 2005; Cooper, Hughes and de Lombaerde 2008), though
this is criticized by some scholars who argue that this distinction is empirically impossible to make (Rosamond 2005a; Hay 2005). While studies
on globalization (in particular Scholte 2012) agree that this process questions the sovereignty of the state and heralds the onset of the Westphalian
system in which the state is the central player, the main idea of new
regionalism goes beyond this assumption. New regionalists argue that
analyses of contemporary regionalization processes require a study of the
internal processes of integration, based on actors, procedures, norms and
cognitive frameworks. Yet, at the same time, it is equally important to
look at the influence of external or global systemic factors on these
phenomena. In-depth studies of regionalization, therefore, must offer
both an endogenous and exogenous perspective and, in so doing, comply
with the important framework developed by Peter Gourevich in his
'Second Image Reversed', which shows the influence of policies led at
global level on the domestic policies of states (Gourevich 2002, 1978;
also Jacoby and Meunier 2010; Diez and Whitman 2002; Warleigh-Lack
2006a).

Forms of regionalization are, therefore, as much influenced by actors
positioned at the heart of the regional bloc as influenced by global
processes. From this point of view, regionalization and globalization
processes are intimately linked to a single phenomenon of global transformation, but which can be just as complementary as they can be
contradictory (Hurrell 2005). Thus, the endogenous perspective emphasizes the similarities that exist between old and new forms of regionalism,
in particular, concerning functionalist and neofunctionalist theorization,
the principal/agent role and long-term transformations of territorial
identities. With the exception of rationalist IPE approaches to regionalization, most contemporary perspectives emphasize the multidimensional nature of integrations; states are just actors among many others.

In the debate on the link between globalization and regionalism, two
themes regularly crop up. First, the degree of complexity characterizing
the globalization process also exists in the regionalization process. In this
context, new regionalism must be understood as a process that unfolds at
different levels and according to different dimensions. Regionalism
occurs in various arenas and is based on a set of extremely heterogeneous

actors who act both 'top-down' and 'bottom-up', linking interests, ideas and identities. According to this interpretation, a large number of elements found in globalization studies can also be found in those referring to regionalization. The latter could, therefore, be seen as a smaller-scale form of globalization.

Secondly, regionalism is often considered to be the vanguard to globalization which allows the region to protect society from the damaging effects of free-market globalization. According to this perspective, regionalization must be understood through globalization.

Complexity and the vanguard

With regard to the complexity issue, regionalization is thus dependent upon a global process, which Hurrell summarizes in several arguments (Hurrell 2005: 53–4):

First, regional integration is the process that best reconciles the changing and increasingly intense pressures of global capitalistic competition, and the need for regulation and political management. Second, it is more likely that coordination and regulation rules will be accepted in a context of profound regional integration, given their greater social consensus. Thirdly, for a number of developing countries and, in particular, ASEAN countries, regionalism can accelerate their integration into a globalized economic system. For developed countries in particular, regionalism allows a reconciliation of free-market economies with a degree of social protection and, thereby, to some extent, reinforces or reinstates their autonomy. One of the ways for states to pursue their autonomy is by institutionalizing cooperation in the area of economic integration.

With regard to this last point, the IPE approach offers a set of coherent questions that link the internal dynamics of the EU, the internal policies of states and the process of globalized change. In this context, Helen Milner uses rational choice theory and the two-level game approach (see Chapter 3) to compare active forces in the preparations running up to the Maastricht (EU) and NAFTA Treaty. The author argues that national elites are more inclined to seek international collaboration in contexts where their economies are interdependent or national conditions are favourable. Thus, the financial liberalization process within the EU, made possible by the Maastricht Treaty, has encouraged governments to seek international cooperation. Financial liberalization is the result of specific constellations at the national level: national governments can accept liberalization only with the support of central actors at the national level, hence the high number of get-out clauses in the Maastricht Treaty (Milner 1998).

Finally, according to Hurrell, new regionalism also addresses the diffusion of regionalization models throughout the world, a research project for which, at the moment, there is a very limited number of empirical studies where the diffusion process is hinted at but not proven. It would be extremely interesting to understand if, and in which way, different regional integration models have influenced others. For example, did the renewed launch of European integration by the end of the 1980s trigger other regional integration schemes? This is generally understood, but a rigorous research agenda would allow us to better understand if, and precisely how, this process has taken place.

Is there a globalization–regionalization correlation?

Linked to this problem is the question of whether it is possible to establish a correlation or even causality between globalization and regionalization. Two groups of studies tackle this problem: while the first group of scholars concentrates on this question generally, the second group has developed a quantitative research design based on policy analysis.

The first group of researchers questions the linkage between regionalization and globalization more generally. One of the starting points is Karl Polanyi's economic theory (Hettne 1999, 2003), according to which enlargement and deeper market cooperation is generally followed by political intervention to defend societal interests. According to Björn Hettne, this dual movement represents a qualified understanding of globalization compared to the dichotomy that distinguishes globalization (as a pressure exerted on regionalization) from regionalization (as an obstacle to globalization). In this regard, regionalization is a movement that not only contributes to liberalization but also encourages a more protectionist stance. This means that the trend towards the creation of regional formations throughout the world can be seen as one political attempt among others to manage the social upheaval that comes with radical deregulation, until today unseen in terms of its global scope.

Such an interpretation that brings in political actors as agents of change allows regionalism to be considered explicitly as a political process. The first sequence takes as a starting point the observation the deliberate institutionalization of a liberalized market and the destruction of institutions created to provide social protection. This movement has been described as 'deregulation' and is associated with the idea of financial globalization. At the same time, and as the analyses of a large number of public policy scholars and comparative politics scholars show (Thatcher 2007), this movement subsequently leads to a new re-regulation, generally following a period of major social upheaval. While the globalization project is generally conceptualized as the first step towards the institutionalization of the free-market system at the global level, this research movement argues that a variety of political forces will attempt to influence and politicize this process. Thus, there are actors whose interests are neither compatible nor necessarily 'good'.

Peter Katzenstein (2005) argues that since the end of the Cold War, regions have become solutions to overcome problems. The author puts forward the hypothesis that globalization and internationalization create porous regions but at the same time offer solutions to the tensions that exist between the state and the market, security and insecurity, nationalism and cosmopolitanism.

The second group of studies concentrates more specifically on the comparison of specific policy fields. These studies show two effects of integration processes: those cases where globalization and Europeanization are working in the same direction, such as finance, and those where European integration slows down or resists the influence of globalization, such as EU Structural Funds (Verdier and Breen 2001). Similarly, in studying the liberalization processes of telecommunication and electricity policies, Levi-Faur (2004) argues that globalization only takes place in fields where European integration is not as strongly developed. European as well as domestic actors use globalization pressures to being about regulatory change (Humphreys and Padgett 2006).

These studies show well how globalization and Europeanization are intertwined. Future research might perhaps concentrate on a larger set of examples to enable us to better understand the conditions that determine when globalization is blocked by European integration, and when globalization is used to foster European regulation.

As it stands, there are limits in conceptualizing the link between globalization and regionalization. Existing scholarship has illustrated, however, that what is won and what is lost in this 'game' does not depend on the power of the state, as classical realists so firmly believe. On the contrary, these approaches start from the assumption that complex systems emerged, managed by a set of norms created by international institutions such as the WTO and the UN. In this context, it is arguable that regional integration influences this 'normalization' or juridicization process undertaken by international organizations. However, as scholars have shown, the potential to influence negotiations is linked for these regions to the capacity to create coalitions with other regional actors (Meunier, Mansfield and Milner 1997), an assumption that helps to explain the establishment of privileged relations between the EU and the Mercosur, the ASEAN or the creation of the Mediterranean Union in the context of the Barcelona Process.

One of the factors that makes this link between globalization and regionalization so important, particularly in the analysis of European integration, is the correlation between exogenous and endogenous factors. The EU is not only interpreted as a more or less coherent political system, but also as a system upon which a number of external actors exert pressure. This dialectic is rarely analysed neither theoretically nor

Table 11.5   *Comparative regionalism perspectives*

Perspectives	Main assumptions	Authors
Old regionalism		
• Neofunctionalism	Regional integration is based on spill-over and transfer of loyalty	Nye 1966, 1970
• Interdependence and elite-centred approaches	The main variables explaining regional integration are the degree of (economic, cultural and political) interdependence as well as the socialization of elites	Russett 1967 Etzioni 1965
New regionalism		
• IPE	Concentrates on the correlation between economic and political interdependence and the increasing powers and competencies of international institutions	Schulz et al. 2001 Hettne 2001 Hettne and Söderbaum 2000
• Constructivism	Regional integration processes must be analysed through the lenses of national culture	Katzenstein 2005 Slocum and van Langehove 2005 Checkel and Katzenstein 2009
• Rationalist approaches to comparative political economy	Regional integration explained through three variables 1 member states' perception of the need for integration 2 stability and continuity of intergovernmental cooperation linked to the degree of acceptance of institutional and political integration 3 the degree of economic integration	Mansfield and Milner 1999 Mattli 1999 Hurrell 2005
Beyond the old-new regionalism divide	Regionalization is dependent on three main factors: the context of the genesis of regional integration, its functionality, and the degree of socialization reached. Regionalization is defined as a dynamic concept, implying fluidity and movement	Warleigh-Lack 2008
Globalization and regionalization	Regionalization and globalization processes are intimately linked to a single phenomenon of global transformation, but which can be just as complementary as they can be contradictory	Hettne et al. 1999 Fawcett and Hurrell 1995 Hettne and van Langenhove 2005 Hurrell 2005

empirically by contemporary international relations studies, which concentrate more on the influence exerted by the EU (diffusion approach (Chapter 6); NPE perspective (Chapter 10)). New regionalism might allow us to study these intertwined influences better as it is based explicitly on a comparative research design, whose aim is to study the dynamics of change in regional integration schemes. The variables developed to explain these dynamics help us to understand both external and internal elements of change much better than the approaches concentrating only on the impact of the EU on the global system.

Conclusion

New regionalism approaches put forward two largely under-conceptualized and under-investigated phenomena for studying European integration: the influence of external phenomena on regional integration, on the one hand, and the relationship between regional integration and globalization, on the other. While these elements help European studies in particular to go beyond their concentration with Europe and to start being interested how European integration compares to and fits into global politics in general, new regionalism as a broad concept still is theoretically in want of slightly more comparative research designs. While a number of studies have developed falsifiable hypotheses or multiple correlations between factors that lead to and transform various forms of regionalization, they are not yet very cumulative and might refer to each other more explicitly. For instance, the question of exporting or disseminating regional integration models or, indeed, importing other models developed by specialists on non-European forms of regional integration has yet to be the subject of theoretical or empirical research. While this is partially done already, this research seems very promising to help us understand the developments of international relations in general through the lenses of regionalism. They offer convincing, albeit as for yet sectoral, conceptual frameworks for understanding European integration in a global perspective.

Finally, while a distinction between the new and old regionalism seems to have secured a certain consensus for a decade or so, critiques and new frameworks are now emerging (Fawcett 1995; Mattli 1999; Caporaso 1998). The differentiation between 'new' and 'old' regionalism seems exaggerated. Thus, the attempt to create a new conceptual perspective opposed to the 'old' regionalism might be erroneous. Only at first sight does it create a homogeneous set of hypotheses (Warleigh-Lack 2006a). The avenues for future research identified in this chapter, including a clearer comparative research design that goes beyond regional or policy case studies, and more analysis of the relationship between regionalization and globalization – seem particularly promising in this respect.

Linking more closely the wealth of EU studies concepts and theories (which are much broader than neofunctionalist research designs, as this book has shown) with comparative regional integration studies would allow us to generalize regionalization processes. This would signify a huge step forward in terms of mainstreaming theories and concepts of European integration.

Conclusion

The last sixty years of European integration have seen the development of a wide range of theories and conceptual tools to explain the why, how and whereto of the regional integration process. This volume has had two aims: First, to explain these theoretical and conceptual innovations, and to put them into perspective with those developments that have taken place in the disciplines of political science and international relations more generally. The second objective was to develop arguments in favour of reintroducing concepts stemming from international relations – more specifically, of concentrating on actors and their representations – into the mainstreaming movement of European studies. This conclusion brings us back to two key questions that run through all the chapters: What have these theories managed to do? And which features of the political system that is the EU still need closer scrutiny?

The process of theoretical thinking: mainstreaming and conceptual robustness

One of the central elements of theoretical approaches to EU studies, at least until the year 2000, was how theory responded to empirical developments. Throughout the book, we have seen that close links exist between empirical developments in European integration and theoretical inventions explaining these phenomena. Theories that have been pronounced dead, such as neofunctionalism (Chapter 2), revive with a different set of real-world events through which they are both challenged and reinforced. This 'cyclical character' of many theories and conceptual frameworks is one of the central features of European studies (see also Paterson 2010). Theories and conceptual frameworks are cyclically challenged and reinforced by empirical developments. For instance, the inter-war period and the period immediately following the Second World War saw the emergence of analytical frameworks seeking to explain the reasons for, and means of, establishing regional institutions. Thus functionalists and federalists argued that regional integration was the most efficient means to prevent future wars by slowly but surely seeking to prevent the outbreak of national sentiments. The creation of the ECSC in 1951 and its institutionalization were the subject of in-depth monographical and comparative analyses, which led to the creation of the first wave of 'European studies'. The Empty Chair Crisis of 1965/66 then brought a period where, after an initial phase of intergovernmental explanations (Chapter 3), few theoretical or conceptual developments could be observed, despite institutional changes in the 1970s such as the establishment of the EMS and EPC, the introduction of a European Council and the first European Parliamentary elections in 1979. Renewed and refined theories and conceptual tools to analyse European integration finally reappeared at the end of the 1980s – when new life was breathed into European integration with the signing of the SEA in 1986 and the Maastricht Treaty in 1992.

These events yielded a rich harvest of new theoretical approaches. Insisting first on the *sui generis* nature of this regional integration phenomenon, conceptual tools progressively brought more general theoretical frameworks initially developed to analyse the state into studies of the EU. These conceptual frameworks took European integration as a given, and shift the emphasis from explaining and advocating regional integration to the study of its actual functioning (Wiener and Diez 2009: 247). This 'mainstreaming' of European studies went through a number of stages. By using tools developed in public policy, comparative politics and political theory, the exceptional nature of European integration was minimized and the political processes under way finally made explicit (Chapters 4 to 9). This is particularly evident in the use of neo-institutionalist frameworks, the concept of governance and, to a lesser extent, political theory. In particular the last perspective developed highly promising concepts in response to questions over the democratic nature of the EU – a topic of widespread academic interest by the mid-1990s. These theoretical and conceptual frameworks, initially developed to study the state ('bottom-up mainstreaming'), led to a qualitative improvement of and quantitative increase in European studies. As in the 1950s and 1960s, this brought the study of integration closer to the analysis of mainstream political science. It allowed scholars to compare domestic phenomena with those occurring in the political system at the European level. While establishing a market for new journals such as the *Journal of Common Market Studies* (1962), *Journal of European Integration* (1978), *Journal of European Public Policy* (1993), and, more recently, *European Union Politics* (2000), this also produced the institutional result of inserting a large number of articles on European integration into mainstream political science journals such as *Governance* (1987), *Political Studies* (1952), *Comparative Politics* (1968), *Public Administration* (1922), *West European Politics* (1978) and *Comparative Political Studies* (1968).

However, because of their reticence to take an interest in conceptual frameworks developed by international relations, and their argument that European integration was best analysed by tools forged to study the state, two key elements were overlooked. First, a general empirical element: despite increased integration, European governance is still characterized by intergovernmental processes and bargaining between state representatives. Thus, member states are still seen as institutional and cognitive reference frameworks, either pushing the European integration process forward or, conversely, holding it back (for an excellent analysis see Thompson 2010). By concentrating mainly on the pillar 1 policies, bottom-up mainstreaming approaches have somewhat neglected pillar 2 and 3 policies – foreign, security and defence policy as well as JHA, pushing these policy areas in specific fields of studies. Only rarely were these policy areas included in more mainstream theorizing. Secondly, it seems that critiques of international relations approaches often jump the gun, and forget that this discipline has evolved since the emergence of structural realism in the 1970s. Studies concerning symbolism in international relations, the dissemination of norms, the social construction of sovereignty or, indeed, those that are part of the critical IPE movement or comparative regionalism more generally are certainly worth taking seriously in European studies. These conceptual approaches enhance our understanding of contemporary transformations of the state because, instead of arguing the obsolescence of state sovereignty or advocating intergovernmentalism, they conceptualize sovereignty and intergovernmental relations by analysing their development and their use over time. According to these approaches, the sovereign functions of the State have not been abolished; they have been transformed and have left their mark, as illustrated by the obvious stakes at play at every EU summit. The negotiations to reform the functioning of European institutions indeed show each state's deep-rooted attachment to its own individual representation within the Commission or to the number of votes at its disposal in QMV procedures, which has become today the ordinary voting procedure. Among other things, this behaviour emphasizes the sensitivity of public opinion and national media to the different expressions of national representation. Finally, one observes that anti-European or even alternative-EU contestations are rarely organized at a transnational basis (Imig and Tarrow 2001). Again, this would seem to underline the importance of national policy and political frames, even after 60 years of European regional integration. It is thus crucial to clearly conceptualize this fact in terms of the theoretical frameworks available in EU studies.

Finally, while it is important to point out that theories and conceptual frameworks are always located in time and space (Cox 1981), and can therefore not be taken as fixed objects, the purpose of this book has been to show that these theoretical and conceptual tools are necessary to structure academic analysis of EU policy-making. However, despite the richness and, at the same time, robustness of contemporary theoretical approaches, a number of obstacles remain that should be tackled head on.

Are there still elements missing?

Having studied the multitude of theories and concepts of European integration, it is possible to identify two major challenges that still lie ahead: first, overcoming the fragmentation of these concepts; and second, developing new tools to analyse the two closely related questions of contemporary European integration: how to explain the political and social consequences of the world economic turmoil and how to take the increased politicization or resistance to European integration into consideration. All in all, EU studies was generally a 'good weather' theory (Paterson 2010). The question of their viability in stormy weather must be raised.

With regard to the fragmentation or, in other words, the limited cumulativeness of theoretical concepts in EU studies (see also Paterson 2010), i.e. that theories do not build on each other but are instead pulling in different direction, is there a particularly pertinent approach or theory emerging to explain all the processes of European and/or regional construction? Or, in other words, is there a possibility for us to build bridges between these conceptual frameworks, which avoid scholars constantly to sit on – if not ideologically but methodologically – 'separate tables' (Almond 1988)?

As far as this first question is concerned, the history of European integration theory and the critical analysis undertaken in this book show that no single theoretical approach seems to be sufficient to analyse all the phenomena and processes of European integration. As highlighted in the Introduction, the idea that the characteristics of this integration process are not covered by any single all-encompassing theory or conceptual framework is broadly accepted today. In this sense, Robert Puchala's (1972) metaphor referring to European studies as an elephant that is seen as a different entity according to the perspective you use to look at it, seems to be the basis for consensus, at least in the majority of approaches to analysing policy development in the former first pillar. This is true to a much lesser extent in foreign, security and defence issues, where conceptual insights usually look at the EU as an international actor, either arguing that it is one, or denying its existence as such independent entity. This idea, taken up again in the 1990s (Bomberg and Peterson 2000), argues that it is possible to attribute a different set of conceptual frameworks to different types of decision-making processes in order to explain European integration phenomena. In this context, the EU is seen as a multi-level system of governance. There seems to be an underlying agreement in contemporary research that a continuum of three types of decisions – history-making, policy-setting and policy-shaping decisions can be distinguished in European integration. Depending on the decision-making level, the type of decision and actors will change. Thus, decisions taken at the super-systemic level have a history-making nature involving the European Council, national governments and the ECJ. The systemic level that the authors place just below is 'policy-setting' where the Council of Ministers, COREPER and the European Parliament are the key players. The lowest level is policy-shaping. At this level the central actors are said to be the Commission, the Council's working groups and the European Parliament's committees. This allows Peterson and Bomberg (1999) to attribute a particular conceptual framework to each decision-making level: the most appropriate at the super-systemic (treaty negotiations) level is liberal inter-governmentalism, or inter-governmentalism more generally, at the systemic level (policy-making at the European level), neo-institutionalism, Europeanization approaches and at the sub-systemic level (day-to-day policy implementation or agenda setting), network governance.

This multitude of approaches leads to the question of whether one conceptual framework is more valid than others to analyse the EU as a whole, and more specifically EU policy-making processes. While I agree with Ben Rosamond, who advocates adopting theoretical as well as methodological pluralism in order to analyse European integration (Rosamond 2006), this raises two major questions: do we need to first understand all the theoretical and conceptual work out there in order to determine which are insufficient (and then to distance ourselves from them)? – and, by extension – how can we develop rigorous, in-depth, constructive critiques, instead of superficially categorizing the approaches we disagree with, and dismissing them as 'mainstream' or 'marginal'?

Is it not time to start thinking in more general terms about European integration, as has been done in four recent projects (Bartolini 2005; Zielonka 2006; Fligstein 2009; Leuffen, Rittberger and Schimmelfennig 2012)? These studies share the characteristics that they ask very broad questions which go beyond the specific nature of a policy sector or a particular group of actors, such as why heterogeneity matters, under which conditions the demand for differentiation is translated into actual differentiated integration (Leuffen et al. 2012), or whether the EU is a new state form (Bartolini 2005).

Why is it preferable to conceptualize European integration consistently as a mosaic (Wiener and Diez 2004, 2009), where we no longer appear to debate grand theories but increasingly focus on methodological issues such as the establishment of extremely useful large-scale datasets or, on the contrary, making a case for trying to understand European integration by studying micro-subjects such as specific policy decisions or voting attitudes in a specific context? The warning issued by Jean Leca on this subject is of importance: '"One more Grand Theory" should not be held in contempt without a careful examination; we need it, or otherwise risk staying trapped in the dark while the much-vaunted "reflexivity" is supposed to reign – unless we content ourselves with an underhand "Grand Theory" that holds that people need not know what they are doing, provided they do it out of a "strategy of domination.' (Leca 2009: 340).

Faced with such an abundance of conceptual frameworks, it is useful to remember that the main objective of theoretical approaches is to try to answer general questions with regard to developments in European integration and to structure its empirical analysis. In recent years and, in particular, since the failure of the Constitutional Treaty in 2005 (and despite the adoption of the Lisbon Treaty in 2009), questions have emerged to which conceptual frameworks of European studies do not seem to have precise answers: how can we explain the results of national referenda which influence the European integration process so profoundly? How can we explain the relationship between public opinion and politics more generally (Hooghe and Marks 2009)? And finally how can we explain the political and economic reaction of the EU to the international economic and financial turmoil?

These questions are of particular importance in light of recent events, with conceptual frameworks called upon to explain these phenomena in a systematic manner. The increasing politicization of the European public sphere (Hooghe and Marks 2009) – which is not necessarily linked to a higher level of Euroscepticism, but has certainly led to more contentious politics (Paterson 2010) and opposition at both domestic and European level to certain aspects of the European project – has brought renewed attention to conceptual difficulties. Bartolini (2005) and Fligstein (2009) underline how the ever-expanding economic and legal scope of integration puts both domestic systems of political legitimation and well as citizens' loyalty and identity under stress. This also reflects Schmitter's (1963, 2004) curvilinear hypothesis where he argues that, up to a certain point of integration, the relationship between integration and homogeneity is linear (more commercial transactions lead to the creation of a more homogenous group). However, when changes become too rapid, actors are inclined to adopt Eurosceptic attitudes once more. The result of this pressure seems to be forming a movement of general resistance. Both public contestation, and the resulting politicization of European issues, exert a greater influence on legal outcomes, while identity remains a central factor in helping to explain the form that opposition to European integration takes (Hooghe and Marks 2009). Thus, a theory that helps us to understand this debate must be profoundly grounded in the understanding of domestic politics and not a *sui generis* framework only applicable to European integration. This is precisely what bottom-up mainstreaming approaches discussed in Part II of the book managed particularly well.

Very much linked to the question of politicization more generally is the specific challenge for EU studies to analyse the economic turmoil the EU is experiencing along with the rest of the world. EU policies in response to economic and financial crisis call for a conceptual framework that is able to link domestic politics to the European level. Decisions to support specific member states financially, thus, to realize a financial transfer from relatively economically stable to economically troubled member states, has led to worries in governmental parties about the electoral consequences of their European policies. The German government's reticence to financially support Greece in the recent financial crisis in order to avoid an economic breakdown of the country was taken in the context of fierce political battles at the domestic level. As Hooghe and Marks rightly emphasize (2009: 15), citizens are extremely reticent to redistribute income to individuals who are not perceived to belong to the same community. In other terms, the general question becomes: how does regional integration proceed when it concerns not only regulatory issues but also large-scale redistributive issues, and goes beyond the 0.75 per cent of the European GDP the EU actually spends through its agricultural and cohesion policies? Is replacing elected politicians by technocrats (*Economist*, 16 November 2011) a solution in line with the very first hypothesis of the functionalist theory of European integration? To tackle this question, we need to include the link between different levels of governance, the role of different institutions and the way they play with their role, such as the Central European Bank or the European Commission, and the positions of the member states in this debate.

It is to answer these very questions that renewed, even revitalized and broad conceptual frameworks are necessary, linking well-established bottom-up mainstreaming to contemporary top-down mainstreaming perspectives. In other words, a combination between comparative politics and international relations is crucial to explain changes in EU policies. These frameworks must offer us a way of analysing the overlap between international, European and national levels. They will help interpret actors' behaviour and would seem most appropriate and beneficial for structuring future research. It is here that the tools developed to analyse the state and those developed to interpret international relations need, more than ever, to talk to each other.

References

Aalberts, T.E. (2004) 'The Future of Sovereignty in Multilevel Governance Europe – A Constructivist Reading', *Journal of Common Market Studies* 42(1): 23–46.

Aalberts, T.E. (2012) *Constructing Sovereignty between Politics and Law*. London, Routledge.

Abdelal, R., M. Blyth and C. Parsons (2010) *Constructing the International Economy*. Ithaca, NY: Cornell University Press.

Abromeit, H. (1998) *Democracy in Europe: Legitimising Politics in a Non-State Polity*. New York: Berghahn.

Acharya, A. (2002) 'Regionalism and the Emerging World Order: Sovereignty, Autonomy, Identity', in B. Rosamond, S. Breslin, C.W. Hughes and N. Philips (eds), *New Regionalism in the Global Political Economy, Theories and Cases*. London: Routledge.

Adler-Nissen, R. (2008) 'The Diplomacy of Opting Out: A Bourdieudian Approach to National Integration Strategies', *Journal for Common Market Studies* 46(3): 663–84.

Adler-Nissen, R. (2009) 'Late Sovereign Diplomacy', *Hague Journal of Diplomacy* 4: 121–41.

Adler-Nissen, R. and T. Gammeltoft-Hansen (eds) (2008) *Sovereignty Games: Instrumentalizing State Sovereignty in Europe and Beyond*. Basingstoke: Palgrave Macmillan.

Adler, E. (1997) 'Seizing the Middle Ground: Constructivism in World Politics', *European Journal of International Relations* 3(3): 319–63.

Adler, E. (2002) 'Constructivism and International Relations', in W. Carlsnaes, T. Risse and B. Simmons (eds), *Handbook of International Relations*. London: Sage, 95–118.

Adler, E. and M. Barnett (1998) *Security Communities*. Cambridge: Cambridge University Press.

Aggestam, L. (2004) 'Role Identity and the Europeanization of Foreign Policy', in B. Tonra and T. Christiansen (eds), *Rethinking European Union Foreign Policy*. Manchester: Manchester University Press, 81–98.

Aggestam, L. (2008) 'Ethical Power Europe?', *International Affairs* 84(1): 1–11.

Allen, D., R. Rummel and W. Wessels (1982) *European Political Cooperation: Towards a Foreign Policy for Western Europe*. London: Butterworth Scientific.

Allison, G.T. (1971) *The Essence of Decision: Explaining the Cuban Missile Crisis*. Boston: Little, Brown.

Almond, G.A. (1988) 'Separate Tables: Schools and Sects in Political Science', *Political Science and Politics* 21(4): 828–42.

Alter, K. (2001) *Establishing the Supremacy of European Law: The Making of an International Rule of Law in Europe*. New York/Oxford: Oxford University Press.

Alter, K. (2009) *The European Court's Political Power: Selected Essays*, Oxford: Oxford University Press.

Alves, R.H. (2007) 'European Union and (Fiscal) Federalism', in John McCombie and Carlos Rodriguez (eds), *The European Union*. Basingstoke: Palgrave Macmillan, 154–72.

Anderson, B. (1991) *Imagined Communities: Reflections on the Origin and Spread of Nationalism* (rev. ed.). London: Verso.

Ansell, C.K., C.A. Parsons and K.A. Darden (1997) 'Dual Networks in European Regional Development Policy', *Journal of Common Market Studies* 35(3): 347–75.

Armstrong, K. and S. Bulmer (1998) *The Governance of the Single European Market*. Manchester: Manchester University Press.

Aron, R. (1962) *Paix et guerre entre les nations*. Paris: Calmann-Lévy.

Ashley, R. (1982) 'The Poverty of Neorealism', in R.O. Keohane (ed.), *Neorealism and its Critics*. New York: Columbia University Press: 255–300.

Aspinwall, M. and G. Schneider (2001) (eds) *The Rules of Integration: Institutionalist Approaches to the Study of Europe*. Manchester: Manchester University Press.

Atkinson, M. and W. Coleman (1986) 'Strong States and Weak States: Sectoral Policy Networks in Advanced Capitalist Economies', *British Journal of Political Science* 19(1): 47–67.

Bach, D.C. (1999) (ed.) *Regionalisation in Africa: Integration and Disintegration*. Harvester: Wheatsheaf.

Bach, M. (1999) *Die Bürokratisierung Europas: Verwaltungseliten, Experten und Politische Legitimität in der EU*. Frankfurt am Main: Campus.

Bach, M. (2000) 'Die Europäisierung der nationalen Gesellschaften? Problemstellungen und Perspektiven. Eine Soziologie der Europäischen Integration', *Kölner Zeitschrift für Soziologie und Sozialpsychologie* 40: 11–36.

Bache, I. (1998) *The Politics of European Union Regional Policy*. Sheffield: Sheffield Academic Press.

Bache, I. and M. Flinders (2004) (eds) *Multi-level Governance*. Oxford: Oxford University Press.

Bache, I. and S. George (2006) (eds) *Politics in the European Union*, Oxford: Oxford University Press.

Bache, I. and A. Jordan (2006) (eds) *The Europeanization of British Politics*. Basingstoke: Palgrave Macmillan.

Bailey, D.J. (2006) 'Governance or the Crisis of Governmentality? Applying Critical State Theory at the European Level', *Journal of European Public Policy* 13(1): 16–33.

Baisnée, O. and R. Pasquier (2007) (eds) *L'Europe telle qu'elle se fait: Européanisation et sociétés politiques nationales*. Paris: Éditions du CNRS.

Balibar, E. (1992) *Les frontières de la démocratie*. Paris: La Découverte.

Balme, R. and D. Chabanet (2002) 'Introduction: Action collective et gouvernance de l'Union européenne', in R. Balme, D. Chabanet and V. Wright (eds), *L'Action collective en Europe*. Paris: Presses de Sciences Po.

Balme, R. and D. Chabanet (2008) *European Governance and Democracy: Power and Protest in the EU*. New York: Rowman & Littlefield.

Barrera, M. and E.B. Haas (1969) 'The Operationalization of Some Variables Related to Regional Integration: a Research Note', *International Organization* 23(1): 150–60.

Bartolini, S. (2005) *Restructuring Europe*. Oxford: Oxford University Press.

Beach, D. (2009) 'Leadership and Intergovernmental Negotiations in the European Union', in M. Egan, N. Nugent and W.E. Paterson (eds), *Research Agendas in EU Studies: Stalking the Elephant*. Basingstoke: Palgrave Macmillan: 92–116.

Beaud, O. (2007) *Théorie de la federation*. Paris: Presses Universitaires de France.

Beck, U. and E. Grande (2007) *Cosmopolitan Europe*. London: Polity Press.

Begg, I., M. Buti, M. Weale, H. Enderlein and W. Schelkle (2004) 'Symposium Reforming Fiscal Policy Co-ordination under EMU: What Should Become of the Stability and Growth Pact', *Journal of Common Market Studies* 42(5): 1023–59.

Béland, D. (2009) 'Ideas, Institutions, and Policy Change', *Journal of European Public Policy* 16(5): 701–18.

Béland, D. and R.H. Cox (eds) (2011) *Ideas and Politics in Social Science Research*. Oxford: Oxford University Press.

Bellamy, R. (1999) *Liberalism and Pluralism*. London: Routledge.

Bellamy, R. and D. Castiglione (2003) 'Legitimizing the Euro-Polity and its Regime: The Normative Turn in EU Studies', *European Journal of Political Theory* 2: 7–34.

Bellamy, R. and A. Warleigh (1998) 'From Ethics of Integration to an Ethics of Participation: Citizenship and the Future of the European Union', *Millennium: Journal of International Studies* 27(3): 447–70.

Belot, C. (2002) 'Les logiques sociologiques de soutien au processus d'intégration européenne: éléments d'interprétations', *Revue internationale de politique comparée* 9(1): 11–29.

Belot, C. (2010) 'Le tournant identitaire des études consacrés aux attitudes à l'égard de l'Europe. Genèse, apports et limites', *Politique européenne* 30: 17–44.

Bennett, C.J. (1991) 'What is Policy Convergence and What Causes It?', *British Journal of Political Science* 21(2): 215–33.

Bennett, C.J. and M. Howlett (1992) 'The Lessons of Learning: Reconciling Theories of Policy Learning and Policy Change', *Policy Sciences* 25(3): 275–94.

Benz, A. (2003) 'Compound Representation in EU Multi-level Governance', in B. Kohler-Koch (ed.), *Linking EU and National Governance*. Oxford: Oxford University Press.

Benz, A. and Y. Papadopoulos (2006) 'Actors, Institutions and Democratic Governance: Comparing across Levels', in A. Benz and Y. Papadopoulos (eds), *Governance and Democracy. Comparing National, European and International Experiences*. London: Routledge: 273–95.

Berenskoetter, F. and M. Williams (eds) (2007) *Power in World Politics*. London; New York: Routledge.

Berger, P. and T. Luckmann (1966) *The Social Construction of Reality: A Treatise in the Sociology of Knowledge*. New York: Doubleday.

Berger, S. (ed.) (1981) *Organising Interests in Western Europe*. Cambridge: Cambridge University Press.

Berman, S. (1998) *The Primacy of Politics: Social Democracy and the Making of Europe's Twentieth Century*. New York: Cambridge University Press.

Berman, S. (2006) *The Primacy of Politics: Social Democracy and the Making of Europe's Twentieth Century*. New York: Cambridge University Press.

Beyers, J. (2005) 'Multiple Embeddedness and Socialization in Europe: The Case of Council Officials', *International Organization* 59(4): 899–936.

Beyers, J. (2010) 'Conceptual and Methodological Challenges in the Study of European Socialization', *Journal of European Public Policy* 17(6): 911–22.

Bially Mattern, J. (2005) 'Why "Soft Power" Isn't Soft: Representational Forces and the Sociolinguistic Construction of Attraction in World Politics', *Millennium: Journal of International Studies* 33(3): 583–612.

Bickerton, C.J. (2011) *European Union Foreign Policy: From Effectiveness to Functionality*. Basingstoke: Palgrave Macmillan.

Bickerton, C.J. et al. (eds) (2007) *Politics without Sovereignty: A Critique of Contemporary International Relations*. London: University College Press.

Biersteker, T.J. and C. Weber (eds) (1996) *State Sovereignty as Social Construct*. Cambridge: Cambridge University Press.

Bigo, D. (1996) *Polices en réseaux*. Paris: Presses de Sciences Po.

Bigo, D. (2006) 'Une sociologie politique des processus d'européanisation en constitution?', in A. Cohen et al., *Les formes de l'activité politique*. Paris: Presses Universitaires de France.

Blyth, M. (1997) '"Any More Bright Ideas?" The Ideational Turn in Comparative Political Economy', *Comparative Politics* 29(2): 229–50.

Blyth, M. (2002) *The Great Transformation: Economic Ideas and Institutional Change in the 20th century*. Cambridge: Cambridge University Press.

Bomberg, E. and J. Peterson (2000) 'Policy Transfer and Europeanization: Passing the Heineken Test?', *Queen's Papers on Europeanisation* 2.

Borrás, S. (2009) 'The Politics of the Lisbon Strategy: Explaining the Changing Role of the Commission', *West European Politics* 32(1): 97–118.

Borrás, S. and T. Conzelmann (2007) 'Democracy, Legitimacy and Soft Modes of Governance in the EU: The Empirical Turn', *Journal of European Integration* 29(5): 531–48.

Borrás, S. and K. Jacobsson (2004) 'The Open Method of Coordination and the New Governance Patterns in the EU', *Journal of European Public Policy* 11(2): 185–208.

Börzel, T.A. (1999) 'Towards Convergence in Europe? Institutional Adaptation in Germany and in Spain', *Journal of Common Market Studies* 37(4): 573–96.

Börzel, T.A. (2001) 'Non-compliance in the European Union: Pathology or Statistical Artefact?', *Journal of European Public Policy* 8(5): 803–24.

Börzel, T.A. and T. Risse (2000) 'When Europe Hits Home: Europeanization and Domestic Change', *European Integration Online Papers (EIOP)* 4(15), http://eiop.or.at/eiop/texte/2000–015a.htm.

Börzel, T.A. and T. Risse (2003) 'Conceptualizing the Domestic Impact of Europe', in K. Featherstone and C.M. Radaelli (eds), *The Politics of Europeanisation*. Oxford: Oxford University Press: 57–80.

Börzel, T.A. and T. Risse (2012) 'When Europeanization Meets Diffusion. Exploring New Territory', *West European Politics* 35(1): 192–207.

Börzel, T.A. et al. (2010) 'Obstinate and Inefficient. Why Member States Do Not Comply with European Law', *Comparative Political Studies* 43(11): 1363–90.

Boswell, C. (2003) 'The External Dimension of EU Immigration and Asylum Policy', *International Affairs* 79(3): 619–38.

Boswell, C. (2009) *The Political Uses of Expert Knowledge: Immigration Policy and Social Research*. Cambridge: Cambridge University Press.

Brattberg, E. and M. Rhinard (2012) 'The EU as a Global Counter-terrorism Actor in the Making', *European Security* 21(4): 557–77.

Braun, D. and Y. Papadopoulos (2001) 'Niklas Luhmann et la gouvernance', *Politix* 55: 15–24.

Bretherton, C. and J. Vogler (2006) *The European Union as a Global Actor*. London: Routledge.

Bruno, I., S. Jacquot and L. Mandin (2006) 'Europeanization through its Instrumentation: Benchmarking, Mainstreaming and OMC: Toolbox or Pandora's Box?', *Journal of European Public Policy* 13(4): 519–36.

Buchet de Neuilly, Y. (2005) *L'Europe de la politique étrangère*. Paris: Economica.

Bull, H. (1977) *The Anarchical Society: A Study of Order in World Politics*. London: Macmillan.

Bull, H. (1982) 'Civilian Power Europe: A Contradiction in Terms', *Journal of Common Market Studies* 21(1–2): 142–64.

Bulmer, S. (1983) 'Domestic Politics and European Community Policy-making', *Journal of Common Market Studies* 21(4): 349–63.

Bulmer, S. (1993) 'The Governance of the European Union: A New Institutionalist Approach', *Journal of Public Policy* 13(4): 351–80.

Bulmer, S. (1994) 'Institutions and Policy Change in the European Communities: the Case of Merger Control', *Public Administration* 72(3): 425–46.

Bulmer, S. (2009) 'Politics in Time Meets the Politics of Time: Historical Institutionalism and the EU Timescale', *Journal of European Public Policy* 16(2): 307–24.

Bulmer, S. and K. Armstrong (1998) *The Governance of the Single European Market*. Manchester: Manchester University Press.

Bulmer, S., D. Dolowitz, P. Humphreys et al. (2007) *Policy Transfer in EU Governance: Regulating the Utilities*. London/New York: Routledge.

Bulmer, S. and S. Padgett (2004) 'Policy Transfer in the European Union: An Institutionalist Perspective', *British Journal of Political Science* 35: 103–26.

Bulmer, S. and C.M. Radaelli (2004) 'The Europeanization of National Policy', *Queen's Papers on Europeanisation* 1.

Burgess, M. (2000) *Federalism and European Union: The Building of Europe, 1950–2000*. London: Routledge.

Burgess, M. (2004) 'Federalism', in A. Wiener and T. Diez (eds), *European Integration Theory*. Oxford: Oxford University Press: 25–43.

Burgess, M. (2006) *Comparative Federalism: Theory and Practice*. London: Routledge.

Burgess, M. (2009) 'Federalism', in W. Antje and D. Thomas (eds), *European Integration Theory*. Oxford, Oxford University Press: 25–44.

Burley, A.M. and W. Mattli (1993) 'Europe before the Court: A Political Theory of Legal Integration', *International Organizations* 47(2): 41–76.

Cafruny, A. and M. Ryner (2007) *Europe at Bay: In the Shadow of US Hegemony*. Boulder, CO: Lynn Rienner.

Cafruny, A.W. and J. M. Ryner (2009) 'Critical Political Economy', in A. Wiener and T. Diez (eds), *European Integration Theory* (2nd edn). Oxford: Oxford University Press: 221–40.

Campbell, D. (1992) *Writing Security: United States Foreign Policy and the Politics of Identity*. Minneapolis: University of Minnesota Press.

Canovan, M. (1996) *Nationhood and Political Theory*. Cheltenham: Edward Elgar.

Cantori, L.J. and S.L. Speigel (1970) *The International Relations of Regions: A Comparative Approach*. Englewood Cliffs, NJ: Prentice Hall.

Caporaso, J.A. (1998) 'Regional Integration Theory: Understanding Our Past and Anticipating Our Future', in W. Sandholtz and A. Stone Sweet (eds), *European Integration and Supranational Governance*. Oxford: Oxford University Press.

Caporaso, J.A. (1999) 'Toward a Normal Science of Regional Integration', *Journal of European Public Policy* 6(1): 160–4.

Caporaso, J.A. and J. Jupille (1998) 'States, Agency and Rules: The European Union in Global Environmental Politics', in C. Rhodes (ed.), *The European Union in the World Community*. Boulder, CO: Lynn Rienner: 213–29.

Caporaso, J.A. and J. Keeler (1995) 'The European Union and Regional Integration Theory', in C. Rhodes (ed.), *The State of the European Union*, vol. 3. Boulder, CO: Lynne Rienner: 29–62.

Cederman, L.E. (2001) *Constructing Europe's Identities: The External Dimension*. Boulder, CO: Lynne Rienner.

Cederman, L.E. and C. Daase (2003) 'Endogenizing Corporate Identities: The Next Step in Constructivist IR Theory', *European Journal of International Relations* 9(1): 5–35.

Checkel, J.T. (1999) 'Social Construction and Integration', *Journal of European Public Policy* 6(4): 545–60.

Checkel, J.T. (2001a) 'Social Constriction and Integration', in T. Christiansen, K.E. Joergensen and A. Wiener (eds), *The Social Construction of Europe*. London: Sage: 50–64.

Checkel, J.T. (2001b) 'Why Comply? Social Learning and European Identity Change' *International Organization* 55(3): 553–88.

Checkel, J.T. (2003) '"Going Native" in Europe? Theorizing Social Interaction in European Institutions', *Comparative Political Studies* 36(1–2): 209–31.

Checkel, J.T. (2005) 'International Institutions and Socialization in Europe: Introduction and Framework', *International Organization* 59(4): 801–26.

Checkel, J.T. (2006) 'Constructivist Approaches to European Integration', *ARENA Working Paper* 6, http://www.sv.uio.no/arena/english/research/publications/arena-publications/workingpapers/working-papers2006/wp06_06.xml, accessed 20 September 2012).

Checkel, J.T. (2007) 'Constructivism and EU Politics', in K.E. Jorgensen, M. Pollack and B. Rosamond (eds), *The Handbook of EU Politics*. London: Sage: 57–76.

Checkel, J. T., and P.J. Katzenstein (eds) (2009) *European Identity*. Cambridge: Cambridge University Press.

Checkel, J.T. and M. Zürn (2005) 'Getting Socialized to Build Bridges: Constructivism *and* Rational Choice, Europe and the Nation State', *International Organization* 59(4): 1045–79.

Cheneval, F. (2005) *La cité des peuples: mémoires de cosmopolitismes*. Paris: Cerf.

Christiansen, T., A. Føllesdal and S. Piattoni (2003) 'Informal Governance in the European Union: An Introduction', in T. Christiansen and S. Piattoni (eds), *Informal Governance in the European Union*. Cheltenham: Edward Elgar.

Christiansen, T., K.E. Joergensen and A. Wiener (1999) 'The Social Construction of Europe', *Journal of European Public Policy* 6(4): 528–44.

Christiansen, T., K.E. Joergensen and A. Wiener (2001) 'Introduction', in T. Christiansen, K.E. Joergensen and A. Wiener (eds), *The Social Construction of Europe*. London: Sage: 1–19.

Christiansen, T. and S. Piattoni (eds) (2003) *Informal Governance in the European Union*. Cheltenham: Edward Elgar.

Christiansen, T. and B. Tonra (2004) (eds) *Rethinking European Union Foreign Policy*. Manchester: Manchester University Press.

Christin, T., S. Hug and T. Schulz (2005) 'Federalism in the European Union: The View from Below (If There Is Such a Thing)', *Journal of European Public Policy* 12(3): 432–47.

Chryssochoou, D.N. (1994) 'Democracy and Symbiosis in the European Union: Towards a Confederal Consociation?', *West European Politics* 17(4): 1–14.

Chryssochoou, D.N. (2008) *Theorizing European Integration*. Abingdon: Routledge.

Chryssochoou, D.N. (2009) *Theorizing European Integration* (2nd edn). London and New York: Routledge.

Cini, C. (1996) *The European Commission: Leadership, Organization and Culture in the EU Administration*. Manchester: Manchester University Press.

Cini, M. (2007) *From Integration to Integrity: Administrative Ethics and Reform in the European Commission*. Manchester: Manchester University Press.

Citi, M. and M. Rhodes (2007a) *New Modes of Governance in the EU: Common Objectives Versus National Preferences*. European Governance Papers (EUROGOV) N-07-01, http://www.connex-network.org/eurogov/ pdf/egp-newgov-N-07-01.pdf.

Citi, M. and M. Rhodes (2007b) 'New Modes of Governance in the European Union: A Critical Survey and Analysis', in K.E. Jorgensen, M. Pollack and B. Rosamond (eds), *The Handbook of EU Politics*. London: Sage: 463–82.

Claude, I.L. (1964) *Swords into Plowshares*. London: University of London Press.

Claude, I.L. (1968) 'The OAS, the UN and the United States', in J. Nye (ed.), *International Regionalism*. Boston: Little, Brown.

Clift, B. and C. Woll (2012) 'Economic Patriotism: Reinventing Control over Open Markets', *Journal of European Public Policy* 19(3): 307–23.

Cobb, R.W. and C.D. Elder (1970) *International Community: A Regional and Global Study*. New York: Holt, Rinehart & Winston.

Cohen, A., Y. Dezalay and D. Marchetti (2007) 'Esprits d'Etat, entrepreneurs d'Europe', *Actes de recherche en science sociale* 166–7: 5–13.

Cohen, J. and C. Sabel (1997) 'Directly-Deliberative Polyarchy', *European Law Journal* 3(4): 313–40.

Cohen, A. and A. Vauchez (eds) (2007) *La constitution européenne: Élites, mobilisations, votes*. Brussels: Éditions de l'Université de Bruxelles.

Collard-Wexler, S. (2006) 'Integration under Anarchy: Neorealism and European Integration', *European Journal of International Relations* 12(3): 397–432.

Conant, L. (2002) *Justice Contained: Law and Politics in the EU*. Ithaca, NY: Cornell University Press.

Cooper, A.F., C.W. Hughes and P. De Lombaerde (eds) (2008) *Regionalisation and Global Governance: The Taming of Globalisation?* London: Routledge.

Costa, O. (2001) *Le Parlement européen*. Brussels: Université Libre de Bruxelles.

Costa, O., N. Jabko, C. Lequesne and P. Magnette (eds) (2001) 'L'Union européenne: Une démocratie diffuse?', *Revue française de science politique* 51(6): 859–948.

Costa, O. and K.E. Jörgensen (2012a) 'The Influence of International Institutions on the European Union: A Framework for Analysis', in O. Costa and K.E. Jörgensen (eds), *The Influence of International Institutions on the European Union: When Multilateralism Hits Brussels*. Basingstoke: Palgrave Macmillan: 1–22.

Costa, O. and K.E. Jörgensen (eds) (2012b) *The Influence of International Institutions on the European Union: When Multilateralism Hits Brussels*. Basingstoke: Palgrave McMillan.

Costa, O. and P. Magnette (2003) 'The European Union as a Consociation? A Methodological Assessment', *West European Politics* 26(3): 1–18.

Costa, O., A. Roger and S. Saurugger (eds) (2008) 'Les remises en cause de l'intégration européenne', *Revue internationale de politique comparée* 15(4): 533–685.

Cox, R. (1981) 'Social Forces, States and World Order', in R. Keohane (ed.), *Neorealism and Its Critics*. New York: Columbia University Press: 204–54.

Croisat, M. and J.-L. Quermonne (1999) *L'Europe et le fédéralisme* (2nd edn). Paris: Montchrestien.

Crone, D. (1993) 'Does Hegemony Matter? The Reorganization of the Pacific Political Economy', *World Politics*, 45(4): 501–25.

Crouch, C. (1999) *Social Change in Western Europe*. Oxford: Oxford University Press.

Crouch, C., P. Le Galès, C. Triglia and H. Voelzkow (2004) *Changing Governance and Local Economics*. Oxford: Oxford University Press.

Crouch, C. and F. Traxler (1995) *Organized Industrial Relations in Europe: What Future?* Aldershot: Avebury.

Dahl, R A. (1961) *Who Governs?* New Haven, CT: Yale University Press.

Dahl, R A. (1970) *Polyarchy, Participation and Opposition*. New Haven, CT: Yale University Press.

Dakowska, D. (2003) 'Usages et mésusages du concept de gouvernance appliqué à l'élargissement de l'Union européenne', *Politique européenne* 10: 99–120.

Daugbjerg, C. (1999) 'Reforming the CAP: Policy Networks and Broader Institutional Structures', *Journal of Common Market Studies* 37(3): 407–28.

Dehousse, R. (1991) *Le fédéralisme et les relations internationales*. Brussels: Bruylant.

Dehousse, R. (1997) 'Regulation by Networks: The Role of European Agencies', *European Journal of Public Policy* 14(2): 240–61.

Dehousse, R. (1998) *The European Court of Justice: The Politics of Judicial Integration*. Basingstoke: Palgrave Macmillan.

Dehousse, R. (1999) 'Towards a Regulation of Transitional Governance? Citizen's Rights and the Reform of Comitology Procedures', in C. Jörges and E. Vos (eds), *EU Committees. Social Regulation, Law and Politics*. Oxford: Hart.

Dehousse, R. (2004a) 'La méthode ouverte de coordination: Quand l'instrument tient lieu de politique', in P. Lascoumes and P. Le Galès (eds), *Gouverner par les instruments*. Paris: Presses de Sciences Po: 331–56.

Dehousse, R. (ed.) (2004b) *L'Europe sans Bruxelles? Une analyse de la méthode ouverte de coordination*. Paris: l'Harmattan.

Dehousse, R. (ed.) (2011) *The Community Method*. Basingstoke: Palgrave Macmillan.

Delanty, G. (2005) 'The Idea of a Cosmopolitan Europe: On the Cultural Significance of Europeanization', *International Review of Sociology* 15(3): 405–21.

Delanty, G. and C. Rumford (2005) *Rethinking Europe*. Abingdon: Routledge.

Dell, S.S. (1966) *A Latin American Common Market?* New York: Oxford University Press.

Deutsch, K.W. (1968) *The Analysis of International Relations*. Englewood Cliffs, NJ: Prentice Hall.

Deutsch, K.W., S.A. Burrell, R.A. Kann, M. Lee, M. Lichterman, R.E. Lindgren, F.L. Loewenheim and R.W. van Wangeren (1957) *Political Community and the North Atlantic Area: International Organization in the Light of Historical Experience*. Princeton, NJ: Princeton University Press.

De Vreese, C. H. (2007) 'A Spiral of Euroscepticism: The Media's Fault?' *Acta Politica* 42(2): 271–86.

de Wilde, J.H. and H. Wiberg (eds) (1996) *Organized Anarchy in Europe: The Role of States and Intergovernmental Organizations*. London: I.B.Tauris.

Dezalay, Y. and B. Garth (2002) *The Internationalization of Palace Wars: Lawyers, Economists and the Contest for Latin American States*. Chicago: University of Chicago Press.

Diez Medrano, J. (2003) *Framing Europe: Attitudes to European Integration in Germany, Spain and the United Kingdom*. Princeton, NJ: Princeton University Press.

Diez Medrano, J. (2009) 'The Public Sphere and the European Union's Political Identity', in J.T. Checkel and P. Katzenstein (eds), *European Identity*. Cambridge: Cambridge University Press.

Diez, T. (1999) 'Speaking Europe: The Politics of Integration Discourse', *Journal of European Public Policy* 6(4): 598–613.

Diez, T. (2005) 'Constructing the Self and the Changing Others: Reconsidering "Normative Power Europe"', *Millennium: Journal of International Studies* 33(3): 613–36.

Diez, T. and R. Whitman (2002) 'Analysing European Integration: Reflecting on the English School – Scenarios for an Encounter', *Journal of Common Market Studies* 40(1): 43–67.

DiMaggio, P.J. and W.A. Powell (eds) (1991) *The New Institutionalism in Organizational Analysis.* Chicago/London: University of Chicago Press.

Dimitrova, A. and M. Rhinard (2005) 'The Power of Norms in the Transposition of EU Directives', *European Integration Online Papers* 9(16).

Dinan, D. (2004) *Europe Recast: A History of the European Union.* Boulder, CO: Lynne Rienner.

Dolowitz, D.P. (2000) *Policy Transfer and British Social Policy.* Buckingham: Open University Press.

Dolowitz, D.P. (2006) 'Bring Back the State: Correcting for the Omission of Globalization', *International Journal of Public Administration* 29(4): 263–80.

Dolowitz, D.P. and D. Marsh (1996) 'Who Learns What from Whom: A Review of the Policy Transfer Literature', *Political Studies* 44(2): 343–57.

Dolowitz, D.P. and D. Marsh (2000) 'Learning from Abroad, the Role of Policy Transfer in Contemporary Policy-making', *Governance* 13(1): 5–23.

Dosenrode, S. (2007a) (ed.) *Approaching the European Federation.* Aldershot: Ashgate.

Dosenrode, S. (2007b) 'The European Federation', in D. Soeren (ed.), *Approaching the European Federation.* Aldershot: Ashgate: 185–210.

Duchêne, F. (1973) 'The European Community and the Uncertainties of Interdependence', in M. Kohnstamm and W. Hager (eds), *A Nation Writ Large? Foreign Policy Problems before the European Community.* London: Macmillan.

Duchesne, S. and A.-P. Frognier (1995) 'Is there a European Identity?', in O. Niedermayer and R. Sinnott (eds), *Public Opinion and Internationalized Governance.* Oxford, Oxford University Press.

Duchesne, S. and A.-P. Frognier (2002) 'Sur les dynamiques sociologiques et politiques de l'identification à l'Europe', *Revue française de science politique* 52(4): 355–73.

Duchesne, S., F. Haegel, E. Fraser, V. van Ingelgom, G. Garcia and A.-P. Frognier (2010) 'Europe between Integration and Globalisation Social Differences and National Frames in the Analysis of Focus Groups Conducted in France, Francophone Belgium and the United Kingdom', *Politique européenne* 30: 67–105.

Dür, A. and G. Matteo (2010) 'Bargaining Power and Negotiation Tactics: The Negotiations on the EU's Financial Perspective', *Journal of Common Market Studies* 48(3): 557–78.

Dyson, K. and K.H. Goetz (eds) (2003) *Germany, Europe and the Politics of Constraint.* Oxford: Oxford University Press.

Eberlein, B. and E. Grande (2005) 'Beyond Delegation: Transnational Regulatory Regimes and the EU Regulatory State', *Journal of European Integration* 12(1): 89–112.

Eberlein, B. and D. Kerwer (2004) 'New Governance in the EU: A Theoretical Perspective', *Journal of Common Market Studies* 42(1): 121–42.

Egan, M., N. Nugent and W.E. Paterson (eds) (2010) *Research Agendas in EU Studies: Stalking the Elephant.* Basingstoke: Palgrave Macmillan

Egeberg, M. (ed.) (2006) *Multilevel Union Administration. The Transformation of Executive Politics in Europe.* Basingstoke: Palgrave Macmillan.

Eilstrup-Sangiovanni, M. (2006) *Debates on European Integration: A Reader.* Basingstoke: Palgrave Macmillan.

Elgie, R. (2002) 'The Politics of the European Central Bank: Principal Agent Theory and the Democratic Deficit', *Journal of European Public Policy* 9(2): 186–200.

Epstein, D. and S. O'Halloran (1999) *Delegating Powers: A Transaction Cost Politics Approach to Policy Making under Separate Powers.* New York: Cambridge University Press.

Eriksen, E. and J. Fossum (eds) (2000) *Democracy in the European Union: Integration through Deliberation?* London: Routledge.

Erne, R. (2008) *European Unions: Labours Quest for a Transnational Democracy.* Ithaca, NY: Cornell University Press.

Etzioni, A. (1965) *Political Unification: A Comparative Study of Leaders and Forces*. New York: Holt, Rinehart & Winston.

Etzioni, A. (2001) *Political Unification Revisited: On Building Supranational Communities*. Lanham, MD: Lexington Books.

European Commission (2001) *European Governance: A White Paper*. Brussels, 25 July, COM 428 final.

Evans, P., D. Rueschemeyer and T. Skocpol (eds) (1985) *Bringing the State Back In*. New York: Cambridge University Press.

Exadaktylos, T. and C.A. Radaelli (2009) 'Research Design in European Studies: the Case of Europeanizations', *Journal of Common Market Studies* 47(3): 507–30.

Exadaktylos, T. and C.A. Radaelli (eds) (2012) *Research Methods in European Studies: Research Design in Europeanization*. Basingstoke: Palgrave Macmillan.

Fairclough, N. (1992) *Discourse and Social Change*. Cambridge: Polity Press.

Falkner, G. (ed.) (2011) *The EU's Decision Traps: Comparing Policies*. Oxford: Oxford University Press.

Falkner, G., M. Hartlapp and O. Treib (2007) 'Worlds of Compliance: Why Leading Approaches to European Union Implementation Are Only "Sometimes-true Theories"', *European Journal of Political Research* 3: 395–416.

Falkner, G., M. Hartlapp, O. Treib and S. Leiber (2005) *Complying with Europe: EU Harmonisation and Soft Law in the Member States*. Cambridge: Cambridge University Press.

Farrell, M., B. Hettne and L. van Langenhove (eds) (2005) *Global Politics of Regionalism: Theory and Practice*. London: Pluto Press.

Faucher-King, F. and P. Le Galès (2010) *The New Labour Experiment: Change and Reform Under Blair and Brown*. Stanford, CA: Stanford University Press.

Favell, A. (2007) 'The Sociology of EU Politics', in K. E. Jorgensen, M. Pollack, and B. Rosamond (eds) *The Handbook of EU Politics*. London: Sage: 122–137.

Favell, A. (2008) *Eurostars and Eurocities: Free Movement and Mobility in an Integrating Europe*. Oxford: Blackwell.

Favell, A. and V. Guiraudon (eds) (2011) *The Sociology of the European Union*. Basingstoke: Palgrave Macmillan.

Fawcett, L. (1995) 'Regionalism in Historical Perspective', in L. Fawcett and A. Hurrell (eds), *Regionalism in World Politics: Regional Organization and International Order*. Oxford: Oxford University Press: 9–36.

Fawcett, L. and A. Hurrell (eds) (1995) *Regionalism in World Politics: Regional Organization and International Order*. Oxford: Oxford University Press.

Featherstone, K. and C.M. Radaelli (eds) (2003) *The Politics of Europeanization*. Oxford: Oxford University Press.

Ferrera, M. (2005) *The Boundaries of Welfare: European Integration and the New Spatial Politics of Social Protection*. Oxford: Oxford University Press.

Ferrera, M. and M. Rhodes (eds) (2000) *Recasting European Welfare States*. London: Frank Cass, 2000.

Ferry, J.M. (2000) *La question de l'Etat européen*. Paris: Gallimard.

Ferry, J.M. (2005) *Europe: La voie kantienne*. Paris: Éditions du Cerf.

Ferry, J.M. (2006) 'Du politique au-delà des nations', *Politique européenne* 19: 5–20.

Finnemore, M. (1996) *National Interests in International Society*. Ithaca, NY: Cornell University Press.

Finnemore, M. and K. Sikkink (1998) 'International Norm Dynamics and Political Change', *International Organization* 52(4): 887–917.

Fligstein, N. (2008) *Euroclash: The EU, European Identity, and the Future of Europe*. Oxford: Oxford University Press.

Fligstein, N. and I. Mara-Drita (1996) 'How to Make a Market: Reflections on the European Union's Single Market Program', *American Journal of Sociology* 102: 1–33.

Fligstein, N. and F. Mérand (2002) 'Globalization or Europeanization: Changes in the European Economy, 1980–2000', *Acta Sociologica* 45: 7–22.

Fligstein, N. and A. Stone Sweet (2002) 'Constructing Polities and Markets: An Institutionalist Account of European Integration', *American Sociological Review*, 107(5): 1206–43.

Føllesdal, A. (2003) 'The Political Theory of the White Paper on Governance: Hidden and Fascinating', *European Public Law* 9(1): 73–86.

Føllesdal, A. (2006) 'EU Legitimacy and Normative Political Theory', in M. Cini and A.K. Bourne (eds), *Palgrave Advances in EU Studies*. Basingstoke: Palgrave Macmillan: 151–73.

Føllesdal, A. (2007a) 'The Legitimacy Deficits of the European Union', *Journal of Political Philosophy* 14(4): 441–68.

Føllesdal, A. (2007b) 'Normative Political Theory and the European Union', in K.E. Jorgensen, M. Pollack and B. Rosamond (eds), *The Handbook of EU Politics*. London: Sage: 316–35.

Føllesdal, A. and S. Hix (2006) 'Why there is a Democratic Deficit in the EU: A Response to Majone and Moravcsik', *Journal of Common Market Studies* 44(3): 533–62.

Foret, F. (ed.) (2007) *L'espace public européen à l'épreuve du religieux*. Brussels: Editions Université de Bruxelles.

Foret, F. (2008) *Légitimer l'Europe : Pouvoir et symbolique à l'ère de la gouvernance*. Paris: Presses de Sciences Po.

Foucault, M. and S. Cochinard (2007) 'Economics of Enhanced Cooperation: a European Defence Perspective', *Revue d'économie politique* 2.

Fouilleux, E. (2000) 'Entre production et institutionnalisation des idées: la réforme de la Politique agricole commune', *Revue française de science politique* 50(2): 277–305.

Freeman, L. (1965) *The Political Process: Executive Bureau–Legislative Committee Relations*. New York: Random House.

Friedrich, C.J. (1962) 'Federal Constitutional Theory and Emergent Proposals', in A.W. Macmahon (ed.), *Federalism, Mature and Emergent*. New York: Russell & Russell.

Fukuyama, F. (1992) *The End of History and the Last Man*. London: Penguin.

Gabel, M. (1998) 'The Endurance of Supranational Governance: A Consociational Interpretation of the European Union', *Comparative Politics* 30(4): 463–75.

Gabel, M., S. Hix and G. Schneider (2002) 'Who Is Afraid of Cumulative Research? Improving Data on EU Politics', *European Union Politics* 3(4) 481–500.

Garrett, G. (1992) 'International Cooperation and Institutional Choice: The European Community's Internal Market', *International Organization* 46(2): 533–60.

Garrett, G., R.D. Kelemen and H. Schulz (1998) 'Legal Politics in the European Union', *International Organization* 52(1): 149–76.

Garrett, G. and G. Tsebelis (2000) 'Legislative Politics in the European Union', *European Union Politics* 1(1): 9–36.

Garrett, G. and B. Weingast (1993) 'Ideas, Interests and Institutions: Constructing the European Community's Internal Market', in J. Goldstein and R. Keohane (eds), *Ideas and Foreign Policy*. Ithaca, NY: Cornell University Press: 173–206.

Gauchet, M. (2005) *La condition politique*. Paris: Gallimard.

Gegout, C. (2010) *European Foreign and Security Policy: States, Power, Institutions, and American Hegemony*. Toronto: University of Toronto Press.

Georgakakis, D. (2008) 'La sociologie historique et politique de l'Union européenne: un point de vue d'ensemble et quelques contrepoints', *Politique européenne* 25: 53–86.

Georgakakis, D. and M. Delassalle (2004) 'Les directeurs généraux de la Commission européenne. Premiers éléments d'une enquête prosopographique', *Regards sociologiques* 27–8: 6–69.

Gifford, C. (2008) *The Making of Eurosceptic Britain*. Aldershot: Ashgate.

Gilardi, F. (2010) 'Who Learns From What in Policy Diffusion Processes?', *American Journal of Political Science* 54(3): 650–66.

Gilardi, F. and C. Meseguer (2009) 'What Is New in the Study of Policy Diffusion?', *Review of International Political Economy* 16(3): 527–43.

Gilbert, M. (2008) 'Narrating the Process: Questioning the Progressive Story of European Integration', *Journal of Common Market Studies* 46(3): 641–62.

Gilpin, R. (1987) *The Political Economy of International Relations*. Princeton, NJ: Princeton University Press.

Ginsberg, R. (2001) *The European Union in International Politics: Baptism by Fire*. Lanham, MD: Rowman & Littlefield.

Ginsberg, R. H. (1989) *Foreign Policy Actions of the European Community: The Politics of Scale*. Boulder, CO: Lynne Rienner.

Giraud, O. (2001) 'La Steuerungstheorie. Une approche synthétique de l'action publique contemporaine', *Politix* 55: 85–93.

Goetschy, J. (2003) 'The European Employment Strategy. Multilevel Governance and Policy Coordination', in J. Zeitlin and D. Trubeck (eds), *Governing Work and Welfare in a New Economy: European and American Experiments*. Oxford: Oxford University Press.

Goetz, K. (2008) 'Governance as a Path to Government', *West European Politics* 31(1/2), 258–79.

Goetz, K.H. and S. Hix (2000) 'Introduction: European Integration and National Political Systems', *West European Politics* 23(4): 1–26.

Goetze, S. and B. Rittberger (2010) 'A Matter of Habit? The Sociological Foundations of Empowering the European Parliament', *Comparative European Politics* 8(1): 37–54.

Gofas, A. and C. Hay (2010) 'The Ideational Turn and the Persistence of Perennial Dualisms', in A. Gofas and C. Hay (eds), *The Role of Ideas in Political Analysis: A Portrait of Contemporary Debates*. London: Routledge.

Goffman, E. (1959) *The Presentation of Self in Everyday Life*. Garden City, NY: Doubleday Anchor Books.

Goffman, E. (1969) *Strategic Interaction*. Philadelphia: University of Pennsylvania Press.

Goldstein, J. and R.O. Keohane (eds) (1993) *Ideas and Foreign Policy: Beliefs, Institutions and Political Change*. Ithaca, NY: Cornell University Press.

Golub, J. (1999) 'In the Shadows of the Vote? Decision-Making in the European Community', *International Organization* 53: 733–64.

Gourevitch, P.A. (1978) 'The Second Image Reversed: The International Sources of Domestic Politics', *International Organization* 32(4): 881–912.

Gourevitch, P.A. (2002) 'Domestic Politics and International Relations', in W. Carlsnaes, T. Risse and B. Simmons (eds), *Handbook of International Organizations*. London: Sage: 309–28.

Graham, E., C. Volden and C.R. Shipan (2008) 'The Diffusion of Policy Diffusion'. Paper presented at the Congress of the American Political Science Association, Boston, 27–31 August.

Grande, E. (1996) 'The State and Interest Groups in a Framework of Multi-level Decision-making: The Case of the European Union', *Journal of European Public Policy* 3(3): 318–38.

Grande, E. (2000) 'Post-National Democracy in Europe', in M. Th. Greven and L. W. Pauly, *Democracy Beyond the State? The European Dilemma and the Emerging Global Order*. Lanham, MD: Rowman & Littlefield: 115–38.

Gravier, M. (2003) 'D'une loyauté à l'autre. Eléments d'analyse sur la fonction publique européenne (1951–2003)', *Politique européenne* 11: 79–98.

Graziano, P.R. and M.P. Vink (eds) (2007) *Europeanization: New Research Agendas*. Basingstoke and New York: Palgrave Macmillan.

Grieco, J.M. (1988) 'Anarchy and the Limits of Cooperation: A Realist Critique of the Newest Liberal Intergovernmentalism', *International Organization* 42(3): 485–508.

Grieco, J M. (1993) 'Understanding the Problem of International Cooperation: The Limits of Neoliberal Institutionalism and the Future of Realist Theory', in D.A. Baldwin (ed.), *Neorealism and Neoliberalism*. New York: Columbia University Press: 301–38.

Grieco, J.M. (1995) 'The Maastricht Treaty, Economic and Monetary Union, and the Neorealist Research Programme', *Review of International Studies* 21(1): 21–40.

Grieco, J.M. (1996) 'State Interests and International Rule Trajectories: A Neorealist Interpretation of the Maastricht Treaty and European Economic and Monetary Union', *Security Studies* 5(2): 176–222.

Griffin, K. and R. Ffrench-Davis (1965) 'Customs Union and Latin American Integration', *Journal of Common Market Studies* 4(1): 1–21.

Groom, J. and P. Taylor (1975) *Functionalism: Theory and Practice in International Relations*. New York: Crane, Russak.

Grossman, E. (2006) 'Europeanization as an Interactive Process: German Public Banks Meet EU State Aid Policy', *Journal of Common Market Studies* 44(2): 325–48.

Guiraudon, V. (2000) 'L'espace sociopolitique européen, un champ encore en friche?', *Cultures et Conflits* 38–9: 7–37, http://www.conflits.org/document290.html#bodyftn33 (accessed 20 February 2008).

Guiraudon, V. (2006) 'The EU through Europeans' Eyes: Political Sociology and EU Studies', *EUSA Review* 19(1): 1–7.

Guiraudon, V. and G. Lahav (2000) 'A Reappraisal of the State Sovereignty Debate', *Comparative Political Studies* 33(2): 163–95.

Guzzini, S. (1998) *Realism in International Relations and Political Economy: The Continuing Story A Death Foretold*. London: Routledge.

Guzzini, S. (2000) 'A Reconstruction of Constructivism in International Relations', *European Journal of International Relations* 6(2): 147–82.

Guzzini, S. and A. Leander (eds) (2006) *Constructivism and International Relations: Alexander Wendt and his Critics*. London: Routledge.

Haas, E.B. (1958) *The Uniting of Europe: Political, Social, and Economic Forces: 1950–1957*, Stanford, CA: Stanford University Press.

Haas, E.B. (1964) *Beyond the Nation State: Functionalism and International Organization*. Stanford, CA: Stanford University Press.

Haas, E.B. (1968) *The Uniting of Europe: Political, Social, and Economic Forces, 1950–1957* (2nd edn). Stanford, CA: Stanford University Press.

Haas, E.B. (1971) 'The Study of Regional Integration: Reflections on the Joy and Anguish of Pretheorizing', in L.N. Lindberg and S.A. Scheingold (eds), *Regional Integration: Theory and Research*. Cambridge, MA: Harvard University Press.

Haas, E.B. (1975) *The Obsolescence of Regional Integration Theory*. Berkeley: Institute of International Studies Working Paper.

Haas, E.B. (1990) *When Knowledge is Power: Three Models of Change in International Organizations*, Berkeley, University of California Press.

Haas, E.B. (2001) 'Does Constructivism Subsume Neofunctionalism?', in T. Christiansen, K.E. Joergensen and A. Wiener (eds), *The Social Construction of Europe*. London: Sage: 22–31.

Haas, E.B. (2004) *The Uniting of Europe: Political, Social, and Economic Forces 1950–1957* (3rd edn, foreword by Desmond Dinan, new introduction by Ernst B. Haas). Notre Dame, IN: University of Notre Dame Press.

Haas, E.B. and P.C. Schmitter (1964) 'Economics and Differential Patterns of Political Integration: Objections about Unity in Latin America', *International Organization* 18(3): 705–35.

Haas, P. (1992) 'Knowledge, Power and International Policy Coordination', *International Organization* 46(1), 1–35.

Habermas, J. (1968) *Technik und Wissenschaft als "Ideologie"*. Frankfurt am Main: Suhrkamp.

Habermas, J. (1981) *Theorie des kommunikativen Handelns* (Vol. 1: *Handlungsrationalität und gesellschaftliche Rationalisierung*, Vol. 2: *Zur Kritik der funktionalistischen Vernunft*). Frankfurt: Suhrkamp.

Habermas, J. (1995a) 'Reconciliation through the Public Use of Reason: Remarks on John Rawls's Political Liberalism', *Journal of Philosophy* 92: 109–31.

Habermas , J. (1995b) *Sociologie et théorie du langage*. Paris: Armand Colin.

Habermas, J. (1996) *La paix perpétuelle: le bicentenaire d'une idée kantienne*. Paris: Éditions du Cerf.

Habermas, J. (2001) *The Postnational Constellation: Political Essays*. Cambridge, MA: MIT Press.

Habermas, J. (2003) 'Towards a Cosmopolitan Europe', *Journal of Democracy* 14(4): 86–100.

Halberstam, D. (2008) 'Comparative Federalism and the Role of the Judiciary', in K. Whittington, D. Kelemen and G. Caleindra (eds), *The Oxford Handbook of Law and Politics*. Oxford: Oxford University Press: 142–64.

Hall, P. (1986) *Governing the Economy: The Politics of State Intervention in Britain and France*. New York: Oxford University Press.

Hall, P. (1993) 'Policy Paradigms, Social Learning and the State. The Case of Economic Policy-making in Britain', *Comparative Politics* 25(3): 275–96.

Hall, P. (1997) 'The Role of Interests, Institutions and Ideas in the Comparative Political Economy of the Industrialized Nations', in M. Lichbach and A. Zuckerman (eds), *Comparative Politics: Rationality, Culture and Structure*. Cambridge: Cambridge University Press: 174–207.

Hall, P. and D. Soskice (2001) (eds) *Varieties of Capitalism: The Institutional Foundations of Comparative Advantage*. Oxford: Oxford University Press.

Hall, P. and R. Taylor (1996) 'Political Science and the Three New Institutionalisms', *Political Studies*, 44: 936–57.

Hallerberg, M., R. Strauch and J. van Hagen (2010) *Fiscal Governance: Evidence from Europe*. Cambridge: Cambridge University Press.

Haltern, U. (2004) 'Integration through Law', in A. Wiener and T. Diez (eds), *European Integration Theory*. Oxford: Oxford University Press: 177–96.

Hanrieder, W. (1967) 'Compatibility and Consensus: A Proposal for the Conceptual Linkage of External and Internal Dimensions of Foreign Policy', *American Political Science Review* 61(4): 971–82.

Harmsen, R. and M. Spiering (2005) *Euroscepticism: Party Politics, National Identity and European Integration*. Amsterdam: Rodopi.

Hay, C. (1999) 'Crisis and the Structural Transformation of the State. Integrating Processes of Change', *British Journal of Politics and International Relations* 1(3): 317–44.

Hay, C. (2001) 'The Crisis of Keynesianism and the Rise of Neoliberalism in Britain: An Ideational Institutionalist Approach', in J.L. Campbell and O. Pedersen (eds), *The Rise of Neoliberalism and Institutional Analysis*. Princeton, NJ: Princeton University Press: 193–218.

Hay, C. (2004) 'Ideas, Interests, and Institutions in the Comparative Political Economy of Great Transformations', *Review of International Political Economy* 11(1): 204–26.

Hay, C. (2010) 'Ideas and the Construction of Interests', in D. Béland and R. Cox (eds), *Ideas and Politics in Social Science Research*. Oxford: Oxford University Press: 65–82.

Hay, C. and B. Rosamond (2002) 'Globalization, European Integration and the Discursive Construction of Economic Imperatives', *Journal of European Public Policy* 9(2): 147–67.

Hayes-Renshaw, F. and H. Wallace (2006) *The Council of Ministers*. Basingstoke: Palgrave Macmillan.

Heclo, H. (1994) 'Ideas, Interests and Institutions', in L. Dodd and C. Jillson (eds), *The Dynamics of American Politics: Approaches and Interpretations*. Boulder, CO: Westview Press.

Héritier, A. (1999) 'Elements of Democratic Legitimation in Europe: an Alternative Perspective', *Journal of European Public Policy*, 6(2): 269–282.

Héritier, A. (2007) *Explaining Institutional Change in Europe*. Oxford: Oxford University Press.

Héritier, A. and D. Lehmkuhl (2008) 'Introduction. The Shadow of Hierarchy and New Modes of Governance', *Journal of Public Policy* 28(1): 1–17.

Héritier, A. et al. (2001) *Differential Europe : The European Union Impact on National Policymaking*. Lanham, MD: Rowman & Littlefield.

Hettne, B. (1999) 'Globalization and the New Regionalism: The Second Great Transformation', in B. Hettne et al. (eds), *Globalism and the New Regionalism*. Basingstoke: Palgrave Macmillan.

Hettne, B. (2001) 'Regionalism, Security and Development: A Comparative Perspective', in B. Hettne, A. Inotai and O. Sunkel (eds), *Comparing Regionalisms: Implications for Global Development*. Basingstoke: Palgrave Macmillan: 1–53.

Hettne, B. (2002) 'The Europeanization of Europe: Endogenous and Exogenous Variables', *Journal of European Integration* 24(4): 325–40.

Hettne, B. (2003) 'The New Regionalism Revisited', in F. Söderbaum and T. Shaw (eds), *Theories of New Regionalisms: A Palgrave Reader*. Basingstoke: Palgrave Macmillan: 325–40.

Hettne, B. and F. Söderbaum (2000) 'Theorising the Rise of Regionness', *New Political Economy* 5(3): 457–72.

Hettne, B. et al. (eds) (1999) *Globalism and New Regionalism*. Basingstoke: Palgrave Macmillan.

Hill, C. (1993) 'The Capability-Expectations Gap: Or Conceptualizing the EU's International Role', *Journal of Common Market Studies* 31(3): 305–28.

Hill, C. (1998) 'Closing the Capability-Expectations Gap?', in J. Peterson and H. Sjursen (eds), *A Foreign Policy for Europe?* London: Routledge.

Hirschman, A. (1970) *Exit, Voice, Loyalty: Responses to Decline in Firms, Organizations, and States*. Cambridge, MA: Harvard University Press.

Hix, S. (1994) 'The Study of the European Community: The Challenge to Comparative Politics', *West European Politics* 17(1): 1–30.

Hix, S. (1998) 'The Study of the European Union II: The "New Governance" Agenda and its Rival', *Journal of European Public Policy* 5(1): 38–65.

Hix, S. (2002a) 'Legislative Behaviour and Party Competition: An Application of Nominate to the EU', *Journal of Common Market Studies* 39(4), 663–88.

Hix, S. (2002b) 'Parliamentary Behavior with Two Principals: Preferences, Parties and Voting in the European Parliament', *American Journal of Political Science* 46(3): 688–98.

Hix, S. and B. Hoyland (2011) *The Political System of the European Union*. London: Palgrave Macmillan.

Hix, S., A. Noury and G. Roland (2007) *Democratic Politics in the European Parliament*. Cambridge: Cambridge University Press.

Hodson, D. and I. Maher (2004) 'Soft Law and Sanctions: Economic Policy Co-ordination and Reform of the Stability and Growth Pact', *Journal of European Public Policy* 11(5): 798–813.

Hoffmann, S. (1954) *Organisations internationales et pouvoirs politiques des États*. Paris: Armand Colin.

Hoffmann, S. (1956) 'Les oraison funèbres: Du vote du 30 août au vote du 30 décembre 1954', in R. Aron and D. Lerner (eds), *La querelle de la CED: Essais d'analyse sociologique*. Paris: Armand Colin.

Hoffmann, S. (1964) 'The European Process at Atlantic Cross Purposes', *Journal of Common Market Studies* 3(2): 85–101.

Hoffmann, S. (1966) 'Obstinate or Obsolete? The Fate of the Nation-state and the Case of Western Europe'. *Daedalus* 95(3), 862–915.

Hoffmann, S. (1987) 'International Organization and International System', in S. Hoffmann, *Janus and Minerva: Essays in the Theory and Practice of International Politics*. Boulder, CO: Westview Press.

Hoffmann, S. (1995a) 'Obstinate or Obsolete? France, European Integration, and the Fate of the Nation State', in S. Hoffman, *The European Sisyphus: Essays on Europe, 1964–1995*. Boulder, CO: Westview Press.

Hoffmann, S. (1995b) 'Reflections on the Nation State in Western Europe Today', in S. Hoffman, *The European Sisyphus: Essays on Europe, 1964–1995*. Boulder, CO: Westview Press: 215–19.

Hoffmann, S. (1995c) 'The European Community and 1992', in S. Hoffman, *The European Sisyphus: Essays on Europe, 1964–1995*. Boulder, CO: Westview Press.

Hogwood, B.W. and B.G. Peters (1985) *The Pathology of Public Policy*. Oxford: Clarendon Press.

Holland, M. (ed.) (1991) *The Future of European Cooperation, Essays on Theory and Practice*. London: Macmillan.

Hollis, M. and S. Smith (1991) *Explaining and Understanding International Relations*, Oxford, Oxford University Press

Hooghe, L. (2001) *The European Commission and the Integration of Governance*. Cambridge: Cambridge University Press.

Hooghe, L. (2005) 'Several Roads Lead to International Norms, but Few via International Socialization: A Case Study of the European Commission', *International Organization* 59(4): 861–98.

Hooghe, L. and G. Marks (2007) 'The Sources of Euroscepticism: Introduction', *Acta Politica* 42 (2–3): 119–354.

Hooghe, L. and G. Marks (2009) 'A Postfunctionalist Theory of European Integration: From Permissive Consensus to Constraining Dissensus', *British Journal of Political Science* 39: 1–23.

Hosli, M., A. van Deemen and M. Widgren (eds) (2002) *Institutional Challenges in the European Union*. London: Routledge.

Howlett, M. and M. Ramesh (1993) 'Patterns of Policy Instrument Choice: Policy Styles, Policy Learning and the Privatization Experience', *Policy Studies Review* 2(1–2): 3–24.

Howorth, J. (2004) 'Discourse, Ideas and Epistemic Communities in European Security and Defence Policy', *West European Politics* 27(1): 29–52.

Howorth, J. (2005) 'From Security to Defence: the Evolution of the CFSP', in C. Hill and M.E. Smith (eds), *International Relations and the European Union*. Oxford: Oxford University Press: 179–204.

Howorth, J. (2007) *Security and Defence Policy in the European Union*. Basingstoke: Palgrave Macmillan.

Huber, J.D. and C.R. Shipan (2003) *Deliberate Discretion: The Institutional Foundations of Bureaucratic Autonomy*. New York: Cambridge University Press.

Humphreys, P. and S. Padgett (2006) 'Globalization, the European Union, and Domestic Governance in Telecoms and Electricity', *Governance* 19(3): 383–406.

Hurrell, A. (1992) 'Latin America and the New World Order: A Regional Bloc in the Americas', *International Affairs* 68(1): 121–39.

Hurrell, A. (1995) 'Regionalism in Theoretical Perspective', in L. Fawcett and A. Hurrell (eds), *Regionalism in World Politics: Regional Organization and International Order*. Oxford: Oxford University Press.

Hurrell, A. (2005) 'The Regional Dimension in International Relations Theory', in M. Farrell, B. Hettne and L. van Langenhove (eds), *Global Politics of Regionalism:. Theory and Practice*. London: Pluto Press: 38–53.

Hurrell, A. (2007) *On Global Order: Power, Values and the Constitution of International Society*. Oxford: Oxford University Press.

Hurrell, A. and A. Menon (1996) 'Politics Like Any Other? Comparative Politics, International Relations and the Study of the EU', *West European Politics* 19(2): 386–402.

Hurrell, A. and A. Menon (2003) 'International Relations, International Institutions, and the European State', in J. Hayward and A. Menon (eds), *Governing Europe*. Oxford: Oxford University Press: 395–412.

Hyde-Price, A. (2006) 'Normative' Power Europe: A Realist Critique', *Journal of European Public Policy* 13(2): 217–34.

Hyde-Price, A. (2008) 'A Tragic Actor? A Realist Perspective on Ethical Power Europe', *International Affairs* 84: 29–44.

Imig, D. and S. Tarrow (2001) *Contentious Europeans*. Lanham: Rowman & Littlefield.

Immergut, E.M. (1992a) *The Political Construction of Interests*. Cambridge: Cambridge University Press.

Immergut, E.M. (1992b) 'The Rules of the Game: The Logic of Health Policy-making in France, Switzerland and Sweden', in K. Thelen, S. Steinmo and F. Longstreth (eds), *Structuring Politics: Historical Institutionalism in Comparative Analysis*. Cambridge: Cambridge University Press: 57–89.

Immergut, E.M. (2006) 'Historical Institutionalism in Political Science and the Problem of Change', in A. Wimmer and R. Kössler (eds), *Understanding Change. Models, Methodologies and Metaphors*. New York: Palgrave Macmillan: 237–59.

Irondelle, B. (2003) 'Europeanization without the European Union? French Military Reforms 1991–1996', *Journal of European Public Policy* 10(2): 208–26.

Jabko, N. (2006) *Playing the Market: A Political Strategy for Uniting Europe, 1985–2005*. Ithaca, NY/London: Cornell University Press.

Jabko, N. (2010) 'The Hidden Face of the Euro', *Journal of European Public Policy* 17(3): 318–34.

Jachtenfuchs, M. (2001) 'The Governance Approach to European Integration', *Journal of Common Market Studies* 39(3): 249–64.

Jachtenfuchs, M. and B. Kohler-Koch (2004) 'Governance and Institutional Development', in A. Wiener and T. Diez (eds), *European Integration Theory*. Oxford: Oxford University Press: 97–115.

Jacobsen, J.K. (1996) 'Are All Politics Domestic? Perspectives on the Integration of Comparative Politics and International Relations Theories', *Comparative Politics* 29(1): 93–115.

Jacoby, W. and S. Meunier (2010a), 'Europe and Globalization', in M. Egan, N. Nugent and W.E. Paterson (eds), *Research Agendas in EU Studies: Stalking the Elephant*. Basingstoke: Palgrave Macmillan: 354–74.

Jacquot, S. and C. Woll (2004a) 'Introduction: Usages et travail politiques: une sociologie compréhensive des usages de l'intégration européenne', in S. Jacquot and C. Woll (eds), *Les usages de l'Europe: Acteurs et transformations européennes*. Paris: L'Harmattan: 1–29.

Jacquot, S. and C. Woll (eds) (2004b) *Les usages de l'Europe: Acteurs et transformations européennes*. Paris: L'Harmattan.

Jacquot, S. and C. Woll (2008) 'Action publique européenne: les acteurs stratégiques face à l'Europe', *Politique européenne* 25: 161–92.

Jacquot, S. and C. Woll (2010) 'Using Europe: Strategic Action in Multi-level Politics', *Comparative European Politics* 8(1): 110–26.

James, O. and M. Lodge (2003) 'The Limitations of Policy Transfer and Lesson Drawing for Public Policy Research', *Political Studies Review* 1: 179–93.

Jenson, J. and F. Merand (2010) 'Sociology, Institutionalism and the European Union', *Comparative European Politics* 8(1): 74–92.

Jepperson, R., A. Wendt and P.J. Katzenstein (1996) 'Norms, Identity, and Culture in National Security', in P. J. Katzenstein (ed.), *The Culture of National Security: Norms and Identity in World Politics*. New York: Columbia University Press: 33–75.

Jobert, B. and P. Muller (1987) *L'Etat en action: Politiques publiques et coropratismes*. Paris: Presses Universitaires de France.

Joerges, C. (1996) 'Taking the Law Seriously: On Political Science and the Role of Law in the Process of European Integration', *European Law Journal* 2(2): 105–35.

Joerges, C. (1999) 'Bureaucratic Nightmare, Technocratic Regime and the Dream of Good Transnational Governance', in C. Joerges and E. Voss (eds), *EU-Committees: Social Regulation, Law and Politics*. Oxford: Hart: 3–17.

Joerges, C. and R. Dehousse (eds) (2002) *Good Governance in Europe's Integrated Market*. Oxford: Oxford University Press.

Joerges, C. and J. Neyer (1997) 'Transforming Strategic Interaction into Deliberative Problem-Solving: European Comitology in the Foodstuff Sector', *Journal of European Public Policy* 4 (4): 609–25.

Johnston, A.I. (2005) 'Conclusion and Extensions: Toward Mid-Range Theorizing and Beyond Europe', *International Organization* 59: 1013–44.

Jong Choi, Y. and J.A. Caporaso (2002) 'Comparative Regional Integration', in W. Carlsnaes, T. Risse and B. Simmons, *Handbook of International Relations*. London: Sage.

Jordan, A. and A. Schout (2006) *Co-ordination of European Governance*. Oxford: Oxford University Press.

Jordan, G. (1990) 'Sub-government, Policy Communities and Networks: Refilling the Old Bottles', *Journal of Theoretical Politics* 2(2): 319–38.

Jordan, G. and K. Schubert (1992) 'A Preliminary Ordering of Policy Network Labels', *European Journal of Political Research* 21(1): 7–27.

Jupille, J. (2006) 'Knowing Europe: Metatheory and Methodology in European Union Studies', in M. Cini and A. Bourne (eds), *Palgrave Advances in European Studies*. Basingstoke: Palgrave Macmillan: 209–32.

Jupille, J. and J. Caporaso (1999) 'Institutionalism and the European Union: Beyond Comparative Politics and International Relations', *Annual Review of Political Science* 2: 429–44.

Kaiser, W. (2008) 'History Meets Politics. Overcoming the Interdisciplinary Volapük in Research on the EU', *Journal of European Public Policy* 15(2): 200–313.

Kaiser, W. (2010) 'From Isolation to Centrality: Contemporary History Meets European Studies', in W. Kaiser and A. Varsori (eds), *European Union History. Themes and Debates*. Basingstoke: Palgrave Macmillan: 45–65.

Kaiser, W., B. Leucht and M. Rasmussen (eds) (2009) *The History of the European Union: Origins of a Trans- and Supranational Polity, 1950–1972*. London: Routledge.

Kaiser, W. et al. (eds) (2005) *Transnational European Union: Towards a Common Political Space*. London: Routledge.

Kassim, H. (1994) 'Policy Networks, Networks and European Policy Making: A Sceptical View', *West European Politics* 17(4): 15–27.

Kassim, H. and A. Menon (2003) 'The Principal-Agent Approach and the Study of the European Union: Promise Unfulfilled?', *Journal of European Public Policy* 10(1): 121–39.

Katzenstein, P. (ed.) (1978) *Between Power and Plenty*. Madison: University of Wisconsin Press.

Katzenstein, P. (1996) 'Regionalism in Comparative Perspective', *Cooperation and Conflict* 31(2): 123–59.

Katzenstein, P. (2005) *A World of Regions: Asia and Europe in the American Imperium*. Ithaca, NY: Cornell University Press.

Kaunert, C. (2010) 'Europol and EU Counterterrorism: International Security Actorness in the External Dimension', *Studies in Conflict and Terrorism* 33(7): 652–71.

Kaunert, C. and S. Leonard (2011) 'European Security Governance after the Lisbon Treaty: Neighbourhood and New Actors in a Changing Security Environment', *Perspectives on European Politics and Society* 12(4): 361–70.

Kauppi, N. (2010) 'The Political Ontology of European Integration' *Comparative European Politics* 8(1): 19–36.

Kauppi, N. and M. Rask Madsen (2008) 'Institutions et acteurs: rationalité, réflexivité et analyse de l'UE', *Politique européenne* 25: 87–113.

Kelemen, D.R. (2003) 'The Structure and Dynamics of EU Federalism', *Comparative Political Studies* 36(1–2): 184–208.

Kelemen, D.R. (2006) 'Federalism and Democratization: The United States and European Union in Comparative Perspective', in A. Menon and M. Schain (eds), *Comparative Federalism: The European Union and the United States in Comparative Perspective*. Oxford: Oxford University Press: 221–44.

Kelemen, R.D. (2004) *The Rules of Federalism: Institutions and Regulatory Politics in the EU and Beyond*. Cambridge, MA: Harvard University Press.

Kelemen, R.D. and K. Nicolaïdis (2007) 'Bringing Federalism Back In', in K.E. Jorgensen, M. Pollack and B. Rosamond (eds), *The Handbook of EU Politics*, London: Sage: 301–16.

Kelstrup, M. and M. Williams (eds) (2000) *International Relations Theory and the Politics of European Integration*. London: Routledge.

Keohane, R.O. (1988) 'International Institutions: Two Approaches', *International Studies Quarterly* 32(4): 379–96.

Keohane, R.O. and S. Hoffmann (eds) (1991) *The New European Community: Decision-Making and Institutional Change*. Boulder, CO: Westview Press.

Keohane, R.O. and J.N. Nye (1972) *Transnational Relations and World Politics*. Cambridge, MA: Harvard University Press.

Keohane, R.O. and J.N. Nye (1977) *Power and Interdependence: World Politics in Transition*. Boston: Little, Brown.

Key, O.V., Jr (1961) *Public Opinion and American Democracy*. New York: Knopf.

Kickert, W.J.M. et al. (1997) *Managing Complex Networks: Strategies for the Public Sector*. London: Sage.

King, G., R.O. Keohane and S. Verba (1994) *Designing Social Enquiry: Scientific Inference in Qualitative Research*. Princeton, NJ: Princeton University Press.

King, P. (1982) *Federalism and Federation*. London: Croom Helm.

Klüver, H. (2009) 'Measuring Interest Group Influence Using Quantitative Text Analysis', *European Union Politics* 10(4): 535–49.

Knodt, M. and S. Princen (2003) 'Introduction. Puzzles and Prospects in Theorizing the EU's External Relations', in M. Knodt and S. Princen (eds), *Understanding the European Union's External Relations*. London: Routledge: 1–16.

Kohler-Koch, B. (1996) 'Catching Up With Change: The Transformation of Governance in the European Union', *Journal of European Public Policy* 3(3): 359–80.

Kohler-Koch, B. (1999) 'The Evolution and Transformation of European Governance', in B. Kohler-Koch and R. Eising (eds), *The Transformation of Governance in the European Union*. London: Routledge.

Kohler-Koch, B. (2000) 'Framing: the Bottleneck of Constructing Legitimate Institutions', *Journal of European Public Policy* 7(4): 513–31.

Kohler-Koch, B. and R. Eising (eds) (1999) *The Transformation of Governance in the European Union*. London: Routledge.

Kohler-Koch, B. and B. Rittberger (eds) (2007) *Debating the Democratic Legitimacy of the European Union*. Lanham, ND: Rowman & Littlefield.

König, T. (1998) 'Introduction: Modeling Policy Networks', *Journal of Theoretical Politics*, 10(4): 387–8.

König, T. (2008) 'Why do Member States Empower the European Parliament?', *Journal of European Public Policy* 15(2): 167–88.

König, T. and D. Junge (2009) 'Why Don't Veto Players Use Their Power?', *European Union Politics* 10(4): 507–34.

König, T. and B. Luetgert (2009) 'Troubles with Transposition? Explaining Trends in Member State Notification and the Delayed Transposition of EU Directives', *British Journal of Political Science* 39(1): 163–94.

Kooiman, J. (ed.) (1993) *Modern Governance: New Government-Society Interactions*. London: Sage.

Koopmans, R., A. Klein, L.Klein, C. Lahusen, D. Rucht and H.-J. Trenz (eds) (2003) *Bürgergesellschaft, Öffentlichkeit und Demokratie in Europa*. Frankfurt: Leske & Budrich.

Kopecky, P. and C. Mudde (2002) 'The Two Sides of Euroscepticism: Party Positions on European Integration in East Central Europe', *European Union Politics*, 2(3): 297–326.

Krasner, S.D. (ed.) (1983) *International Regimes*. Ithaca, NY/London: Cornell University Press.

Krasner, S.D. (1984) 'Approaches to the State: Alternative Conceptions and Historical Dynamics', *Comparative Politics* 16: 223–46.

Krasner, S.D. (1993) 'Westphalia and All That', in J. Goldstein and R.O. Keohane (eds), *Ideas and Foreign Policy: Beliefs, Institutions and Political Change*. Ithaca, NY: Cornell University Press.

Kratochwil, F. (1989) *Rules, Norms and Decisions*. Cambridge: Cambridge University Press.

Kreher, A. and Y. Meny (eds) (1997) 'European Agencies.' *Journal of European Public Policy* 4(2), Special Issue.

Kreppel, A. (1999) 'The European Parliament's Influence over EU Policy Outcomes', *Journal of Common Market Studies* 37(3): 521–38.

Kreppel, A. (2001) *The European Parliament and Supranational Party System: A Study in Institutional Development.* New York: Cambridge University Press.

Kriesi, H.P., E. Grande, R. Lachat, M. Dolezal and T. Frey (2008) *West European Politics in the Age of Globalization.* Cambridge: Cambridge University Press.

Kröger, S. (2006) 'When Learning Hits Politics: Or Social Policy Coordination Left to Administrations and the NGOs?', *European Integration Online Papers* 10(3).

Kröger, S. (2009) 'The Open Method of Coordination: Underconceptualisation, Overdetermination, De-politicisation and Beyond', *European Integration Online Papers* 13(1).

Kurowska, X. and F. Breuer (2011) (eds), *Explaining the EU's Common Security and Defence Policy.* Basingstoke: Palgrave Macmillan.

Lacroix, J. (2008) *La pensée française à l'épreuve de l'Europe.* Paris: Grasset.

Lacroix, J. (2009) 'Does Europe Need Common Values? Habermas vs. Habermas', *European Journal of Political Theory*, 8(2): 141–56.

Lacroix, J. and R. Coman (eds) (2007) *Les resistances à l'Europe: Cultures nationales, ideologies et strategies d'acteurs.* Brussels, Éditions de l'Université de Bruxelles.

Lacroix, J. and P. Magnette (2008) 'Théorie politique', in C. Belot, P. Magnette and S. Saurugger (eds), *Science politique de l'Union européenne.* Paris: Economica: 5–27.

Ladrech, R. (1994) 'The Europeanization of Domestic Politics and Institutions: The Case of France', *Journal of Common Market Studies* 32(1): 69–88.

Ladrech, R. (2010) *Europeanization and National Politics.* Basingstoke: Palgrave Macmillan.

Laïdi, Z. (2008) *Norms over Force: The Enigma of European Power.* Basingstoke: Palgrave Macmillan.

Lascoumes, P. and P. Le Galès (eds) (2004) *Gouverner par les instruments.* Paris: Presses de Sciences Po.

Lascoumes, P. and P. Le Galès (2007) 'Understanding Public Policy through Its Instruments – From the Nature of Instruments to the Sociology of Public Policy Instrumentation', *Governance* 20(1): 1–21.

Laursen, F. (ed.) (2003) *Comparative Regional Integration: Theoretical Approaches.* Aldershot: Ashgate.

Laursen, F. (ed.) (2010) *Comparative Regional Integration: Europe and Beyond.* Aldershot: Ashgate.

Lavenex, S. (2006) 'Shifting Up and Out: The Foreign Policy of European Migration Control', *Western European Politics*, 29(2): 329–50.

Lavenex, S. (2010) 'Justice and Home Affairs: Communitarization with Hesitation', in H. Wallace, M. Pollack and A. Young (eds), *Policy-Making in the European Union* (6th edn). Oxford: Oxford University Press.

Lavenex, S. and W. Wallace (2005) 'Justice and Home Affairs. Towards a European Public Order?', in H. Wallace, W. Wallace and M. Pollack (eds), *Policy-Making in the European Union* (5th edn). Oxford: Oxford University Press: 457–80.

Lavenex, S. and N. Wichmann (2009) 'The External Governance of EU Internal Security', *Journal of European Integration*, 31(1): 83–102.

Le Galès, P. (1998) 'Régulation, gouvernance et territoire', in J. Commaille and B. Jobert (eds), *La régulation politique.* Paris: LGDJ.

Le Galès, P. (2002) *European Cities, Social Conflicts and Governance.* Oxford: Oxford University Press.

Le Goff, J. (2003) *L'Europe est-elle née au Moyen-Âge?,* Paris: Seuil.

Lebessis, N. and J. Peterson (2000) 'Développer de nouveaux modes de gouvernance', *Working Papers de la Cellule de Perspective de la Commission européenne.*

Leca, J. (2001) *Pourquoi la philosophie politique: Petit traité de théorie et de science politique.* Paris: Presses de Sciences Po.

Leca, J. (2009) '"The Empire Strikes Back!" An Uncanny View of the European Union. Part I – Do We Need A Theory of the European Union?', *Government and Opposition* 44(3): 285–340.

Leca, J. (2010) '"The Empire Strikes Back!" Part II – Empire, Federation or What?", *Government and Opposition* 45(2): 208–93.

Leconte, C. (2010) *Understanding Euroscepticism*. Basingstoke: Palgrave Macmillan.

Legro, J. and A. Moravcsik (1999) 'Is Anybody Still a Realist?', *International Organization* 24(2): 5–55.

Lehning, P. and A. Weale (eds) (1997) *Citizenship, Democracy and Justice in the New Europe*. London: Routledge.

Lerch, M. and Schwellnus, G. (2006) 'Normative by Nature? The Role of Coherence in Justifying the EU's External Human Rights Policy'. *Journal of European Public Policy* 13(2): 304–21.

Leuffen, D., Rittberger, B., and Schimmelfennig, F. (2012) *Differentiated Integration: Explaining Variation in the European Union*. Basingstoke: Palgrave Macmillan.

Leuffen, D. et al. (2012) *Differentiated Integration: Explaining Variation in the European Union*. Basingstoke: Palgrave Macmillan.

Levi-Faur, D. (2004) 'On the "Net Impact" of Europeanization: the EU's Telecoms and Electricity Regimes Between the Global and the National', *Comparative Political Studies* 37(1): 3–29.

Lewis, J. (1998) 'Is the Hard Bargaining Image of the Council Misleading? The Committee of Permanent Representatives and the Local Elections Directive', *Journal of Common Market Studies* 36(4): 479–504.

Lewis, J. (2000) 'The Methods Community EU Decision-making and Administrative Rivalry in the Council's Infrastructure', *Journal of European Public Policy* 7(2): 261–89.

Lewis, J. (2005) 'The Janus Face of Brussels: Socialization and Everyday Decision Making in the European Union', *International Organization* 59(4): 937–71.

Lewis, J. (2008) 'Strategic Bargaining, Norms and Deliberation: Modes of Action in the Council of the European Union', in D. Naurin and H. Wallace (eds), *Unveiling the Council: Games Governments Play in Brussels*. Basingstoke: Palgrave Macmillan: 165–84.

Lijphart, A. (1968) *The Politics of Accommodation: Pluralism and Democracy in the Netherlands*. Berkeley: University of California Press.

Lijphart, A. (1977) *Democracy in Plural Societies*. New Haven, CT: Yale University Press.

Lijphart, A. (1999) *Patterns of Democracy: Government Forms and Performance in Thirty-Six Countries*. New Haven, CT/London: Yale University Press.

Lindberg, L.N. (1963) *The Political Dynamics of European Economic Integration*. Stanford, CT: Stanford University Press.

Lindberg, L.N. and S.A. Scheingold (1970) *Europe's Would-be Polity: Patterns of Change in the European Community*. Englewood Cliffs, NJ: Prentice Hall.

Lindberg, L.N. and S.A. Scheingold (eds) (1971) *Regional Integration: Theory and Research*. Cambridge, MA: Harvard University Press.

Lindner, J. and B. Rittberger (2003) 'The Creation, Interpretation and Contestation of Institutions – Revisiting Historical Institutionalism', *Journal of Common Market Studies* 41(3): 444–73.

Linklater, A. (1998) *The Transformation of Political Community: Ethical Foundations of the Post Westphalian Era*. Columbia: University of South Carolina Press.

Lodge, J. (1994) 'Transparency and Democratic Legitimacy', *Journal of Common Market Studies* 32: 343–68.

Lord, C. and D. Beetham (1998) *Legitimacy and the European Union*. London, New York: Longman.

Lord, C. and P. Magnette (2004) 'E Pluribus Unum? Creative Disagreement about Legitimacy in the EU', *Journal of Common Market Studies* 42(1): 193–202.

Lord, C. and J. Pollak (2010) 'The EU's Many Representative Modes: Colliding? Cohering?', *Journal of European Public Policy* 17(1): 117–36.

Lowi, T. (1969) *The End of Liberalism*. New York: Norton.

MacCormick, N. (1999) *Questioning Sovereignty: Law, State, and Nation in the European Commonwealth*. Oxford: Oxford University Press.

Magnette, P. (2000) 'Towards "Accountable Independence"? Parliamentary Control of the European Central Bank and the Rise of a New Democratic Model', *European Law Journal* 6(4): 326–40.

Magnette, P. (2004) 'La convention européenne: argumenter et négocier dans une assemblée constituante multinationale', *Revue française de science politique* 54(1): 5–42.

Magnette, P. and K. Nicolaïdis (2004) 'The European Convention: Bargaining in the Shadow of Rhetoric', *West European Politics* 27(3): 381–404.

Magnette, P. and Y. Papadopoulos (2008) 'On the Politicization of the European Consociation: A Middle Way between Hix and Bartolini', *European Governance Papers (EUROGOV)* C-08–01, http://www.connex-network.org/eurogov/pdf/egp-connex-C-08–01.pdf.

Maher, I., S. Billiet and D. Hodson (2009) 'The Principal-agent Approach to EU Studies: Apply Liberally but Handle with Care', *Comparative European Policy* 7 (3): 409–13.

Mahoney, J. (2000) 'Path Dependency in Historical Sociology', *Theory and Society* 29(4): 507–48.

Mair, P. (2007) 'Political Opposition and the European Union', *Government and Opposition* 42(1): 1–17.

Mair, P. and J. Thomassen (2010) 'Political Representation and Government in the European Union', *Journal of European Public Policy* 17(1): 20–35.

Majone, G. (1996) *Regulating Europe*. London: Routledge.

Majone, G. (1998) 'Europe's "Democratic Deficit": A Question of Standards', *European Law Journal* 4(1): 5–28.

Majone, G. (2005) *Dilemmas of European Integration*. Oxford: Oxford University Press.

Mancini, G.F. (1989) 'The Making of a Constitution for Europe', *Common Market Law Review* 24: 595–614.

Manent, P. (2006) *La raison des nations: Réflexions sur la démocratie en Europe*. Paris: Gallimard.

Manin, B. (1995) *Le gouvernement representative*. Paris: Calmann-Lévy.

Manners, I. (2002) 'Normative Power Europe: A Contradiction in Terms?', *Journal of Common Market Studies* 40(2): 235–58.

Manners, I. (2006) 'Normative Power Europe Reconsidered: Beyond the Crossroads', *Journal of European Public Policy* 13(2): 182–99.

Manners, I. (2007) 'Another Europe is Possible: Critical Perspectives on European Union Politics', in K.E. Jorgensen, M. Pollack and B. Rosamond (eds), *The Handbook of EU Politics*. London: Sage: 77–95.

Manners, I. (2008) 'The Normative Ethics of the European Union', *International Affairs* 81(1): 45–60.

Manners, I. (2009) 'Normative Power Europe: A Transdisciplinary Approach to European Studies', in C. Rumford (ed.), *The Sage Handbook of European Studies*, London: Sage: 561–86.

Manners, I. (2010) 'Global Europa: Mythology of the European Union in World Politics', *Journal of Common Market Studies*, 48(1): 67–87.

Manners, I. (2012) 'The European Union's Normative Power in Global Politics', in H. Zimmermann and A Dür (eds), *Key Controversies in European Integration*. Basingstoke: Palgrave Macmillan: 192–8.

Mansfield, E.D. and H. Milner (1999) 'The New Wave of Regionalism', *International Organization* 53(3): 589–627.

March, J.G. and J.P. Olsen (1984) 'The New Institutionalism: Organizational Factors in Political Life', *American Political Science Review* 78(3): 734–49.

March, J.G. and J.P. Olsen (1989) *Rediscovering Institutions: The Organizational Basis of Politics*. New York: Free Press.

March, J.G. and J.P. Olsen (2006) 'Elaborating the 'New Institutionalism', in R.A.W. Rhodes, S. Binder and B.A. Rockman (eds), *Oxford Handbook of Political Institutions*. Oxford: Oxford University Press: 3–20.

Marin, B. and R. Mayntz (eds) (1991) *Policy Networks: Empirical Evidence and Theoretical Considerations*. Boulder, CO: Westview Press.

Marks, G. and L. Hooghe (2000) 'Optimality and Authority: A Critique of Neoclassical Theory', *Journal of Common Market Studies* 38: 795–816.

Marks, G. and L. Hooghe (2001) *Multi-level Governance and European Integration.* Lanham, MD: Rowman & Littlefield.

Marks, G. and L. Hooghe (2004) 'Contrasting Visions of Multi-level Governance', in I. Bache and M. Flinders (ed.), *Multi-level Governance.* Oxford: Oxford University Press.

Marks, G., L. Hooghe and K. Blanc (1996) 'European Integration since the 1980s, State-Centric versus Multilevel Governance', *Journal of Common Market Studies* 34(3): 343–78.

Marrel, G. and R. Payre (2006) 'Des carriers au Parlement. Longévité des eurodéputés et institutionnalisation de l'arène parlementaire', *Politique européenne* 18: 69–104.

Marsh, D. (ed.) (1998) *Comparing Policy Networks.* Buckingham: Open University Press.

Marsh, D. and J.C. Sherman (2009) 'Policy Diffusion and Policy Transfer', *Policy Studies* 30(3): 269–88.

Marsh, D. and G. Stoker (eds) (1995) *Theory and Method in Political Science.* Basingstoke: Macmillan.

Mastenbroek, E. (2005) 'EU Compliance: Still a Black Hole?', *Journal of European Public Policy* 12(6): 1103–20.

Mattli, W. (1999) *The Logic of Regional Integration: Europe and Beyond.* Cambridge: Cambridge University Press.

Mattli, W. (2005) 'Ernst Haas's Evolving Thinking on Comparative Regional Integration: of Virtues and Infelicities', *Journal of European Public Policy* 12(2): 327–48.

Mattli, W. and A.-M. Slaughter (1995) 'Law and Politics in the European Union. A Reply to Garrett', *International Organization* 49(1): 183–90.

Mattli, W. and A.-M. Slaughter (1998) 'Revisiting the European Court of Justice', *International Organization* 52(1): 177–209.

Mayntz, R. (1987) 'Politische Steuerung und gesellschaftliche Steuerungsprobleme. Anmerkungen zu einem theoretischen Paradigma', *Jahrbuch für Staats- und Verwaltungswissenschaften* 1: 89–110.

Mayntz, R. (1998) *New Challenges to Governance Theory.* Florence: European University Institute, Robert Schuman Center 50.

Mayntz, R. and F. Scharpf (eds) (1995) *Gesellschaftliche Selbstregelung und politische Steuerung.* Frankfurt: Campus.

Mazey, S. and J. Richardson (eds) (1993) *Lobbying in the European Community.* Oxford: Oxford University Press.

McKelvey, R. (1976) 'Intransitivities in Multidimensional Voting. Models and Some Implications for Agenda Control', *Journal of Economic Theory* 12(4): 472–82.

McNamara, K. (1998) *The Currency of Ideas: Monetary Politics in the European Union.* Ithaca, NY/London: Cornell University Press.

McNamara, K. (2006) 'Economic Governance, Ideas and EMU: What Currency Does Policy Consensus have Today?', *Journal of Common Market Studies* 44(4): 803–21.

Mearsheimer, J. (1993) 'Back to the Future: Instability in Europe after the Cold War', *International Security* 15(4): 5–56.

Menon, A. (2003) 'Member States and International Institutions: Institutionalizing Intergovernmentalism in the European Union', *Comparative European Politics* 1(2): 171–201.

Menon, A. and M. Schain (eds) (2006) *Comparative Federalism: The European Union and the United States in Comparative Perspective.* Oxford: Oxford University Press.

Mény, Y. (2002) 'De la démocratie en Europe: Old Concepts and New Challenges', *Journal of Common Market Studies* 41(1): 1–13.

Menz, G. (2011) 'Stopping, Shaping and Moulding Europe: Two-level Games, Non-state Actors and the Europeanization of Migration Policies', *Journal of Common Market Studies* 49(2): 437–62.

Mérand, F. (2006) 'Social Representations in the European Security and Defence Policy', *Cooperation and Conflict* 41(6): 131–52.

Mérand, F. (2008a) 'Les institutionnalistes (américains) devraient-ils lire les sociologues (français)?', *Politique européenne* 25: 23–51.

Mérand, F. (2008b) *European Defence Policy: Beyond the Nation State*. Oxford: Oxford University Press.

Meunier, S. (2005) *Trading Voices: The European Union in International Commercial Negotiations*. Princeton, NJ: Princeton University Press.

Meunier, S., E.D. Mansfield and H. Milner (eds) (1997) *The Political Economy of Regionalism*. New York: Columbia University Press.

Middlemas, K. (1995) *Orchestrating Europe: The Informal Politics of the European Union, 1943–1995*. London: Fontana.

Miller, D. (1995) *On Nationality*. Oxford: Oxford University Press.

Milner, H. (1998) 'Regional Economic Cooperation, Global Markets and Domestic Politics. A Comparison of NAFTA and the Maastricht Treaty', in W.D. Coleman and G.R.D. Underhill (eds), *Regionalism and Global Economic Integration: Europe, Asia and the Americas*. London: Routledge.

Milward, A.S. (1984) *The Reconstruction of Western Europe, 1945–1951*. London: Routledge.

Milward, A.S. (1992) *The European Rescue of the Nation State*. London: Routledge.

Milward, A.S., R. Ruggero, F.M.B. Lynch, F. Romero and V. Dorensen (1993) *The Frontier of National Sovereignty: History and Theory 1945–1992*. London: Routledge.

Mitrany, D. (1933) *The Progress of International Government*. New Haven, CT: Yale University Press.

Mitrany, D. (1943) *A Working Peace System: An Argument for the Functional Development of International Organization*. London: Royal Institute of International Affairs/Oxford University Press.

Moe, T. (1984) 'The New Economics of Organization', *American Journal of Political Science* 28(4): 739–77.

Moran, M. (2002) 'Understanding the Regulatory State', *British Journal of Political Science* 32(2): 391–413.

Moravcsik, A. (1991) 'Negotiating the Single European Act: National Interests and Conventional Statecraft in the European Community', *International Organization* 45(1): 19–56.

Moravcsik, A. (1993a) 'A New Statecraft? Supranational Entrepreneurs and International Cooperation', *International Organization* 53(2): 267–306.

Moravcsik, A. (1993b) 'Preferences and Power in the European Community: A Liberal Intergovernmentalist Approach', *Journal of Common Market Studies* 31(4): 473–524.

Moravcsik, A. (1995) 'Liberal Intergovernmentalism and Integration: A Rejoinder', *Journal of Common Market Studies* 33(4): 611–28.

Moravcsik, A. (1998) *The Choice for Europe: Social Purpose and State Power from Messina to Maastricht*. Ithaca, NY: Cornell University Press.

Moravcsik, A. (1999) 'Is Something Rotten in the State of Denmark? Constructivism and European Integration', *Journal of European Public Policy* 6(5): 669–81.

Moravcsik, A. (2002) 'In Defence of the "Democratic Deficit": Reassessing Legitimacy in the European Union', *Journal of Common Market Studies* 40(4): 603–24.

Moravcsik, A. (2005) 'The European Constitutional Compromise and the Neofunctionalist Legacy', *Journal of European Public Policy* 12(2): 349–86.

Morgan, G. (2005) *The Idea of a European Superstate: Public Justification and European Integration*, new edn. Princeton, NJ: Princeton University Press.

Mörth, U. (2005) *Soft Law in Governance and Regulation*. Cheltenham: Edward Elgar.

Muller, P. and B. Jobert (1987) *L'Etat en action*. Paris, Presses Universitaires de France.

Mutimer, D. (1989) '1992 and the Political Integration of Europe: Neofunctionalism Reconsidered', *Journal of European Integration* 13(1): 75–101.

Nanz, P. (2006) *Europolis: Constitutional Patriotism: Beyond the Nation-State*. Manchester: Manchester University Press.

Navari, C. (1995) 'David Mitrany and International Functionalism', in D. Long and P. Wilson (eds), *Thinkers of the Twenty Years Crisis: Inter-War Idealism Reassessed*. Oxford: Clarendon Press.

Navarro, J. (2009) *Les députés européens et leur rôle: Sociologie interpretative des pratiques parlementaires*. Brussels: Éditions de l'Université de Bruxelles.

Neyer, J. (2002) 'Politische Herrschaft in nicht-hierarchischen Mehrebenensystemen', *Zeitschrift für Internationale Beziehungen* (1): 9–74.

Nicolaïdis, K. (2004) 'We The European Peoples ...', *Foreign Affairs* Nov.–Dec.: 97–110.

Nicolaïdis, K. and R. Howse (2001) 'Introduction: The Federal Vision. Levels of Governance and Legitimacy', in K. Nicolaidis and R. Howse (eds), *The Federal Vision*. Oxford: Oxford University Press: 1–27.

Niemann, A. (2006) *Explaining Decisions in the European Union*. Cambridge: Cambridge University Press.

North, D. (1990) *Institutions, Institutional Change and Economic Performance*. Cambridge: Cambridge University Press.

Nugent, N. (ed.) (2000) *At the Heart of the Union*. New York: St. Martin's Press.

Nugent, N. (2001) *The European Commission*. Basingstoke: Palgrave Macmillan.

Nuttall, S. (1992) *European Political Cooperation*. Oxford: Clarendon Press.

Nye, J.N. (1966) *International Political Communities: An Anthology*. New York: Doubleday.

Nye, J.N. (ed.) (1968) *International Regionalism*. Boston: Little, Brown.

Nye, J.N. (1970) 'Comparing Common Markets: A Revised Neofunctionalist Model', *International Organization* 24(4): 796–835.

Nye, J.N. (1971) *Peace in Parts: Integration and Conflict in Regional Organizations*. Boston: Little, Brown.

Nye, J.N. (1995) *Bound to Lead: The Changing Nature of American Power*. New York: Basic Books.

Nye, J.N. (2004) *Soft Power: The Means to Success in World Politics*. New York: Public Affairs.

Nye, J.N. and R. Keohane (1972) *Transnational Relations and World Politics*. Cambridge, MA: Harvard University Press.

Nye, J.N. and R. Keohane (1977) *Power and Interdependence: World Politics in Transition*. Boston: Little, Brown.

OECD (ed.) (2001) *Governance in the 21st Century*. Paris: OECD.

Offe, C. (2000) 'The German Welfare State: Principles, Performance and Prospects after Unification', *Thesis Eleven* 63(1): 11–37.

Ohmae, K. (1993) 'The Rise of the Region State', *Foreign Affairs* 72(2): 78–87.

Olsen, J.P. (2007) *Europe in Search of Political Order: An Institutional Perspective on Unity/Diversity, Citizens/Their Helpers; Democratic Design/Historical Drift, and the Co-existence of Orders*. Oxford: Oxford University Press.

Olsen, J.P. (2009) 'Change and Continuity: An Institutional Approach to Institutions of Democratic Government', *European Political Science Review* 1(1): 3–32.

Onuf, N. (1989) *World of Our Making: Rules and Rule in Social Theory and International Relations*. Columbia: University of South Carolina Press.

Orbie, J. (2006) 'Review Essay. Civilian Power Europe. Review of the Original and Current Debates', *Cooperation and Conflict* 41(1): 123–6.

Pahre, R. (1997) 'Endogenous Domestic Institutions in Two-level Games and Parliamentary Oversight of the European Union', *Journal of Conflict Resolution* 41(1): 147–74.

Palier, B. and Y. Surel (2005) 'Les 'trois I' et l'analyse de l'Etat en action', *Revue française de science politique* 55(1): 7–32.

Palier, B. and Y. Surel (2007) 'Analyser l'européanisation des politiques publiques', in B. Palier, Y. Surel et al., *L'Europe en action*. Paris: L'Harmattan: 13–85.

Panke, D. (2007) 'The European Court of Justice as an Agent of Europeanization: Inducing Compliance with EU Law', *Journal of European Public Policy* 14(6): 847–66.

Papadopoulos, Y. (1995) *Complexité sociale et politiques publiques*. Paris: Montchrestien.

Papadopoulos, Y. (2003) 'Cooperative Forms of Governance: Problems of Democratic Accountability in Complex Environments', *European Journal of Political Research* 42: 473–501.

Papadopoulos, Y. (2007) 'Problems with Democratic Accountability in Network and Multi-level Governance', *European Law Journal* 13(4): 469–86.

Papadopoulos, Y. (2010) 'Accountability and Multi-Level Governance: More Accountability, Less Democracy?', *West European Politics* 33(5): 1030–49.

Parsons, C. (2002) 'Showing Ideas as Causes: The Origins of the European Union', *International Organization* 55(1): 47–84.

Parsons, C. (2004) *A Certain Idea of Europe*. Ithaca, NY: Cornell University Press.

Parsons, C. (2010) 'How – and How Much – are Sociological Approaches to the EU Distinctive?', *Comparative European Politics*, 8(1): 143–59.

Pasquier, R. and J. Weisbein (2004) 'L'Europe au microscope du local. Manifeste pour une sociologie politique de l'intégration communautaire', *Politique européenne* 12: 5–21.

Paterson, W.E. (2010) 'Hastening Slowly: European Studies –Between Reinvention and Continuing Fragmentation', in M. Egan, N. Nugent and W.E. Paterson (eds), *Research Agendas in EU Studies: Stalking the Elephant*. Basingstoke: Palgrave Macmillan: 398–420.

Patterson, L.A. (1997) 'Agricultural Policy Reform in the European Community: A Three level Game Analysis', *International Organization* 51(1): 135–65.

Pedersen, T. (1998) *Germany, France, and the Integration of Europe: A Realist Interpretation*. London and New York: Frances Pinter.

Pedersen, T. (2002) 'Cooperative Hegemony: Power, Ideas and Institutions in Regional Integration', *Review of International Studies* 28(4): 677–96.

Pentland, C. (1973) *International Theory and European Integration*. London: Faber & Faber.

Pernice, I. (1999) 'Multilevel Constitutionalism and the Treaty of Amsterdam: European Constitution-making Revisited'. *Common Market Law Review* 36: 703–50.

Peters, B.G. (2005) *Institutional Theory in Political Science: The New Institutionalism*. London: Continuum.

Peters, B.G. and S. Borrás (2010) 'Governance and European Integration', in M. Egan, N. Nugent and W.E. Paterson (eds), *Research Agendas in EU Studies: Stalking the Elephant*. Basingstoke: Palgrave Macmillan: 117–33.

Peters, B.G., C. Levine and F. Thompson (1990) *Public Administration in the United States: Problems and Prospects*. Boston: Little, Brown.

Peters, B.G. and J. Pierre (2004) 'Multi-level Governance and Democracy: A Faustian Bargain?', in I. Bache and M. Flinders (eds), *Multi-level Governance*. Oxford: Oxford University Press.

Peters, B.G. and J. Pierre (2009) 'Governance Approaches', in A. Wiener and T. Diez (eds), *European Integration Theory*. Oxford: Oxford University Press: 91–104.

Peterson, J. (2003) 'Policy Networks'. Political Science Series. Vienna: Institute for Advanced Studies.

Peterson, J. (2009) 'Policy Networks', in A. Wiener and T. Diez (eds), *European Integration Theory*. Oxford: Oxford University Press: 105–24.

Peterson, J. and E. Bomberg (1999) *Decision-Making in the European Union*. London: Macmillan.

Petiteville, F. (2006) *La politique internationale de l'Union européenne*. Paris: Presses de Sciences Po.

Piattoni, S. (2010) *The Theory of Multi-Level Governance: Conceptual, Empirical, and Normative Challenges*. Oxford: Oxford University Press.

Pierre, J. and B.G. Peters (2000) (eds) *Governance, Politics and the State*. Basingstoke: Palgrave Macmillan.

Pierson, P. (1994) *Dismantling the Welfare States? Reagan, Thatcher and the Politics of Retrenchment*. Cambridge: Cambridge University Press.

Pierson, P. (1996) 'The Path to European Integration: A Historical Institutionalist Analysis', *Comparative Political Studies* 29(2): 123–63.

Pierson, P. (2000) 'Path Dependency, Increasing Returns and the Study of Politics', *American Political Science Review* 94(2): 251–67.

Pierson, P. (2004) *Politics in Time, History, Institutions and Social Analysis.* Princeton, NJ: Princeton University Press.

Pinder, J. (1992) *Altiero Spinelli and the British Federalists.* Oxford: Oxford University Press.

Pitkin, H.F. (1967) *The Concept of Representation.* Berkeley: University of California Press.

Poguntke, T., N. Aylott, R. Ladrech, E. Carter and K.R. Luther (eds) (2007) *The Europeanization of National Political Parties: Power and Organizational Adaptation.* London: Routledge.

Pollack, M.A. (1996) 'The New Institutionalism and EC Governance: The Promise and Limits of Institutional Analysis', *Governance* 9(4): 429–58.

Pollack, M.A. (1997) 'Delegation, Agency, and Agenda Setting in the European Community', *International Organization* 51(1): 99–134.

Pollack, M.A. (2001) 'International Relations Theory and European Integration', *Journal of Common Market Studies* 39(2): 221–44.

Pollack, M.A. (2003) *The Engines of European Integration, Delegation, Agency and Agenda Setting in the EU.* Oxford: Oxford University Press.

Pollack, M.A. (2004) 'The New Institutionalisms and European Integration', in A. Wiener and T. Diez (eds), *European Integration Theory.* Oxford: Oxford University Press: 154–5.

Pollack, M.A. (2005) 'Theorizing the European Union: International Organization, Domestic Polity, or Experiment in New Governance?', *Annual Review of Political Science* 8: 357–98.

Pollack, M.A. (2007) 'Rational Choice and EU Politics', in K.E. Joergensen et al. (eds), *Handbook of European Union Politics.* London: Sage: 31–55.

Portela, C. (2010) *European Union Sanctions and Foreign Policy: When and Why Do They Work?* Routledge: London.

Princen, S. and M. Rhinard (2006) 'Crashing and Creeping: Agenda-Setting Dynamics in the European Union', *Journal of European Public Policy* 13(7): 1119–32.

Przeworski, A. and H. Teune (1982) *The Logic of Comparative Social Enquiry.* Malabar: Krieger.

Puchala, R. D. (1972) 'Of Blind Men, Elephants and International Integration', *Journal of Common Market Studies* 10(3): 427–60.

Puchala, R.D. (1981) 'Integration Theory and the Study of International Relations', in R.W. Merritt and B.M. Russett (eds), *From National Development to Global Community: Essays in Honour of Karl Deutsch.* London: George Allen & Unwin.

Puetter, U. (2006) *The Eurogroup: How a Secretive Circle of Finance Ministers Shape European Economic Governance.* Manchester: Manchester University Press.

Puetter, U. (2012) 'Europe's Deliberative Intergovernmentalism: The Role of the Council and the European Council in EU Economic Governance', *Journal of European Public Policy* 19(2): 161–78.

Putnam, R. (1988) 'Diplomacy and Domestic Politics. The Logic of Two-Level Games', *International Organizations* 42: 427–60.

Quaglia, L., F. De Francesco and C. Radaelli (2008) 'Committee Governance and Socialization in the EU', *Journal of European Public Policy*, 15(1): 155–66.

Radaelli, C.M. (2000) 'Policy Transfer in the European Union', *Governance* 13(1): 25–43.

Radaelli, C.M. (2001) 'The Domestic Impact of European Public Policy: Notes on Concepts, Methods and the Challenge of Empirical Research', *Politique européenne* 5:107–42.

Radaelli, C.M. (2008) 'Europeanization, Policy Learning, and New Modes of Governance', *Journal of Comparative European Policy Analysis* 10(3): 239–54.

Rasmussen, M. (2008) 'The Origins of Legal Revolution: The Early History of the European Court of Justice', *Journal of European Integration History* 14(2): 77–98.

Rawls, J. (1993) *Political Liberalism*. New York: Columbia University Press.

Reif, K.H. and H. Schmitt (1980) 'Nine Second Order National Elections: A Conceptual Framework for the Analysis of European Elections', *European Journal of Political Research* 8(1): 3–44.

Reuter, P. (1956) 'La Communauté européenne du charbon et de l'acier', in G. Berger et al., *Le fédéralisme*. Paris: Presses Universitaires de France.

Rhodes, R. (2003) 'What is New about Governance and Why Does it Matter?', in J. Hayward and A. Menon (eds), *Governing Europe*. Oxford: Oxford University Press.

Rhodes, R., I. Bache and S. George (1996) 'Policy Networks and Policy Making in the European Union: A Critical Appraisal', in L. Hooghe (ed.), *Cohesion Policy and European Integration: Building Multilevel Governance*. Oxford: Clarendon Press.

Richardson, J. (1995) 'The Market for Political Activism: Interest Groups as a Challenge to Political Parties', *West European Politics* 18(1): 116–39.

Richardson, J.J. (1996a) 'Actor-Based Models of National and EU Policy Making', in H. Kassim and A. Menon (eds), *The EU and National Industrial Policy*. London: Routledge: 26–51.

Richardson, J.J. (1996b) 'Approches de la décision politique nationale et européenne fondées sur l'acteur : communautés de politique publique, réseaux par questions et communautés épistémiques', in P. Le Galès and M. Thatcher (eds), *Les réseaux en politique publique*. Paris: L'Harmattan.

Riker, W. (1964) *Federalism: Origin, Operation, Significance*. Boston: Little, Brown.

Riker, W. (1980) 'Implications from the Disequilibrium of Majority Rule for the Study of Institutions', *American Political Science Review* 74(3): 432–47.

Risse, T. (1996) 'Exploring the Nature of the Beast: International Relations Theory and Comparative Policy Analysis Meet the European Union', *Journal of Common Market Studies* 34(1): 53–80.

Risse, T. (2000) '"Let's Argue!" Communicative Action in World Politics', *International Organization*, 54(1): 1–40.

Risse, T. (2001) 'A European Identity? Europeanization and the Evolution of Nation State Identities', in M. Green Cowles, J. Caporaso and T. Risse (eds), *Europeanization and Domestic Change*. Ithaca, NY: Cornell University Press: 198–216.

Risse, T. (2003) 'The Euro between National and European Identity', *Journal of European Public Policy* 10(4): 487–503.

Risse, T. (2004a) 'Global Governance and Communicative Action', *Government and Opposition* 39 (2): 288–313.

Risse, T. (2004b) 'Social Constructivism and European Integration', in A. Wiener and T. Diez (eds), *European Integration Theory,* Oxford: Oxford University Press: 159–76.

Risse, T. (2005) 'Neofunctionalism, European Identity and the Puzzles of European Integration', *Journal of European Public Policy* 12(2): 291–309.

Risse, T. (2009) 'Social Constructivism and European Integration', in A. Wiener and T. Diez (eds), *European Integration Theory*. Oxford: Oxford University Press: 159–76.

Risse, T. (2010) *A Community of Europeans? Transnational Identities and Public Spheres*. Ithaca, NY: Cornell University Press.

Risse, T., M. Green Cowles and J. Caporaso (2001a) 'Europeanization and Domestic Change: Introduction', in M. Green Cowles, J. Caporaso and T. Risse (eds), *Transforming Europe: Europeanization and Domestic Change*. Ithaca, NY: Cornell University Press.

Risse, T., M. Green Cowles and J. Caporaso (eds) (2001b), *Transforming Europe: Europeanization and Domestic Change*. Ithaca, NY: Cornell University Press.

Risse, T. and A. Wiener (1999) '"Something Rotten" and the Social Construction of Social Construction: A Comment on Comments', *Journal of European Public Policy* 6(5): 775–82.

Risse-Kappen, T. (1994) 'Ideas Do Not Float Freely: Transnational Coalitions, Domestic Structures and the End of the Cold War', *International Organization* 48 (2): 185–214.

Risse-Kappen, T. (1996) 'Exploring the Nature of the Beast: International Relations Theory and Comparative Policy Analysis Meet the European Union', *Journal of Common Market Studies* 34(1): 53–80.

Rittberger, B. (2005) *Building Europe's Parliament: Democratic Representation Beyond the Nation State*. Oxford: Oxford University Press.

Rittberger, B. (2009) 'The Historical Origins of the EU's System of Representation', *Journal of European Public Policy* 16(1): 43–61.

Rittberger, B. (2010) 'Democracy and European Union Governance', in M. Egan, N. Nugent and W.E. Paterson (eds), *Research Agendas in EU Studies: Stalking the Elephant*. Basingstoke: Palgrave Macmillan: 134–167.

Roberts, A. (1993) 'The United Nations and International Security', *Survival* 35(2): 3–30.

Rosamond, B. (1995) 'Mapping the European Condition: The Theory of Integration and the Integration of Theory', *European Journal of International Relations*, 1(3): 391–408.

Rosamond, B. (1999) 'Discourses of Globalization and the Social Construction of European Identities', *Journal of European Public Policy*, 6(4): 652–68.

Rosamond, B. (2000) *Theories of European Integration*. Basingstoke: Palgrave Macmillan.

Rosamond, B. (2005a) 'Conceptualizing the EU Model of Governance in World Politics', *European Foreign Affairs Review*, 10(4): 463–78.

Rosamond, B. (2005b) 'The Uniting of Europe and the Foundation of EU Studies: Revisiting Neo-functionalism of Ernst B. Haas', *Journal of European Public Policy* 12(2): 237–54.

Rosamond, B. (2006) 'The Future of European Studies: Integration Theory, EU Studies and Social Science', in M. Eilstrup-Sangiovanni, *Debates on European Integration: A Reader*. Basingstoke: Palgrave Macmillan: 448–60.

Rosamond, B. (2007) 'The Political Sciences of European Integration: Disciplinary History and EU Studies, in K.E. Joergensen, M.A. Pollack and B. Rosamond (eds), *Handbook of European Union Politics*. London: Sage: 7–30.

Rosecrance. R. (1991) 'Regionalism and the Post-Cold War Era', *International Journal* 46(3): 373–93.

Rosenau, J.N. (ed.) (1969) *Linkage Politics: Essays on the Convergence of National and International Systems*. New York: Free Press.

Rosenau, J.N. (1997) *Along the Domestic-Foreign Frontier: Exploring Governance in a Turbulent World*. Cambridge: Cambridge University Press.

Rosenau, J.N. (2004) 'Strong Demand, Huge Supply: Governance in an Emerging Epoch', in I. Bache and M. Flinders (eds), *Multi-level Governance*. Oxford: Oxford University Press.

Rosenau, J.N. and E.O. Czempiel (eds) (1992) *Governance without Government: Order and Change in World Politics*. Cambridge: Cambridge University Press.

Ross, G. (1994a) *Jacques Delors and European Integration*. Oxford/New York: Polity Press/Oxford University Press.

Ross, G. (1994b) 'Inside the Delors Cabinet', *Journal of Common Market Studies* 32(4): 499–523.

Ross, G. (2008) 'What do Europeans Think? Analyses of the EU's Current Crisis by European Elites', *Journal of Common Market Studies* 46(2): 389–412.

Ruggie, J.G. (1998a) *Constructing the World Polity: Essays on International Institutionalisation*. London: Routledge.

Ruggie, J.G. (1998b) 'What makes the World Hang Together? Neoutilitarism and the Social Constructivist Challenge', *International Organization* 62(4):855–85.

Ruggie, J.G., P. Katzenstein, R.O. Keohane and P.C. Schmitter (2005) 'Transformations in World Politics: The Intellectual Contributions of Ernst B. Haas', *Annual Review of Political Science* 8: 271–96.

Rumford, C. (2002) *The European Union: A Political Sociology*. London: Blackwell.

Rumford, C. (2008) *Cosmopolitan Spaces: Europe, Globalization, Theory*. London: Routledge.

Rumford, C. (ed.) (2009) *The Sage Handbook of European Studies*. London: Sage.

Russett, B. (1967) *International Regions and the International System: A Study in Political Ecology*. Chicago: Rand McNally.

Rynning, S. (2003a) 'A Fragmented External Role. The EU, Defence Policy and New Atlanticism', in M. Knodt and S. Princen (eds), *Understanding the European Union's External Relations*. London: Routledge: 19–34.

Rynning, S. (2003b) 'Toward a Strategic Culture for the EU', *Security Dialogue* 34(4): 479–96.

Rynning, S. (2006) 'Return of the Jedi: Realism and the Study of the European Union', *Politique européenne* 17: 11–34.

Sabatier, P. and H. Jenkins-Smith (eds) (1993) *Policy Change and Learning: An Advocacy Coalition Approach*. Boulder, CO: Westview Press.

Sabel, C. and J. Zeitlin (2008) 'Learning from Difference: The New Architecture of Experimentalist Governance in the EU', *European Law Journal* 14(3): 271–327.

Sandholtz, W. (1993) 'Choosing the Union: Monetary Politics and Maastricht', *International Organization* 47(1): 1–40.

Sandholtz, W. (1996) 'Membership Matters: Limits of the Functional Approach to European Institutions', *Journal of Common Market Studies* 34(3): 403–29.

Sandholtz, W. and A. Stone Sweet (eds) (1998) *European Integration and Supranational Governance*. Oxford: Oxford University Press.

Sandholtz, W. and J. Zysman (1989) 'Recasting the European Bargain', *World Politics* 42(1): 95–128.

Sangiovanni, A. (2013) 'Solidarity in the European Union', *Oxford Journal of Legal Studies* 33(2): 1–29.

Sassen, S. (1996) *Losing Control? Sovereignty in an Age of Globalisation*. New York: Columbia University Press.

Saurugger, S. (2008) 'Interest Groups and Democracy in the EU', *West European Politics* 31(6): 1274–91.

Saurugger, S. (2009) 'Sociology and European Studies', *Journal of European Public Policy* 16(6): 937–50.

Saurugger, S. (2013) 'Constructivism and Public Policy Approaches in the EU: From Ideas to Power Games', *Journal of European Public Policy*, 20(6): 888–906.

Saurugger, S. and F. Mérand (eds) (2010) 'Mainstreaming Sociology in EU Studies', *Comparative European Politics* 8(1), Special Issue.

Saurugger, S. and C.M. Radaelli (2008) 'The Europeanization of Public Policies: Introduction', *Journal of Comparative Policy Analysis* 10(3): 213–19.

Saurugger, S. and Y. Surel (2006) 'L'européanisation comme transfert de politiques publiques', *Revue internationale de politique comparée* 13(2): 179–211.

Sbragia, A. (2008) 'Review Article: Comparative Regionalism: What Might It Be?', *Journal of Common Market Studies* 46(1): 29–49.

Sbragia, A. (ed.) (1991) *Europolitics: Institutions and Policy-Making in the 'New' European Community*. Washington, DC: Brookings Institution.

Schäfer, A. (2004) 'Beyond the Community Method: Why the Open Method of Coordination Was Introduced in EU Policy-making', *European Integration Online Papers* 13(1).

Scharpf, F.W. (1988) 'The Joint-decision Trap: Lessons from German Federalism and European Integration', *Public Administration* 66(3): 239–78.

Scharpf, F.W. (1997) *Games Real Actors Play, Actor-Centered Institutionalism in Policy Research*. Boulder, CO: Westview Press.

Scharpf, F.W. (1999) *Governing in Europe: Effective and Democratic?* Oxford: Oxford University Press.

Scharpf, F.W. (2002) 'La diversité légitime: nouveau défi de l'intégration européenne', *Revue française de science politique* 52(5–6): 609–39.

Scharpf, F.W. (2006) 'The Joint-decision Trap Revisited', *Journal of Common Market Studies* 44(4): 845–64.

Scheingold, S.A. (1964) *The Rule of Law in European Integration*. Montreal: McGill University Press.

Schelkle, W. (2012) 'European Fiscal Union: From Monetary Back Door to Parliamentary Main Entrance'. *CESifo Forum* 13 (1): 28–34.

Schepel, H. and R. Wesseling (1997) 'The Legal Community: Judges, Lawyers, Officials and Clerks in the Writing of Europe', *European Law Journal* 3(2): 165–88.

Schimmel, C., M. Ronzoni and A. Benaï (2011) (eds) *Social Justice, Global Dynamics.* London, Routledge.

Schimmelfennig, F. (2000a) 'Goffman Meets IR: Dramaturgical Action in International Community', *International Review of Sociology* 12(3): 417–37.

Schimmelfennig, F. (2000b) 'International Socialisation in the New Europe: Rational Action in an Institutional Environment', *European Journal of International Relations* 6(1): 109–39.

Schimmelfennig, F. (2004) 'Liberal Intergovernementalism', in A. Wiener and T. Diez (eds), *European Integration Theory*. Oxford: Oxford University Press: 75–94.

Schimmelfennig, F. and U. Sedelmeier (2002) 'Theorizing Enlargement: Research Focus, Hypotheses, and the State of Research', *Journal of European Public Policy* 9 (4): 500–28.

Schimmelfennig, F. and U. Sedelmeier (2004) 'Governance by Conditionality: EU Rule Transfer to the Candidate Countries of Central and Eastern Europe', *Journal of European Public Policy* 11 (4): 669–87.

Schimmelfennig, F. and U. Sedelmeier (eds) (2005) *The Europeanization of Central and Eastern Europe*. Ithaca, NY: Cornell University Press.

Schlesinger, P. and F. Foret (2006) 'Political Roof and Sacred Canopy? Religion and the EU Constitution', *European Journal of Social Theory* 9(1): 59–81.

Schlesinger, P., and D. Kevin (2000) 'Can the European Union Become a Sphere of Publics?', in E.O. Eriksen and J. Fossum (eds), *Democracy in the European Union: Integration Through Deliberation?*, London: Routledge: 277–305.

Schmidt, S. (1998) 'Commission Activism: Subsuming Telecommunications and Electricity under European Competition Law', *Journal of European Public Policy* 5(1): 169–84.

Schmidt, S. (2000) 'Only an Agenda-Setter? The European Commission's Power over the Council of Ministers', *European Union Politics* 1(1): 37–61.

Schmidt, V.A. (2001) 'The Politics of Economic Adjustment in France and Britain: When Does Discourse Matter?', *Journal of European Public Policy* 8(2): 247–64.

Schmidt, V.A. (2002) *The Futures of European Capitalism*. Oxford: Oxford University Press.

Schmidt, V.A. (2004) 'The European Union: Democratic Legitimacy in a Regional State?', *Journal of Common Market Studies* 42(4): 975–98.

Schmidt, V.A. (2006) *Democracy in Europe: The EU and National Politics*. Oxford: Oxford University Press.

Schmidt, V.A. (2008) 'Discursive Institutionalism: The Explanatory Power of Ideas and Discourses', *Annual Review of Political Science* 11: 303–26.

Schmidt, V.A. (2010a) 'Give Peace a Chance: Reconciling Four (not Three) Institutionalisms', in D. Béland and R.H. Cox (eds), *Ideas and Politics in Social Science Research*. Oxford: Oxford University Press.

Schmidt, V.A. (2010b) 'Taking Ideas and Discourses Seriously: Explaining Change through Discursive Institutionalism as the Fourth "New Institutionalism"', *European Political Science Review* 2(1): 1–25.

Schmidt, V.A. and C.M. Radaelli (2004) 'Conclusions', *West European Politics* 27(2): 364–79.

Schmitt, P. and J. Thomassen (eds) (1999) *Political Representation and Legitimacy in the European Union*. Oxford, Oxford University Press.

Schmitter, P.C. (1969) 'Three Neofunctionalist Hypothesis about International Integration', *International Organization* 23(1): 161–6.

Schmitter, P.C. (1970) 'A Revised Theory of Regional Integration', *International Organization* 24(4): 836–68.

Schmitter, P.C. (1971) 'A Revised Theory of European Integration', in L.N. Lindberg and S.A. Scheingold (eds), *Regional Integration: Theory and Research*. Cambridge, MA: Harvard University Press.

Schmitter, P.C. (2000) *How to Democratize the European Union – And Why Bother?* London: Rowman & Littlefield.

Schmitter, P.C. (2004) 'Neo-Neofunctionalism', in A. Wiener and T. Diez (eds), *European Integration Theory*. Oxford: Oxford University Press: 45–74.

Schmitter, P.C. and A. Niemann (2009) 'Neofunctionalism', in A. Wiener and T. Diez (eds), *European Integration Theory*. Oxford: Oxford University Press: 45–74.

Schmitter, P.C. and W. Streeck (1991) 'From National Corporatism to Transnational Pluralism: Organized Interests and the Single European Market', *Politics and Society* 19(2): 133–64.

Schmitter, P.C. and F. Traxler (1995) 'The Emerging Euro-Polity and Organized Interests', *European Journal of International Relations* 1(2): 191–218.

Schneider, G., D. Finke and K. Baltz (2007) 'With a Little Help from the State: Interest Intermediation in the Domestic Pre-negotiations of EU Legislation', *Journal of European Public Policy* 14(3): 444–59.

Schneider, G., P. Moser and G. Kirchgässner (2000) *Decision Rules in the EU: A Rational Choice Perspective*. London: Macmillan.

Schneider, V. (2004) 'State Theory, Governance and the Logic of Regulation and Administrative Control', in A. Warntjen and A. Wonka (eds), *Governance in Europe*. Baden-Baden: Nomos: 25–41.

Scholte, J.A. (2012) *Globalization: A Critical Introduction*. Basingstoke, Palgrave Macmillan.

Schulz, M., F. Söderbaum and J. Ojendal (2001) 'A Framework for Understanding Regionalization', in M. Schulz, F. Söderbaum and J. Ojendal (eds), *Regionalisation in a Globalizing World*. London: Zed Books: 1–21.

Searle, J. (1996) *Mind, Language and Society*. New York: Basic Books.

Sedelmeier, U. and R. Epstein (2008) 'Beyond Conditionality: International Institutions in Postcommunist Europe after Enlargement', *Journal of European Public Policy* 15 (6): 795–805.

Shepsle, K. (1979) 'Institutional Arrangements and Equilibrium in Multi-dimensional Voting Models', *American Journal of Political Science* 23(1): 27–60.

Shepsle, K. and B. Weingast (1984) 'Uncovered Bets and Sophisticated Voting Outcomes with Implications for Agenda Control', *American Journal of Political Science* 28(1): 49–74.

Shipan, C.R. and C. Volden (2008) 'The Mechanisms of Policy Diffusion', *American Journal of Political Science* 52(4): 840–57.

Shore, C. (2000) *Building Europe: The Cultural Politics of European Integration*. London: Routledge.

Simmel, G. (1955) *Conflict and the Web of Affiliations*. New York: Free Press.

Sjursen, H. (2006) 'What Kind of Power?'. *Journal of European Public Policy* 13(2): 169–81.

Slocum, N. and L. van Langenhove (2005) 'Identity and Regional Integration', in M. Farrell, B. Hettne and L. van Langenhove (eds), *Global Politics of Regionalism: Theory and Practice*. London: Pluto Press: 49–50.

Smismans, S. (ed.) (2006) *European Governance and Civil Society*. Cheltenham: Edward Elgar.

Smith, A. (2004) *Le gouvernement de l'Union européenne: Une sociologie politique*. Paris: LGDJ.

Smith, D.L. and J.L. Ray (1993) 'The 1992 Project', in D.L. Smith and J.L. Ray (eds), *The 1992 Project and the Future of Integration in Europe*. Armonk, NY: Sharpe 1993: 3–18.

Smith, H. (2002) *European Foreign Policy: What It Is and What It Does*. London: Pluto Press.

Smith, K. (2005) 'Beyond the Civilian Power EU Debate', *Politique européenne* 17: 63–82.

Smith, M.E. (2003) *Europe's Foreign and Security Policy: The Institutionalization of Cooperation*. Cambridge: Cambridge University Press.

Snidal, D. (2002) 'Rational Choice and International Relations', in W. Carlsnaes, B. Simmons and T. Risse (eds), *The Handbook of International Relations*. New York: Sage: 73–94.

Söderbaum, F. and T.M. Shaw (2003) 'Conclusion: What Futures for New Regionalism?', in F. Söderbaum and T. M. Shaw (eds), *Theories of New Regionalism: A Palgrave Reader*. Basingstoke: Palgrave Macmillan: 211–25.

Stacey, J. and B. Rittberger (2003) 'Dynamics of Formal and Informal Institutional Change in the EU', *Journal of European Public Policy* 10(6): 858–83.

Stein, E. (1981) 'Lawyers, Judges, and the Making of a Transnational Constitution', *American Journal of International Law* 75: 1–27.

Steinmo, S., K. Thelen and F. Longstreth (eds) (1992) *Structuring Politics: Historical Institutionalism in Comparative Analysis*. Cambridge: Cambridge University Press.

Stoker, G. (1995) 'Introduction', in D. Marsh and G. Stoker (eds), *Theory and Methods in Political Science*. London: Macmillan.

Stone Sweet, A. and J. Caporaso (1998) 'From Free Trade to Supranational Polity: The European Court and Integration', in W. Sandholtz and A. Stone Sweet (eds), *European Integration and Supranational Governance*. New York: Oxford University Press: 92–133.

Stone Sweet, A. and W. Sandholtz (1997) 'European Integration and Supranational Governance', *Journal of European Public Policy* 4(3): 297–317.

Stone Sweet, A., W. Sandholtz and N. Fligstein (eds) (2001) *The Institutionalization of Europe*. Oxford: Oxford University Press.

Stone Sweet, A., A-M. Slaughter and J. Weiler (eds) (1998) *The European Court and the National Courts: Legal Change in its Social, Political, and Economic Context*. Oxford: Hart.

Strange, S. (1988) *States and Markets: An Introduction to International Political Economy*. London: Frances Pinter.

Strange, S. (1996) *The Retreat of the State: The Diffusion of Power in the World Economy*. Cambridge: Cambridge University Press.

Streeck, W. and K. Thelen (2007) 'Introduction: Institutional Change in Advanced Political Economies', in W. Streeck and K. Thelen (eds), *Beyond Continuity: Institutional Change in Advanced Political Economies*. Oxford: Oxford University Press: 1–39.

Surel, Y. (2000) 'The Role of Cognitive and Normative Policy-Making', *Journal of European Public Policy* 7(4): 495–512.

Szczerbiak, A. and P.A. Taggart (2002) *The Party Politics of Euroscepticism in EU Member and Candidate States*. Sussex European Institute (online) SEI Working Paper 51.

Szczerbiak, A. and P.A. Taggart (2008) *Opposing Europe?* Oxford: Oxford University Press.

Tallberg, J. (2002a) 'Delegation to Supranational Institutions: Why, How and With What Consequences?' *West European Politics* 25(1): 20.

Tallberg, J. (2002b) 'Paths to Compliance: Enforcement, Management and the European Union', *International Organization* 56(3): 609–44.

Tallberg, J. (2003) 'The Agenda Shaping Powers of the EU Council Presidency', *Journal of European Public Policy* 10(1): 1–19.

Talliaferro, J. W. (2000/2001) 'Security Seeking Under Anarchy: Defensive Realism Revisited', *International Security* 25(3): 128–61.

Taylor, P. (1993) *International Organization in the Modern World: The Regional and the Global Process*. London: Frances Pinter.

Taylor, P. (1996) *The European Union in the 1990s*. Oxford: Oxford University Press.

Taylor, P. (1998) 'Consociationalism and Federalism as Approaches in International Integration', in A.J.R. Groom and P. Taylor (eds), *Frameworks for International Cooperation*. London: Frances Pinter: 172–84.

Telo, M. (2007) 'Introduction: Globalization, New Regionalism and the Role of the European Union', in M. Telo (ed.), *European Union and New Regionalism: Regional Actors and Global Governance in a Post-Hegemonic Era* (2nd edn). London: Ashgate.

Terpan, F. (ed.) (2004) *La politique européenne de sécurité et de défense. L'UE peut-elle gérer les crises?* Toulouse: Presses de l'Institut d'Études Politiques de Toulouse.

Thatcher, M. (1995) 'Les réseaux de politique publique: bilan d'un sceptique', in P. Le Galès and M. Thatcher (eds), *Les réseaux en politique publique*. Paris: L'Harmattan.

Thatcher, M. (1998) 'The Development of Policy Network Analysis. From Modest Origins to Overarching Frameworks', *Journal of Theoretical Politics* 10(4): 389–416.

Thatcher, M. (2004) 'Winners and Losers in Europeanization: Reforming the National Regulation of Telecommunications', *West European Politics* 27 (2): 284–309.

Thatcher, M. (2007) *Internationalization and Economic Institutions: Comparing European Experience*. Oxford: Oxford University Press.

Thelen, K. and S. Steinmo (1992) 'Historical Institutionalism in Comparative Politics', in S. Steinmo, K. Thelen and F. Lonstreth (eds), *Structuring Politics: Historical Institutionalism in Comparative Analysis*. Cambridge: Cambridge University Press: 1–32.

Thibaud, P. and J.M. Ferry (1992) *Discussion sur l'Europe*. Paris: Calmann-Lévy.

Thompson, H. (2010) 'The Character of the State', in C. Hay (ed.), *New Directions in Political Science: Responding to the Challenges of an Interdependent World*. Basingstoke: Palgrave Macmillan: 130–47.

Thomson, R., F. Stokman, C. Achen and T. König (eds) (2006) *The European Union Decides*. Cambridge: Cambridge University Press.

Thorlakson, L. (2003) 'Comparing Federal Institutions: Power and Representation in Six Federations', *West European Politics* 26(1): 1–22.

Thorlakson, L. (2005) 'Federalism and the European Party System', *Journal of European Public Policy* 12(3): 468–87.

Tonra, B. (2001) *The Europeanisation of National Foreign Policy: Dutch, Danish and Irish Foreign Policy in the European Union*. Aldershot: Ashgate.

Toshkov, D. (2010) 'Taking Stock: A Review of Quantitative Studies of Transposition and Implementation of EU Law', *EIF Working Paper* 01.2010, February.

Tranholm-Mikkelsen, J. (1991) 'Neofunctionalism: Obstinate or Obsolete? A Reappraisal in the Light of the New Dynamism of the EC', *Millennium: Journal of International Studies* 20(1): 1–21.

Trauner, F. (2009) 'From Membership Conditionality to Policy Conditionality. EU External Governance in South Eastern Europe', *Journal of European Public Policy* 16(5): 774–90.

Traxler, F., S. Blaschke and B. Kittel (2001) *National Labour Relations in Internationalised Markets*. Oxford: Oxford University Press.

Treib, O. (2008) 'Implementing and Complying with EU Governance Outputs', *Living Reviews in European Governance* 3(5), http://www.livingreviews. org/lreg-2008-5.

Trenz, H.J. (2011) 'Social Theory and European Integration', in A. Favell and V. Guiraudon (eds), *Sociology of the European Union*. Basingstoke: Palgrave Macmillan: 193–214.

Tsebelis, G. (1990) *Nested Games: Rational Choice in Comparative Politics*. Berkeley: University of California Press.

Tsebelis, G. (2002) *Veto Players: How Political Institutions Work*. Princeton, NJ: Princeton University Press.

Tsebelis, G. and G. Garrett (1997) 'Agenda Setting, Vetoes, and the European Union's Codecision Procedure', *Journal of Legislative Studies* 3(3): 74–92.

Tsebelis, G., C.B. Jensen, A. Kalandrakis and A. Kreppel (2001) 'Legislative Procedures in the European Union', *British Journal of Political Science* 31(4): 573–99.

Tulmets, E. (2006) 'L'adaptation de la méthode ouverte de coordination à la politique d'élargissement de l'UE: l'expérience des jumelages institutionnels en Estonie et en Hongrie', *Politique européenne* 18: 155–89.

Vachudova, M.A. (2008) 'Tempered by the EU? Political Parties and Party Systems Before and After Accession', *Journal of European Public Policy* 15 (6): 861–79.

Van der Eijk, C., and M.N. Franklin (2004) 'Potential for Contestation on European Matters at National Elections in Europe', in G. Marks and M.R. Steenbergen (eds),

European Integration and Political Conflict, Cambridge: Cambridge University Press: 32–50.

van Evera, S. (2001) *Causes of War*. Ithaca, NY: Cornell University Press.

Vanke, J. (2010) *Europeanism and the European Union: Interests, Emotions and Systemic Integration in the Early European Economic Community*. Bethesda, MD: Academica Press.

Van Parijs, P. (2011) *Just Democracy*. London: ECPR Press.

van Waarden, F. (1992) 'Dimensions and Types of Policy Networks', *European Journal of Political Research* 21(1–2): 29–52.

Vauchez, A. (2008) 'The Forces of a Weak Field: Laws and Lawyers in the Government of the European Union', *International Political Sociology* 2(1): 128–44.

Vauchez, A. and A. Cohen (eds) (2006) 'Les juristes et l'ordre politique européen', *Critique international* 26: 97–158.

Vayssière, B. (2006) *Vers une Europe fédérale? Les espoirs et actions fédéralistes au sortir de la Seconde Guerre mondiale*. Brussels: Peter Lang.

Verdier, D. and R. Breen (2001) 'Europeanization and Globalization: Politics against Markets in the European Union', *Comparative Political Studies* 34: 227–62.

Versluis, E. (2007) 'Even Rules, Uneven Practices: Opening the Black Box of EU Law in Action', *West European Politics* 30(1): 50–67.

Viroli, M., and N. Bobbio (2003) *The Idea of the Republic*. Polity: Cambridge.

Von Apeldoorn, B. (2002) *Transnational Capitalism and the Struggle over European Integration*. London: Routledge

von Beyme, K. (2005) 'Assymetric Federalism between Globalization and Regionalization', *Journal of European Public Policy* 12(3): 432–47.

Waever, O. (1995) 'Identity, integration and Security: Solving the Sovereignty Puzzle in EU Studies', *Journal of International Affairs* 48(2): 389–431.

Walker, N. (2001) 'The White Paper in Constitutional Context', Jean Monnet Programme Working Paper, New University Law School, 1 June.

Walker, N. (2003) 'Late Sovereignty in the European Union', in N. Walker (ed.), *Sovereignty in Transition*. Oxford: Hart: 3–33.

Walker, N. (2007) 'Post-Constituent Constitutionalism. The Case of the European Union', in M. Loughlin and N. Walker (eds), *The Paradox of Constitutionalism: Constituent Power and Constitutional Form*. Oxford: Oxford University Press: 247–68.

Walker, N. (2008) 'Taking Constitutionalism Beyond the State', *Political Studies*, 56: 519–43.

Walker, R.B.K. (1993) *Inside/Outside: International Relations as Political Theory*. Cambridge: Cambridge University Press.

Wallace, H., M. Pollack and A. Young (eds) (2010) *Policy Making in the European Union*. Oxford: Oxford University Press

Wallace, W. (1990) 'Introduction: the Dynamics of European Integration', in W. Wallace (ed.), *The Dynamics of European Integration*. London: Frances Pinter.

Wallace, W. (1999) 'The Sharing of Sovereignty: The European Paradox', *Political Studies* 47(3): 503–21.

Walt, S.M. (1987) *The Origins of Alliances*. Ithaca, NY: Cornell University Press.

Waltz, K. (1979) *Theory of International Politics*. Reading: AddisonWesley.

Warleigh-Lack, A. (1998) 'Better the Devil You Know? Synthetic and Confederal Understandings of European Unification', *West European Politics* 21(3): 1–18.

Warleigh-Lack, A. (2003) *Democracy in the European Union*. London: Sage.

Warleigh-Lack, A. (2004) 'In Defence of Intra-disciplinarity: 'European Studies', the 'New Regionalism', and the Issue of Democratisation', *Cambridge Review of International Studies*, 17(2): 301–18.

Warleigh-Lack, A. (2006a) 'Conceptual Combinations: Multilevel Governance and Policy Networks', in M. Cini and A. Bourne (eds), *Palgrave Advances in European Union Studies*. Basingstoke: Palgrave Macmillan: 77–95.

Warleigh-Lack, A. (2006b) 'Learning from Europe? EU Studies and the Rethinking of International Relations', *European Journal of International Relations* 12(1): 31–51.

Warleigh-Lack, A. (2006c) 'Towards a Conceptual Framework for Regionalisation: Bridging "New Regionalism" and "Integration Theory"', *Review of International Political Economy*, 13(5): 750–71.

Warleigh-Lack, A. (2007) 'The European and the Universal Process? European Union Studies, New Regionalism and Global Governance', in K.E. Joergensen, M.A. Pollack and B. Rosamond (eds,) *Handbook of European Union Politics*. London: Sage: 561–75.

Warleigh-Lack, A. (2008) 'Studying Regionalisation Comparatively. A Conceptual Framework', in A.F. Cooper, C.W. Hughes and P. de Lombaerde (eds), *Regionalization and Global Governance: The Taming of Globalization*. London: Routledge: 43–60.

Warleigh-Lack, A., Robinson, N., and Rosamond, B. (eds) (2011) *New Regionalism and the European Union. Dialogues, Comparisons and New Research Directions*. London: Routledge.

Warleigh-Lack, A. and B. Rosamond (2010) 'Across the EU Studies–New Regionalism Frontier: Invitation to a Dialogue', *Journal of Common Market Studies* 48(4): 993–1013.

Weber, M. (1980) *Wirtschaft und Gesellschaft. Grundriss einer verstehenden Soziologie*. Tübingen: Winkelmann.

Weiler, J.H.H. (1981) 'The Community System: The Dual Character of Supranationalism', *Yearbook of European Law* 1: 267–306.

Weiler, J.H.H. (1991) 'The Transformation of Europe', *Yale Law Journal* 100: 2403–83.

Weiler, J.H.H. (1995) *The State "über alles": Demos, Telos and the German Maastricht Decision*. New York: Jean Monnet Center for International and Regional Economic 'Law and Justice.

Weiler, J.H.H. (1997) 'Does Europe Need a Constitution? Reflections on Demos, Telos, Ethos and the Maastricht Decision', in P. Gowan and P. Anderson (eds), *The Question of Europe*. London: Verso.

Weiler, J.H.H. (2002) 'A Constitution for Europe? Some Hard Choices', *Journal of Common Market Studies* 40(4): 563–80.

Weisbein, J. (2006) 'Des mobilisation sous (inter)dépendances. Une approche configurationnelle du militantisme fédéraliste en Europe', in A. Cohen et al. (eds), *Les formes de l'activité politique*. Paris: Presses Universitaires de France.

Weisbein, J. (2008) 'L'Europe à contrepoint. Objets nouveaux et classicisme théorique pour les études européennes', *Politique européenne* 25: 115–36.

Weiss, T.G. (2000) 'Governance, Good Governance and Global Governance: Conceptual and Actual Challenges', *Third World Quarterly* 21(5): 795–814.

Wendt, A. (1999) *Social theory of international politics*. Cambridge: Cambridge University Press.

Wessels, W. (1997) 'An Ever Closer Fusion? A Dynamic Macropolitical View on Integration Processes', *Journal of Common Market Studies* 35(2): 267–99.

Wessels, W. and D. Rometsch (eds) (1996) *The European Union and Member States. Towards Institutional Fusion?* Manchester: Manchester University Press.

White, J. (2010) 'European Integration By Daylight', *Comparative European Politics* 8(1): 55–73.

Whitman, R. (eds) (2011) *Normative power Europe: empirical and theoretical perspectives*. Basingstoke: Palgrave Macmillan.

Whitman, R.G. (1998) *From Civilian Power to Superpower? The International Identity of the EU*. Basingstoke: Palgrave Macmillan.

Wiener, A. (2006) 'Constructivism and Sociological Institutionalism', in M. Cini and A.K. Bourne (eds), *Palgrave Advances in European Union Studies*. Basingstoke: Palgrave Macmillan: 35–55.

Wiener, A. (2007) 'Contested Meanings of Norms: A Research Framework', *Comparative European Politics* 5(1): 1–17.

Wiener, A. (2008) *The Invisible Constitution of Politics. Contested Norms and International Encounters*. Cambridge: Cambridge University Press.

Wiener, A. and T. Diez (eds) (2004) *European Integration Theory*. Oxford: Oxford University Press.

Wiener, A. and T. Diez (2009) 'Taking Stock of Integration Theory', in A. Wiener and T. Diez (eds), *European Integration Theory*. Oxford: Oxford University Press: 241–52.

Willits, P. (1978) *The Non-Aligned Movement*. London: Frances Pinter.

Wincott, D. (1995) 'Institutional Interaction and European Integration: Towards an Everyday Critique of Liberal Intergovernmentalism', *Journal of Common Market Studies* 33(4): 597–609.

Wionczek, M. (1970) 'The Rise and Decline of Latin American Economic Integration', *Journal of Common Market Studies* 9(1): 49–66.

Wolff, S., N. Wichmann, N. and G. Mounier (eds) (2010) *The External Dimension of Justice and Home Affairs: A Different Security Agenda for the European Union?* London: Routledge.

Woll, C. (2006) 'Research Agenda: Lobbying in the European Union: From *Sui Generis* to a Comparative Perspective', *Journal of European Public Policy* 13(3): 456–70.

Woll, C. (2008) *Firm Interests: How Governments Shape Business Lobbying on Global Trade*. Ithaca, NY: Cornell University Press.

Woll, C. and B. Clift (eds) (2012) 'Economic Patriotism: Political Intervention in Open Economies', *Journal of European Public Policy* 19(3): 307–23.

Wonka, A. and B. Rittberger (2011) 'Perspectives on EU Governance: An Empirical Assessment of the Political Attitudes of EU Agency Professionals', *Journal of European Public Policy* 18(6): 888–908.

World Bank (1997) *World Development Report: The State in a Changing World*. Oxford: Oxford University Press.

Zahariadis, N. (2008a) 'Ambiguity and Choice in European Public Policy', *Journal of European Public Policy* 15(4): 514–30.

Zahariadis, N. (2008b) 'Europeanization as Program Implementation: Effective and Democratic?', *Journal of Comparative Policy Analysis* 10(3): 221–38.

Zeitlin, J. (2005) 'Conclusion', in J. Zeitlin and P. Pochet (eds), *The Open Method of Coordination in Action*. Brussels: PIE–Peter Lang: 447–503.

Zielonka, J. (2006) *Europe as Empire: The Nature of the Enlarged European Union*. Oxford: Oxford University Press.

Zürn, M. (1998) *Regieren jenseits des Nationalstaates: Denationalisierung und Globalisierung als Chance*. Frankfurt am Main: Suhrkamp.

Zürn, M. and J.T. Checkel (2005) 'Getting Socialized to Build Bridges: Constructivism and Rationalism, Europe and the Nation State', *International Organization* 59(4): 1045–79.

Index

acquis communautaire 89, 99, 125, 140
agency 28, 78, 83, 91, 95, 96, 104, 108, 117, 120 188
Independent 92, 119, 199
Amsterdam Treaty 161
Aron, Raymond 67, 88
ASEAN 12, 71, 230, 236, 239–41, 245, 248, 251, 253, 255

balancing 71, 72, 165
bargaining
intergovernmental 19, 56, 68, 77, 80, 83
international 65, 75, 82, 92
power 75, 99, 222
Bartolini, Stefano 21, 61–2, 85, 187–199, 211–12, 263–8
Börzel, Tanja 135–46, 152, 182
Bulmer, Simon 2–12, 83, 87, 90, 100, 102–18, 146, 150–3
Burgess, Michael 34, 42
Burley, Anne-Marie 55, 61

Caporaso, James 7, 12, 50, 54, 87, 96, 135, 137, 152, 218, 227, 233, 257
Christiansen, Thomas 105, 109, 128, 161, 162, 173
Common Agricultural Policy (CAP) 38, 50–1, 67, 70, 83, 125–6, 228
Common Foreign and Security Policy (CFSP) 181, 225–31
communities
policy 128
political 33, 46, 53
Community Method 62, 247
comparative federalism 36–42
comparative politics 11–19, 32, 87, 89, 100, 110, 113, 131, 146, 183, 215–18, 233
compliance 88–96, 140–3, 152–3, 208–12, 224
confederation 32–3, 195–6
consociation 32–42
cosmopolitanism 183, 204, 213, 255
Coudenhove-Kalergi, Richard Count 26

Council of Ministers 33, 37, 42, 50, 62, 76, 89, 97, 126, 161
European 37, 64, 89, 98, 151, 161, 210, 218, 220, 222, 260, 263
Cox, Robert W. 156, 159, 261

De Gaulle, General Charles 24, 44, 50–1, 64, 67, 78, 222
Delors, Jacques 80
democratic deficit 36, 107, 169, 172, 181, 185, 195, 205–8
Deutsch, Karl 30–1, 42, 54, 158, 174
Diez, Thomas 15–17, 231, 233, 248, 252, 260, 263
Dolowitz, David 146–52

Economic and Monetary Union 39, 72, 89, 104, 138, 222, 223–8
'empty chair crisis' 24, 44, 50, 55, 64, 67, 222
epistemic communities 106, 151
Etzioni, Amitai 53–4, 174, 242, 256
Euratom 58
European Central Bank (ECB) 91, 94, 104
European Coal and Steel Community (ECSC) 44, 49, 58, 174
European Commission 13, 23, 44, 47–8, 50, 55, 61, 76, 83, 89, 93–5, 104–5, 107, 113, 117, 121, 129, 131, 142, 149, 168, 179, 197, 247, 265
European Court of Justice (ECJ) 14, 33
European Movement 34–5
European Parliament 14, 23, 35, 37, 83, 97, 1969, 181, 185, 189, 206–8, 210, 260, 263
euroscepticism 37, 52, 137, 139, 140, 145, 166, 201–3, 208–9, 264

Falkner, Gerda 39, 42, 226, 239, 140–3, 152
federalism 33–43, 116, 12à
federation 33–5, 37, 40–1, 43, 48, 53–4, 115, 195–7, 213, 234, 242
feedback loop 83, 93
Ferry, Jean-Marc 201, 202, 204–5
Fligstein, Neil 20, 56, 62, 85, 186–7, 191, 263–4

Føllesdal, Andreas   117, 128, 194, 198, 207, 208, 211
foreign policy   14, 28, 67, 73, 218, 226, 230, 232, 245, 249

Garrett, Geoffrey   92, 96, 108
General Agreement on Tariffs and Trade (GATT)   75, 241
governance
  good   113, 117, 118
  multi-level   41, 73, 112–13, 118, 120–4, 130, 147, 204, 211, 262
  network   15, 118, 124–6, 128, 130, 263
grand theory   18, 58, 77, 82, 85, 88, 110
Grieco, Joseph   72, 88

Haas, Ernst B.   51–4, 57, 65, 58, 151, 158, 164, 174, 220, 240, 250
Hall, Peter   89, 90, 100, 102, 109, 110, 167, 169, 190
high authority   47, 49, 52, 104, 197
high politics   84, 226
Hix, Simon   12, 21, 87, 97, 108, 133–4, 138, 145, 152, 162, 207, 211, 215
Hoffmann, Stanley   67–9, 77, 84, 174, 226, 238
Hooghe, Liesbet   57, 61, 112, 117, 120–3, 130, 143, 170, 194, 202, 217, 264–5
Hurrell, Andrew   12, 71, 171, 233, 244–5, 247, 249, 252, 253, 256

inertia   29, 68, 141, 145, 152–3
integration
  differentiated   263
  legal   55, 61, 96
  market   37
interdependence   6, 28–9, 32, 65, 69, 70, 78, 82, 84, 120–1, 124–5, 127–8, 132, 137, 146, 154, 168, 182, 237, 240–2, 246–7, 251–6

Jabko, Nicolas   167–8, 170, 180, 220, 233
Jachtenfuchs, Markus   105–9, 131, 132
Jacquot, Sophie   32, 143–4, 152, 180–1, 191, 270
joint decision trap   38, 42, 116
Jorgensen, Knud Erik   161, 162, 173, 227
judicial politics   96
Justice and Home Affairs (JHA)   12, 82

Kaiser, Wolfram   31, 70, 83–4
Kant, Immanuel   26–7, 196–7, 201, 204, 211, 213
Katzenstein, Peter   89, 100, 158, 237, 248, 254, 256

Kohler-Koch, Beate   112–13, 116, 118, 120, 123, 125, 130, 132, 204, 208, 210

Lewis, Jeffrey   83, 163, 222
Lijphart, Arend   40
Lindberg, Leon   45, 48–50, 65, 164, 194, 206
Lisbon Treaty   19, 38, 62, 129, 151, 207, 227, 264
logic
  of appropriateness   104, 157
  of arguing   157
  of consequentialism   104–5, 157
low politics   68–9, 84
loyalty, transfer of   44, 49, 52–3, 55, 57, 61, 62, 110, 164, 243, 256
Luxembourg compromise   50, 55, 97

Maastricht Treaty   19, 35, 71–2, 78, 95, 112, 119, 221, 133, 172, 194, 206–7, 233, 236, 253, 260
mainstreaming
  bottom-up   12, 19, 87, 216, 218, 219, 234, 244, 260, 264–5
  top-down   13, 19, 87, 255
Majone, Giandomenico   37, 119, 130, 198, 199, 207
Manners, Ian   174, 130
Marks, Gary   112, 120–3, 130, 161, 194, 202, 217, 264–5
McNamara, Kathleen   107, 166–7, 170, 180
Mearsheimer, John   71, 84
Menon, Anand   12, 33, 36, 42, 82, 94–5, 100, 218, 233
Merand, Frédéric   10, 171, 172, 176–8, 180–2, 187, 191, 226, 232
MERCOSUR   12, 50, 71, 217, 236, 240, 241, 245, 249, 255
Meunier, Sophie   75, 84–6, 225, 229, 252, 255
Milward, Alan   65, 69, 70–1, 78, 83, 285, 174
Mitrany, David   27–30, 42, 46
Monnet, Jean   35, 45, 49, 80
Moravcsik, Andrew   66, 69–70, 72, 77–86, 99, 131, 161, 198, 203, 208, 225, 250

n=1 problem   216, 236
national interest   12, 13, 19, 20, 32, 40, 48, 50, 51, 54, 65, 70, 77, 80, 94, 96, 98, 161, 215, 217, 219–21, 225, 233–4, 277

nationalism   23, 50, 55, 57, 119, 192, 255
neorealism   45, 66, 72, 218
new public management (NPM)   116, 129
Nye, Joseph   28, 29, 53, 221, 232, 237, 238, 240, 256

ontology   17, 177
Open Method of Coordination (OMC)   37, 62, 129
opt-out   172, 206, 223

Parsons, Craig   107, 126, 167–8, 170, 177, 180, 229
path dependency   101–3, 11, 145
permissive consensus   194, 206
Pierson, Paul   58, 83, 100–3, 109, 145, 215
Pollack, Mark   12, 21, 27, 77, 92, 94, 96–8, 103, 108, 215
pooling sovereignty   93
positivism   88, 159
post-positivism   88
principal-agent theory   92, 95, 97, 99, 108
Putnam, Robert   73–5, 84, 86, 161

Qualified Majority Voting (QMV)   55, 76, 97, 121, 222, 261

Radaelli, Claudio   107, 125, 133, 135–6, 138, 145–6, 149–52, 163–4, 170, 181–2, 191
reflexivity   174, 263
regime theory   29
regionalisation   59, 216, 236–7, 239–40, 242, 244–6, 250–8
regulatory state   113, 118–20, 130, 199
Risse, Thomas   52, 57, 61, 83, 87, 122, 135–8, 140, 145–6, 152, 157, 159, 162–3, 165–6, 168, 170, 176, 182, 218
Rittberger, Berthold   21, 95, 102–3, 108–9, 113, 119, 130, 181, 185, 191, 197, 204, 208, 210–11, 263
Rome Treaty   78

Rosamond, Ben   15, 24, 28, 46, 56, 62, 69, 105, 109, 164–5, 174, 237, 252, 263

Sandholtz, Wayne   56, 61, 83
Sbragia, Alberta   36–7, 42, 244
Scharpf, Fritz   36, 38, 42, 103, 115–16, 119, 130, 199–200, 209, 220, 221, 233
Scheingold, Stuart   45, 50, 174, 206
Schimmelfennig, Frank   21, 24, 56, 77, 82, 98, 108, 140, 150, 152, 158, 162–3, 263
Schmitter, Philippe   47, 52, 53, 55–6, 58–62, 198, 264
Schuman, Robert   45, 49, 70
security communities   27, 31, 42, 158
Single European Act (SEA)   14
spill-back   50, 52
spillover   44, 47, 49–52, 54–5, 58–62, 80, 256
  functional   49
  political   49, 50, 242
Spinelli, Altiero   35
state sovereignty   48, 54, 65, 69, 86, 204, 217, 221, 224, 229, 235, 246, 261
structure and agency   56, 192

Thelen, Kathleen   70, 100–3, 109
thematic networks   128
transactionalism   16, 19, 24, 30, 42–3
transaction costs   78, 80, 82, 90, 92–3, 95, 102, 248
Tsebelis, George   92, 96–9, 108
two-level games   65, 73–4, 84

Ventotene Manifesto   34

Waltz, Kenneth   64
Weiler, J.W.   33, 36, 55, 61, 200–8
Wessels, Wolfgang   135, 236
Wiener, Antje   15, 17, 24, 161–2, 170, 173
World Trade Organization (WTO)   215, 217, 241, 255